CIVIL DIALOGUE ON ABORTION

Civil Dialogue on Abortion provides a cutting-edge discussion between two philosophy scholars on each side of the abortion debate. Bertha Alvarez Manninen argues for her pro-choice view, but also urges respect for the life of the fetus, while Jack Mulder argues for his pro-life view, but recognizes that for the pro-life movement to be consistent, it must urge society to care more for the vulnerable. Coming together to discuss their views, but also to seek common ground, the two authors show how their differing positions nevertheless rest upon some common convictions. The book helps to provide a way forward for a divide that has only seemed to widen the aisle of public discourse in recent years.

This engaging book will prove essential reading for students across multiple disciplines, including applied ethics, medical ethics, and bioethics, but will also be of interest to students of religious studies and women's studies.

Bertha Alvarez Manninen is Associate Professor of Philosophy at Arizona State University, USA.

Jack Mulder, Jr. is Associate Professor of Philosophy at Hope College, USA.

CIVIL DIALOGUE ON ABORTION

Bertha Alvarez Manninen and Jack Mulder, Jr.

LONDON AND NEW YORK

First published 2018
by Routledge
2 Park Square, Milton Park, Abingdon, Oxon OX14 4RN

and by Routledge
711 Third Avenue, New York, NY 10017

Routledge is an imprint of the Taylor & Francis Group, an informa business

© 2018 Bertha Alvarez Manninen and Jack Mulder, Jr.

The right of Bertha Alvarez Manninen and Jack Mulder, Jr. to be identified as authors of this work has been asserted by them in accordance with sections 77 and 78 of the Copyright, Designs and Patents Act 1988.

All rights reserved. No part of this book may be reprinted or reproduced or utilised in any form or by any electronic, mechanical, or other means, now known or hereafter invented, including photocopying and recording, or in any information storage or retrieval system, without permission in writing from the publishers.

Trademark notice: Product or corporate names may be trademarks or registered trademarks, and are used only for identification and explanation without intent to infringe.

British Library Cataloguing in Publication Data
A catalogue record for this book is available from the British Library

Library of Congress Cataloging in Publication Data
A catalog record for this book has been requested

ISBN: 978-1-138-20586-4 (hbk)
ISBN: 978-1-138-20587-1 (pbk)
ISBN: 978-1-315-21365-1 (ebk)

Typeset in Bembo
by Taylor & Francis Books

For our students.

CONTENTS

Acknowledgments viii
Bertha Alvarez Manninen

Acknowledgments x
Jack Mulder, Jr.

Introduction 1
Bertha Alvarez Manninen and Jack Mulder, Jr.

1 Why I am pro-choice 11
  Bertha Alvarez Manninen

2 Why I am pro-life 65
  Jack Mulder, Jr.

3 A response to Mulder 113
  Bertha Alvarez Manninen

4 A response to Manninen 149
  Jack Mulder, Jr.

5 Convergences and divergences 172
  Bertha Alvarez Manninen and Jack Mulder, Jr.

Conclusion 213
Bertha Alvarez Manninen and Jack Mulder, Jr.

Index *216*

ACKNOWLEDGMENTS

Bertha Alvarez Manninen

First and foremost, I want to thank my co-author Jack Mulder. He has been one of my best friends from our graduate school days at Purdue University in the philosophy department, and he has always welcomed and embraced me with an open mind and heart, even in areas where we vehemently disagree. This sentiment is also extended to his wife, Melissa, who is also one of my closest friends from our grad school days, and their beautiful children Maria and Luke. Thank you all for exemplifying for me what loving, rational, and civil disagreement looks like. On the days I feel like society is at a standstill, where we seem unable to talk to or teach each other, when I want to give up on the "other side," all of you remind me that it *is* possible to move forward and to dialogue. Thank you for making me a better person. Your friendship has been invaluable.

Thank you to Rebecca Shillabeer, Routledge publishers, and to our anonymous reviewer for all your help and support. You have made this whole process remarkably smooth, and I am appreciative of the opportunity to co-write this book for you.

Thank you to Arizona State University, and all my colleagues in the New College of Interdisciplinary Arts and Sciences, for all the years of research support, camaraderie, and friendship.

Thank you to Paul, Linda, and Caitlin Draper for over 20 years of care, mentorship, and love, and for adopting my family as part of your own.

To Letty Sanchez – your 30 years of sisterhood has kept me going in my most difficult moments. Every day you remind me that you don't have to share blood to be family.

And then there is my family – the ones who are always waiting for me whenever I come home and who have given me endless support throughout my educational and career endeavors. I am forever grateful to all of you for always standing by my side. My friends keep me grounded and remind me how much more there is to life than academic work. This is a reminder I often need, and one for which I am always appreciative.

My most endless bounty of love and support comes always from my husband Tuomas Manninen, and my children, Michelle and Julia, who make life so much more beautiful and meaningful in every conceivable way. It's because I have held you both in my womb, felt you kick and grow, and watched your development in awe that I had to think long and hard about the things I have written in this book. Just your presence alone inspires me to be a better person every day. And thank you to Tuomas for raising these precious souls with me.

Finally, to the loved ones I have lost this year (2017) – my world is much emptier without you, but I hope that you have somehow found each other.

ACKNOWLEDGMENTS

Jack Mulder, Jr.

My friend Bertha Alvarez Manninen is a hard act to follow. I'm very grateful for her friendship, kindness, and willingness to discuss this issue and many others. I, too, draw much hope from her desire for more meaningful dialogue. She is the trailblazer. I've learned a great deal from her and continue to do so. My thinking on the abortion issue is inseparable from my friendship with her both because I may never have thought as deeply about the issue if not for her challenges, and because she simply began inviting me to talk and write with her more often once it became clear we had enough to talk about on this issue. We disagree, of course, but we have always been able to challenge each other in ways that only work in the context of friendship. I can only offer my hearty thanks as well to her husband, Tuomas, and their children, Michelle and Julia, for sparing their wife and mother for this work.

My wife, Melissa Manchester Mulder, and our two children, Maria, and Luke, teach me every day how to be more deeply and consistently pro-life. I have a long way to go, but perhaps not quite as long a way thanks to them. The faith we share in a God who teaches us how to love the whole person from conception to natural death is the greatest gift I know. My parents, Jack and Pat Mulder, and John and Therese Manchester, have always encouraged my thinking in these areas through their ideas about what it might mean to be pro-life. Thanks also to current and former colleagues Melissa Mulder, Jared Ortiz, Joe LaPorte, Lyra Pitstick, Jeff Polet, and David Ryden for their insights. A number of past students have also offered helpful ideas, including Chikara Saito and Taylor Mills.

Thanks to Stephen Law, *Think*, and The Royal Institute of Philosophy for permission to use material for my article "A Short Argument Against Abortion Rights." I was heartened to find the journal receptive to my paper. Thanks also to Rebecca Shillabeer at Routledge for her very helpful work on this project.

INTRODUCTION

Bertha Alvarez Manninen and Jack Mulder, Jr.

In 2008, the late Soran Reader wrote,

> There can be no real question about whether abortion can be justified. To "debate" such a question is to harm women, just as to "debate" Apartheid would be to harm black South Africans. The fact that something so necessary for women is treated as a "debate" shows a worrying lack of respect.[1]

As this passage shows, the abortion issue is particularly difficult and sensitive. The trouble is that it is difficult and sensitive precisely because people care about it very deeply and do so often for different reasons, though at times surprisingly symmetrical ones. For instance, the "pro-choice" writer (we will discuss terminology in a moment) has serious reasons assembled to say what Reader does in the epigraph here. But the "pro-life" writer also has serious reasons assembled to say precisely what Reader does about another marginalized population, namely, the very young and defenseless (as pro-life writers see it) who have not yet been born. No doubt each side sees the other evincing a "worrying lack of respect" in the sense that a marginalized population is dealt a bad hand by the policies she or he rejects, but as far as persuading the other side that he or she should change course, it will hardly do to shrug off rational and civil arguments from the other side and retreat to one's ideological bubble (though of course we do not mean to attribute this further step to Reader herself).

In our age of information overload and partisan spin that threatens to undo the facts themselves, there is simply no substitute for earnest dialogue and, indeed, friendship across ideological lines. That is what we hope to exhibit in this book. Why friendship? Because every mechanism for dialogue with tightly written rules will feel stifling and unproductive at some point, especially when trust is already developed. We must invest in one another and care for one another as people and when that happens, some more direct forms of speech and argumentative critique can be productive that would not be productive without friendship, or at least mutual respect. Some scholars of intergroup dialogue attempt to differentiate between terms such as "debate," "discussion," and "dialogue," and this does have some usefulness. Patricia Gurin and her coauthors write

> Dialogue is collaborative and honors the intellectual and experiential diversity among participants. It strives for understanding, not agreement. Unlike debate, which is usually oppositional and in which people try to convince each other so that one side wins, dialogue strives to build mutual understanding ... In debate, one may listen to identify weaknesses in others' arguments in order to counter them. In discussion, one may listen just to know when it is time to enter and express a point of view. In dialogue, one is able to listen and share in a connected way.[2]

Now it is surely right to identify missteps that can occur when power inequities hamper productive discussion, and nothing prevents someone from holding out a term like "dialogue" for when all of that is going right. Nevertheless, the structure of this book and our vocations as philosophers do allow us to take turns in the discussion, they do allow us to learn from one another (as we have done often over the years), and they do allow us to critique our various arguments. It may turn out that, on some people's definitions of "debate," "discussion," and "dialogue," we are doing one or another at various points in the book. Moreover, we already know that we disagree, and there is a sense in which of course we would like to persuade the other that he or she is wrong, since we both believe that we are talking about matters of justice. But because we are friends, we know that scoring a point in a debate is not worth it if it comes at the cost of a friendship and a more polarized discussion.

Now Reader is right in the epigraph, if we assume her pro-choice premises, that debating abortion is worrying. But what is the solution? Surely a multi-pronged answer is the right one. Legislative advocacy and peaceful protest both have their place (as both sides should admit). But any plan for what to do about our current cultural divides about abortion that does not include serious debate and dialogue, undertaken by scholars with charitable motives, would be deeply flawed. Partisanship on abortion can escalate far beyond respectful dialogue, and anyone who cannot admit that some protest(or)s on both sides have gone beyond ordinary standards of civility may want to check his or her ideological pulse.

In 2015, Robert L. Dear was apprehended after he allegedly murdered three individuals at a Planned Parenthood clinic in Colorado Springs, Colorado. At his trial, Dear referred to himself as a "warrior for the [unborn] babies," defending his actions under the guise of saving infants from being murdered. This is a similar justification to the one used by Scott Roeder who was found guilty of first degree murder and two counts of aggravated assault for the killing of Dr. George Tiller, who was known in Wichita, Kansas as being one of the few physicians in the

United States willing to perform late-term abortions (abortions after 20 weeks gestational age). On the other hand, in 2012, the home of Keith and Jennifer Mason, leaders of the pro-life group Personhood USA, was attacked and vandalized while they, and their three small children, slept. Rocks were hurled through their window, and their house was spray-painted with images of coat hangers. In 2010, the home of Joe and Ann Scheidler, directors of the Pro-Life Action League, was also vandalized when large chunks of asphalt were thrown through their window. Make no mistake about it – advocates on both sides of the abortion debate have engaged in violent behavior toward individuals with opposing perspectives. These examples are extreme, but they illustrate some of the worst-case scenarios that come when we replace dialogue and discussion with anger and violence.

But even without this extreme kind of violence, both pro-life and pro-choice advocates share a history of mutually vilifying each other, as is illustrated in a 1989 study by Marsha Vanderford. This kind of reciprocated slander ultimately leads to alienation between opponents, and renders it unlikely that any fruitful dialogue can emerge. For example, pro-choice members of the Abortion Rights Council of Minnesota, as Vanderford documents, largely dismissed pro-life advocates with accusations of religious extremism and accused them of wanting to relegate women back into oppression. Pro-lifers were charged with being motivated by sexism, elitism, and authoritarianism. The pro-life position was often fallaciously depicted as one of "compulsory pregnancy" and "mandatory motherhood," rather than as a genuine concern over the lives and welfare of perceived innocent human beings.[3]

Likewise, Vanderford also notes, pro-choice advocates were equally vilified by pro-life members of the group Minnesota Citizens Concerned for Life. Citing the support of abortion in communist China in adherence to the one-child policy, pro-life advocates accused any pro-choice advocate of communism (a term that incited much fear during the Cold War era). Pro-choice advocates argued for freedom to choose abortion, but their real goal, they claimed, was one of compulsory abortions. And when pro-choice supporters advocate for state or federal financial aid in order to help poor women fund their abortions, their real desires, it was argued, are racist in nature; what they actually believe is that "poor (and black) people have not the brains, the will, or the morals to be anything but promiscuous, so we must watch over them with a paternal eye and abort their babies every season."[4] Feminist pro-choice supporters often face accusations of being anti-family and anti-child. At a 1992 Iowa fundraiser, Christian fundamentalist preacher Pat Robertson denied that the goals of the feminist movement were equal rights for women, stating instead that it is "a socialist, anti-family political movement that encourages women to leave their husbands, kill their children, practice witchcraft, destroy capitalism and become lesbians."[5]

Moreover, the individuals most affected by abortion (fetuses and pregnant women) are also often referred to with dehumanizing terms that serve to, effectively, rob them of their moral status and moral sympathy. Women who procure abortions are oftentimes called "selfish" or "murderers" and accused of sexual promiscuity. Accusing women who abort of being careless monsters means we do not have to engage in very real stories of struggle and heartache. It becomes easier to oppose abortion when one refuses to immerse oneself in the lives of the women who choose it, and it becomes easy to refuse this immersion when one relies on stereotypes and slurs, rather than on the individual humanity of the pregnant woman.

Fetuses, however, fare no better. They are often referred to by pro-choice advocates as nothing but "tissue," "clumps of cells," or "products of conception." Often, they will be derided as being neither really human nor alive (as if they were another species altogether or not growing organisms themselves). These terms psychologically erase the fetus from moral consideration and deny them any moral value. If we don't regard them as human beings whose lives are being terminated (whether rightly or wrongly) by abortion, it becomes easier not to empathize with their deaths. Both sides want to simplify the others' perspective because it renders it psychologically easier to hold their respective views when the other side is rendered clearly immoral or irrational. But easier is not always better. Dehumanizing either pregnant women or human fetuses effectively means we do not have to engage in the very real and complex moral questions that come with abortion.

Violence, lewd or rude conduct, and name-calling are not productive ways to participate in a deliberative democracy, though protesting and advocacy (in addition to rational argument) can be. In response to an Easter attack in Pakistan, Pope Francis recently said "I repeat, once again, that violence and murderous hatred lead only to pain and destruction; respect and fraternity are the only way to achieve peace."[6] While only one of us is a practicing Catholic (though the other was raised Catholic, and still harbors some affinity toward the tradition), surely the Pope's words here ring true. Whether what we need more of is respect for women and their rights (and surely we do) or we need more respect for the unborn, or both (which is both our views), disrespectful treatment of adults with whom we disagree is hardly the most effective way to any of these goals.

That is why we have put together this book, and the desire for civility has shaped how we have chosen to put it together. Charles C. Camosy, in a thoughtful book of his own,[7] offers four general traits and dispositions that are important in this discussion, and these seem eminently worth our support. They are humility, solidarity with our conversation partners, avoiding dismissive words and phrases that erect fences, and leading with what we are for instead of what we are against.[8] Throughout the process of writing this book and our years of friendship prior to doing so, we have learned from and laughed with one another and tried to understand our positions on their own terms. These are important parts of effective civil dialogue.

It may also be worthwhile here to stake out some working ideas about civil dialogue[9] itself and some rules. For instance, we take it that a subjective definition with some objective constraints is helpful. Thus, we might say that civil discourse occurs when people of sincere conviction (a subjective condition) who are willing (also subjective) to submit their opinions to the (metaphorical) court of argument and rational discourse (this is at least *more* objective in the sense that we can agree on certain logical rules that can be articulated for any debate) are therefore invited to the table of conversation and not disinvited unless they refuse to make their case in such a fashion. There also needs to be a demonstrated capacity for doing this, which in some manner needs to be objective, but once someone shows it, their voice should be considered, investigated, and listened to on its own terms. What we mean by this is that it won't be the case that just *any* pro-life person, say, must be admitted to a moral and political conversation of consequence on the issue of abortion. Rather, we must ask that such people offer reasons for their view, and these should be reasons, if such people hope to be taken seriously, that can be entertained by people across a wide array of ideological convictions. As Mulder himself notes, the pro-life position will not adopt the most effective strategy if it articulates its views using only language belonging to a particular faith tradition, especially in an increasingly pluralistic public square.[10] Nevertheless, if this argumentative burden is accepted, those participating in civil discourse and dialogue should be willing to give all such arguments a serious hearing.

This cannot happen if we mischaracterize each other's views in the hasty desire for a catchy bumper sticker or placard. Placards and bumper stickers have their place, but those that are overly negative and question-begging usually serve only to drive a wedge between ideologically divided groups. Thus, because we listen to each other's views on their own terms, one rule we will observe is that Mulder will not refer to Manninen's position as "pro-abortion" because Manninen herself does not see this as a helpful way to understand her position. Also, Manninen will not call Mulder's position "anti-choice" because Mulder himself does not see this as a helpful way to understand his position. This is not even because we are persuaded these terms are inaccurate in regard to the other side; rather this usage is a decision we've made to respect the other person's view as rationally defensible. Using terms the other accepts is a way to honor the other person as a full partner in dialogue and to recognize that this is a complex debate that will never truly be won by ideological sleight of hand.

It is not necessary to argue over the negative terms that each rejects about her or his position, but we can note something about the positive terms each embraces. For those who embrace a "pro-life" position, at least the version Mulder stakes out in this book, to take direct action against any human life (and indeed, some cases of non-human animal life) transgresses the definition of "pro-life," whether the patient of the action is young or old. Mulder also holds that all forms of unjust discrimination would also fail the test of being "pro-life" since these, as he holds abortion does, take a member of the human family to be less than what she is and somehow deserving of less moral consideration. The point is that "pro-life" is a term that should suggest, although it often does not, a holistic view of how one must respect all human life (and non-human animal life in important ways). For just such a reason, although neither of us will be detained by a serious scholarly argument to this effect, we both hold that capital punishment fails this test and that such a position is entailed by a consistently "pro-life" view.

We will also not be characterizing abortion as anything other than a difficult decision that few undertake lightly. Certainly, Camosy is right that some individuals have at times taken a flaunting, cavalier attitude toward abortion, but we suspect that the very public examples he gives have more to do with the attempt to put a right deemed so necessary for women firmly and comfortably past the "debate" that worries Soran Reader in the epigraph.[11] Further, terms like "murder" are out of place when talking about abortion. Manninen holds that this is true because she thinks abortions are not cases of violating anyone's right to life in that the fetus does not have the right to draw upon the woman's sustaining aid without her consent. While Mulder holds that abortion, unless the fetus survives, does result in the death of a person, "murder" is a legal term that connotes culpability and violent intent. This, Mulder thinks, is simply not an accurate way to understand the choices going on in virtually all abortions.

It will also become clear that we actually disagree on whether pro-lifers *should* consider abortion an act of murder. Interestingly, it is Manninen who thinks they should. She alleges that abortion, on pro-life principles, should be thought so grievous as to constitute not just homicide or manslaughter, but first-degree murder. She simply thinks that the pro-life principles that would generate this conclusion are mistaken. Mulder holds the pro-life position but believes that there are reasons to think that nearly all acts of abortion could not qualify as murder. Murder, as most penal codes recognize, requires malicious intent.[12] As Manninen discusses at length in her initial chapter, we know enough about many women's motivations for abortion to believe that the attribution of malicious intent to them is implausible. Mulder simply holds that they would still lack malice even if it turned out they were mistaken about whether their autonomy extended to abortion or about whether the fetus were a person, or some other such belief that is commonly used to justify abortion. Add to this that in our culture there are widespread disagreements about this issue, as well as politicians who shift their positions in sometimes alarming ways to grasp hold of or continue in power.[13] These factors (some more than others) significantly impact our ability to assess the culpability of those involved in abortion.

Manninen's preferred term of "pro-choice" reinforces her view that abortion should be a choice for the woman involved, and it also reflects her preferred strategy in arguing for the abortion right. Her defense of this right relies on the issue of autonomy, and how far she takes that autonomy to extend. Significantly, her view is that "the pro-choice community needs to acknowledge the value of fetal life."[14] Given that fetal life has some genuine value, Manninen can admit that abortion is in some manner unfortunate. Past members of the United States Democratic Party had famously used phrases like "safe, legal, and rare" of abortion, though in more recent years, the word "rare" has often disappeared, especially from more recent party platforms.[15] But Manninen's views about the value of fetal life allow her to be in an interesting position with regard to dialoguing with people who identify as pro-life, since, while affirming that the choice of whether to continue or to terminate a pregnancy must remain available to women, Manninen nevertheless can consistently hold (as some pro-choice thinkers could not) that abortion should be rare for good socioeconomic reasons among others.

It's also important to remember that we will not finally agree. This is not a "compromise" book. Manninen will argue that abortion ought to always remain legal and accessible, whereas Mulder will argue that abortion is a serious moral and social wrong and should not be legal. Nevertheless, both agree that they would like to see a reduction of instances of abortion. For Manninen, this is because studies show that a portion of women who choose abortion do so because they feel they must due to social and economic pressures. Being a champion of choice, she argues that no abortion should ever be coerced, whether by another person or by social or economic circumstances. Mulder will certainly admit that all positive coercion in sexual and reproductive matters is bad, and that there are important ways we can help reduce the need for abortion, for instance by providing stronger societal support for intact families and those whose poverty might otherwise suggest abortion in dire situations of financial need. But neither author will "finally come around" to the other's viewpoint.

Yet this fact does not mean we have nothing to talk about. In his 1995 encyclical *Evangelium Vitae*, then Pope (now St.) John Paul II wrote

> In a case like the one just mentioned, when it is not possible to overturn or completely abrogate a pro-abortion[16] law, an elected official, whose absolute personal opposition to procured abortion was well known, could licitly support proposals aimed at limiting the harm done by such a law and at lessening its negative consequences at the level of general opinion and public morality. This does not in fact represent an illicit cooperation with an unjust law, but rather a legitimate and proper attempt to limit its evil aspects.[17]

Here we have a well-known pro-life advocate urging that it is perfectly possible to make progress in the legislative sphere with pro-choice advocates who disagree. "Compromises" are, in that sense, possible, as long as presumably both parties understand that such political "solutions" are always temporary. Pro-life thinkers cannot simply sit comfortably back in their chairs upon passing some incremental law that might limit some "evil aspect" of one or another law, but it is possible to engage in dialogue with meaningful outcomes.

There are two outcomes that are particularly notable. First, dialogue allows us to engage in the moral complexity of these issues, when we may be tempted to give them the "bumper sticker" treatment and simplify them. But earnest engagement allows us to see the world from another perspective, adding depth and complexity to our moral lives, and it also gives us the opportunity to defend our views in the face of opposition. The ability to do this renders our own position much stronger and formidable. As utilitarian philosopher John Stuart Mill puts it:

> He who knows only his own side of the case knows little of that. His reasons may be good, and no one may have been able to refute them. But if he is

equally unable to refute the reasons on the opposite side, if he does not so much as know what they are, he has no ground for preferring either opinion ... Nor is it enough that he should hear the opinions of adversaries from his own teachers, presented as they state them, and accompanied by what they offer as refutations ... He must be able to hear them from persons who actually believe them ... he must know them in their most plausible and persuasive form.[18]

The second outcome is arguably the most important one. As we saw above, consistently being at each other's throats, denying ourselves interaction and discussion with those with whom we disagree, very often results in caricaturing and dehumanizing others. Dehumanizing others can, at worst, result in acts of violence, but even without that violence, it often results in a society where resentment and anger are frequently brewing at the surface. Striving for a society of mutual respect and care *requires* us to look each other in the eye, to interact with each other, to treat each other as persons *simpliciter* first, and only as persons-with-disagreements secondly. When we dehumanize others, we become increasingly less empathetic and sympathetic; we are far more likely to do harm to them, or, at least, regard any harm that befalls them as justified. However, when we seek to dialogue with each other, even when we have no intention (or at least expectation) of actually changing each other's minds, animosity sometimes tends to melt away.

An excellent example of this can be seen in Dr. Susan Wicklund's book *This Common Secret*, which chronicles her years as an abortion provider, including many times she has come in contact with pro-life activists. She tells a story of a young man, who was vehemently pro-life and with whom she engages in hours of face-to-face dialogue. After these various conversations, Wicklund writes about the mutual esteem they gained for each other, even though their respective views on abortion were unaffected:

I gained respect for his convictions and earnest beliefs. He, I think, learned a few things about the realities of abortion and the tough life dilemmas women are faced with. Several times over the ensuing months we met and talked more. The last time we spoke was just before he was entering a seminary. At the end of the conversation, before we parted ways, he said, "You know, I can't hate you anymore."[19]

This is the effect we should strive to achieve, not just when it comes to the issue of abortion, but with all controversial, divisive issues. In a world where we refuse to listen to each other, we tend to slander, vilify, vandalize, hurt, and sometimes kill each other. In a world where we talk, dialogue, trade arguments, genuinely try to understand each other, and still shake hands after all is said and done, we come one step closer to saying to our former adversaries: "I can't hate you anymore."

Finally, it is probably best to acknowledge that the discussion in this book reflects the concerns of a largely American audience, although certainly other nations and cultures will be mentioned along the way. This is because abortion remains a far more contentious issue in the United States than in other countries. By contrast, William LaFleur has detailed how a kind of majority consensus seems to have developed in Japan regarding abortion.[20] We will mention at points how various other countries have dealt with abortion, but it is also significant that both the authors were raised in the United States. Both are accustomed to a political, social, and moral environment in which the topic of abortion matters. Both are accustomed to challenges to their views, and both authors have had to learn to treat those with whom they disagree with respect. We believe that our ability to continue to dialogue with one another and to learn from one another on an issue that matters to both of us makes us well-suited to offer this book, in which we detail our divergences and attempt to glimpse some convergences related to abortion, a momentous but complicated issue. We have always been "abortion adversaries," but this has never mitigated our 17 years of friendship and mutual care and esteem.

Notes

1 Soran Reader, 2008, "Abortion, Killing, and Maternal Moral Authority," *Hypatia*, 23: 132–149, at p. 132.
2 See Patricia Gurin, et al. 2013, "Intergroup Dialogue: Its Role in Contemporary Society," in Patricia Gurin, Biren (Ratnesh) A. Nagda, and Ximena Zúñiga, eds., *Dialogue Across Difference: Practice, Theory, and Research on Intergroup Dialogue* (New York: Russell Sage Foundation), pp. 11–31 at p. 29.
3 Marsha Vanderford, 1989, "Vilification and Social Movements: A Case Study of Pro-Life and Pro-Choice Rhetoric," *Quarterly Journal of Speech*, 75.2: 166–182, at p. 170.
4 Vanderford, 1989, p. 174.
5 *New York Times*, 1992, "Robertson Letter Attacks Feminists." Available at: http://www.nytimes.com/1992/08/26/us/robertson-letter-attacks-feminists.html
6 Pope Francis made these comments after praying the *Regina Caeli* in Saint Peter's Square on Easter Monday, 28 March 2016. See Pope Francis, 2016: http://w2.vatican.va/content/francesco/en/angelus/2016/documents/papa-francesco_regina-coeli_20160328.html.
7 Charles C. Camosy, 2015, *Beyond the Abortion Wars: A Way Forward for a New Generation* (Grand Rapids: Eerdmans).
8 See Camosy, 2015, p. 13.
9 We'll use "discourse" and "dialogue" more or less interchangeably in this book.
10 Mulder will discuss this a bit more in his initial chapter.
11 See Camosy, 2015, pp. 17–18.
12 "Malice aforethought" is how the United States Code puts it. See 18 U.S. Code 1111 – Murder, at https://www.law.cornell.edu/uscode/text/18/1111.
13 See Camosy, 2015, chapter 1.
14 See Bertha Alvarez Manninen, 2014, *Pro-Life, Pro-Choice: Shared Values in the Abortion Debate* (Nashville: Vanderbilt University Press), p. 92.
15 As in the Democratic Party 2016 party platform. See: https://www.democrats.org/party-platform.
16 This is John Paul II's term. We have agreed not to use (in our own voices) the terms "pro-abortion" and "anti-choice" in this book, though we are not engaging the question of whether they are accurate terms in this book.
17 See Pope John Paul II, 1995, *Evangelium Vitae*, 73 at: http://w2.vatican.va/content/john-paul-ii/en/encyclicals/documents/hf_jp-ii_enc_25031995_evangelium-vitae.html.

18 John Stuart Mill, 2004, *On Liberty and Other Essays*, ed. Stefan Collini (Cambridge: Cambridge University Press), p. 38.
19 Susan Wicklund, 2007, *This Common Secret: My Journey as an Abortion Doctor* (New York: Public Affairs Publishing), pp. 238–239.
20 See William R. LaFleur, 1990, "Contestation and Consensus: The Morality of Abortion in Japan," *Philosophy East and West*, 40: 529–542.

References

18 U.S. Code 1111 – Murder. Available at: https://www.law.cornell.edu/uscode/text/18/1111
Camosy, Charles. 2015. *Beyond the Abortion Wars: A Way Forward for a New Generation*. Grand Rapids, MI: Eerdmans.
Democratic Party. 2016. Party Platform. Available at: https://www.democrats.org/party-platform
Francis, Pope. 2016. "Regina Caeli." Available at: http://w2.vatican.va/content/francesco/en/angelus/2016/documents/papa-francesco_regina-coeli_20160328.html
Gurin, Patricia, Biren (Ratnesh) A. Nagda, Cookie White Stephan, and Walter G. Stephan. 2013. "Intergroup Dialogue: Its Role in Contemporary Society," in Patricia Gurin, Biren (Ratnesh) A. Nagda, and Ximena Zúñiga (eds.), *Dialogue Across Difference: Practice, Theory, and Research on Intergroup Dialogue*. New York: Russell Sage Foundation, pp. 11–31.
John Paul II, Pope. 1995. *Evangelium Vitae*. New York, NY: Random House Inc.
LaFleur, William R. 1990. "Contestation and Consensus: The Morality of Abortion in Japan." *Philosophy East and West*, 40. 4: 529–542.
Manninen, Bertha Alvarez. 2014. *Pro-Life, Pro-Choice: Shared Values in the Abortion Debate*. Nashville: Vanderbilt University Press.
Mill, John Stuart. 1991. *On Liberty and Other Essays*. New York: Oxford University Press.
New York Times. August 26, 1992. "Robertson Letter Attacks Feminists." Available at: http://www.nytimes.com/1992/08/26/us/robertson-letter-attacks-feminists.html
Reader, Soran. 2008. "Abortion, Killing, and Maternal Moral Authority." *Hypatia*, 23. 2: 132–150.
Vanderford, Marsha. 1989. "Vilification and Social Movements: A case study of Pro-Life and Pro-Choice Rhetoric." *Quarterly Journal of Speech*, 75. 2: 166–182.
Wicklund, Susan. 2007. *This Common Secret: My Journey as an Abortion Doctor*. New York: Public Affairs Publishing.

1

WHY I AM PRO-CHOICE

Bertha Alvarez Manninen

I. What does it mean (for me) to be pro-choice (and what does it not mean)?

I am pro-choice. Before I tell you why, I want to first clarify what that means from my perspective. Pro-choice does not mean pro-abortion for me. I neither celebrate abortions, nor think women should be pushed or pressured into obtaining one. Forced abortions, from my perspective, are as bad as forced gestations. I do not regard abortions as merely medical procedures with no moral dimensions. I do not regard abortions cavalierly, nor think anyone else should either. Even though I believe women should retain the right to obtain an abortion (within certain limits, as I will discuss below), I also think that everyone who supports abortion choice should always remember that in abortion, a death occurs. And that it is the death of a nascent human life (in that fetuses are members of the species *Homo sapiens*). Obtaining an abortion is not equivalent to removing an organ or getting a haircut. Whether this species membership renders fetuses bearers of moral and legal rights will be explored below. However, I am neither anti-family, nor anti-child. I have children of my own who are my light and my world; in fact, it was the experience of being pregnant and having them that really tested my pro-choice views, and required that I deeply examine them.

I feel the necessity to begin with this disclaimer because there is rampant mischaracterization of pro-choice advocacy. Admittedly, some of these accusations are not without merit. There are many pro-choice philosophers who have made claims about fetal life that I not only dispute, but find deeply morally troubling. Mary Anne Warren,[1] Peter Singer,[2] and Michael Tooley,[3] for example, all argue that a necessary prerequisite for personhood is the possession of certain cognitive capacities, such as self-consciousness, reasoning abilities, autonomy (the ability to self-govern and make rational choices), and moral agency (the ability to make morally significant choices). As such, no fetus ever has a right to life, and abortions may be performed for any reason whatsoever. They also hold, for similar reasons, that infanticide is not intrinsically immoral because neonates, also, possess none of these cognitive capacities. This point was argued more recently by Alberto Giubilini and Francesca Minerva in an article entitled "After-Birth Abortion: Why Should the Baby Live." Here, they argue that infanticide, or "after-birth abortion" should be permissible for the same reason abortion is: neither the fetus, nor the newborn infant, possesses sufficiently robust mental properties to qualify as persons with a right to life.[4] In response, I published a criticism of their arguments from a pro-choice perspective, and argued that there was nothing intrinsic about pro-choice advocacy that would lead to the conclusion that newborns have no right to life.[5] Aside from academia, however, I have also heard pro-choice advocates argue for their position in morally concerning ways. They argue that a fetus isn't human, that it isn't alive, or that it is just a clump of cells. In her book *Why I am an Abortion Doctor*, Dr. Suzanne Poppema, although providing an excellent perspective on why abortions should remain legal and accessible, constantly derides fetal life by referring to fetal remains as mere "tissue" and even wantonly derides a plumber who begins to cry upon realizing that a disposal system he was installing would be used to break up fetal parts. Poppema describes the remains after an abortion as, "organic material that once was living but now is not living. It was tissue contained in a woman who made a conscious decision that she no longer wanted this tissue in her body."[6] From this perspective, disposing of fetal remains is no different than disposing of any other post-operative organ or tissue.

While there certainly are pro-choice supporters who take a dismissive attitude against fetal life, there are many feminist pro-choice advocates who do not. In my writings, I have consistently called for pro-choice advocates to argue in favor of their position in a way that does not entail robbing the fetus of its humanity and moral worth.[7] In her article "Is There Life After *Roe*?" Frances Kissling, a leading Catholic pro-choice advocate and former president of Catholics for a Free Choice, chastises the abortion movement for its failure to display adequate respect for fetal life:

> The precise moment when the fetus becomes a person is less important than a simple acknowledgement that whatever category of human life the fetus is, it nonetheless has value, it is not nothing ... I am deeply struck by the number of thoughtful, progressive people who have been turned off to the prochoice movement by the lack of adequate and clear expressions of respect for fetal life, people who are themselves grappling with the conflict between upholding women's rights and the right to conscience and respecting the value of nascent human life. There is a strong distaste of the prochoice community in many facets of society because of the inability or unwillingness to acknowledge one iota of value in fetal life. It almost seems as if there has been a "hardening of the heart" resulting from the prochoice position.[8]

Feminist philosopher Margaret Olivia Little argues that, ultimately, the decision whether or not to gestate remains with the pregnant woman alone. Nevertheless, she too argues that abortions should always be approached with a profound appreciation for the life that is taken: "burgeoning human life, we might put it, is respect-worthy. Abortion involves loss. Not just loss of the hope that various parties might have invested, but loss of something valuable in its own right."[9] Pro-choice feminist Linda Francke's book *The Ambivalence of Abortion* begins with her writing about her own abortion experience, and how it deepened her view of the moral ambiguity that may accompany exercising the choice she had fought so hard to protect. In response to her husband's attempt at comfort, telling her that an early embryo is "not a life ... it's a bunch of cells smaller than my fingernail," Francke thinks to herself: "any woman who has had children knows that certain feeling in her taut, swollen breasts, and the slight but constant ache in her uterus signals the arrival of life. Though I would march myself into blisters for a woman's right to exercise the option of motherhood, I discovered there in the waiting room that I was not the modern woman I thought I was."[10]

In my book *Pro-Life, Pro-Choice: Shared Values in the Abortion Debate*, I spend a whole chapter emphasizing why it is so vitally important that pro-choice advocates move away from defending their positions on reproductive liberty in a way that fails to accord fetal life proper value and respect. Some of the more philosophical reasons why I think this will be explored below, but here I will focus on one important point that I think Francke's words highlight: she assumes that acknowledging the moral worth of fetal life is inconsistent with being a pro-choice feminist, or a "modern woman." But why should this be so? Even in cases where women choose to procure abortions, very few approach it wantonly, or experience it as the mere extraction of unwanted cells or tissue. Quite the contrary – many women who obtain abortions recognize that a morally significant life has ended; if pro-choice advocates fail to recognize that, then they fail to emotionally and mentally support the very women whose reproductive rights they fight so vehemently to protect. Take, for example, a woman interviewed for Leslie Cannold's book *The Abortion Myth* when another woman referred to fetuses being discarded after an abortion like unwanted trash: "The whole handling of the abortion issue is wrong. You don't toss [the fetus] in the garbage. I mean, I've had an abortion, it was an incredibly painful experience. I didn't toss it in the garbage. And I find it really distressing to hear it referred to in that way."[11] Two other women's experiences highlight the way pro-choice advocacy has failed to meet many women's emotional needs after experiencing an abortion.

> I desperately wanted a feminist article, pamphlet, speech, anything that would let me have both the abortion and my own ambivalence ... I wanted to deal with the moral balance sheet of abortion, not to have to deny that one existed for me. Instead people kept telling me I was misguided, brainwashed by the patriarchy. They patiently explained that the fetus was just a bunch of cells.[12]

Heidi also feels alienation from reproductive rights activists, whom she feels treat abortion too casually. She says, "I find myself not being a great supporter of the pro-choice movement. When I ask myself why that is, since I believe in the right to choose, what comes back as my answer is that it is something you are killing." Heidi laments that so much of the pro-choice side "tries to pretend that's not true."[13]

In Japan, women who procure abortions sometimes take part in a Buddhist-themed *mizuko kuyo* ritual, a memorial rite for either miscarried or aborted fetuses, or stillborn infants. In many of the rituals, the bodhisattva Jizo, who is "traditionally associated with the care of travelers in the six realms of birth, and also known as the special protector of children,"[14] is invoked. Sculptures of him are often adorned with baby clothes and toys, and prayers to the aborted fetus are typically attached. Many scholars have focused on the therapeutic role the rituals can serve for women who have aborted, as well as for a society that largely regards abortion as "a painful social necessity."[15] Despite the general societal consensus that abortion must remain legal and available, one role of the *mizuko kuyo* rituals is to remind people that abortion does indeed constitute the taking of a human life and that, therefore, it should not be regarded wantonly. Indeed, the debate in the U.S. regarding the fetus' personhood and moral status is largely absent in Japan. As one Buddhist bishop puts it: "*Mizuko* is not a different kind of life – your life and the *mizuko* life are the same, same nature."[16] Here we have a situation that would strike many in America as puzzling: the fetus is clearly regarded as subject of moral value and concern, and its death can be mourned in the same manner as the death of any other human being, and yet abortion remains permissible and available.

It should be emphasized that the fact that *some* women have moral difficulties when obtaining an abortion does not mean *all* women do. There is evidence that the abortion experience is often regarded favorably by women.[17] Yet the fact that some women experience difficulties is sometimes taken as evidence in favor of the existence of Post-Abortion Syndrome, allegedly a kind of Post-Traumatic Stress Disorder that is supposed to be intrinsic when procuring an abortion.[18] No medical or psychological organization recognizes Post-Abortion Syndrome as a clinical disease. In 2008, the American Psychological Association reviewed a variety of articles in psychology and mental health journals in order to come to a more definitive conclusion concerning the existence of Post-Abortion Syndrome. They found that "the best scientific evidence indicates that the relative risk of mental health problems among adult women who have an unplanned pregnancy is no greater if they have an elective first trimester abortion than if they deliver that pregnancy."[19]

None of this mitigates the moral obligation I believe pro-choice advocates possess to approach the issue of abortion with frank honesty about the life that is being taken. Dr. Lisa Harris, an abortion provider, also implores the pro-choice community to do the same. She admits that "[t]here is violence in abortion, especially in second trimester procedures"[20] but that it is perfectly understandable why pro-choice advocacy has been reticent to engage in this difficult conversation for fear that it would be used against them as grounds for eradicating abortion rights. Nevertheless, it is a conversation that we need to embrace, for successfully arguing in favor of abortion rights in light of these difficulties only strengthens the position.

It may seem odd to simultaneously argue in favor of abortion rights while acknowledging that fetal life has value. The two, however, are not mutually exclusive. Take, for example, how we approach euthanizing our pets – even if we acknowledge that the death was justifiable given certain medical afflictions, we still mourn the loss of our animal companion, and we certainly don't approach its death wantonly. The same applies in some cases of passive euthanasia for our human loved ones. Sometimes we have family members or friends who are so ill that they refuse life-sustaining treatment or, in cases when they cannot choose for themselves, their medical proxies decide for them. Sometimes we are also faced with removing life-sustaining treatment, e.g., respirators or feeding tubes, when we think that it is no longer prolonging their lives in any meaningful way. In these cases, someone has actively opted for death over continued life, yet even with this choice oftentimes there is sadness involved, as well as a deep feeling of loss and mourning, when we acknowledge that something morally significant – the life of our loved ones – has been lost. Choosing death for something is not mutually exclusive with valuing their lives, or mourning their loss. This applies to abortion choice as well.

II. Are human fetuses persons?

If pressed, individuals who argue in favor of abortion rights by denying the fetus' humanity do not really intend to deny that it is a member of our species, or that it is biologically alive. Instead, they are making a claim about the fetus' moral status, and whether it is the kind of being that is the bearer of moral (and therefore legal) rights. This is not a question concerning the fetus' biological species membership, but rather about their moral personhood. Ultimately, I will argue that it is possible to be in favor of abortion rights regardless of whether the fetus is granted the moral and legal status of persons. However, because the question of fetal personhood comes up so often in the abortion debate, I would be remiss not to discuss it here. I will first consider the view that fetuses are not persons because they lack certain (allegedly necessary) mental capacities – what I will call the "cognitive account of moral personhood." Then, I will discuss the view that seems most prevalent amongst those who deny abortion rights – that moral status and personhood begin from the moment of conception. I will call this the "genetic account of moral personhood." My intention is to show that these two views, which lie on extreme ends to each other, have grave difficulties that make them, for different reasons, impractical and morally concerning to hold. I will then propose a middle ground between these views, and argue that there are good reasons to believe that moral status begins sometime in mid-gestation, when the fetus attains the capacity for some degree of conscious life.

The cognitive account of moral personhood

As abovementioned, some philosophers deny the fetal right to life on the grounds that, in order for any human being to qualify as a person, several rather robust mental traits must be possessed as a pre-requisite. Here, I will present reasons why this approach is deeply flawed.

Kicking a chair in anger is a vastly different kind of action than kicking a child in anger. Disposing of a cell phone when it no longer meets your needs or desires is a very different kind of action than disposing of a child if she becomes too difficult to parent. While we should all be careful not to wantonly destroy any life, stepping on an ant hill is a different kind of action than killing a human being. In general, chairs, cell phones, and ants are not regarded as beings that have rights, particularly a right to life, whereas children, clearly, do have such rights. On what basis do we make such distinctions?

In her article "On the Moral and Legal Status of Abortion," Mary Ann Warren offers this non-exhaustive, but philosophically common, list of the allegedly necessary mental traits that any being must possess in order to qualify for moral status, and subsequently, a right to life.

1. Consciousness (of objects and events external and/or internal to the being), and in particular the capacity to feel pain [i.e. sentience];
2. Reasoning (the *developed* capacity to solve new and relatively complex problems);
3. Self-motivated activity (activity which is relatively independent of either genetic or direct external control);
4. The capacity to communicate, by whatever means, messages of an indefinite number of possible contents, but on indefinitely many possible topics;
5. The presence of self-concepts, and self-awareness, either individual or racial, or both.[21]

Peter Singer, also, offers a similar list: "rationality, self-consciousness, awareness, capacity to feel, etc."[22] Both Singer and Warren pick out two of these characteristics as fundamental for defining a person: self-consciousness and rationality. This is also central to Michael Tooley's analysis of what it means to have a right to life, and why fetuses, according to him, do not possess such a right. According to both Singer and Tooley, a being cannot possess a right to life unless that being is at least capable of desiring continued existence, and in order to have this capacity, this being must be able to conceive of herself as a distinct entity existing over time – that is, she must possess some degree of self-consciousness.[23] Similarly, Singer argues that "…if the right to life is the right to continue existing as a distinct entity, then the desire relevant to possessing a right to life is the desire to continue existing as a distinct entity. But only a being who is capable of conceiving herself as a distinct entity over time – that is, only a person – could have this desire. Therefore only a person could have a right to life."[24]

Tooley argues that there is a correlation between rights and desires. He maintains that violating A's right to X is, essentially, to thwart a desire of A to obtain X.

> To ascribe a right to an individual is to assert something about the *prima facie* obligations of other individuals to act, or to refrain from acting, in certain

ways. However, the obligations in question are conditional ones, being dependent upon the existence of certain desires of the individual to whom the right is ascribed. Thus if an individual asks one to destroy something to which he has a right, one does not violate his right to that thing if one proceeds to destroy it. This suggests the following analysis: "A has a right to X" is roughly synonymous with "If A desires X, then others are under a *prima facie* obligation to refrain from actions that would deprive him of it"... "A has a right to X" is roughly synonymous with "A is the sort of thing that is subject of experiences and other mental states, A is capable of desiring X, and if A does desire X, then others are under a *prima facie* obligation to refrain from actions that would deprive him of it."[25]

It would make no sense to bestow a right to life onto cell phones, chairs, and ants because they lack the kind of consciousness necessary in order to possess the relevant desire for such a right – the desire for continued existence. In another of his writings, Tooley explains it this way:

The basic intuition is that a right is something that can be violated and that, in general, to violate an individual's right to something is to frustrate the corresponding desire. Suppose, for example, that you own a car. There I am under a *prima facie* obligation not to take it from you. However, the obligation is not unconditional: it depends in part upon the existence of a corresponding desire in you. If you do not care whether I take your car, then I generally do not violate your right by doing so.[26]

It is true that fetuses lack any capacity for self-awareness. By mid-gestation they are sentient and conscious creatures, but a fetus' mental life is never so advanced that it leads to them being aware of themselves as distinct individuals who exist over time. Consequently, according to Tooley, a fetus is simply cognitively unable to possess the relevant desire for continued existence, and so there exists no basis in grounding a right to life for them.

These Singer/Tooley/Warren-esque arguments are flawed. It is quite clear that someone could have a right to something even if she lacks either the actual, or even potential, corresponding desire. I would still violate someone's property rights if I stole her car regardless of whether or not she actively desires the car. If a piece of property is bequeathed onto a young child, to take it from the child would still be regarded as stealing, and a violation of the child's rights, even though she may be too young to even understand that she is the owner of any property at all. If self-awareness is what is required for possessing the relevant desire for having a right to life, not even infants or toddlers would possess a right to life, for they lack the capacity to regard themselves as individuals who subsist over time (Tooley does acknowledge that his argument entails the moral permissibility of infanticide, but it also entails the moral permissibility of homicide as well in regards to very young children, at least until they are able to desire continued existence).

While we can debate, in general, whether anyone possesses a moral right to healthcare or education, certainly one reason we *wouldn't* argue against someone possessing such a right is because they lack the cognitive capacity to desire it. Suppose a child with a developmental disability lacks the capacity to desire an education that would increase her conceptual or physical capacities – surely she has a right to that education (assuming anyone has a right to education at all) regardless of whether she has the capacity to desire it. Similarly, individuals with extreme cognitive impairments, infant, toddlers, or maybe even an elderly person with dementia may all lack the capacity to desire medical treatment (and if you are a parent, you will know that often times children very clearly *do not* desire medical treatment, especially when it involves needles), yet we wouldn't deny them medical treatment for this reason alone; we wouldn't say, for example, that an infant has no right to a life-saving heart surgery because he lacks the conceptual capacity to desire that surgery, or to continue living at all. While alive, my father suffered from dementia and Type 2 diabetes. Because of the former ailment, he did not understand that he also had the latter. Therefore he was cognitively unable to desire his insulin injections. However, this inability did not mitigate the need for those injections and, therefore, had we not given them to him, it would have harmed him. My father, while alive, had the same right to his insulin injection as anyone else who needs it – regardless of whether he could actively desire it.

While a full exposition of the nature of rights (what it is, who has them, what purposes they serve) lies beyond the scope of our present topic, it does not seem controversial to hold that one of the purposes of rights is to protect their bearers from harm. Stealing my property, curtailing my freedom of worship and speech, and killing me all harm me in some fashion or another, and as such ascribing rights to me protects me from harm by also ascribing corresponding obligations to others (not to steal from me, or invade my freedom of speech and religion, or kill me), and consequences if they refuse to meet those obligations. One central issue concerning whether any being ought to be given a right to life is whether depriving that being of continued existence inflicts any harm on it, and clearly whether or not someone can be harmed by being deprived of life is not contingent at all on whether one has the capacity to desire life (just as one can be harmed by being deprived of medical care even if one is unable to desire that medical care).

Therefore, it seems to me that the cognitive account of moral personhood, insofar as it is used to ascribe a right to life onto any being, including human embryos or fetuses, fails – not only philosophically (as I believe I have shown here) but practically as well. It would deny a right to life to embryos and infants, but also toddlers, very young children, the severely mentally disabled, and individuals suffering from advanced dementia – anyone, essentially, who lacks a robust sense of self-consciousness. To me, these are the kinds of beings who need the *most* protection because of their vulnerabilities. When it comes to the applicability of moral theories, Singer writes that "ethics is not an ideal system that is noble in theory but no good in practice. The reverse of this is closer to the truth: an ethical judgment that is no good in practice must suffer from a theoretical defect as well, for the whole point of ethical judgments is to guide practice."[27] It is for this very reason these arguments should be rejected; the cognitive account of moral personhood is not something that can be put into practice without leading to deeply morally troubling consequences.

The genetic account of moral personhood

In 1983, Sheila Hodgers died an excruciating death in Ireland after being denied cancer treatment because she was pregnant and the Catholic hospital where she was being treated refused to engage in any action that could harm her fetus. Hodgers ended up giving birth to a premature baby girl who died immediately thereafter; she then died two days later from a cancer that had spread throughout her body.[28] In 2012, Savita Halappanavar was rushed to University Hospital Galway in Ireland while experiencing a septic miscarriage of her 17-week-old fetus after her uterus had ruptured. Halappanavar requested an abortion in order to avoid any further complications after it was discovered that the fetus could not be saved. The hospital refused the abortion so long as the fetus had a detectable heartbeat. Four days after she was admitted, she delivered a dead fetus, slipped into a coma, and died four days later. Dr. Sabaratnam Arulkumaran, a London professor of obstetrics and gynecology, noted that had Halappanavar received an abortion and been aggressively treated with antibiotics, she might have survived.[29]

Hodgers' and Halappanavar's deaths can be traced back to Ireland's strict prohibition of abortion given that fetal life is constitutionally protected from conception onward by their 8th Amendment, which states that "the State acknowledges the right to life of the unborn and, with due regard to the equal right to life of the mother, guarantees in its laws to respect, and, as far as practicable, by its laws to defend and vindicate that right."[30] In the wake of Halappanavar's death, the Irish Protection of Life During Pregnancy Act of 2013 slightly loosened some of its anti-abortion policies, now allowing for hospitals to perform abortions in cases where a woman's life is endangered. However, Hodgers' and Halappanavar's respective cases force us to think about the practical consequences of enshrining a fetal right to life as part of our laws or social policies, for many in the United States would like to adopt a similar constitutional amendment.[31]

In some election years, various states have tried to pass Personhood Amendments (also called Human Life Amendments) which aim at codifying into law that embryos and fetuses are persons, with all the full rights therein, from conception. In 2008, Colorado, Montana, Georgia, and South Dakota all had such an initiative on their state ballots. In 2010, many more states joined in, including Florida, Michigan, Mississippi, Nevada, and Virginia. As of now, all of them have failed to pass, but its supporters have vowed to continually press for new versions of the initiative in subsequent voting years. The intentions of those who support the amendment are clear – they regard it as an important step in repealing *Roe v. Wade*. In reference to Georgia's 2008 initiative, Richard Thompson, the President and Chief Counsel of the Thomas More Law Center states:

The Human Life Amendment provides Georgia with the best legal means of overturning the central holding of *Roe v Wade*. At the very least, it ensures that Georgia immediately becomes a pro-life state the moment the shackles of Roe are broken … The adoption of this amendment will place Georgia at the forefront of the battle to restore the sanctity of innocent human life.[32]

Advocates of Personhood Amendments clearly wish to criminalize abortions, and this desire is what primarily fuels their persistence. Yet regarding embryos and fetuses as persons, and granting them all the rights of persons, has implications that reach beyond abortion. I ended the section above by endorsing the view that moral theories and stances need to be applicable as a reason to reject the cognitive account – I want to begin this section by doing the same. Suppose we do succeed in officially designating embryos and fetuses as persons from conception – that is, let us assume that simply being a member of the species *Homo sapiens* is sufficient for being ascribed full and equal moral and legal rights. This means that we would have to treat embryos and fetuses *in exactly the same way*, in regards to their rights, as we treat any other person. As we can see from Hodgers' and Halappanavar's cases, the practical implications of doing this are morally problematic. Let me discuss two additional concerns that also illustrate this.

At the age of 18, Carmen Guadalupe Vasquez Aldana was sentenced to 30 years in jail in El Salvador. She delivered a stillborn baby, who was conceived after she had been raped by her employer, and was convicted of aggravated homicide. Aldana claimed that she had lost her son because of medical complications late in the pregnancy. In other words, Aldana was convicted of murder and imprisoned for having a late-term miscarriage. There are at least a dozen other women serving time for similar sentences in El Salvador. Aldana was released on January 21, 2015 after widespread international outcry, and currently other women are hoping for a similar pardon.

Aldana's conviction is a direct result of Article 1 of the Salvadorian constitution, which grants all embryos and fetuses the status of personhood from the moment of conception. Given this, what happened to Aldana is not exactly surprising. When infants or children die, typically some kind of investigation ensues and if anyone is found responsible for that death, then that person is punished accordingly. Granting the moral and legal equivalence between fetal life and all other extra-uterine life, if a fetus is miscarried, or stillborn, a similar procedure would have to be followed. The pregnant woman would likely be subjected to some degree of scrutiny in order to determine if anything she did "caused" the fetus' death. So while miscarriage *per se* would not be subject to criminalization any more than the accidental death of persons would render someone legally liable (fetuses often die in the womb for reasons unrelated to anyone's actions), determining whether the death of an embryo or fetus was indeed accidental means that women, in the midst of grieving their loss, would be subject to some degree of investigation.

In 2011, House Republican Bobby Franklin introduced a bill to the Georgia Legislature that would have rendered all abortions the legal equivalent to murder and would require any instance of prenatal death, including spontaneous miscarriages, to be investigated for criminal activity. Anyone found guilty of "prenatal murder," defined as any instance of embryonic or fetal death due to "human involvement," would face either a life sentence or even the death penalty:

> [t]he State of Georgia has the duty to protect all innocent life from the moment of conception until natural death. We know that life begins at conception ... The Georgia Constitution, at Article I, Section I, Paragraph II, provides: "Protection to person and property is the paramount duty of government and shall be impartial and complete. No person shall be denied the equal protection of the laws." Because a fetus is a person, constitutional protection attaches at the moment of conception. It is therefore the duty of the General Assembly to protect the innocent life that is being taken.[33]

Because the fetus is considered a person according to this bill, its death is regarded as equivalent to the death of any other person. A person's death is typically investigated in order to determine if it was accidental or a product of someone else's deliberate actions; if the latter is found, a charge of some degree of murder ensues, and punishment is bestowed upon any guilty party. Therefore, given the ascription of personhood onto a fetus, its death would need to be dealt with in a similar manner.

Francis Beckwith, a pro-life philosopher, disagrees that ascribing personhood onto a fetus would necessarily lead to these consequences. For starters, he writes that investigating a miscarriage would not be necessary, since "[p]eople die all the time, but we do not ask those closest to the deceased to prove that they did not commit a murder."[34] But clearly this isn't true – when people die and the cause of death is not immediately clear (as would be the case for many women who experience a miscarriage), the people and circumstances that surround them are, indeed, subject to investigation. Given the fetus' location in a woman's body, and given the effects her actions may have on it, even a cursory investigation of the circumstances of its death will involve probing a woman's body and any actions she took that may have affected the fetus. Beckwith also argues that "not all miscarriages would be suspect, but only those for which there are reasonable grounds to suspect that deliberate killing was involved."[35] But how shall we define such "reasonable grounds"? And how would we even know why a particular fetus died without first conducting an investigation as to the cause of its death? The fact that a woman's actions during pregnancy could be subject to such a level of scrutiny would not only result in a grave violation of her rights and privacy during a time of grieving and loss, it could also potentially lead to severe stress for *all* pregnant women, who now have to worry about their own welfare were their pregnancies to take a tragic turn.

Let's consider some implications of assigning personhood onto embryos that exist outside the womb. When individuals undergo In Vitro Fertilization (IVF), a woman's egg and a man's sperm are combined in a petri dish to create the embryo, which is then transferred into a woman's uterus in the hopes it successfully implants and gestates. Often, more embryos are created than are initially implanted, in case pregnancy does not occur the first time. As a result, there exist thousands of surplus embryos in frozen storage in various fertility clinics across the United States. Often, after individuals no longer wish to have children, the frozen embryos will be destroyed. If embryos are given the same moral status and rights as the ones we enjoy, then such an act would be tantamount to homicide. The sponsors of Mississippi's Personhood Amendment admit that this is the case; while it would not affect the legality of IVF treatments, it would be the case that "unused embryos cannot be destroyed."[36]

In 1992, Tennessee Supreme Court adjudicated *Davis v. Davis*, the first embryo disposition case. Here, a formerly married couple were fighting over the fate of their seven surplus frozen embryos, which were left over after repeated and unsuccessful IVF treatments. Mrs. Davis asked the court to allow her to implant the embryos, since it was the only remaining chance she had to become pregnant; Mr. Davis argued that he no longer wanted to share children with his ex-wife. The Tennessee Supreme Court ruled that implanting the embryos against Mr. Davis' consent would violate his procreative liberty.

> ... disputes involving the disposition of preembryos produced by in vitro fertilization should be resolved, first, by looking to the preferences of the progenitors. If their wishes cannot be ascertained, or if there is dispute, then their prior agreement concerning disposition should be carried out. If no prior agreement exists, then the relative interests of the parties in using or not using the preembryos must be weighed. *Ordinarily, the party wishing to avoid procreation should prevail*, assuming that the other party has a reasonable possibility of achieving parenthood by means other than use of the preembryos in question. If no other reasonable alternatives exist, then the argument in favor of using the preembryos to achieve pregnancy should be considered.[37]

If embryos are considered persons, with all the full rights therein, this decision would have been exactly the opposite – the party wishing to keep the embryos and bring them to term would always win, since this is the best way to ensure that they won't be destroyed. Now turn the tables and suppose that the party wanting the embryos to be gestated is the man, whereas the woman is the one refusing. It would seem to follow that the woman can be compelled into implanting the embryos and gestating them, since considerations of bodily autonomy are outweighed by the embryos' right to life (according to those who support Personhood Amendments as a way to ban abortions). Similarly, what should happen to the thousands of embryos already existing in fertility clinics? The only way to avoid their destruction (which, remember, would be morally equivalent to homicide if they are persons) is to implant them in women for gestation. But who would provide these uteruses? The respective egg donor? If she is unwilling, can she be forced? If she is no longer available, can other women be forced to gestate them? This would mean that these women would undergo a forced implantation of these embryos in addition to forced gestation. These are complications I do not believe supporters of Personhood Amendments anticipate.

In general, I think supporters of such amendments, and of the belief that fetuses have full and equal moral status with born humans, only consider the alleged implications this view has for abortion rights, without stopping to consider the implications it can have in other areas as well. However, while I believe I have shown why holding to such a view of moral status leads to morally concerning consequences, rendering its applicability suspect, this does not logically entail that the genetic account of moral personhood is incorrect. Perhaps a pro-life advocate is willing to bite the bullet on many of these concerns. Other than leading to unfavorable consequences, is there any other reason to reject the genetic account?

There are two reasons why the genetic account of moral status has been difficult for me to accept. First, it has never been made sufficiently clear to me why simply belonging to a certain species, even our own, is sufficient for moral status – that is, it is unclear how a biological fact about species membership *in and of itself* is supposed to translate into a moral fact. While I am sympathetic to the view that human beings have a moral status higher than that of other animals, the reasons I believe this extend beyond simply our membership in a certain species: we are sentient creatures, with fairly complex minds. This means we can be bearers of harm in ways that other animals cannot be (but, to the extent that other animals can be the bearers of harm, they too deserve the corresponding rights to protect them). For example, we have a right to freedom of worship because to impede on something as intimate and vital to a human being as their relationship with their version of the divine can cause great emotional and mental distress. My dogs, however, do not have this right because they are simply incapable of worshipping any divine entity, and so are not harmed by not being given such a right. Now consider whether it would make sense to bestow a right to freedom of religion onto an embryo in a petri dish – I do not think many would disagree that such an idea is an absurd one. To bestow such a right upon an embryo would be meaningless, since an embryo cannot be harmed by not being allowed to worship. Simply being a member of the species *Homo sapiens* is not sufficient for ascribing this right to the embryo because doing so serves no function in this context.

If we agree that rights exist in order to prevent their bearers from suffering harm, a pro-life advocate would likely argue that ascribing the right to life to an embryo does make sense because it *is* protecting a vital interest – the interest in continued existence. The embryo can be harmed by the deprivation of its life, and as such it is as entitled to being ascribed a right to life as any other human being. This is essentially what Don Marquis argues in his famous essay "Why Abortion is Immoral":

> The future of a standard fetus includes a set of experiences, projects, activities, and such which are identical with the futures of adult human beings and are identical with the futures of young children. Since the reason that is sufficient to explain why it is wrong to kill human beings after the time of birth is a

reason that also applies to fetuses, it follows that abortion is prima facie seriously morally wrong.[38]

In what may strike my readers as a surprise, I actually think Marquis' argument is mostly correct. I agree with him that killing any being (not just *human* beings) is morally wrong in relation to the extent that killing her deprives her of a valuable future and existence. Because Marquis does not limit his argument to simply the ethics of killing human beings, he is not making the claim that mere membership in a species is sufficient (or necessary) for moral status. However, in applying it to human embryos Marquis is making another assumption that I find problematic; he is making a tacit identity claim, that the embryo is the *same individual* who will go on to enjoy that life and who, therefore, will be harmed by its deprivation. In his influential *Evangelium Vitae*, Pope John Paul II also appears to be making similar identity claims:

> [P]rocured abortion is the deliberate and direct killing, by whatever means it is carried out, of a human being *in the initial phase of his or her existence* ... Some people try to justify abortion by claiming that the result of conception, at least up to a certain number of days, cannot yet be considered a personal human life. But in fact, "from the time that the ovum is fertilized, a life is begun which is neither that of the father nor the mother; it is rather the life of a new human being with his own growth ... It has been demonstrated that from the first instant there is established the programme of what this living being will be: a person, this individual person with his characteristic aspects already well determined."[39]

In other words, if we are to claim that in destroying an embryo or a fetus we are depriving this being of the rest of its future, what we are saying is that this future properly *belongs* to the embryo or fetus; that it is the *same* individual who would have gone on to live that future. While this may seem obvious to some, I think it can be called into question. The phrase "life begins at conception" is true in one capacity – it is at conception that we have a new genetically unique human organism. What is not clearly true to me is that this new human organism shares an identity relationship with any future person. That is, while it is clear to me that my genetic blueprint came into existence when my parents' gametes came together to form an embryo, it is not at all clear to me that *I* came into existence then.

In this sense we can begin to see something intrinsically fascinating about philosophical discourse – that, sometimes, certain ethical questions are vitally dependent on more foundational questions in other areas of philosophy as well, in this case metaphysics. The issue of diachronic personal identity (what is it that makes me the same individual over time) is a perennial one in philosophy. In order for the genetic account of moral personhood to function in the capacity pro-life advocates desire (to thwart abortion rights), it must somehow be the case that our personal identities began to exist whenever our unique genetic organism began to exist, a view that is known as animalism (for those who are religious and believe in the existence of immaterial souls, they may believe that God infuses the human organism with a soul upon conception). Again, this is because if an embryo or fetus is to be ascribed a right to life, it must be because death harms it in some way – because death deprives it of the rest of its life. As such, it must be *its* life to begin with, and so the embryo and fetus must be the *same* individual as the one who would have lived that life had it not been aborted.

Animalism has many supporters, e.g., Eric Olson and David DeGrazia[40] (although animalism may be a necessary metaphysical position to hold in order to argue that embryos and fetuses have a right to life (Don Marquis has admitted to holding this view, for example) it should be noted that not all animalists are pro-life; DeGrazia, for example, is not), and it is a philosophically respectable position to hold. The fact that pro-life advocates are making such a claim about identity (if only tacitly) when arguing in favor of the genetic account of moral personhood is not in itself an argument against the latter, but I do think it is evidence that pro-life advocates have to think about metaphysical issues in a way that they were perhaps not anticipating.

Nevertheless, I believe I have shown why granting embryos and fetuses moral status and rights from conception is, for various reasons, problematic, and these reasons extend beyond the issue of abortion. In a society that grants embryos and fetuses personhood from conception onwards, I do not see how we could escape similar cases like that of Carmen Aldana, where women who miscarry would be subject to suspicion, possible investigation during what is surely an emotionally difficult time, or, at the very worst, may face conviction if they are deemed "responsible" for their respective fetus' death. What to do with existing surplus embryos from IVF treatments would also be a concern, since letting them die, or donating them to research, would now be akin to murder. Philosophically, I remain unconvinced that species membership is, in and of itself, sufficient to automatically grant embryos and fetuses equal moral (and legal) status to human persons, and it appears to me that the metaphysical claims that would have to be true to establish an identity relation between an embryo and a future human being are also problematic. I will say much about this latter claim in Chapter 3, when I respond to some of the arguments Mulder makes in Chapter 2.

The interest view of moral status and the embodied mind account of identity

In this section, I want to offer an alternative account of moral status (and identity) that walks a "middle ground" between the two views above that places the onset of moral status along radically different lines in human development. According to the cognitive account, the embryo/fetus *never* possesses moral status, not even right before birth (or even right after birth). According to the genetic account, the embryo/fetus possesses moral status from the very moment it begins to exist. Neither of these positions correspond to the general public's views on the morality of abortion.

A 2013 Gallup Poll on where Americans stand on abortion notes that "26% of Americans saying abortion should be legal under any circumstances and 20% saying it should be illegal in all circumstances. The majority, 52%, opt for something in between."[41] Most Americans oppose late-term abortions, whereas early trimester abortions are considered more acceptable. So a common view seems to be that the embryo/fetus *gains* moral status some time during pregnancy. Some philosophers, for example Norman Gillespie, agree that there is a morally significant difference between an early- and late-term abortion, but that this does not mean that we have to pin-point exactly when in pregnancy this change takes place (Gillespie favors a more gradualist approach to moral status[42]). However, if we were to try to demarcate a significant time in pregnancy when the fetus undergoes a substantial change, one that renders it a being with moral status, I think the strongest possible candidate is whenever in pregnancy the fetus becomes a sentient, conscious being. There are both moral and metaphysical reasons that can be offered in defense of this view (the latter related to the issue of personal identity); let's address each in turn.

Above I argued that cell phones and chairs are not typically regarded as the kinds of things which are rights-bearers. This is not, however, because these things lack the capacity to desire rights (we saw why this was problematic), but because cell phones and chairs, while they can be destroyed, cannot be *harmed* by that destruction. If the owner of a cell phone no longer wants to keep it, we don't typically believe the cell phone has been harmed when she exchanges it for a newer model, and the older one is destroyed. Yet consider the same actions directed toward an older pet. If the owner wants to just "trade" in his dog for a "younger model," many would likely recoil and accuse him of being a bad pet owner. If he didn't want his pet vaccinated, many would argue that the pet should get vaccinated anyway *for its own sake* (in contrast, no one would say that you should download the newest update for the cell phone's own sake).

According to Joel Feinberg, a being possesses an interest in x, "when he stands to gain or lose depending on the nature or the condition of x."[43] An individual's collection of interests "consists in all of those things in which one has a stake ... what promotes them is to his advantage or *in his interest*; what thwarts them is to his detriment or *against his interest*."[44] This is why an infant, or a pet, or an elderly person afflicted with dementia has an interest in her continued health even if she is incapable of desiring, or taking an interest in, her continued health. Feinberg argues that harming any being should always be "conceived as the thwarting, setting back, or defeating of an interest."[45] Therefore, only beings that are capable of having interests are viable candidates for moral status. Cell phones have no interests of their own, whereas animals and infants clearly do. What is it exactly that infants and animals have, that cell phones lack, that render the former, but not the latter, subjects of interests and, therefore, moral status?

As we saw above, the wrong answer to this question is one that ties in moral status to robust mental *capacities* – one need not be aware of their interests in order to have them. However, that does not mean that having some sort of mental life is not relevant. Cell phones and chairs cannot be subjects of interests because they cannot be harmed or benefited, and this is because they lack the capacity for any kind of sentience or conscious awareness. Nothing *matters* to nonsentient, nonconscious creatures. Bonnie Steinbock argues that "it is this notion of mattering that is key to moral status. Beings that have moral status must be capable of caring about what is done to them. They must be capable of being made, if only in a rudimentary sense, happy or miserable, comfortable or distressed."[46]

The most rudimentary form of consciousness is basic sentience – the ability to feel pain and pleasure, and therefore the ability to suffer and be affected by the actions of others. An animal that is sentient is capable of deriving enjoyment from pleasurable experiences and suffering from painful ones. It matters to the animal *herself* that suffering is not inflicted upon her, since *she* is the one undergoing the painful experiences. If an animal is burned in a forest fire, this elicits sympathy in us in a way that a tree being burned does not, and that's because we understand that the animal suffered whereas the tree did not. Given this, a minimally conscious being possesses at least two interests: an interest in not experiencing pain and an interest in experiencing pleasure. Because it has these interests, it can be harmed by the violation of these interests. Because it is the type of being that can be harmed or benefited, this is sufficient to impose upon other moral agents a *prima facie* moral duty not to violate that being's interests. Sentience, then, is necessary and sufficient to render a being part of the moral community.

One of the most telling reasons for why we ought to avoid inflicting needless pain is that if we were to "shift our perspective and see things *from another's point of view*, we will regard ourselves as having reasons provided by his pain [to avoid inflicting needless suffering]."[47] This captures another important reason for attributing moral status only to conscious beings. We can sympathize with them, and feel that we have obligations to them, because they have a *point of view*, an inner life, that is affected by our treatment of them. A being that can have experiences, be a locus for consciousness, not just an object, but rather a *subject*. As Thomas Nagel writes:

> ... an organism has conscious mental states if and only if there is something that it is like to *be* that organism – something it is like *for* the organism. We may call this the subjective character of experience ...[48]

Nonconscious objects, having no such phenomenology, can have no point of view, no inner life, that is affected by our treatment of them, and thus they cannot suffer or benefit from anything done to them. To borrow from Ludwig Wittgenstein,

> And can one say of the stone that it has a soul and *that* is what has the pain? What has a soul, or pain, to do with a stone? ... Look at a stone and imagine it having sensations. – One says to oneself: How could one so much as get the idea of ascribing a *sensation* to a *thing*.[49]

This passage eloquently captures the essence of what is called the "interest view" of moral status. Given that stones are inanimate things that lack the capacity to feel pain and to have consciousness, this tells us "about the kind of thing that stones are – what falls within and what exceeds the sense of their *type*."[50] Nonsentient beings are not the types of beings to whom we owe moral consideration because nothing at all is important *to them*.

If we accept this view of moral status, what this means for embryos and fetuses is that they become the kinds of beings that possess interests and can be harmed when they acquire the capacity for consciousness. When in pregnancy this occurs will be discussed below, but suffice it to say, for now, that we have a fair amount of evidence to conclude that early embryos and fetuses simply do not have the necessary neurological maturity to possess this capacity. Nevertheless, once they do acquire the capacity for sentience, while this may be enough to attribute at least one interest to them, the interest in avoiding pain, this alone does not show us that fetuses have an interest in continued existence. There is no clear correlation between sentience and an interest in continued existence; the interest in avoiding pain could still be respected if the being in question is killed as painlessly as possible. H.J. McCloskey argues this point as well:

> It is clear that, as it becomes more probable that a creature has a capacity for pain the more relevant becomes the case for refraining from acting towards it in ways which would cause it pain, if it could experience pain. This is distinct from there being a reason for abstaining from painlessly killing it. More important for the purposes of this paper, both are different from ascribing an animal a right to life ... whilst sentience seems to mark a morally profound difference in the world between those things that possess it, and those that lack it, sentience alone also seems not to qualify a being as a possessor of rights.[51]

A sentient fetus is a being that possesses some degree of moral status, and in that way is significantly different than a nonsentient fetus, but there is nothing in the interest view alone that entails that it has an interest in continued existence that being ascribed a right to life protects.

I suggest that, when it comes to the welfare of a human fetus, we move away from focusing on its capacity for sentience *simpliciter*, a move towards a deeper understanding of what that capacity means for issues of identity. It's not just that a sentient fetus has the capacity to feel pain, rather sentience brings with it something that the fetus never had before: a mental life. With sentience comes the rudimentary beginning of a phenomenology for the fetus, and for those who believe (as I do) that personal identity is intimately related to the capacity for having a mental life of some sort, it is at this point that the fetus becomes identical with the human being who would go on to live the rest of its life if it is not killed. It is here, then, that the fetus' death harms it in some fashion, because at this point you are actually robbing some*one* of the rest of its life. Or, put it this way: because I believe that I continue to exist as long as I retain the capacity for consciousness, I didn't begin to exist until I acquired the capacity for consciousness. Once I did begin to exist, killing my fetal life would have deprived *me* of my continued life, but before then, it would only have *prevented* me from coming into existence (and I do not believe that we have moral obligations to bring potential people into existence, though I will not argue this point here). If one believes that personal identity commences at the onset of the "birth" of a rudimentary mental life (rather than at the creation of one's organism at conception), then this is known as the Embodied Mind Account of Personal Identity (EMAPI).

In 1983, a young woman named Nancy Beth Cruzan lost control of her car, crashed, and was discovered lying face-down in a ditch. She had gone without oxygen for at least 15 minutes by the time the paramedics restored her breathing and heartbeat. She was diagnosed as being in a persistent vegetative state, and she never regained consciousness. Her family engaged in a years-long struggle with the hospital to remove her feeding tube, allowing her body to die. This was finally done on December 14, 1990, and she died 12 days later. The inscription on her tombstone is interesting for our purposes because it lists two "death dates": "Departed January 11, 1983; At Peace December 26, 1990." A similar inscription is found on the tombstone of Terri Schiavo, who collapsed in her home in 1990 after a heart attack. She too was in a persistent vegetative state for years, and her death was stalled by the legal battles between her husband and parents for guardianship and treatment. After her death (also via the removal of a feeding tube) in 2005, her husband had inscribed on her tombstone: "Departed this Earth February 25, 1990; At Peace March 31, 2005."

What interests me about these inscriptions is that they convey an intuition that I think many people share: when the mind is completely eradicated, when the capacity for consciousness is forever lost, the person had died, even if her body continues to function. According to the EMAPI, Cruzan and Schiavo died the day they went into a vegetative state, because it was then that their brains were no longer able to sustain the capacity for consciousness. Jeff McMahan argues in favor of the EMAPI and describes it as follows:

> I suggest that the corresponding criterion for personal identity is the continued existence and functioning ... of enough of the same brain to be capable of generating mental activity. This criterion stresses the survival of one's basic psychological capacities, in particular the capacity for consciousness. It does not require continuity of any particular *contents* of one's mental life. This allows that one ... continues to exist through the progress of Alzheimer's disease, until the disease destroys one's capacity for consciousness ...[52]

According to this view, it does not matter whether an individual possesses robust mental capacities in order to retain an identity throughout time. To put it in a way that is relevant to our purposes here, the EMAPI is the metaphysical companion of the interest view of moral status, not the cognitive account of moral status. Philosophers who defend the latter have also defended a metaphysical account of identity that rests upon possessing robust mental capacities and contents. For example, Peter Singer argues that personal identity does not extend back into infancy because we do not share any mental contents with our infant self.

> I am not the infant from whom I developed. The infant could not look forward to developing into the kind of being that I am, or even into any intermediate being, between the being I now am and the infant. I cannot even recall being the infant; there are no mental links between us.[53]

Mary Anne Warren argues along a similar vein.

> [W]e are essentially people if we are essentially anything at all. Therefore, if fetuses and gametes are not people, then we were never fetuses and gametes, though one might say that we emerged from them. The fetus which later became you was not you because you did not exist at that time ... [s]o if it had been aborted nothing whatever would have been done to you, since you would have never existed.[54]

From this perspective, we would lose any identity relationship with ourselves if we ever entered into a state of advanced dementia. Someone with severe cognitive disabilities would not only lack a moral right to life according to the cognitive account, but also would never really seem to have any kind of subsisting personal identity, since she may never be able to form or sustain any kind of robust mental links. This is quite different from what is entailed by the EMAPI. Someone in the advanced stages of dementia may have lost all his robust mental capacities (e.g., memories, rational abilities, self-consciousness) but he still retains an identity relationship with his pre-dementia self because he still retains the capacity for consciousness. Even the most mentally disabled human being would still subsist as the same human being over time so long as she retains the basic capacity for conscious life. However, once the brain loses the capacity to generate *any* conscious awareness at all, the individual has, for all intents and purposes, stopped existing. Death occurs not necessarily when one's organism stops functioning, but when one's mind is forever eradicated. Most of the time, the two happen simultaneously. When they do not, as in the cases of Cruzan and Schiavo, we can make a distinction between the death of the person and the death of the body.

But if we make this distinction at the end of life, consistency requires that we make this distinction, also, at the beginning of life. Just as the organism can continue to function after the death of the person, the organism can come into existence and function before the person begins to exist as well. If the EMAPI is true, we do not begin to exist until our brains are capable of generating some kind of conscious awareness, even in the most rudimentary sense. While it is true that fetal brain waves can be detected early in pregnancy, this does not mean that the brain is mature enough to generate conscious activity. Individuals in persistent vegetative states are often erroneously referred to as "brain dead," however other parts of the brain can still function even if the cerebral cortex, the part of the brain responsible for consciousness, no longer functions.

The cortex is responsible for "conscious experience, pain perception, and voluntary movements ... an intact, normally functioning cerebral cortex is indispensable for human cognitive abilities."[55] Indeed, the most common consensus among experts in this area is that a functioning cerebral cortex is vital in order to possess the capacity for conscious awareness of any kind, including conscious awareness of pain. J.A. Burgess and S.A. Tawia write:

> It has long been recognized that a (relatively) undamaged brain, in particular, a (relatively) undamaged cerebral cortex is a fundamental requirement of normal consciousness in humans. There is now overwhelming evidence that *particular* disorders of consciousness are associated with damage to *specific* regions of the parietal lobes ... If, as this evidence seems overwhelmingly to suggest, widespread and severe cortical damage is enough to deprive a subject of consciousness, then this would indicate that the content of consciousness is at least largely a product of – perhaps identical with – some kind of activity in the cortex.[56]

In order to be consciously aware of pain, it is necessary to have a functioning central nervous system, which is made up of the spinal cord and the brain. The two most important parts of this system that contribute to the conscious perception of pain are the thalamus and cortex. The thalamus is a small, bean-like mass in the brain that serves as the reception area for sensory input. It resides in the human brain-stem, which is responsible for many of our reflexes, including rooting, sucking, and swallowing, which are all feeding reflexes critical for survival in infancy, respiratory reflexes, heart rate, interactions involving eye movements, and facial expressions.[57] Noxious stimuli originate as a signal in some innervated area of the body that contains nociceptors (receptors specialized for picking up potentially painful stimuli). The signal travels up the spinal cord to the thalamus as electrical impulses through sensory nerves. Once the electrical signal reaches the thalamus, the thalamus relays the electrical signals via its projection fibers (neurons that serve to connect various parts of the brain) to the appropriate area in the cerebral cortex.[58] It is when noxious stimuli are transferred to the cortex that pain is *perceived*; it is only at this point where it can be rightly said that a human being is conscious or aware of pain. If the projection fibers at the thalamus are not connected to the cortex, or if there is no cortical function for some reason, a noxious stimulus cannot be perceived; an individual cannot be *aware* of pain.

A first trimester fetus cannot be conscious of pain, or of anything at all, because the projection fibers that connect the thalamus to the cortex do not start developing until 18 weeks gestational age.[59] Indeed, the projection fibers in the thalamus do not even begin to connect with the cortex until approximately 20 to 22 weeks gestational age.[60] Some have even argued that conscious awareness does not commence until even later than this. Burgess and Tawia, for example, argue that fetal consciousness most likely begins at 30–35 weeks gestational age, almost towards the end of gestation, because it is here that cortical function in the fetus begins to resemble cortical function in a normal child or adult.

If we combine the view of moral status we get from the interest view, with the view of identity we get from the EMAPI, what we get is that fetuses have no interests at all until they become sentient, conscious beings, but that after they do, some time in mid-gestation, they not only gain some degree of moral status, they gain an interest in continued existence, since they now have an identity relationship with a future person. Therefore, to destroy the fetus after this point robs it of what is now properly its future. McMahan explains this as follows:

> The Embodied Mind Account of Identity has immediate implications for the morality of abortion. For, according to that account, we do not begin to exist until our organism develops the capacity to generate consciousness. Only then is there *someone* present rather than merely *something* ... An early abortion does not kill anyone; it merely prevents someone from coming into existence ... If we assume that the capacity for consciousness arises at approximately twenty weeks after conception ... it follows that an abortion performed later than twenty weeks after conception involves the killing of some*one* rather than merely some*thing* ... before twenty weeks, no one suffers the loss of a future like ours; after twenty weeks, someone does.[61]

Does fetal personhood matter?

In a way, this entire section is really irrelevant as to the reasons why I identify as pro-choice. I do believe both the cognitive account and the genetic account of moral personhood are flawed for the reasons explained here. And while I also think the interest view of moral status, and the embodied mind account of identity, are strong positions to hold, they, also, are not free of difficulties. The fetal organism, while not yet a some*one* in the first half of pregnancy, is a some*thing* with the potential to become some*one*, and in other venues I have argued that this potential is indeed morally relevant, and should be taken into account to some extent when determining whether the fetus has an interest in continued existence (although I also argue that this determination is dependent on considerations of personal identity).[62] When I was pregnant, I was equally in awe of the life that grew within me regardless of the gestational age of that life. Whereas I do believe that later-term fetuses are more morally significant beings than early-term fetuses and embryos for the reasons I have explained here, I am not prepared to say that early-term fetuses categorically lack moral significance.

Consequently, I do not want my actual argument in favor of abortion rights to stand or fall on the issue of fetal personhood or human identity. I think this is especially important for practical reasons – any arguments in favor of abortion rights should be able to withstand any possible challenge that may present itself if ever a Personhood Amendment were to pass on a state, or even federal, level. The problem is that I do not think the arguments presented by the Supreme Court Justices who decided *Roe v. Wade* could withstand such scrutiny. In the next section, I will explain why I think these arguments are vulnerable, but then I will present an alternative argument in favor of abortion rights that I do believe could withstand any moral, or legal, defense of fetal personhood.

III. The argument from bodily autonomy

The inadequacies of Roe v. Wade

In 1973, the Supreme Court decided, in *Roe v. Wade*, that the United States Constitution guarantees a right to privacy under the 14th Amendment, which includes a woman's right to obtain an abortion. Despite the claims made by some pro-life advocates, *Roe* does not guarantee "abortion on demand." Within the first trimester (implantation to 3 months), the decision to abort is left exclusively in the hands of the pregnant woman, meaning that any state's attempt to prohibit her from obtaining an abortion would be deemed unconstitutional. Within the second trimester (3–6 months), states could pass laws regulating abortion only in the interest of securing maternal health, which is less of an issue now than it was in 1973 given the increased safety of abortion procedures. Within the third trimester (6–9 months), after the fetus is considered "viable" (capable of surviving outside the womb, even with technology aiding it), states may implement restrictions on abortion in the interest of protecting fetal life, with exceptions being made for maternal health. The 1992 case *Planned Parenthood v. Casey* further affirmed that states have a right to restrict abortion access *whenever* a fetus is deemed viable, even if medical technology pushes viability back earlier into the second trimester (the decision also allows states to regulate abortions so long as doing so is not regarded as placing an "undue burden" upon the woman[63]). As of this writing, 43 states have laws prohibiting or severely restricting abortion after the fetus has achieved viability (at about 25 weeks gestational age), and sometimes even earlier, e.g., at 20 weeks gestational age.[64]

The *Roe* decision came on the heels of two other significant reproductive rights decisions: in 1965, *Griswold v. Connecticut* struck down a ban on issuing contraception to married couples, and then in 1972, *Eisenstadt v. Baird* extended the same right to unmarried individuals. In the latter case, the Justices wrote: "If the right of privacy means anything, it is the right of the individual, married or single, to be free from unwarranted governmental intrusion into matters so fundamentally affecting a person as the decision whether to bear or beget a child."[65] In 1977, *Carey v. Population Services International* further asserted this interpretation when the Justices contended that: "Regulations imposing a burden on a decision as fundamental as whether to bear or beget a child may be justified only by compelling state interests, and must be narrowly drawn to express only those interests."[66]

Justice Harry Blackmun referred to *Roe* as the next logical step after *Griswold* and *Eisenstadt* in outlining what is entailed by a right to procreative liberty (meaning that the government can neither force someone to become a parent, nor can they prohibit someone from becoming a parent). The Justices who decided *Roe* argued that abortion was a legitimate exercise of the right to privacy *qua* the right to procreative liberty:

> This right of privacy ... is broad enough to encompass a woman's decision whether or not to terminate her pregnancy. The detriment that the State

would impose upon the pregnant woman by denying this choice altogether is apparent. Specific and direct harm medically diagnosable even in early pregnancy may be involved. Maternity, or additional offspring, may force upon the woman a distressful life and future. Psychological harm may be imminent. Mental and physical health may be taxed by child care. There is also the distress, for all concerned, associated with the unwanted child, and there is the problem of bringing a child into a family already unable, psychologically and otherwise, to care for it.[67]

Most of these considerations focus on the extreme burdens that come with unwanted social parenthood. Therefore, these considerations were taken to be legitimate reasons for aborting fetal life for two-thirds of a woman's gestational period. However, note that these reasons in favor of abortion can only be successful *if the fetus is not considered a person*. If I were to lose my job now, become unable to pay my bills, and possibly end up homeless, I cannot appeal to these worries as justification for killing my currently existing children. This is because my currently existing children are persons with their own right to life that cannot be compromised due to any social burdens, no matter how severe. As Christopher Kaczor puts it "one cannot exercise the right not to remain a social parent at the expense of one's progeny's well-being ... the right not to be a social mother does not allow one to endanger or neglect the life of one's progeny."[68]

The Supreme Court Justices who decided *Roe* noted that the "Constitution does not define 'person' in so many words" but that typically the term applies "only postnatally. None indicates, with any assurance, that it has any possible prenatal application."[69] However, they stopped short of affirming that fetuses were absolutely not moral or legal persons by essentially writing off the question as a philosophical, religious, and ultimately intractable one:

> We need not resolve the difficult question of when life begins. When those trained in the respective disciplines of medicine, philosophy, and theology are unable to arrive at a consensus, the judiciary, at this point in the development of man's knowledge, is not in a position to speculate as to the answer.[70]

Yet at the same time, Justice Potter Stewart, when questioning Attorney Sarah Weddington, noted that "if it were established that an unborn fetus is a person, with the protection of the Fourteenth Amendment, you would have almost an impossible case here," to which she admitted that she "would have a very difficult case." This effectively admits that, despite their claims to the contrary, the arguments proffered by the Supreme Court Justices in favor of abortion rights tacitly assert that fetuses are not persons, neither in the moral or legal sense, and therefore have no rights, including the right to life. If fetuses were accorded such rights, one could not defend the abortion right on the grounds that forcing women to have unwanted children would impose severe social burdens on them. While it may indeed be true that unwanted children create burdens on the parents who do not want them, this would be insufficient for defending a right to destroy fetal life, lest we also offer this right to the parents of born children in situations where continuing to care for them imposes severe social burdens.

This, then, is my worry. Since *Roe* made abortion access legal across the country, there have been, and will continue to be, attempts to pass Personhood Amendments. If any one of these amendments moves up to federal court, and becomes adopted, they may pose a serious threat to abortion rights as they currently stand. Pro-life organizations know this, noting that Personhood Amendments are the "silver bullet to kill *Roe v. Wade*" and that "the right to an abortion ... is living on borrowed time."[71] Pro-choice supporters need to admit that *Roe* is vulnerable in this way, and offer new arguments in favor of abortion rights that are not dependent on whether fetuses are considered (moral or legal) persons.

Judith Jarvis Thomson's Kantian argument in favor of abortion rights

In 1971, Judith Jarvis Thomson wrote what is one of the most well-known essays in defense of the right to an abortion entitled, appropriately, "A Defense of Abortion." Thomson begins her essay with the disclaimer that she herself does not believe that fetuses are persons from conception, but that they do begin to resemble human infants rather early in pregnancy. Because she believes that, when it comes to the question of when we should ascribe personhood to the fetus, "the prospects for 'drawing a line' in the development of the fetus look dim,"[72] she grants, for the sake of argument, that fetuses are indeed persons from conception. She then goes on to offer this thought experiment, meant to test the reader's intuition concerning what exactly follows from anyone's (not just a fetus') right to life:

> You wake up in the morning and find yourself back to back in bed with an unconscious violinist. A famous unconscious violinist. He has been found to have a fatal kidney ailment, and the Society of Music Lovers has canvassed all the available medical records and found that you alone have the right blood type to help. They have therefore kidnapped you, and last night the violinist's circulatory system was plugged into yours, so that your kidneys can be used to extract poisons from his blood as well as your own. The director of the hospital now tells you, "Look, we're sorry the Society of Music Lovers did this to you – we would never have permitted it if we had known. But still, they did it, and the violinist now is plugged into you. To unplug you would be to kill him. But never mind, it's only for nine months. By then he will have recovered from his ailment, and can safely be unplugged from you." Is it morally incumbent on you to accede to this situation? No doubt it would be very nice of you if you did, a great kindness. But do you *have* to accede to it?[73]

Thomson argues that the answer here is clearly no. Undoubtedly the violinist is an innocent person with a right to life – this is never called into question. However, the violinist's right to life (like all of our rights) has limitations, one of which is that he cannot be given whatever is necessary for his continued survival if doing so entails forcing another human being to use her body to sustain his life.

> I am not arguing that people do not have a right to life … I am arguing only that a right to life does not guarantee having either a right to be given the use of or a right to be allowed continued use of another person's body – even if one needs it for life itself. So the right to life will not serve the opponents of abortion in the very simple and clear way in which they seem to have thought it would.[74]

Most pro-life advocates do not deny that women have a right to bodily autonomy. However, they do appear to hold that, in a situation where the woman's right to bodily autonomy is potentially at odds with the fetus' right to life, the rights of the fetus supervene over the rights of the woman. Thomson's violinist example is meant to combat this assumption.

Consider other situations, outside the context of abortion, where the same two rights (bodily autonomy and right to life) appear to be in *prima facie* conflict. Suppose your local hospital is experiencing dire blood shortages, and people who need blood transfusions are dying because of a lack of available supply. Hospital workers will likely go out into the city, enticing people as much as they can, in the hopes that they will voluntarily donate. However, no one would ever suggest that potential donors be strapped down and their blood forcibly extracted, even if it were the case that this would be the only option available to keep hospital patients from dying. No doubt these patients possess a right to life. No doubt they are innocent, vulnerable persons. Their deaths would be, without question, sad and tragic. Nevertheless, *none* of this entails that other people can be forced to use their body in a manner in which they simply do not consent in order to save those patients' lives. In fact, the right to bodily autonomy is so sacrosanct in our society that we often refuse to violate it even after death. Take, as an example, that we honor the decision many people make against organ donation even after their deaths, even though there exists a critical short supply of organs, and that many people die on waiting lists. To violate the wishes of dead patients, and extract organs from every suitable corpse after death, would potentially save thousands of lives. Yet, there is little push to change our organ donation laws. Those who would eradicate abortion rights would effectively give a pregnant woman less of a right over her body than we give to dead persons over their organs, and would bestow upon fetuses not just a right to life, but an additional right to forcibly use another's body for sustenance – a right no extra-uterine person possesses.

Philosophical support for Thomson's thesis can be found in the writings of ethicist Immanuel Kant. In his book *Groundwork of the Metaphysics of Morals*, Kant proposes one of the most influential moral laws in both normative and applied ethics, referred to by ethicists as the formula of humanity version of the categorical imperative: "Act in such a way that you treat humanity, whether in your own person or in the person of another, always at the same time as an end and never simply as a means."[75] Because of our rational capacities, all persons are to be treated in a manner that accords them proper respect and dignity. They may never be dehumanized or instrumentalized, treated as mere tools, in order to attain some other goal. This moral law has a prominent place in bioethics. For example, in studies involving human subjects, it is imperative those running the study acquire informed consent to ensure that the patient is making an autonomous decision about their involvement. To fail to do so treats the subject not as a person with intrinsic worth, but as a mere instrument for the benefit of the study. One of the gravest human rights violations in American history was the Tuskegee study of untreated syphilis, where poor and sick African-American men were lied to about receiving healthcare from the government for their syphilis when, in fact, investigators were not treating their disease at all. Instead, the investigators opted to watch them deteriorate over time in order to study the effects of the disease. The experiment took an even more appalling turn when penicillin was confirmed as a treatment for syphilis, and yet denied to these subjects so that the experiment would continue uninterrupted. Clearly the welfare of the men themselves was simply unimportant for the investigators. They lied to them and allowed them to suffer and die, even when an effective medicine was readily available, in order to continue their study. From a Kantian perspective, even if it were the case that the study produced invaluable knowledge about syphilis, it would still be gravely morally wrong to treat these men as mere instruments to achieve that end.

A pregnant woman is not simply renting her uterus to a tenant whose presence minimally impacts her – pregnancy can often result in severe and permanent health issues for women. Savita Halappanavar's death because of her septic pregnancy highlights these dangers, but there are many more: hyperemesis gravidarum (extreme and persistent nausea and vomiting during pregnancy), pre-eclampsia (pregnancy-related high blood pressure, that results in protein in the urine, kidney ailments, and can lead to a stroke), gestational diabetes (which increases your chances of becoming a type two diabetic in the future), anemia, ectopic pregnancy (which can lead to fallopian tubes rupturing), placenta previa (which may necessitate bed rest, or result in heavy bleeding), increase in the possibility of urinary tract infections and yeast infections, possible cesarean section, or vaginal tearing. If we, as a society, do not force the comparatively minor physical discomfort of blood donation in order to save the lives of ailing patients (who are undoubtedly persons with a right to life), we will be hard pressed to find legitimate reasons to force a woman to undergo the possible, more severe, perils of pregnancy to save fetuses, even if we assume that they, too, are persons with a right to life.

But the consequences of pregnancy extend far beyond possible health complications; pregnancy also represents a time of incredible emotional and mental intimacy. Margaret Olivia Little highlights that pregnancy represents a time of:

> *extraordinary* physical enmeshment with another – a person whose blood is being oxygenated by another's lungs, a person whose hormonal activity in turn affects another's brain and metabolism, a person whose growing size

enlarges another's physical boundaries ... To be pregnant is to be *inhabited*. It is to be *occupied*. It is to be in a state of physical intimacy of a particularly thoroughgoing nature.[76]

Christine Overall relays a similar experience: "being 'with child' was sufficiently engrossing, disturbing, even overpowering at times, to persuade me that no woman should ever have to go through this experience – an experience that philosopher Caroline Whitbeck has suggested is akin to literally being possessed or taken over by another being – against her will."[77] In Caroline Lundquist's essay on the phenomenology of forced pregnancy, she writes:

> In one sense, women who never positively identify with their pregnancies ... experience progressive awareness of changes in their bodies, eventually become conscious of some "other" within them, and await delivery in much the same sense as the expectant mother. Even so, the splitting of bodily subjectivity seems more akin to the splitting of the transcendent from the immanent flesh described by existential phenomenologists, and the differentiation between mother and child is not felt by the mother as that of two subjects, but rather of herself and something radically other. Even following delivery, mothers who reject their pregnancies may not feel any sense of attachment to the newly born infant ...[78]

Lundquist emphasizes that women who are forced to undergo pregnancy are being compelled to "experience one's own flesh as a vessel for something radically other ... in cases of rejected pregnancy, women tend to undergo the basic psychological processes of pregnancy, though they subjectively experience them in a radically different way from women with chosen pregnancies."[79]

Appreciating this aspect about pregnancy advances Thomson's argument in ways even she perhaps did not anticipate. It is easy to read Thomson as advocating the view that we have control over our bodies in the same way we have control over our private properties, and as no one may be allowed on our properties against our consent, so no one may use our bodies without our consent. But a focus on the *sui generis* phenomenology of pregnancy highlights that forced pregnancy would not be akin to an invasion of our house or our land; it is an invasion of our *person*, of our *selves*. To deny women access to abortion, therefore, is to compel them to use their body in a way that brings with it intrinsic dangers to their physical health, and also imposes upon them a mental and emotional state that ultimately alienates a woman from her very body, and therefore from herself. As Susan Bordo puts it, protecting bodily autonomy is extremely important because

> in a very real sense, [it is] a protection of the *subjectivity* of the person involved – that is, it is an acknowledgement that the body can never be regarded merely as a site of quantifiable processes that can be assessed objectively, but must be

treated as invested with personal meaning, history, and value that are ultimately determinable only by the subject who lives "within" it.[80]

A fetus is not just renting out a room in someone's "home"; the fetus' presence occupies another person *completely* – in both body and mind. It is precisely this profound intimacy that may render pregnancy a beautiful and transcendental experience for women who voluntarily choose it; for those who do not, it represents a profound violation. Forced pregnancy clearly violates Kant's formula of humanity. Once a woman has made a rational, autonomous, decision not to gestate, compelling her to do so ignores her decision in this regard, treats her in a way to which she has not consented, and forces her into a potentially dangerous and intimate physical and mental state. Her body is reduced to an incubator for the fetus against her will and therefore, *she* is reduced to an incubator against her will. Donald Regan puts this excellently when he writes:

> Pregnancy is painful. It involves a significant risk of death. It represents an intrusion into the most intimate parts of the woman's body … the woman who is compelled to carry a fetus she does not want is in effect being used as an incubator. She is being used as a physical object … laws forbidding abortion involve the requisitioning of the woman's body by the state … [it] relegate[s] [women] to the status of a broodmare (for this is how the pregnant woman may well view the matter) by society at large …[81]

Bordo also argues that depriving women of the right to obtain an abortion "is necessarily also to mount an assault on her personal integrity and autonomy (the essence of personhood in our culture) and to treat her merely as pregnant *res extensa*, material incubator of fetal subjectivity."[82]

Ultimately, this is the main reason I defend abortion rights: I think Thomson gets it right. Although I do personally believe that there is a significant difference in terms of moral status between a pre-conscious fetus and one who possesses some kind of mental life, I also recognize that the issue of fetal personhood is sufficiently difficult and philosophically complex so that I have no hopes to ever "solve" it any definitive way. Moreover, even if the fetus is not considered a person, as a living human being it is still worthy, I think, of profound respect. However, as Thomson emphasizes, regarding the fetus as a being with moral status and a rights bearer simply does not lead to the conclusion that abortions are impermissible any more than any of our statuses as persons lead to the conclusion that another human being can be forced to use their body to sustain our lives. To give the fetus this right against a woman's body does not just grant it a right to life – but grants it an *additional* right that no other extra-uterine person possesses. I have yet to encounter a pro-life argument that convinces me that intra-uterine life should be granted *more* rights than extra-uterine persons.

To be fair, there have been many objections to Thomson's argument – far too many to exhaustively cover here. In what follows I will briefly discuss three objections that have most challenged me, and will show why, ultimately, they have failed to convince me that Thomson's argument is fatally flawed.

Some difficulties (and responses) to Thomson's argument

David Boonin's book *A Defense of Abortion* covers a wide variety of objections against Thomson's argument and offers convincing responses to all of them. The three I will cover here are the ones that have, personally, most challenged me as a defender of abortion rights.

When I teach Thomson's essay in class, many students often object that the violinist example fails to be analogous to pregnancy in two ways. First, in the violinist example, the person kidnapped is taken against her will, and has not contributed to the violinist's illness in any way. Pregnancy is importantly different; unless a woman was sexually assaulted, most women know that engaging in sexual intercourse, even with contraception, may result in pregnancy. Therefore, women (and also men) are responsible for the fetus' existence and subsequent dependence on her body; she therefore does indeed have a moral obligation to continue to gestate it. This is known in the literature as the Responsibility Objection to Thomson's argument. John Wilcox explains it thus:

> In the violinist scenario, you do nothing to get yourself into the mess; you wake up one morning and simply "find yourself" hooked up to the violinist … [b]ut in the normal case of pregnancy, one has voluntarily engaged in the sexual relations which lead to conception … A woman voluntarily engages in sexual intercourse, knowing full well what the consequences may be. Might we say sensibly that in the ordinary case she *has* given the fetus special rights to her body, that she has voluntarily given herself some responsibility for the fetus, and so that she does then do it an injustice if she aborts it?[83]

In order to assess whether this objection works against Thomson's example, let's begin with trying to decipher the underlying principle supporting the objection. It seems to be something like this:

> Voluntarily engaging in action x with the foresight that it may result in consequence y creates an obligation to take responsibility for the circumstances that come with y if y does indeed materialize.

Francis Beckwith seems to understand the objection this way. He writes: "we hold drunk people whose driving results in manslaughter responsible for their actions, even if they did not intend to kill someone prior to becoming intoxicated."[84] If we replace the variables in the above principle, we obtain the following imperative: "Voluntarily engaging in drunk driving with the foresight that it may result in hitting and hurting or killing someone creates an obligation to take responsibility for those circumstances if they indeed happen to materialize." While the principle clearly holds in this instance, there are alternative examples that call the principle into question. For example: "voluntarily walking down the street of a crime infested neighborhood in the middle of the night with the foresight that it may result in being raped or being the victim of assault creates an obligation to take responsibility for those circumstances if they indeed happen to materialize." Here, the principle clearly *does not* hold. What we have to ask, then, is what makes it the case that it holds in the former instance but not the latter, and to which one is pregnancy most analogous?

David Boonin counters Beckwith's drunk driving example as follows:

> ... in the case of drunk or negligent driving, we already agree that people have a right not to be run over by cars, and then determine that a person who risks running over someone with cars can be held culpable if he has an accident that results in a violation of this right ... from this we derive a right that people not negligently act in ways that risk unintentionally causing these things to occur.[85]

Similarly, we already agree that women have a right not to be raped, or that people have a right to walk down the streets without being assaulted. It is because we consider this right inalienable that a woman does not forfeit it by walking down the street of a dangerous neighborhood. However, as Boonin points out, this is *precisely* the issue at stake when it comes to abortion, i.e., the very question at hand is whether the fetus has a right to use the woman's body for sustenance in the first place.

While I do agree with Boonin's argument here, I believe, like Thomson, it would be more fruitful to grant the key premise; that is, let's assume, for the sake for argument, that a woman has indeed incurred some level of responsibility for the fetus' existence and welfare given her voluntarily engagement in sexual intercourse. Even granting this, I do not think we can arrive at the conclusion that a pregnant woman can be compelled to surrender her body for the fetus' sustenance. This is because there are some rights that we simply do not give up, even in situations where we could rightly be called careless in our choices (I am not saying that women who become pregnant unintentionally are automatically careless – I am just granting as many potential pro-life principles as possible in order to show that the conclusion in question still does not follow). Thomson alludes to a response like this in her essay:

> If the room is stuffy, and I therefore open a window to air it, and a burglar climbs in, it would be absurd to say, "Ah, now he can stay, she's given him a right to the use of her house – for she is partially responsible for his presence there, having voluntarily done what enabled him to get in, in full knowledge that there are such things as burglars, and that burglars burgle." It would be still more absurd to say this if I had had bars installed outside my windows, precisely to prevent burglars from getting in, and a burglar got in only because of

a defect in the bars. It remains equally absurd if we imagine it is not a burglar who climbs in, but an innocent person who blunders or falls in. Again, suppose it were like this: people-seeds drift about in the air like pollen, and if you open your windows, one may drift in and take root in your carpets or upholstery. You don't want children, so you fix up your windows with fine mesh screens, the very best you can buy. As can happen, however, and on very, very rare occasions does happen, one of the screens is defective, and a seed drifts in and takes root. Does the person-plant who now develops have a right to the use of your house? Surely not – despite the fact that you voluntarily opened your windows, you knowingly kept carpets and upholstered furniture, and you knew that screens were sometimes defective.[86]

This is what I understand Thomson to be saying: some rights are so imperative to the well-being of their bearers that they cannot be easily waived, even in situations where one deliberately acted in a way that may lead to a right being violated. It does not matter if I left my doors and windows wide open while a murderer or rapist was on the loose. Perhaps I should have been more careful, of course, but I do not forfeit my property rights to my home (and so the criminal may not come into my home uninvited), I do not forfeit my right to my body and sexual autonomy (and so raping me is still impermissible), and I do not forfeit my right to my life (and so killing me is still impermissible). The fetus, of course, is unlike a murderer in that it is not *deliberately* acting in a way that it knows violates the woman's bodily autonomy, but this difference is not relevant here. Even most pro-life supporters already agree that women (that all persons) have a right to bodily security that should be, at least *prima facie*, respected as much as possible. For all the reasons I have argued above, to compel a woman to remain pregnant deeply violates that bodily autonomy (the violator here is not the fetus, but the state and its laws that would prevent abortion access). Because of the extraordinary physical sacrifices that can come with pregnancy, and the emotional and mental effects compelled pregnancy can have, the right to bodily autonomy in this instance is a good candidate for a right that cannot simply be forfeited because of one's "careless" actions; it is a right that remains with the bearer alone unless she voluntarily chooses to gestate.

The upshot, then, is that even if we do assume that a woman who engages voluntarily in sexual intercourse is responsible for the fetus' aid and dependence to some degree, this alone is not sufficient to render abortion impermissible. It must be *further* illustrated that the woman is *so* responsible that she can be forced to use her body to sustain the fetus, and this is an argument that advocates of the Responsibility Objection typically do not provide.

The second objection I will discuss also relies on an alleged relevant dissimilarity between the violinist example and typical cases of pregnancy. In Thomson's example, the violinist is a stranger to you – he is not a family member or even a close friend. Family members and friends have moral obligations to each other that are missing amongst strangers. But fetuses are importantly different – a fetus is a woman's child. Parents clearly have a moral responsibility toward their children that they lack to complete strangers. As such, while it may be true that you have no moral obligation to sustain the life of a stranger through the use of your body, you would indeed have this moral obligation when it comes to your children. Consequently, the objection goes, a woman does have a moral obligation to sustain the life of her fetus given that she shares this very special relationship with it, one that is utterly lacking in Thomson's example. As Stephen Schwartz writes:

> The person hooked up to the violinist (we are assuming) has no duty to sustain him, for he is a total stranger, standing in a relation to him that is most unnatural. This is exactly the opposite of the mother-child relation, which is most natural and proper. We do not have the obligation to sustain strangers artificially hooked up to us, but we do have the obligation to sustain our own children. So, the very thing that makes it plausible to say that the person in bed with the violinist has no duty to sustain him, namely, that he is a stranger unnaturally hooked up to him, is precisely what is absent in the case of the mother and her child.[87]

This is often called, in the literature, the Special Relationship objection.

As a parent myself, this objection is emotionally striking. There is nothing I would not do for my children, and I would undoubtedly offer blood, bone marrow, organs – anything that would be necessary to keep them alive and healthy. However, this immediate emotional reaction is not enough to show the objection succeeds. Instead, we have to ask two questions here. First, what is it *exactly* that grounds moral obligations between family members, in this case between parents and children? Second, assuming that there *are* certain moral obligations that exist amongst family members that don't exist amongst strangers, are those obligations *so strong* that they entail that anything at all can be demanded of our family members? Are there limits of what we can expect them to do for us, and would compelled bodily intrusion surpass that limit?

A woman and her fetus are biologically related (except in cases of surrogacy). Of course, for some women, that relationship extends far deeper – women who choose and desire their pregnancies already regard themselves as a mother to her fetus in every relevant sense of the term. However, what we have to ask here is whether biological relationships alone ground our moral obligations to our family, and between parents and children in particular. My oldest daughter looks exactly like her father and very little like me. If it were revealed to me tomorrow that she was not, biologically, my child, it would seem odd to contend that the last eight years of raising her are for naught, and that I no longer had any moral responsibilities to her. Likewise, parents of adopted children have moral obligations to them regardless of their lack of genetic relations. On the other hand, gamete donors may have many biological children that they will never meet, and there seems to be little moral obligation (if any at all) that exists between them and any biological children. What grounds our moral obligations to our family members seems much less about our biological connections, and much more about our emotional connections and shared experiences. Nancy Jecker highlights this as well:

> the ethical requirement of respect takes different shapes when placed against a *backdrop of personal relationships*. Where an *antecedent* tie or bond exists between the person who makes some sacrifice and the person who benefits, the requirements of respect subtly shift. Relationships vary in the degree to which they are personal, and the closer and more personal a relationship is, the stronger the claim it can make ethically on our allegiance ...[88]

If a woman chooses to abort, she may not have the same emotional connections or shared experiences with that fetus as a woman who desires the pregnancy (though this is not to say that women who abort categorically do not have emotional connections to the fetuses – in my study of abortion ethics, I have read many personal stories of women who, for varying reasons, aborted fetuses to whom they felt a personal connection), and there is certainly no antecedent tie or bond that exists between woman and fetus. She may *choose* to engage in an emotional relationship with her fetus, but I have yet to read an argument that she is *morally required* to engage in such a relationship. As such, even though the fetus is indeed a woman's biological progeny that *alone* seems insufficient for maintaining that she has moral obligations to it.

However, let's assume that a woman does indeed have some moral obligations toward the fetus in virtue of their genetic relationships – would that obligation include allowing the fetus use of her body for sustenance? She can, of course, volunteer, but can she be compelled? It seems clear here that the answer is still no. This is one of the moral questions raised in Jodi Picoult's 2004 novel *My Sister's Keeper*. Picoult tells the story of Anna, a 13-year-old girl who was deliberately conceived in order to provide blood and bone marrow for her sister Kate, who continually battles leukemia. When Anna is informed that she is expected to donate a kidney to Kate, she sues her parents for medical emancipation, which she successfully attains. One of the moral dilemmas in the book is whether one person can be compelled to sacrifice her body in order to save another person. While the reader feels sympathy for the dying and struggling Kate, the exploitation of Anna's body, and therefore of Anna herself, is also a cause for deep moral concern. It seems clear that Anna cannot be forced to give Kate her kidney, even though Kate's personhood and right to life are never questioned, and even though they are siblings with a close relationship. This is something that Donald Regan also brings up: "no state imposes on parents (or, I think, would impose if a case came up) the burdens that would be most comparable to the burdens of pregnancy, such as the burdens of a genuinely dangerous rescue or of compulsory organ donation."[89] Constitutional scholar Robin West agrees:

> A parent is not required to donate even a milliliter of blood, much less a kidney, or bone marrow, even to save the life of his born child, and even

though the parents of the born child quite willfully and consensually brought the child into the world ... Furthermore, should the born child – perhaps a grown child – attempt to extract the blood or kidney from the parent by force, without the consent of the unwilling parent, perhaps by drugging him and strapping him to a gurney, the state would step in when called upon to help the parent ward off the child's attack. The child, not the parent, would be charged with a crime.[90]

The above assessment may seem heartless to some given the incredible lengths parents often go through to care for their children – however, again, it must be emphasized that the dedication parents often have to their children is a result of their intimate relationship, not merely their biological connection. Perhaps the following example can test our intuitions more reliably: would I be morally obligated (and could be compelled by my government) to donate, say, bone marrow for a newly discovered genetic sibling I never knew I had, or even for a person who is biologically my progeny but raised by a whole other family (keeping in mind that bone marrow donation is still far less physically intrusive than pregnancy)? I think here it is not at all clear that I have such moral obligations, but it does seem clear that forcing me to do so would be a grave violation of my bodily autonomy and moral rights. The relationship between a pregnant woman and fetus seems much more analogous to these two examples than that between a parent and a child who share an antecedent intimate relationship. Therefore, the Special Relationship objection also appears to fall short.

The last objection I will consider does not attempt to draw a disanalogy between the violinist example and cases of pregnancy, rather it presents a problem with the Kantian defense I have offered. I have argued that Kant's formula of humanity would be violated against a pregnant woman who is compelled to gestate, however it appears that abortion would violate the same imperative against the fetus. This is something that is often brought up by my students: while it is possible to argue that compelling pregnancy treats women as mere means to the end of gestating a fetus, aborting said fetus treats it as a mere means to whatever end the woman hopes to attain when obtaining the abortion (e.g., to be able to continue her education).

One immediate response is to deny that fetuses are persons in the *Kantian* sense of the term, which many ethicists interpret as something that approximates the cognitive account of personhood. In his *Metaphysics of Morals*, Kant clearly defines "person" as a moral agent; as a being with certain cognitive capacities, "a subject whose actions can be imputed to him. Moral personality is therefore nothing other than the freedom of a rational being under moral laws."[91] To be fair, there is disagreement amongst Kantian scholars concerning whether Kant meant to denote only currently rational agents as moral persons, or whether this would apply, also, to all members of the human species, whether they be potential rational agents (as fetuses and infants would be), current rational agents, or former rational agents (as someone with severe dementia would be).[92] However, even Kantian ethicists who do not believe this is what Kant meant still believe that potentially rational humans, and formerly rational humans, are worthy of some level of respect.[93]

Suppose fetuses are considered only persons in a potential sense, from a Kantian perspective. One argument is that, although the fetus' potential personhood ought to be respected, it cannot be respected to the extent that entails violating the formula of humanity against a currently existing person. Susan Feldman puts it this way: "the fetus ... is valuable as a potential rational being ... but a potential value must in every case be less than that value fully realized."[94] It isn't that human fetuses aren't valuable entities, nor are they not entitled to some degree of respect. To the extent that both a pregnant women and a fetus could be mutually respected, then this should be done as much as possible. However, when respecting a potential person directly involves treating an actual person, an actual autonomous agent (as the pregnant woman surely is), as a mere means, from a Kantian perspective, one has to opt for respecting the formula of humanity *vis-à-vis* the actual person.

However, keeping in line with Thomson's view, suppose we assume, for the sake of argument, that fetuses have the same moral standing as all other persons. It seems that we are at an impasse here: no matter what we choose, one person will be treated as a mere means towards the ends of the other person. At this point, I can only appeal to consistency in the way we handle similar situations outside the realm of pregnancy. One time, when I was donating blood, I remember feeling very faint, and was told repeatedly by the medical staff that I could stop the donation at any time, even if this means that the donation was incomplete. Suppose we assume that there was a person in the neighboring hospital in dire need of my blood (and that my blood was the only one that would have helped her given that we share a rare blood type), I would still be allowed to stop the donation whenever I wanted, even if the reason I did so was because I no longer wanted to feel faint. The health of the patient in need succumbs to my decisions about my body; this is true whether the need be for bodily fluids, or non-vital organs, or any other thing that necessitates an invasion of my body. In other words, as Regan puts it, the potential Good Samaritan in these cases always has the final say:

> When I suggest that the woman should not be compelled to subordinate her interests to those of the fetus, I sometimes meet with the response: "But if she is allowed to have an abortion, the fetus is subordinated. It is just a question of who shall be subordinated to whom." In a sense, of course, this is correct. There is a conflict of interest between the woman and the fetus, and someone is going to lose. But that is true in every Samaritan situation. There is a conflict between the distressed party's need for aid and the potential rescuer's desire not to give it. The point is that our law generally resolves this conflict in favor of the potential Samaritan.[95]

In this sense, one of the strengths of Thomson's argument is not only that it can be defended using a philosophically rich moral theory, as Kantian normative ethics surely is, but also that we see many examples in the "real world" that substantiate it.

The practical implications of Thomson's argument

As aforementioned, one mark of a good theory, particularly in ethics, is whether it can successfully transfer over to practical use. The fact that both the genetic and cognitive account of personhood leads to morally concerning consequences are good reasons to call them into question. With Thomson's argument, the opposite is the case. There are many "real world" scenarios that vindicate Thomson's main points: not only is bodily autonomy considered an almost sacrosanct right in our society, but when such a right is in tension, or direct conflict, with some other person's right to life, the right to bodily autonomy typically supervenes.

The legal right to bodily integrity has been repeatedly affirmed by several courts, including the United States Supreme Court. For example, there is the 1891 case *Union Pacific Railway Company v. Botsford*. Clara Botsford sued the Pacific Railway Company for negligence after an upper berth in a sleeping car fell on her head in the railroad car she was riding in, causing damages to the membranes of her brain and spinal cord. The lawyers for Union Pacific Railway argued that they had a right, against Botsford's consent, to have her submit to an examination by their own lawyers in order to assess the extent of her injuries. The United States Supreme Court disagreed, ruling that:

> No right is held more sacred, or is more carefully guarded by the common law, than the right of every individual to the possession and control of his own person, free from all restraint or interference of others, unless by clear and unquestionable authority of law.[96]

In the 1996 case *Stamford Hospital vs. Vega*, the Supreme Court of Connecticut ruled that a patient, in this case a Jehovah's Witness, has a right to refuse a blood transfusion, even if necessary to save his own life, and that a hospital's interest in preserving the lives of its patients was not sufficient to override the patient's right to bodily integrity.[97] Indeed, the right to self-determination in regards to medical treatment, in particular the right to refuse life-sustaining treatment, is well established. In the 1985 case *Winston vs. Lee*, the U.S. Supreme Court ruled that law enforcement could not force a suspected criminal to undergo surgery to remove a bullet lodged in his chest, which the state wanted to use as evidence that he was involved in an armed robbery: "surgery without the patient's consent ... involves a virtually total divestment of the patient's ordinary control over surgical probing beneath his skin."[98] The Illinois Appellate Court, in the 1994 case *Doe v. Doe*, upheld a woman's right to refuse to undergo a caesarian section, even if doing so goes against the attending physician's advice that normal vaginal delivery may be detrimental to the life and health of her baby. But the clearest instance of a person's right to bodily integrity being upheld over another person's right to life when preserving the latter would entail violating the former is the 1978 Pennsylvania court ruling of *McFall v. Shimp*.

After slowly losing his battle with aplastic anemia, Robert McFall asked his cousin, David Shimp, to undergo testing to determine if he would be a match for a bone marrow transfusion. Shimp agreed to the testing, but after it was determined that he was, indeed, a match, he refused to undergo the extraction procedure. McFall sued Shimp in the hopes that the Court would force Shimp to undergo the extraction. As the Court stated, the main ethical and legal question at stake was whether "in order to save the life of one of its members by the only means available, may society infringe upon one's absolute right to his 'bodily security?'"[99] The 10th Pennsylvania District Court answered the question in the negative.

> The common law has consistently held to a rule which provides that one human being is under no legal compulsion to give aid or to take action to save that human being or to rescue ... the rule is founded upon the very essence of our free society ... Our society, contrary to many others, has as its first principle, the respect for the individual, and that society and government exist to protect the individual from being invaded and hurt by another ... For our law to compel the defendant to submit to an intrusion of his body would change the very concept and principle upon which our society is founded. To do so would defeat the sanctity of the individual, and would impose a rule which would know no limits, and one could not imagine where the line would be drawn ... For a society, which respects the rights of one individual, to sink its teeth into the jugular vein or neck of one of its members and suck from it sustenance for another member, is revolting to our hard-wrought concept of jurisprudence ...[100]

It is important to note here that the Courts never denied McFall's moral and legal personhood, nor did they deny that he had a right to life. Rather, their argument was essentially Thomson's thesis: one person's right to life cannot entail that another person can be forced to submit to unwanted bodily intrusion in order to sustain that right. In other words, *McFall v. Shimp* is a "real life" violinist example.

According to Donald Regan, to require women to undergo pregnancy against their will is to require them to do something that no other non-pregnant person is required to do:

> It is a deeply rooted principle of American law that an individual is ordinarily not required to volunteer aid to another individual who is in danger or in need of assistance. In brief, our law does not require people to be Good Samaritans ... if we require a pregnant woman to carry the fetus to term and deliver it – if we forbid abortion, in other words – we are compelling her to be a Good Samaritan ... the equal protection clause forbids imposition of these burdens on pregnant women.[101]

Unlike the United States Supreme Court, the Supreme Court of Canada did defend its decision to legalize abortion based on the preservation of bodily integrity. In the 1988 decision *R v. Morgentaler*, the Justices decided that "[f]orcing a woman, by threat of criminal sanction, to carry a foetus to term unless she meets certain criteria unrelated to her own priorities and aspirations, is a profound interference with a woman's body and thus an infringement of security of the person."[102] Abortion in Canada is considered purely a medical matter and has been removed entirely from the Criminal Code. In her "re-write" of *Roe* Robin West acknowledges her debt to Thomson's argument and concludes that, if abortion is prohibited, "*pregnant women alone* must, by law, give their bodies over to the survival needs of others." Criminalizing abortion, then, reduces "the pregnant woman's body to the status of chattel. And because this is a difference in treatment that cuts so deeply, I believe it is a difference that is unconstitutional under the Fourteenth Amendment."[103]

There is one very clear difference between abortion and these cases. In every case, including the violinist example, what we have are examples of *refusing to provide aid*, whereas abortion, some may argue, is importantly different in that it involves taking direct action to kill the fetus. The former is more morally akin to passive euthanasia, where a terminal patient is, at her request, allowed to die from her underlying disease or affliction by not being given any life-sustaining treatment. This is in opposition to active euthanasia, where the patient, again upon her request, is directly killed by a medical professional, often because she is experiencing intense physical or mental suffering as a result of a terminal disease, but her death does not appear to be occurring any time in the proximate future. The American Medical Association, for instance, argues that these two kinds of euthanasia are significantly morally different, and that while a patient has a right to decide not to undergo any more life-sustaining treatment and be allowed to die, physicians cannot take active steps to kill a patient even at the latter's request.[104] Drawing on this difference, one may argue that in cases such as *McFall v. Shimp*, the person in need of aid was being allowed to die rather than be given access to another's body. Abortion does much more than this – abortion, like active euthanasia, involves the direct and intentional killing of the human fetus. Because of this difference, the objection goes, it would be illegitimate to appeal to these cases of "passive" death in order to justify "active" killing.

My response is to acknowledge this difference, but to deny its relevance. First, I am often suspicious of this argument because I sincerely doubt that if we could devise a way to "unplug" the fetus from a woman in a way more akin to passive euthanasia, pro-life advocates would all of a sudden find abortion permissible. From a pro-life prospective, it is the death of the fetus itself that is morally objectionable, not necessarily how it is killed. Second, up until the time that the fetus is viable, "unplugging" it from the woman necessarily entails its death, regardless of what method of abortion is used. Moreover, because early and mid-term abortions (which constitute 98.8% of all abortions[105]) involve the destruction of a non-sentient life, there is no abortive method that causes the fetus any pain or suffering (which would indeed be a morally relevant consideration were a fetus sentient). That is, if we have already accepted the fact that the woman may "unplug" herself from the fetus, if we acknowledge that this will necessarily entail its death, and if the abortion does not cause the fetus any pain, it seems morally irrelevant *how* the abortion is conducted; there is no "extra" harm that comes to the fetus because of the method in which it is aborted. The abortion methods that are currently used have proven to be most safe for women; when performed by skilled medical professionals under hygienic conditions, fewer than 1% of women of who obtain abortions experience any complications, and the risk of death in a safely conducted first trimester abortion is ten times lower than that of childbirth.[106]

Finally, while it may be possible to argue that there is something intrinsically immoral about actively killing a fetus versus letting it die, even in cases involving non-sentient life, this in itself is a morally controversial distinction that has been debated by bioethicists for decades, particularly in regards to euthanasia. Many philosophers have argued that there is no such intrinsic moral difference – non-action that is directly intended to lead to a person's death is not morally different than direct action intended to lead to a person's death. There is debate about this, of course, but the upshot is that a pro-life advocate who wants to implement this distinction in order to argue that abortion is relevantly dissimilar to the real cases I have cited, and even to Thomson's violinist example, has to contend with the plethora of philosophical literature that denies the moral relevance of the omission versus commission distinction.[107]

This segues into the final point I wish to make in this section. Because Thomson makes clear that the right to an abortion is a subset of the wider right to bodily autonomy (which is possessed by all persons, not just pregnant women), she argues that it is permissible to cause the fetus' death only when doing so is inseparable from allowing the woman to exercise her bodily autonomy. If it is possible to separate the two – that is, if the fetus is no longer dependent on the woman's body for sustenance – then it is impermissible to further demand the fetus' death. Thomson writes:

> [W]hile I am arguing for the permissibility of abortion in some cases, I am not arguing for the right to secure the death of the unborn child. It is easy to confuse these two things in that up to a certain point in the life of the fetus it is not able to survive outside the mother's body; hence removing it from her body guarantees its death. But they are importantly different. I have argued that you are not morally required to spend nine months in bed, sustaining the life of that violinist, but to say this is by no means to say that if, when you unplug yourself, there is a miracle and he survives, you then have a right to turn round and slit his throat. You may detach yourself even if this costs him his life; you have no right to be guaranteed his death, by some other means, if unplugging yourself does not kill him. There are some people who will feel dissatisfied by this feature of my argument. A woman may be utterly devastated by the thought of a child, a bit of herself, put out for adoption and never seen or heard of again. She may therefore want not merely that the child be detached from her, but more, that it die. Some opponents of abortion are inclined to regard this as beneath contempt – thereby showing insensitivity to what is surely a powerful source of despair. All the same, I agree that the desire

for the child's death is not one which anybody may gratify, should it turn out to be possible to detach the child alive.[108]

This is a vital component of Thomson's argument because it clarifies how she conceives the right to an abortion: it is not the right to *kill* the fetus, but rather a right to *evacuate* it if the woman no longer wishes to provide her body for sustenance. This can be read as an argument in support of the Supreme Court's decision to allow states to prohibit non-therapeutic abortion after viability. Demanding a destructive abortion after the fetus is no longer in need of a woman's body transforms the abortion right from one justified under the right to bodily autonomy to a right to kill a human being who is no longer in need of your body for sustenance.

Feminist philosopher Catriona Mackenzie rejects this aspect of Thomson's argument; according to her, arguments in favor of abortion that rely on women's autonomy should not just be restricted to fetal evacuation. Rather, Mackenzie argues that the right to an abortion should include a right to secure the death of the fetus:

> In choosing an abortion … a woman is not merely choosing not to allow the foetus occupancy of her uterus. Nor is she merely choosing not to undertake responsibility for a particular future child. Rather … she is choosing that there be *no being at all* in relation to whom she is in a situation of such responsibility. To require that a woman has no right to secure the death of the foetus, at least in the early stages of pregnancy, thus violates her autonomy.[109]

Mackenzie argues that early fetal life has no intrinsic worth, that its value is purely relational to how others, especially the woman, regard it. While the fetus' intrinsic moral worth increases as it develops, it never approximates the worth of a full-fledged person. According to her, a woman has a right to have a fetus destroyed, not just evacuated, because of her unique physical and mental connection to it:

> Phenomenologically, the experience of pregnancy, particularly in the early stages, is unique in the sense that it defied a sharp opposition between self and other … the fetus is not simply an entity extrinsic to her which happens to be developing inside her body and which she desires either to remove or to allow to develop. It is a being, both inseparable and yet separate from her, both part of and yet soon to be independent from her, whose existence calls into question her own present and future destiny.[110]

I agree with Mackenzie that pregnancy presents a time of extraordinary "psychic and bodily connectedness between woman and fetus"[111] and that it is precisely this unique and intimate connection that renders pregnancy a state of being that a woman must voluntarily assume. Highlighting this phenomenology serves to make Thomson's argument far stronger than she herself may have realized. However, I cannot agree with Mackenzie that this entails that we understand abortion rights *qua* fetal destruction rather than *qua* fetal evacuation. One reason she argues this is because she denies the personhood of the fetus, not just in early pregnancy, but all the way until its birth.[112] Because the fetus lacks personhood and therefore moral rights, it is essentially the woman's property up until the time it is born given her unique relationship to it. To affirm her argument, then, is to take a stance on fetal personhood that I am not able to make with confidence philosophically (as abovementioned, although I do believe the interest view of moral status/the embodied mind account of personal identity is the *best* way to go when it comes to the issue of fetal moral status, I am not unconditionally confident enough to close the book on this question), nor do I think, for all the reasons I have articulated here, that it is a good idea for pro-choice advocates to rely on practically.

As I have argued, interpreting the right to an abortion as a right to deny bodily aid to a dependent human being (rather than a right to kill a human being) allows us two philosophical advantages: we can circumvent the issue of fetal personhood altogether and also use well-established Kantian moral philosophy as our theoretical foundations. Practically, the abortion right stands on a strong ground of legal precedent if interpreted in this way, and survives any challenges thrown at it by impending Personhood Amendments. These are important advantages, even if it entails that women's access to destructive abortions after viability may be curtailed (within relevant considerations of her life and health). Admittedly, this may mean (as per *Planned Parenthood v. Casey*) that the window of opportunity a woman has for obtaining an abortion will shrink as the age of fetal viability increases given advancements in neonatal medicine. However, given that almost 90% of abortions happen in the first 12 weeks of pregnancy, and medical technology is not anywhere near being able to sustain a fetus that young, this concession is not a troubling one to make.

IV. Concluding thoughts: Beyond abortion as a conversation of rights

In 2011, the United States Supreme Court adjudicated *Snyder v. Phelps*, a case that tested our allegiance to the First Amendment right to freedom of speech. Fred Phelps was the lead pastor of the Westboro Baptist Church, whose members are infamous for picketing the funerals of fallen U.S. soldiers and other high-profile deaths. At these protests, members of the Church thank God for these deaths because they consider them to be just divine retribution for a sinful world that embraces homosexuality. The Phelps picketed the funeral of fallen Marine Matthew Snyder, and his father sued the Church for the intentional infliction of emotional distress. In an 8–1 vote, the Supreme Court Justices upheld the Phelps' freedom of speech, stating that, despite the vile content of their speech, the First Amendment protected them as well. From a moral standpoint, one may agree with the Justices here, perhaps citing utilitarian or deontological reasons why freedom of speech should be upheld in a free society. Yet, very few human beings, even the most devout of Christians, support the Phelps' hate speech. While they may have a legal and moral right to say what they please, their decision to exercise their rights in such a way falls way short of any kind of moral virtue or decency.

I use this example to make an important distinction: even if we argue that a person has a right to act in a certain way, this does not exhaust the moral dimensions of the conversation. There are further questions that we can ask, particularly whether persons are using their rights well. I have a right to use my hard-earned money as I see fit, but that does not mean that any exercise of that right is a virtuous one; waving my paycheck in front of a homeless person in order to taunt him would certainly be a morally appalling thing to do, even though I act perfectly within my rights by doing so. On the other hand, there are morally virtuous ways of exercising your rights. You can use your freedom of speech to stand on a corner and read the inspiring speeches of Martin Luther King Jr., and to preach a message of peace, love, and tolerance. You can use your money to feed a homeless family, or buy them some basic necessities.

Thomson argues that this distinction applies equally to abortion rights – while a woman does not commit an act of injustice when obtaining an abortion (as in, no rights are being violated when she does so), that does not mean that abortion choice cannot be subject to accusations of what she calls "moral indecency." She writes:

> [My argument] allows for and supports our sense that, for example, a sick and desperately frightened fourteen-year-old schoolgirl, pregnant due to rape, may *of course* choose abortion, and that any law which rules this out is an insane law. And it also allows for and supports our sense that in other cases resort to abortion is even positively indecent. It would be indecent in the woman to request an abortion, and indecent in a doctor to perform it, if she is in her seventh month, and wants the abortion just to avoid the nuisance of postponing a trip abroad.[113]

Thomson does not elaborate much on this point, particularly what qualifies as a "decent" versus "indecent" abortion. Rosalind Hursthouse takes this up in more detail in her essay "Virtue Theory and Abortion," where she also argues that even if we agree that women have a right to an abortion, this does not mean that there aren't ethical considerations that extend beyond this consideration:

> … in exercising a moral right I can do something cruel or callous, or selfish, light-minded, self-righteous, stupid, inconsiderate, disloyal, dishonest – that is, act viciously. Love and friendship do not survive their parties' constantly insisting on their rights, nor do people live well when they think that getting what they have a right to is of preeminent importance; they harm others, and they harm themselves … The fact that the premature termination of a pregnancy is, in some sense, the cutting off of a new human life, and thereby, like the procreation of a new human life, connects with all our thoughts about human

life and death, parenthood, and family relationships, must make it a serious matter. To disregard this fact about it, to think of abortion as nothing but the killing of something that does not matter, or as nothing but the exercise of some right or rights one has, or as the incidental means to some desirable states of affairs, is to do something callous and light-minded, the sort of thing that no virtuous or wise person would do. It is to have the wrong attitude not only to fetuses, but more generally to human life and death, parenthood, and family relationships.[114]

Here, Hursthouse illustrates how we could apply another normative theory, virtue ethics, to the abortion conversation. Because my primary concern in this chapter is to argue in favor of the moral and legal right to an abortion, it would be beyond the scope of my purposes to get into a conversation on how virtue ethics can be applied here. However, I have written about this extensively in other venues, including how to use the theory to adjudicate between "good" and "bad" reasons for having an abortion.[115]

In her study of pro-life and pro-choice women, Leslie Cannold found that many women in the latter group still thought that there were morally acceptable and unacceptable reasons for choosing abortion:

> Most all the women I interviewed saw the abortion issue as revolving around the pregnant woman's decision-making process. An abortion decision that did not reflect a woman's "feelings" and "love" for her could-be child and other significant people in her life, and that was not motivated by care and protective concern for all those she loves, was just plain wrong ... The younger women I interviewed tended to see safe and legal abortion as their birthright and were more concerned with the morality of the abortion decisions made by individual women ... No matter what their position on the morality of abortion, the women had almost identical views on the ethical issues that should be central in the mind of a woman dealing with the dilemma of an unexpected pregnancy and the concepts pregnant women needed to use to navigate this dilemma: responsibility, motherhood, relationship, and caring.[116]

The choice to abort is not intrinsically indecent or unvirtuous. My years of research on this issue have shown me that most of the time, women choose abortion for careful and considered reasons, often out of respect for the moral obligations they have for others (e.g., a woman who aborts because she has other children for whom she is already having difficulty caring) and for the moral obligations to self-improvement (e.g., a woman who aborts because she deems it necessary in order to continue her education or work prospects). Moreover, oftentimes, many women who abort do so in the midst of feelings of care for the life that grows within them. One of the most touching examples of this is of a woman who, after the abortion was completed, "reached out her beautifully delicate young hand, gently touched the cheek of her newly aborted tiny fetus and said 'I'm sorry, baby.'"[117] Another woman procured an abortion after her fetus was diagnosed with a deformity: "The woman said: 'I don't want to deny that this baby existed.' She gave it a name, had a funeral for it, and buried it in the family plot alongside her grandmother."[118]

The biggest strength of Thomson's argument is that it shows pro-life advocates that a successful argument in favor of abortion rights is possible even if we grant fetal personhood. Another, often unsung, strength is that it shows pro-choice advocates that one need not deprive fetuses of moral value (regardless of where we stand on the issue of fetal personhood) in order to argue in favor of abortion rights, just as we do not need to deride sick patients in need of bone marrow, blood transfusions, or organ donations in order to argue that caring for their welfare cannot entail forcing others into bodily submission. As I mentioned at the onset of this chapter, dismissing the value of fetal life fails to capture the phenomenology of abortion for many women. As a mother, I decided that if I was going to go on paper defending a woman's right to choose abortion, I couldn't do so by dismissing fetuses as mere "clumps of cells" or "tissue" or "products of conception," or whatever term people use to strip the fetus of its humanity. Pro-choice advocates should not, and need not, ground their arguments on a foundation that dismisses fetal life, but should, rather, acknowledge its value and defend abortion rights through that lens.

Abortions will never be eradicated completely, especially as long as sexual assault against women exists. Prohibiting abortion will not significantly affect its prevalence. In Brazil, where abortions are only allowed in cases of rape or incest, more than 200,000 women are hospitalized annually as a result of attempted abortions. In Colombia, abortions are only allowed in cases of rape, incest, or in pregnancies involving fatal fetal abnormalities, yet according to the Colombian government there are more than 300,000 illegal abortions performed every year, and abortion is the third leading cause of maternal mortality.[119] Yet while banning abortions would be ineffective for saving fetal or maternal life, I would like to, as a society, work harder to simultaneously protect women's reproductive liberty while working towards a culture that makes abortion less prevalent. As a pro-choice advocate, I will always maintain that a woman's decision whether to gestate should be free from all kinds of coercion, whether that be by restrictive laws, or by social circumstances. A woman who chooses abortion because of financial or social pressures, when she otherwise would have chosen to gestate the fetus and parent the child, did not really choose her abortion freely; the choice to abort in these circumstances does not reflect her actual desires. Working towards a society that meets the economic, mental, and emotional needs of women who choose abortion for these reasons not only will be actually effective in lowering abortion rates, but will help ensure that women facing unplanned pregnancies have better options so that, if they do choose abortion, it is not because they were coerced into it by these circumstances. This is where I believe pro-choice and pro-life advocates can come together and move away from the vitriolic hate that permeates this debate. It because I care deeply about the rights of women *and* about respecting human life in its earliest stages that I look forward to exploring ways that we can do this alongside Mulder in Chapter 5.

Notes

1 Mary Anne Warren. 1973. "On the Moral and Legal Status of Abortion." *The Monist* 57.1: 43–61.
2 Peter Singer. 1993. *Practical Ethics.* New York: Cambridge University Press.
3 Michael Tooley. 1972. "Abortion and Infanticide." *Philosophy and Public Affairs* 2.1: 37–65.
4 Giubilini and Minerva. 2013. "After-birth Abortion: Why Should the Baby Live?" *Journal of Medical Ethics* 39: 261–263.
5 Bertha Alvarez Manninen. 2013. "Yes, the Baby Should Live: A Pro-Choice Response to Giubilini and Minerva." *Journal of Medical Ethics* 39: 330–335.
6 Susan Poppema. 1996. *Why I am an Abortion Doctor.* New York: Prometheus Books, p. 165.
7 See, for example: Bertha Alvarez Manninen. 2013. "The Value of Choice and the Choice to Value: Expanding the Discussion of Fetal Life within Pro-Choice Advocacy." *Hypatia* 28.3: 663–683.
8 Frances Kissling. 2005. "Is There Life after Roe?: How to Think about the Fetus." *Conscience: The News Journal of Catholic Opinion.* http://www.catholicsforchoice.org/conscience/archives/c2004win_lifeafterroe.asp
9 Margaret Olivia Little. 2002. "The Morality of Abortion." In *Biomedical Ethics*, edited by David DeGrazia, Thomas Mappes, and Jeffrey Brand-Ballard. New York, NY: McGraw Hill, p. 488.
10 Linda Francke. 1978. *The Ambivalence of Abortion.* New York: Random House, p. 5.
11 Leslie Cannold. 1998. *The Abortion Myth: Feminism, Morality, and the Hard Choices Women Make.* Hanover, NH: Wesleyan University Press, p. 36.
12 Lindsy Van Gelder. 1978. "Cracking the Women's Movement Protection Game." *Ms. Magazine,* December, pp. 66–67.
13 Eve Kushner. 1997. *Experiencing Abortion: A Weaving of Women's Words.* New York: Harrington Park Press, p. 148.
14 Ibid.
15 William LaFleur. 1990. "Contestation and Consensus: The Morality of Abortion in Japan." *Philosophy East and West*, 40.4: 529–542, at p. 534. See also LaFleur, 1992, *Liquid Life: Abortion and Buddhism in Japan.* Princeton: Princeton University Press.
16 Jeff Wilson. 2009. *Mourning the Unborn Dead: A Buddhist Ritual Comes to America.* New York: Oxford University Press, p. 37.
17 See Helen Cvejic et al. 1977. "Follow up of 50 Adolescent Girls 2 Years After Abortion." *Canadian Medical Association,* 116.1: 44–46 and Laurie Zabin et al. 1989. "When Urban Adolescents Choose Abortion: Effects on Education, Psychological Status, and Subsequent Pregnancy." *Family Planning Perspective,* 21.6: 248–255.
18 See, for example: David Reardon. 1987. *Aborted Women: Silent No More.* Chicago: Loyola University Press. Here, he argued (quite badly) in favor of such a condition.
19 Brenda Major et al. 2008. "Report of the APA Task Force on Mental Health and Abortion," p. 90. Full report available at http://www.apa.org/pi/wpo/mental-health-abortion-report.pdf.
20 Ibid.
21 Mary Anne Warren. 1973. "On the Moral and Legal Status of Abortion." *The Monist,* 57. 1. In *Contemporary Issues in Bioethics.* Tom Beauchamp and LeRoy Walters (eds.). Belmont, CA: Wadsworth Publishing Company, p. 308.
22 Peter Singer. 1993. *Practical Ethics.* Cambridge: Cambridge University Press, p. 151.
23 Michael Tooley. 1972. "Abortion and Infanticide." *Philosophy and Public Affairs*, Vol. 2, No. 1, p. 44.
24 Singer, 1993, p. 97.
25 Tooley, 1972, p. 48.
26 Michael Tooley. 1985. *Abortion and Infanticide.* New York, NY: Oxford University Press, p. 60.

27 Singer, 1993, p. 3
28 Wendy Holden. 1994. *Unlawful Carnal Knowledge: The True Story of the Irish 'X' Case*. Glasgow: Harper Collins Publishers, pp. 98–100.
29 Shawn Pogatchnik. 2013. "Ireland to Release Report on Savita Halappanavar, Woman Who Died After Denied Abortion." Available from http://www.huffingtonpost.com/2013/06/13/savita-halappanavar-report-ireland-abortion_n_3434769.html
30 Angela Bourke et al. 2002. *The Field Day Anthology of Irish Writing, Vol. V, Irish Women's Writing and Traditions*. Washington Square, NY: New York University Press, p. 341.
31 Many of these arguments can be found in a more detailed exposition in my essay: "Beyond Abortion: The Implications of Human Life Amendments." Manninen. 2012. *Journal of Social Philosophy*, 43.2: 140–160.
32 HLA Coalition, n.d. "The Human Life Amendment." Available from http://www.personhood.net/coalition.html
33 Georgia General Assembly, n.d. See full text of bill here: http://www.legis.ga.gov/Legislation/en-US/display.aspx?Legislation=31965
34 Francis Beckwith. 2007. *Defending Life: A Moral and Legal Case Against Abortion Choice*. New York, NY: Cambridge University Press, p. 171.
35 Ibid.
36 "Real Answers to the Scare-Tactics Being Spread by the Pro-Abortion Minority about the Personhood Amendment." Available at: http://yeson26.net/media/1999/yeson26-faq.pdf
37 Tennessee Supreme Court. 1992. *Davis v. Davis*. Available at: http://biotech.law.lsu.edu/cases/cloning/davis_v_davis.htm
38 Don Marquis. 1989. "Why Abortion is Immoral." *The Journal of Philosophy*, 86.4, p. 192. Here it should be noted that Marquis does not intend his argument to apply to embryos from *conception*, but rather from the time of individuation, when the embryo can no longer divide into separate distinct organisms, which occurs at about two weeks post-conception. Given that individuation happens early on in the embryo's development, definitely by the time a woman learns she is pregnant, this distinction makes no practical difference when it comes to abortion ethics. It *can*, however, be relevant when dealing with the moral status of extra-uterine embryos; Marquis' argument may not apply to surplus IVF embryos, for example, who have not yet passed the two week post-conception mark.
39 Pope John Paul II. 1995. *Evangelium Vitae*. New York, NY: Random House Inc., pp. 104 and 107; emphasis mine.
40 See: Eric Olson. 1997. "Was I Ever a Fetus?" *Philosophy and Phenomenological Research*, 57.1: 95–110; Eric Olson. 1997. *The Human Animal: Personal Identity without Psychology*. New York, NY: Oxford University Press; and David DeGrazia. 2005. *Human Identity and Bioethics*. New York, NY: Cambridge University Press.
41 Lydia Saad. 2013. "Americans' Abortion Views Steady Amid Gosnell Trial." Available at: http://www.gallup.com/poll/162374/americans-abortion-views-steady-amid-gosnell-trial.aspx?utm_source=google&utm_medium=rss&utm_campaign=syndication
42 Norman C. Gillespie. 1977. "Abortion and Human Rights." *Ethics*, 87.3.
43 Joel Feinberg. 1984. *Harm to Others: The Moral Limits of the Criminal Law*. New York, NY: Oxford University Press, p. 34.
44 Ibid.
45 Feinberg, 1984, p. 33.
46 Bonnie Steinbock. 1992. *Life Before Birth: The Moral and Legal Status of Embryos and Fetuses*. New York, NY: Oxford University Press, p. 5.
47 Steinbock, 1992, p. 23.
48 Thomas Nagel. 1974. "What Is It Like to Be a Bat?" *The Philosophical Review*, Vol. 83, No. 4, p. 436.
49 Ludwig Wittgenstein. 1963. *Philosophical Investigations*, G.E.M. Anscombe (trans). Oxford: Basil Blackwell,, par. 283–284.

50 H. Tristam Engelhardt. 1974. "The Ontology of Abortion." *Ethics*, Vol. 84, No. 3, p. 219.
51 H.J. McCloskey. 1975. "The Right to Life." *Mind*, 84.335, p. 411.
52 Jeff McMahan. 2002. *The Ethics of Killing: Problems at the Margins of Life*. New York, NY: Oxford University Press, p. 68.
53 Singer, 1993, p. 97.
54 Mary Anne Warren. 1981. "Do Potential Persons Have Rights?" in *Responsibilities to Future Generations*. E. Partridge (ed.). Buffalo, NY: Prometheus Books, p. 264.
55 Rodrigo O. Kuljis. 1994. "Development of Human Brain; The Emergence of the Neural Substrate for Pain Perception and Conscious Experience," in *The Beginnings of Human Life*. F.K. Beller and R.F. Weir (eds.). Amsterdam, the Netherlands: Kluwer Academic Publishers, pp. 49–50.
56 J.A. Burgess and S.A. Tawia. 1996. "When Did You First Begin to Feel It? – Locating the Beginning of Human Consciousness." *Bioethics*, 10.1, pp. 7–8.
57 Kuljis, 1994, p. 52.
58 UK Parliament. POSTnote to the All-Party Parliament Inquiry into Fetal Awareness. Accessed on February 1, 2005. Available on the World Wide Web: researchbriefings.files.parliament.uk/documents/POST-PN-94/POST-PN-94.pdf
59 Burgess and Tawia, 1996, p. 17.
60 J.C. Laroche. 1981. "The Marginal Layer in the Neocortex of a 7 week-old Human Embryo: A Light and Electron Microscopic Study." *Anatomy and Embryology*, 162. 3, pp. 301–312. Also see V. Glover and N.M. Fisk. 1999. "Fetal Pain: Implications for Research and Practice." *British Journal of Obstetrics and Gynaecology*, 106.9, pp. 881–886.
61 McMahan, 2002, pp. 267–272.
62 See: Bertha Alvarez Manninen. 2007. "Revisiting the Argument of Fetal Potential." *Philosophy, Ethics, and Humanities in Medicine*, 2: 17. Available at: http://www.pehmed.com/content/2/1/7
63 United States Supreme Court. 1992. *Planned Parenthood vs. Casey*.https://www.law.cornell.edu/supremecourt/text/505/833
64 Guttmacher Institute. 2016. "An Overview of Abortion Laws." Available at: http://www.guttmacher.org/statecenter/spibs/spib_OAL.pdf
65 United States Supreme Court. 1972. *Eisenstadt v. Baird*. http://supreme.justia.com/us/405/438/case.html
66 United States Supreme Court. 1977. *Carey v. Population Services International*. http://www.law.cornell.edu/supct/html/historics/USSC_CR_0431_0678_ZS.html
67 United States Supreme Court. 1973. *Roe v. Wade*. http://www.tourolaw.edu/Patch/Roe/
68 Christopher Kaczor. 2005. *The Edge of Life: Human Dignity and Contemporary Bioethics*. Dordrecht: Springer, p. 111.
69 United States Supreme Court. 1973. *Roe v. Wade*. http://www.tourolaw.edu/Patch/Roe/
70 Ibid.
71 Bob Unruh. 2007. "'Personhood' Silver Bullet to Kill *Roe v. Wade*." Available at: http://www.wnd.com/news/article.asp?ARTICLE_ID=57888
72 Judith Jarvis Thomson. 1971. "A Defense of Abortion." *Philosophy and Public Affairs* 1.1, p. 47.
73 Thomson, 1971, pp. 48–49.
74 Judith Jarvis Thomson. 1971. "A Defense of Abortion." *Philosophy and Public Affairs*, 1.1: 47–66, at p. 56.
75 Immanuel Kant. 1981. *Grounding for the Metaphysics of Morals*. Indianapolis: Hackett Publishing Company, p. 36.
76 Margaret Olivia Little. 1999. "Abortion Intimacy, and the Duty to Gestate." *Ethical Theory and Moral Practice*, 2.3: 295–312, at pp. 299 and 301.
77 Christine Overall. 1993. *Human Reproduction: Principles, Practices, and Policies*. Toronto: Oxford University Press, pp. 1–2.

78 Caroline Lundquist. 2008. "Being Torn: Toward a Phenomenology of Unwanted Pregnancy." *Hypatia* 23.3, pp. 145–146.
79 Lundquist, 2008, p. 147.
80 Susan Bordo. 1993. "Are Mothers Persons? Reproductive Rights and the Politics of Subjectivity." In *Unbearable Weight: Feminism, Western Culture, and the Body*. Berkeley, CA: University of California Press, p. 74.
81 Donald H. Regan. 1979. "Rewriting Roe v. Wade." *Michigan Law Review*, 77.7: 1569–1646, at pp. 1616–1617.
82 Bordo, 1993, p. 94.
83 John Wilcox. 1989. "Nature as Demonic in Thomson's Defense of Abortion." In *The Ethics of Abortion*. Amherst: Prometheus Books, p. 262. In addition to Wilcox, other philosophers that have posed the Responsibility Objection against Thomson: e.g., Robert N. Wennberg. 1985. *Life in the Balance: Exploring the Abortion Controversy*. Grand Rapids, MI: Eerdmans Publishing; Paul D. Feinberg. 1978. "The Morality of Abortion" In *Thou Shalt Not Kill: The Christian Case against Abortion*. New Rochelle: Arlington House; Francis Beckwith. 2007. *A Defending Life: A Moral and Legal Case Against Abortion Choice*. New York: Cambridge University Press; Francis Beckwith. 1993. *Politically Correct Death*. Grand Rapids, MI: Baker Books. Even philosophers who are in favor of abortion rights have argued that the Responsibility Objection is a formidable one against Thomson, e.g., Warren, 1973 and Jeff McMahan. 2002. *The Ethics of Killing: Problems at the Margins of Life*. New York: Oxford University Press.
84 Francis Beckwith. 1992. "Personal Bodily Rights, Abortion, and Unplugging the Violinist." *International Philosophical Quarterly*, 32.1: 105–118, at pp. 111–112.
85 David Boonin. 2003. *A Defense of Abortion*. New York, NY: Cambridge University Press, p. 168.
86 Thomson, 1971, pp. 58–59.
87 Stephen Schwartz. 1990. *The Moral Question of Abortion*. Chicago: Loyola University Press, p. 118.
88 Nancy Jecker. 1990. "Conceiving a Child to Save a Child: Reproduction and Filial Ethics." *Journal of Clinical Ethics*, 1.2, p. 102; emphasis added.
89 Regan, 1979, p. 1623.
90 Robin West. 2005. "Concurring with the Judgment." In *What* Roe v. Wade *Should Have Said*, edited by Jack Balkin. New York: New York University Press, p. 133.
91 Immanuel Kant. 1996. *The Metaphysics of Morals*. New York, NY: Cambridge University Press, p. 16.
92 See, for example: Patrick Kain. 2009. "Kant's Defense of Human Moral Status." *Journal of the History of Philosophy*, 47: 59–101.
93 See, for example: Linda Papadaki. 2012. "Abortion and Kant's Formula of Humanity." *Humana.Mente: Journal of Philosophical Studies*, 22: 145–166, and Allen Wood. 1998. "Kant on Duties Regarding Nonrational Nature." *Supplemental Proceedings of the Aristotelian Society*, 72: 189–210.
94 Susan Feldman. 1998. "From Occupied Bodies to Pregnant Persons: How Kantian Ethics Should Treat Pregnancy and Abortion." In *Autonomy and Community: Readings in Contemporary Kantian Social Philosophy*, edited by Jane Kneller and Sidney Axinn. Albany, NY: State University of New York Press, p. 278.
95 Regan, 1979, p. 1610.
96 United States Supreme Court. 1891. *Union Pacific Railway Co. v. Botsford*. http://supreme.justia.com/us/141/250/case.html
97 Connecticut Supreme Court. 1996. *Stamford Hospital vs. Vega*. *Atlantic Reporter*, 674: 821–834.
98 Cited in Bordo, 1993, p. 75.
99 10th Pennsylvania District Court. 1978. *McFall v. Shimp*. http://www.ucs.louisiana.edu/~ras2777/judpol/mcfall.html
100 Ibid.
101 Regan, 1979, p. 1569.

102 Canadian Supreme Court. 1988. *R v. Morgentaler.* http://csc.lexum.umontreal.ca/en/1988/1988scr1-30/1988scr1-30.html
103 West, 2005, p. 134.
104 AMA policy on End-of-Life Care. http://www.ama-assn.org/ama/pub/physician-resources/medical-ethics/about-ethics-group/ethics-resource-center/end-of-life-care/ama-policy-end-of-life-care.page?
105 Guttmacher Institute. 2014. "Facts on Induced Abortion." Available at: http://www.guttmacher.org/pubs/fb_induced_abortion.html
106 R.B. Gold, et al. 1990. *Abortion and Women's Health: A Turning Point for America?* New York: The Alan Guttmacher Institute.
107 See, for example: James Rachels. 1975. "Active and Passive Euthanasia." *New England Journal of Medicine*, 292: 78–80 and Dan Brock. 1992. "Voluntary Active Euthanasia." *The Hastings Center Report* 22.2: 10–22.
108 Thomson, 1971, p. 66.
109 Catriona Mackenzie. 1992. "Abortion and Embodiment." *Australasian Journal of Philosophy*, 70.2, pp. 137–138. In her essay "Abortion, Killing, and Maternal Moral Authority" (Reader, 2008, *Hypatia*, 23.2: 132–150), Soran Reader also argues in favor of understanding the right to an abortion as a right to kill the fetus, but not because she believes that fetuses are morally negligible, but because, she argues, the maternal duty of care can sometimes entail that a woman is justified in taking her child's life. She offers as an example a woman who chooses to kill her infant rather than have the baby return to a life of slavery or other kinds of unimaginable suffering. Discussing Reader's argument in detail would take me beyond the immediate scope of my arguments here, but she does offer a compelling and unique argument in favor of abortion right *qua* fetal destruction in a way not immediately reliant on denying fetal moral worth.
110 Mackenzie, 1992, p. 148.
111 Mackenzie, 1992, p. 151.
112 Mackenzie, 1992, p. 146.
113 Thomson, 1971, pp. 65–66.
114 Rosalind Hursthouse. 1991. "Virtue Theory and Abortion." *Philosophy and Public Affairs*, 20.3, pp. 235–238.
115 See, for example: Manninen. 2014. *Pro-Life, Pro-Choice: Shared Values in the Abortion Debate*. Nashville: Vanderbilt University Press; Manninen. 2013. "The Value of Choice and the Choice to Value: Expanding the Discussion about Fetal Life within Pro-choice Advocacy." *Hypatia: A Journal of Feminist Philosophy*, 28.3: 663–683; and Manninen. 2007. "Pleading Men and Virtuous Women: Considering the Role of the Father in the Abortion Debate." *International Journal of Applied Philosophy*, 21.1: 1–24.
116 Cannold, 1998, pp. xx and 16.
117 Bobbie Jeanne Kennedy. 1988. "I'm Sorry Baby." *American Journal of Nursing*, 88.8, p. 1067.
118 Kennedy, 1988, p. 1068.
119 Pew Research Center. 2008. "Abortion Laws Around the World." Available at: http://www.pewforum.org/2008/09/30/abortion-laws-around-the-world/

References

10th Pennsylvania District Court. 1978. *McFall v. Shimp*. http://www.ucs.louisiana.edu/~ras2777/judpol/mcfall.html

AMA policy on End-of-Life Care. http://www.ama-assn.org/ama/pub/physician-resources/medical-ethics/about-ethics-group/ethics-resource-center/end-of-life-care/ama-policy-end-of-life-care.page?

Beckwith, Francis. 2007. *Defending Life: A Moral and Legal Case Against Abortion Choice*. New York: Cambridge University Press.
Beckwith, Francis. 1993. *Politically Correct Death*. Grand Rapids, MI: Baker Books.
Beckwith, Francis. 1992. "Personal Bodily Rights, Abortion, and Unplugging the Violinist." *International Philosophical Quarterly*, 32. 1: 105–118.
Boonin, David. 2003. *A Defense of Abortion*. New York: Cambridge University Press.
Bordo, Susan. 1993. "Are Mothers Persons? Reproductive Rights and the Politics of Subjectivity," in Susan Bordo and Leslie Heywood (eds), *Unbearable Weight: Feminism, Western Culture, and the Body*. Berkeley: University of California Press, pp. 71–97.
Bourke, Angela, Siobhan Kilfeather, Maria Luddy, *et al.* (eds) 2002. *The Field Day Anthology of Irish Writing, Vol. V, Irish Women's Writing and Traditions*. Washington Square: New York University Press.
Brock, Dan. 1992. "Voluntary Active Euthanasia." *The Hastings Center Report*, 22. 2: 10–22.
Burgess, J.A. and S.A. Tawia. 1996. "When Did You First Begin to Feel It?: Locating the Beginning of Human Consciousness." *Bioethics*, 10. 1: 1–26.
Canadian Supreme Court. 1988. *R v. Morgentaler*. http://csc.lexum.umontreal.ca/en/1988/1988scr1-30/1988scr1-30.html
Cannold, Leslie. 1998. *The Abortion Myth: Feminism, Morality, and the Hard Choices Women Make*. Hanover: Wesleyan University Press.
Connecticut Supreme Court. 1996. *Stamford Hospital vs. Vega.Atlantic Reporter*, 674: 821–834.
Cvejic, Helen, I. Lipper, R.A. Kinch, and P. Benjamin. 1977. "Follow up of 50 Adolescent Girls 2 Years After Abortion." *Canadian Medical Association*, 116. 1: 44–46.
DeGrazia, David. 2005. *Human Identity and Bioethics*. New York: Cambridge University Press.
Engelhardt, H. Tristam. 1974. "The Ontology of Abortion." *Ethics*, 84. 3: 217–234.
Feinberg, Joel. 1984. *Harm to Others: The Moral Limits of the Criminal Law*. New York: Oxford University Press.
Feinberg, Paul D. 1978. "The Morality of Abortion," in Richard Ganz and C. Everett Koop (eds), *Thou Shalt Not Kill: The Christian Case against Abortion*. New Rochelle: Arlington House.
Feldman, Susan. 1998. "From Occupied Bodies to Pregnant Persons: How Kantian Ethics Should Treat Pregnancy and Abortion," in Jane Kneller and Sidney Axinn (eds), *Autonomy and Community: Readings in Contemporary Kantian Social Philosophy*. Albany: State University of New York Press, pp. 265–282.
Francke, Linda. 1978. *The Ambivalence of Abortion*. New York: Random House.
Georgia General Assembly, n.d. "HB 1 – Crimes and Offenses; Prenatal Murder." Available from: http://www.legis.ga.gov/legislation/en-US/display/31965
Gillespie, Norman C. 1977. "Abortion and Human Rights." *Ethics*, 87. 3: 237–243.
Giubilini, Alberto and Francesca Minerva. 2013. "After-birth Abortion: Why Should the Baby Live?" *Journal of Medical Ethics*, 39: 261–263.
Glover, V. and N.M. Fisk. 1999. "Fetal Pain: Implications for Research and Practice." *British Journal of Obstetrics and Gynaecology*, 106. 9: 881–886.
Gold, R.B., S.K. Henshaw, and L.D. Lindberg. 1990. *Abortion and Women's Health: A Turning Point for America?* New York: The Alan Guttmacher Institute. Available at: https://www.guttmacher.org/sites/default/files/pdfs/pubs/2006/05/04/AiWL.pdf
Guttmacher Institute. 2016. "An Overview of Abortion Laws." Available at: http://www.guttmacher.org/statecenter/spibs/spib_OAL.pdf
Guttmacher Institute. 2014. "Facts on Induced Abortion." Available at: http://www.guttmacher.org/pubs/fb_induced_abortion.html
HLA Coalition, n.d. "The Human Life Amendment." Available from http://www.personhood.net/coalition.html

Holden, Wendy. 1994. *Unlawful Carnal Knowledge: The True Story of the Irish 'X' Case*. Glasgow: Harper Collins Publishers.
Hursthouse, Rosalind. 1991. "Virtue Theory and Abortion." *Philosophy and Public Affairs*, 20. 3: 223–246.
Jecker, Nancy. 1990. "Conceiving a Child to Save a Child: Reproduction and Filial Ethics." *Journal of Clinical Ethics*, 1. 2: 99–103.
John Paul II, Pope. 1995. *Evangelium Vitae*. New York, NY: Random House Inc.
Kaczor, Christopher. 2005. *The Edge of Life: Human Dignity and Contemporary Bioethics*. Dordrecht: Springer.
Kain, Patrick. 2009. "Kant's Defense of Human Moral Status." *Journal of the History of Philosophy*, 47. 1: 59–101.
Kant, Immanuel. 1996. *The Metaphysics of Morals*. New York: Cambridge University Press.
Kant, Immanuel. 1981. *Grounding for the Metaphysics of Morals*. Indianapolis: Hackett Publishing Company.
Kennedy, Bobbie Jeanne. 1988. "I'm Sorry Baby." *American Journal of Nursing*, 88. 8: 1067–1069.
Kissling, Frances. 2005. "Is There Life After Roe?: How to Think about the Fetus." *Conscience: The News Journal of Catholic Opinion*. Available at: http://www.catholicsforchoice.org/conscience/archives/c2004win_lifeafterroe.asp
Kuljis, Rodrigo O. 1994. "Development of Human Brain; The Emergence of the Neural Substrate for Pain Perception and Conscious Experience," in F.K. Beller and R.F. Weir (eds), *The Beginnings of Human Life*. Amsterdam: Kluwer Academic Publisher, pp. 49–56.
Kushner, Eve. 1997. *Experiencing Abortion: A Weaving of Women's Words*. New York: Harrington Park Press.
LaFleur, William. 1992. *Liquid Life: Abortion and Buddhism in Japan*. Princeton: Princeton University Press.
LaFleur, William. 1990. "Contestation and Consensus: The Morality of Abortion in Japan." *Philosophy East and West*, 40. 4: 529–542.
Laroche, J.C. 1981. "The Marginal Layer in the Neocortex of a 7 week-old Human Embryo: A Light and Electron Microscopic Study." *Anatomy and Embryology*, 162. 3: 301–312.
Little, Margaret Olivia. 2002. "The Morality of Abortion," in David DeGrazia, Thomas Mappes, and Jeffrey Brand-Ballard (eds), *Biomedical Ethics*. New York: McGraw Hill, pp. 488–492.
Little, Margaret Olivia. 1999. "Abortion Intimacy, and the Duty to Gestate." *Ethical Theory and Moral Practice*, 2. 3: 295–312.
Lundquist, Caroline. 2008. "Being Torn: Toward a Phenomenology of Unwanted Pregnancy." *Hypatia*, 23. 3: 136–155.
Mackenzie, Catriona. 1992. "Abortion and Embodiment." *Australasian Journal of Philosophy*, 70. 2: 136–155.
Major, Brenda, Mark Appelbaum, Linda Beckman et al. 2008. "Report of the APA Task Force on Mental Health and Abortion." Available at: http://www.apa.org/pi/wpo/mental-health-abortion-report.pdf.
Manninen, Bertha Alvarez. 2014. *Pro-Life, Pro-Choice: Shared Values in the Abortion Debate*. Nashville: Vanderbilt University Press.
Manninen, Bertha Alvarez. 2013. "The Value of Choice and the Choice to Value: Expanding the Discussion of Fetal Life within Pro-Choice Advocacy." *Hypatia*, 28. 3: 663–683.
Manninen, Bertha Alvarez. 2013. "Yes, the Baby Should Live: A Pro-Choice Response to Giubilini and Minerva." *Journal of Medical Ethics*, 39: 330–335.

Manninen, Bertha Alvarez. 2012. "Beyond Abortion: The Implications of Human Life Amendments." *Journal of Social Philosophy*, 43. 2: 140–160.
Manninen, Bertha Alvarez. 2007. "Pleading Men and Virtuous Women: Considering the Role of the Father in the Abortion Debate." *International Journal of Applied Philosophy*, 21. 1: 1–24.
Manninen, Bertha Alvarez. 2007. "Revisiting the Argument of Fetal Potential." *Philosophy, Ethics, and Humanities in Medicine*, 2:17. Available at: http://www.pehmed.com/content/2/1/7
Marquis, Don. 1989. "Why Abortion is Immoral." *The Journal of Philosophy*, 86. 4: 183–202.
McCloskey, H.J. 1975. "The Right to Life." *Mind*, 84. 335: 403–425.
McMahan, Jeff. 2002. *The Ethics of Killing: Problems at the Margins of Life*. New York: Oxford University Press.
Nagel, Thomas. 1974. "What is it Like to be a Bat?" *The Philosophical Review*, 83. 4: 435–450.
Olson, Eric. 1997. *The Human Animal: Personal Identity without Psychology*. New York: Oxford University Press.
Olson, Eric. 1997. "Was I Ever a Fetus?" *Philosophy and Phenomenological Research*, 57. 1: 95–110.
Overall, Christine. 1993. *Human Reproduction: Principles, Practices, and Policies*. Toronto: Oxford University Press.
Papadaki, Linda. 2012. "Abortion and Kant's Formula of Humanity." *Humana.Mente: Journal of Philosophical Studies*, 22: 145–166.
Pew Research Center. 2008. "Abortion Laws Around the World." Available at: http://www.pewforum.org/2008/09/30/abortion-laws-around-the-world/
Pogatchnik, Shawn. 2013. "Ireland to Release Report on Savita Halappanavar, Woman Who Died After Denied Abortion." Available from: http://www.huffingtonpost.com/2013/06/13/savita-halappanavar-report-ireland-abortion_n_3434769.html
Poppema, Susan. 1996. *Why I Am an Abortion Doctor*. New York: Prometheus Books.
POSTnote to the All-Party Parliament Inquiry into Fetal Awareness. Available at: researchbriefings.files.parliament.uk/documents/POST-PN-94/POST-PN-94.pdf.
Rachels, James. 1975. "Active and Passive Euthanasia." *New England Journal of Medicine*, 292: 78–80.
Reader, Soran. 2008. "Abortion, Killing, and Maternal Moral Authority." *Hypatia*, 23. 2: 132–150.
Reardon, David. 1987. *Aborted Women: Silent No More*. Chicago: Loyola University Press.
Regan, Donald. 1979. "Rewriting Roe v. Wade." *Michigan Law Review*, 77. 7: 1569–1646.
Saad, Lydia. 2013. "Americans' Abortion Views Steady Amid Gosnell Trial." Available at: http://www.gallup.com/poll/162374/americans-abortion-views-steady-amid-gosnell-trial.aspx?utm_source=google&utm_medium=rss&utm_campaign=syndication
Schwartz, Stephen. 1990. *The Moral Question of Abortion*. Chicago: Loyola University Press.
Singer, Peter. 1993. *Practical Ethics*. New York: Cambridge University Press.
Steinbock, Bonnie. 1992. *Life Before Birth: The Moral and Legal Status of Embryos and Fetuses*. New York, NY: Oxford University Press.
Tennessee Supreme Court. 1992. *Davis v. Davis*. Available at: http://biotech.law.lsu.edu/cases/cloning/davis_v_davis.htm
Thomson, Judith Jarvis. 1971. "A Defense of Abortion." *Philosophy and Public Affairs*, 1. 1: 47–66.
Tooley, Michael. 1985. *Abortion and Infanticide*. New York: Oxford University Press.
Tooley, Michael. 1972. "Abortion and Infanticide." *Philosophy and Public Affairs*, 2. 1: 37–65.
United States Supreme Court. 1992. *Planned Parenthood vs. Casey*. Available at: https://www.law.cornell.edu/supremecourt/text/505/833

United States Supreme Court. 1977. *Carey v. Population Services International*. Available at: http://www.law.cornell.edu/supct/html/historics/USSC_CR_0431_0678_ZS.html

United States Supreme Court. 1973. *Roe v. Wade*. Available at: http://www.tourolaw.edu/Patch/Roe/

United States Supreme Court. 1972. *Eisenstadt v. Baird*. Available at: http://supreme.justia.com/us/405/438/case.html

United States Supreme Court. 1891. *Union Pacific Railway Co. v. Botsford*. Available at: http://supreme.justia.com/us/141/250/case.html

Unruh, Bob. 2007. "'Personhood' Silver Bullet to Kill *Roe v. Wade*." Available at: http://www.wnd.com/news/article.asp?ARTICLE_ID=57888

Van Gelder, Lindsy. 1978. "Cracking the Women's Movement Protection Game." *Ms. Magazine*, December, pp. 66–67.

Warren, Mary Anne. 1981. "Do Potential Persons Have Rights?" in E. Partridge (ed.), *Responsibilities to Future Generations*. Buffalo: Prometheus Books, pp. 261–273.

Warren, Mary Anne. 1973. "On the Moral and Legal Status of Abortion." *The Monist*, 57. 1: 43–61.

Wennberg, Robert N. 1985. *Life in the Balance: Exploring the Abortion Controversy*. Grand Rapids, MI: Eerdmans Publishing.

West, Robin. 2005. "Concurring with the Judgment," in Jack Balkin (ed.), *What Roe v. Wade Should Have Said*. New York: New York University Press, pp. 121–147.

Wilcox, John. 1989. "Nature as Demonic in Thomson's Defense of Abortion," in Robert Baird and Stuart Rosenbaum (eds), *The Ethics of Abortion*. Amherst: Prometheus Books, pp. 257–271.

Wilson, Jeff. 2009. *Mourning the Unborn Dead: A Buddhist Ritual Comes to America*. New York: Oxford University Press.

Wittgenstein, Ludwig. 1963. *Philosophical Investigations*, G.E.M. Anscombe (trans). Oxford: Basil Blackwell.

Wood, Allen. 1998. "Kant on Duties Regarding Nonrational Nature." *Supplemental Proceedings of the Aristotelian Society*, 72: 189–210.

Zabin, Laurie, M.B. Hirsch, and M.R. Emerson. 1989. "When Urban Adolescents Choose Abortion: Effects on Education, Psychological Status, and Subsequent Pregnancy." *Family Planning Perspective*, 21. 6: 248–255.

2
WHY I AM PRO-LIFE[1]

Jack Mulder, Jr.

1 Introduction

I am pro-life. That's a label that in common parlance means that one is opposed to legal abortion. I am. Yet, it is often treated as an objection that to be *really* pro-life, one should be for gun control, for robust measures to help secure racial justice, for a decent family leave policy for mothers and caregivers, for serious state and societal policies to help the poor, against euthanasia, and against capital punishment. I am all too well aware of my failings in each of these areas, but all I can say is that I simply embrace such definitions of the term "pro-life."[2] To me it is painfully obvious that no major political party comes close to being pro-life in this way. Indeed, it may bear saying in our current political climate that I found (and find) the United States presidential campaign (and thus far presidency) of Donald J. Trump odious in many respects and ultimately a failure measured against any serious criteria for being "pro-life." In this chapter, I cannot attempt to discuss an entire pro-life worldview. Instead, I will try to explain why I am pro-life in regard to the abortion issue, and along the way respond to important objections.

When I teach issues of applied ethics, it's common for me to give the students a bit of let-up from the heavy reading in the class and show them the movie *Vera Drake* (2004), a drama set in London in the 1950s on the abortion issue. The movie was mostly a critical success, and Imelda Staunton is, I think, a very compelling lead. Her character, Vera, whom we are to understand as something of a moral saint, is clearly devoted to her family and cares for others in ways that go beyond what we usually think of as morally required. Moreover, nearly everyone in the movie thinks of her in this way, at least until her secret is revealed. Her secret is that she "helps young girls out" by providing illegal abortions. She believes she does this without cost, though she is in fact dispatched to her clients by an unsavory woman, Lily, whom Vera regards as a friend. Lily charges a price well below what a medical facility would charge those who could even qualify for such a procedure (though it's a decent sum when under the table), and the swindler pockets the fee in its entirety.

The reason I enjoy the film, apart from its cinematic virtues, is that it doesn't decide the question. Abortion is a complex issue, and the film presents it that way. There are clearly kind and thoughtful people on both sides of the question. For that matter, there are clearly louts on both sides as well. Indeed, the clients themselves are in varying predicaments. To be sure, most are women rather down on their luck. One client is a prostitute. One has been raped, and one simply cannot imagine another child in her crowded house. However, one memorable episode shows some well-to-do women clearly regarding humble Vera as a laughing-stock and the abortion she has come to perform as just another trifle.

The reason I invoke this film is to emphasize that my goal in this chapter is not to argue that the issue of abortion is simple and obvious. I don't see it that way, and those who do, I think, tend to be overlooking one or another aspect of the topic. Contemporary western culture is too saturated with rhetoric to revert to an Eden before partisan politics, but I think that many who are not already in the grip of a theory would find quite a number of late-term abortions, however rare they may be, to be morally problematic, on a purely intuitive level. Still, many find it similarly difficult to imagine that an early blastocyst, which does not look recognizably human, would be deserving of all the rights and protections of the late-term unborn child. As even pro-life philosopher Christopher Kaczor writes, "In terms of looks and the ability to stir unreflective human emotion, a zygote, embryo, or early fetus utterly fails."[3] Still, we don't make coherent, consistent, and defensible ethical theories merely by raw intuition or emotion. Every theory is going to surprise at least some people, once it is articulated consistently.

Indeed, the fact that something is not obvious does not mean it is not true, and it also does not mean that it cannot be discerned upon careful reflection. In this chapter I will be defending the view that abortion is not morally permissible and, due to the gravity of the moral issue involved, should not be legally permissible. I would define abortion as an intentional act whose sole immediate effect is the termination of a pregnancy and which places a nonviable or viable[4] embryo, fetus, or unborn infant in grave peril by reason of the act itself.[5] In the ordinary case, a person (I maintain) is killed by abortion, but if the fetus survives abortion as evacuation, this does not necessarily mean that the abortion was "botched." This definition means that merely inducing a delivery is not necessarily an abortion, since delivery needs to come at some time or other, and nothing prevents us from using medical science to determine when a better time might be. Nor, though this is more controversial, is the removal of the portion of a fallopian tube in which an embryo is lodged an abortion (this is called an ectopic pregnancy, and the procedure would be a salpingectomy), since the tube's rupture would likely kill the woman, and would certainly kill the nonviable embryo.[6] The sole immediate effect of this action is to heal the woman, whose death at this early stage of pregnancy would certainly mean the death of the embryo as well. However, the deliberate introduction of chemicals into one's uterus that could kill a fetus therein would be an abortion; indeed, that is precisely what Vera Drake is about in the aforementioned movie. Getting clear on the nature of abortion itself will help us sort out some cases later.

2 How not to be pro-life

Although I have never actually protested outside a facility that provides abortions, I do not say that I never shall, because I do not oppose such protests, if they are done with respect and civility. Peaceful protest is a perfectly acceptable way to make one's opinion known in a democratic society. In the United States in particular, recently we have seen grievous injustice, indeed homicide, visited upon black citizens by law enforcement officers tasked with their protection and service.[7] Protest of such injustice is surely a right, and perhaps in some circumstances, a duty. Protests often have the effect of raising the public profile of an issue and the opinion defended within them, and some issues and opinions need exactly that.

While I hold that abortion should not be legally permissible at all, I also recognize that some laws, sometimes termed "incremental," have a defensible role in the opposition to abortion. Since I hold that it is unjust to abort a fetus at any stage of pregnancy, I certainly hold that it is unjust to do so at, say, 20 weeks after fertilization.[8] Since I hold that it is unjust to abort a fetus at any stage of pregnancy, I certainly hold that, morally speaking, minors who seek abortions can be asked to supply the consent of a parent or guardian.[9] Certainly, this has its limits. One should at least respect the process of law enough to make a rationally defensible case for an incremental law. To be clear: just because I'm pro-life, that doesn't mean I think one should bring forward a law that restricted abortion access merely to those days on which the moon is full. As I will go on to discuss here, there are bad ways to hold a good position. But respectful and civil protest (and of course some protests do not meet this standard) of the injustice of abortion needn't be one of them. Incremental laws have their place, too, but the laws proposed should be defensible.[10]

So what are some ways that the pro-life position can go wrong? In the rest of this section, I will discuss some aspects of opposition to abortion that seem wrongheaded to me. I want to be clear in what I say here that I am not attacking the pro-life movement, only offering some suggestions on ways forward that might be more and less fruitful for the sake of dialogue. The first is represented by billboard signs, protester signs, and incremental laws that fall under the heading of what we might call "heartbeat legislation." Many readers will have read a sign that reads "Abortion Stops a Beating Heart" or some such thing. The idea behind "heartbeat legislation" is often to proscribe abortions that take place after the fetus has a detectable heartbeat. While the wisdom of supporting any particular piece of "heartbeat legislation" would have to be decided based on the legislation itself, there is no serious defense available for the idea that the development of a heartbeat is itself the beginning of a human life.

If those of us who claim to be pro-life wish to make people aware of the early stage at which a fetus develops a heartbeat, we should have more moral and philosophical resources at the ready when their emotions are stirred by slogans such as "Abortion Stops a Beating Heart." Again, I do not deny the strategic usefulness of such slogans at various points, nor do I even say I shall never hold such a sign (it is, after all, true that some abortions stop beating hearts), but legislation that proposes to proscribe abortions *merely* on this criterion for humanity is not defensible as such. We should aim for a higher and better public discourse and we should work to make people more reflective than to suggest this as a serious criterion for the beginning of human life and rights.

Another pitfall I want to suggest for the pro-life position to avoid is the error of couching its rhetoric too heavily in religious language when speaking in a public forum. This is neither because I deplore religious language nor because I find it without its uses in the right arena. I am a Catholic Christian and I believe that careful reflection upon Christian Scripture within the Church's tradition ultimately delivers its devoted reader into a worldview where abortion is unjust. I know not all Christians see the matter in this way, but intra-Christian disputes are a topic for another day. They are not the best way to resolve legal disputes in a pluralistic society. Indeed, this was the way the discussion took place in a Right-to-Life group that I attended recently. Evidently there had been a student essay contest, and the finalists were reading their essays. In fairness, this was hardly the spot in the galaxy to drop an unsuspecting philosopher. I kept quiet, and the three young students put their best foot forward in explaining why they were pro-life, and the urgency of the issue for them. The trouble was that, to a person, they articulated their argument in almost entirely Christian terms. While I have no problem with turning to sacred texts for guidance in one's own religious and moral life, when one lives in a religiously pluralistic society, I think one needs to be able to articulate one's convictions about just laws on such important matters as the nature and limits of human life in ways that do not draw all their force from sacred texts one cannot expect the rest of the population to revere.

It may be worth explaining this position a bit here. My reason for adopting this view is primarily strategic. Adherents of any religion with a robust view of the afterlife presumably hold that their religion marks out the best way to live in community, since in what they regard as heaven it will be lived in just that way. Certainly, as a Christian, I can hardly deny that genuinely Christian principles will govern the community that is and will be heaven. Nevertheless, for practical reasons, there are worthwhile principles that are different for preserving the transitory peace we can experience in this temporal order. To take the most obvious, heaven will be, in my view, a monarchy. But earthly government is more effective, in my view, through representative democracy. I do not think that religion is merely a private matter or that it should be excluded from politics per se. In regions with a dominant religion, it can be entirely fitting that the majority culture might bear its mark, and even that some political initiatives might as well, so long as its proverbial doors are as open as they should be to outsiders. For example, if 95% of the residents of a particular locale are Muslim and feel that alcohol should not be sold or that a loud call to prayer should be given special consideration when determining what noise levels count as disturbances of the peace, this can be fitting and good. Indeed, sometimes a religion can itself offer a justification for a moral or political vision that relies on a very different foundation from the one the larger society espouses.[11] In such a case, the religious justification may prove most useful in quasi-public fora where that faith is held predominantly.

Nevertheless, there are also important moral truths that can, and in the right contexts should, be explored without recourse to the special revelation of a particular faith tradition. One reason is that we should care enough about what unites us as humans, especially in a society where there are important religious and cultural divisions, to find some common language for our most significant rights and duties. Another reason is the strategic one: once we have some common language for rights and duties in a civil society that crosses faith traditions, it is wise (and usually advantageous) to use it in settings of public discourse and not to abandon it therein unless it is necessary to do so.

It is also true however, that one cannot expect participants in a democratic society positively to eschew what they regard as compelling moral reasons for a particular view just because those views happen to deliver verdicts that one's religion also thinks are true. Here's what I mean: every major world religion holds that stealing is wrong. But so does any just society. Certainly one is not going to remain agnostic about the moral and legal status of theft out of an otherwise well-placed worry about intrusion of sectarianism into public legal matters. Similarly, the fact that many religions (though by no means all) have prohibitions on abortion[12] does not mean that we should seek to undercut pro-life verdicts on abortion merely because such verdicts would happen to coincide with the verdicts of *some* religions. If a legal battle must be fought in the public square through the use of non-sectarian language, one can't very well place restrictions on the *outcome* of the battle before it is even joined.[13]

Humanist writer Thomas W. Clark writes:

> The faith-based claim that God endows a newly formed embryo with an immortal soul is sectarian since it invokes a religious worldview that many might not hold in a diverse pluralistic society. The naturalist's claim that there is *no* such soul is equally contested and equally sectarian. By contrast, the claim that an embryo is a potential autonomous individual is secular, since whatever your view of ultimate reality, it's likely you accept it.[14]

Clark is right, and helpful, in his claim that neither religious nor naturalist worldviews as such should simply, and without further ado, be adopted for policy purposes. Indeed, it is precisely this sort of understanding that leads Robert P. George and Christopher Tollefsen assiduously to avoid appealing to "premises from revelation or religious authority" as well as the concept of a soul in their pro-life book on embryo research.[15] Nevertheless, what Clark appears to misunderstand is that debates such as that on abortion cannot be resolved simply by appeal to the mere fact of societal pluralism or a kind of methodological agnosticism about metaphysics. As in many other matters, moral and metaphysical neutrality is a myth, and ideological neutrality on an issue can only be championed by those for whom the status quo (or its present tilt) is more or less satisfactory. Rather, the debate must take place using publicly available facts and reason, whether those are drawn from biology or philosophy. The fact is that we do need some metaphysical premises to make a judgment about abortion: we need to know a) what a person is, b) what rights accrue to persons, c) in virtue of what they accrue to such persons, and d) how far these rights extend. All of these matters presuppose metaphysical conclusions of great import and controversy. Indeed, as my coauthor admits, "the arguments given in *Roe* do rely on denying fetal personhood," a denial that entails a metaphysical position on personhood.[16]

Now one might worry that keeping revealed religion at bay for this limited purpose just raises the question: if special revelation can be held at arm's length because people disagree about it, why not metaphysics, and then again why not morality itself?[17] My answer on this point is that it is simply not possible to form a coherent body of law of a sufficiently large size without metaphysics and morality, whereas it is possible to form a coherent body of law of a sufficiently large size without appeal to the revelatory events of the world's major religions. Again: it is not that revealed religion is impermissible in the public square; it is that it is usually unnecessary, and often strategically unhelpful. Manninen and I do not share a religious faith, but we do share many similar moral ideals. These are what will be highlighted in what follows.

Manninen and I will have to tangle a bit about our metaphysics. But coming to metaphysical conclusions that are warranted on the basis of publicly available premises is not the same as being sectarian. Some sort of metaphysic is after all, the right one, and presumably we aim to make laws that operate on the basis of what our own metaphysical, and physical, status is as human beings. If human beings had metallic exoskeletons, we might regard knife-fights as a matter of indifference.[18] If the aroma of a lilac were virulently toxic for humans, then we might proscribe its growth in residential environments. But all of this would be based on the idea that human beings are worthy of moral respect under the law, and we would offer metaphysical reasons for this conviction to differentiate them from, say, bronze sculptures. We generally can, and often should, formulate law without appealing to religions that hold to (actually or merely potentially) competing sources of revelation. We *cannot* formulate law without appealing to *some* metaphysics and moral philosophy, though we will have occasion to discuss this a bit more later.

In what follows, I will begin by discussing why I think we should regard fetuses as human persons under the law, and then explain why I think that women's rights do not extend so far as to allow pregnant women intentionally to procure an abortion. Insofar as my argument will require some moral principles they will be things like (1) intentionally committing an act, or procuring another's act, that directly places a vulnerable person in grave peril is wrong,[19] and (2) that doing so is wrong in a non-consequentialist way; no circumstance makes it right. I will not be arguing for (1) or (2). They are shared (or disputed) widely enough, and good philosophical treatments of them already exist. I also have no particularly novel or comprehensive theory of justice to offer or endorse. However, whether or not one is a Rawlsian about justice in general, I think that John Rawls is right about this much: that in any just society, there should be "equality in the assignment of basic rights and duties" and that "social and economic inequalities, for example, inequalities of wealth and authority, are just *only if* they result in compensating benefits for everyone, and in particular for the least advantaged [I might say "most vulnerable"] members of society."[20] A concern for the most vulnerable is, I think, a fundamental value of a well-ordered society, and that extends to all areas of unjust discrimination. We are all too familiar with, and regrettably too complicit in, many forms of societal discrimination, whether this is racial, ethnic, or gender-related discrimination, to name just a few. I merely see the belief that it is permissible to kill an unborn child due to her condition of dependency upon the mother as another grievous type of discrimination.

3 The personhood argument

If it turns out that the fetus is a full person, then it would have a right to life, as all persons would. As we will see later in this chapter, someone's having a right to life does not answer all the questions, however. For example, Judith Jarvis Thomson famously argues that *even if* the fetus has a right to life, that right does not extend so far as to allow it to draw life-sustaining aid from the mother who wishes to terminate her pregnancy.[21] This is an important argument, and I will discuss it at some length later in the chapter. However, if the fetus is not a person anyway, there is no need for that argument. Consequently, the pro-life view must argue for two things. First, the pro-lifer must argue that a fetus is a person. Second, the pro-lifer must argue that the fetus's right to life extends far enough for its dependence on the mother not to be terminated by killing it. This section will be devoted to the first aim, that of showing that a fetus is a person.

There are essentially two main ways we conceive of personhood that relate to this debate. Drawing on the work of others, Kaczor defines two broad views as the "endowment view" and the "performance view." The first he defines as the view that "each human being has inherent, moral worth simply by virtue of the kind of being it is." The second view, the performance view, holds that "a being is to be accorded respect, if and only if, the being functions in a given way."[22] Kaczor's work and his 2011 book in particular are tremendously helpful on personhood, and give more comprehensive arguments than I can give here. Nevertheless, in this section, I will first offer some reasons to reject the "performance view" and then discuss some reasons to prefer the "endowment view." The most plausible endowment view, I think, is the view that both the fetus and the adult human being are living human organisms that enjoy a right to life.

The view that grounds many of the theories of personhood employed by pro-choice advocates finds its historical genesis in the work of John Locke (1632–1704) in his *An Essay Concerning Human Understanding*. Locke's account is telling, because he gives an account closely related to the rival view we will consider along the way to detailing his own view of personhood. It is worth considering his account in some detail. In context, Locke is attempting to get clear about the identity of various substances through time and in what such identities consist. Thus, when he first considers a "mass of matter," or a more or less random pile of material (think of the weekly load in a dumpster, for example), Locke says that the mass of matter remains the same mass (the same weekly load) when its *organization* changes, but if anything is added or taken away it is a new and different mass (load). What this mass lacks is an "Organization of Parts in one coherent Body partaking of one Common Life."[23] By contrast, an oak tree "continues to be the same Plant as long as it partakes of the same Life, though that Life be communicated to new Particles of Matter vitally united to the living Plant."[24] Locke considers the same point to be true about "brute" animals. That is, a particular zebra, call her Zoe, remains the same zebra from embryo to adult.

When it comes to the question of what it would take for something to be the "same man" or same human being as something, say, in an earlier stage of its life, Locke opts for the same criterion. Indeed, it is noteworthy that Locke *denies* that what guarantees identity through time for a human being is an immaterial soul. He writes "He that shall place the *Identity* of Man in anything else, but like that of other Animals, in one fitly organized Body ... will find it hard, to make an *Embryo*, one of years, mad, and sober, the same Man ..."[25] Locke can make little sense of transmigrating souls that have "past lives." To him it makes no sense to talk about Eleanor Roosevelt, say, being the same human being or "man" (Locke's term) as Socrates, *even if* an immaterial soul bounded from the latter to the former. The two would still not be the same human being because they would not share the same common (organic) life in which all of Socrates' molecules shared. An immaterial soul as such does not make one human being the same human being three years or twenty-five centuries later. Instead, it is the continued common life in which the human being at one stage and the same human being at another stage partake that does that.

Yet, Locke does not consider this concept of "man" or human being, to be the same concept as that of *person*. Thus, he writes "*personal Identity* consists, not in the Identity of Substance, but ... in the Identity of *consciousness* ..."[26] It is consciousness, for Locke, upon which personhood rests, and "as far as this consciousness can be extended backward to any past Action or Thought, so far reaches the Identity of that *Person*."[27] Locke thinks that his concept of person in this sense helps us to track with certain legal intuitions about when someone is responsible for an action. Thus, when we consider insanity pleas for someone accused of a crime, we don't ask whether the defendant is the same organic entity, but whether that person's consciousness at the time was impaired or disconnected in some way from the person he had always been.

Despite some of the interest of Locke's account, however, it is beset with certain problems. Locke himself was forced to admit that if "two distinct incommunicable consciousnesses" were acting by turns in one body (think of Jekyll and Hyde) then these would be two different persons. Further, he also conceded that if the same consciousness were "acting by Intervals two distinct Bodies" these would be one person.[28] The latter suggestion is developed in a vivid (albeit highly fictional) way in the nineteenth episode of the fourth season of the espionage television show *Alias*. A former criminal mastermind turned apparent do-gooder, Arvin Sloane, is tracking, with his CIA team, a man (whom we later find out is named Ned Bolger) who seems to anticipate their every move. Further, he is rumored to *be* Arvin Sloane himself, apparently by those who had not met the real Arvin Sloane in the past. When he is finally brought in for questioning, he remembers with authenticity and vivacity things only Arvin Sloane could remember and know. What is most surprising, however, is that eventually it becomes clear he really *does* remember them, and really *believes* that he is Arvin Sloane. Through methods as far-fetched as the scenario itself, Sloane's team of spies and analysts eventually brings Bolger, a quite ordinary fellow with only a slight physical resemblance to Sloane, back to himself. The implication, which is hard to deflect from a Lockean standpoint, is that during the time when both the *human beings* Sloane and Bolger had the ability to recall and be conscious of past experiences belonging to the life history of Arvin Sloane, they were, at least with regard to the conscious experiences that seem to matter to Locke, the same *person*.

For Locke, the "person" is the consciousness, and the consciousness is neither the physical human being nor the immaterial soul (should there exist such a thing). Rather, it is something else, and this something else could, at least in principle, belong (whatever that means) to more than one body.[29] Or at any rate, it is very hard to discern why we would be warranted in saying that this would be impossible, since Locke himself does not.[30] Locke scholar Samuel C. Rickless writes that, for Locke "persons are neither living bodies nor souls, nor are they combinations of living bodies and souls. If persons are substances, as it seems they must be, then they are *sui generis*."[31] This is exceedingly peculiar. Prominent pro-choice advocates, notably Peter Singer,[32] explicitly note their debt to Locke in terms of his theory of personal identity. But to what exactly has this theory committed us? While I've admitted we need to do some metaphysics to determine policy matters such as that of abortion, we have now introduced an entity that is neither a body, nor a soul (which is controversial enough), nor a body-soul composite, but something else entirely which we're not even sure how to classify. Public policy may require some metaphysics, but presumably we'd at least like to adhere to some version of Ockham's razor, to the effect that we needn't multiply entities without necessity. With some prominent philosophers arguing that consciousness is simply matter,[33] it is unclear why we need to postulate another entity beyond the living human body for the purposes of public policy. We may need metaphysics for public policy, but we would do well to want our metaphysics as parsimonious as possible, and this concept of the self does not seem very parsimonious.[34]

But maybe things aren't that bad for the pro-choice theorist after all. Surely, the fact that Locke's theory delivers some odd results doesn't necessarily mean it can't be salvaged or that it can't be a source of inspiration for better theories of personhood. Indeed, one thing to consider is whether Locke's view is even what Kaczor calls a "performance" view at all, since it seems to introduce an entity with its own set of potentialities,[35] and maybe each (human) consciousness "has inherent, moral worth simply by virtue of the kind of being it is," which would make it a type of "endowment view." As I will be arguing later in this section, when the criterion for personhood shifts from performance to endowment, phenomenological to organic, and from consciousness to body, the pro-life side tends to see the game being played on its own court. So maybe the pro-choice advocate should articulate its position more clearly under the heading of the "performance view."

Mary Anne Warren is one of the more famous voices in this debate to make this same Lockean distinction between human being (where one is "genetically human") and person (or "member of the moral community"), but she offers a set of five criteria for personhood that seem to have to do with what acts one can *perform*. Her criteria are: (1) consciousness (including the capacity to feel pain), (2) reasoning (meaning a *developed* capacity for reasoning), (3) self-motivated activity, (4) the capacity to communicate, and (5) the presence of self-concepts.[36] For Warren these capacities must be developed by performance rather than be merely potentially possessed, and while it is debatable which set might be necessary for personhood or which set might be sufficient for it, Warren thinks that "any being which satisfies *none* of (1)–(5) is certainly not a person."[37] Until a human being reaches this point, it cannot be regarded as possessing a right to life. In other work, Warren suggests that young infants might not meet this criterion, but argues against infanticide because society in general strongly desires to protect infants, and so we should, but until they are born "their equality would mean women's inequality."[38]

Other philosophers hold that the criterion for moral personhood can be reached prior to birth. David Boonin, for instance, argues that the fetus attains a right to life sometime between 25 and 32 weeks after fertilization when it is probably capable of the organized cortical brain activity linked with consciousness.[39] Until then, he thinks, the embryo or fetus has simply not developed the kinds of abilities that make one a moral person in one's own right. The reason he thinks this is significant is partly because the context of the debate is one in which Boonin is responding to Don Marquis's now rather famous argument against abortion.[40] For Marquis, the argument against abortion must be grounded in a wider reason for why killing in general is wrong. For Marquis, the reason it is wrong to kill is that killing deprives someone of something valuable to her. It deprives her of her future. Marquis attempts to construct his account to avoid taking positions on other controversial issues. For instance, he explicitly argues that his account is neutral on matters of animal rights and issues of euthanasia, and he regards this as a virtue of his account.[41] Indeed, he even argues that one of the reasons his view can sidestep so many difficulties is that "the concept of person plays no role whatsoever" in it.[42] For Boonin, however, the vast majority of abortions do not deprive the fetus of its future, because, according to Boonin, the typical fetus is not yet a person and so does not yet possess a "future like ours," the sort upon which Marquis bases his discussion.

Boonin takes the cases of the "(A) fetus, (B) infant, (C) suicidal teenager, (D) temporarily comatose adult, and (E) you or me"[43] and argues that he has a plausible criterion that accounts for why it is wrong to end the lives of (B)-(E) but not (A). He suggests that while the individuals in (B)-(E) have a "present ideal dispositional desire" for their future, the fetus does not, and cannot be wronged by the deprivation of a biologically continuous future because it cannot yet be a person, understood as the subject of desires. By "dispositional desire" Boonin means a desire that we have even if we are not conscious of having it at the moment. So the adulterer is not off the hook simply because his wife is playing bridge and not consciously entertaining the desire that her husband be faithful because she still has the dispositional desire that he be faithful.[44] Similarly, the adulterer's wife has the "ideal" desire that her husband be faithful to her even if she is so distraught over her son's failing health that she claims to her therapist that her attention is so focused on her son that she would not even mind if her husband were cheating on her, because she *would have* the desire that her husband remain faithful to her under conditions that more accurately reflect her real priorities.[45]

So what about the fetus? We are told that the temporarily comatose adult has dispositional desires for a future and that the suicidal teenager has ideal desires for a future, but the fetus does not qualify because it lacks any dispositional and ideal desires and this, in turn, is because it lacks any occurrent or actual desires on which either of those could be based.[46] This, by the way, is what makes Boonin's argument a clear case of what Kaczor called a "performance view." But there are several objections one might raise at this point. For one, why is a past with *some* actual desires (even dispositional ones) morally relevant to purchase ideal ones? Rocks and thermostats, it is true, have no ideal desires because there are no desires they *would* form under more ideal circumstances.[47] But why is an individual's stage of development disqualified from counting as a less than ideal circumstance? Certainly we give children some leeway in our legal systems when they are charged with a crime precisely because we're not comfortable claiming that their actions resulted from a character that had been sufficiently formed in the right sorts of circumstances. Why not say that fetuses are not yet in a position to desire their future but will be as soon as the biological equipment that we believe helps give rise to conscious experience adequately develops? After all, as George and Tollefsen tellingly observe:

> When it is a matter of race or ethnicity, color or gender, origin or outlook, our culture resolutely and rightly holds that what matters is the fact of humanity, not any other property shared by some but not others. But by the same token ... [embryonic humans] should not be regarded as inferior to other members of the human family based on their age, size, location, stage of development, or condition of dependency.[48]

Boonin might respond that there is a difference here because those other features (race, ethnicity, etc.) have to do with human beings who have already attained *personhood*. Equal treatment should be given to anyone with these differing characteristics, but not, so the argument goes, to someone who has not attained personhood. To get clearer on this, let's discuss each element of the "present ideal dispositional desire" account Boonin gives. We've mentioned the ideal desire that the suicidal teenager may have. He does not currently value his future, but he would value it if conditions were more ideal. Boonin says that just as rocks and thermostats have no actual desires on which ideal desires could be based, neither do fetuses. But we've noted that this is a strange comparison. Rocks and thermostats are not even the *kinds* of entities that could develop such desires or the capacities for them. Boonin, however, thinks it is significant that fetuses cannot immediately exercise the capacity for desire. Boonin argues that "only a being with conscious desires is a being that has things matter to it."[49] If this is so, then a lot will depend on when those conscious desires are had.[50] Thus, let us turn to the issue of present and dispositional desires.

Consider the temporarily comatose patient. She will, let us say, desire her future in the, well, future. Boonin notes that the temporarily comatose adult has "actual dispositional desires that he has developed under actual conditions" whereas the fetus does not, and if the *contents* of his dispositional desires are not for his future, then we can turn to ideal desires. This is something of the scaffolding of Boonin's account: a person should have a *present* desire for her future. If she does not have a present occurrent desire (like the bridge player) for her future, then it is enough that she presently has the *disposition* to desire her future. If she does not have a present dispositional actual desire (like the suicidal teenager) then it is enough that she presently has an *ideal* desire for her future. But all of this hangs very much on the under-examined idea that the person in question has a *present* desire. Boonin admits that he offers no rigorous definition of a dispositional desire. Instead, he gives several observations about people who are asleep and would have a certain set of desires if they were awakened and brought up to speed.[51] But all of this depends on it being *presently* the case that an individual has such desires, and it is still quite unclear what it would mean to say that a temporarily comatose patient has desires of any kind *in the present*. The only guess I can hazard is that the temporarily comatose patient has a past narrative of conscious selfhood that, *were it resumed*, would have certain contents based on its past experiences. But if both dispositional and ideal desires hang on the presence of some actual desires, which actual desires does the temporarily comatose patient really have *in the present*? How could such a person in such a state "have" desires in anything but a counterfactual way? How could any counterfactual way in which such a person might have desires not be suitably amended for the fetus? Since any view that will take into account Boonin's cases B-E will eventually have a bottom-floor criterion that will allow for a being with desires that are not plausibly had in the present to count as a person, I believe that even this definition will collapse into an "endowment" view.

What reasons might be offered for preferring the "endowment" view of the human person, then? For endowment views, the important thing is when a human person becomes the "kind of being it is," and since we've moved away from the idea that a human person is a consciousness, and we'd probably like to avoid turning to an immaterial soul unless it becomes necessary to postulate, let's consider the idea that a human person might be something much more ordinary to our experience, that is, a living human body. To do this, we'll have to figure out when a human body is genuinely organically alive. While there is no need here to rehearse the entirety of human embryogenesis, certain salient facts should be discussed briefly so that we can see at what stage an embryo attains an organic integrity sufficient for us to trace its development through to birth and maturation. The process of fertilization of an oocyte (egg) by a sperm involves several stages. Prior to fertilization, though, it is clear that the sperm and oocyte have by themselves, only 23 chromosomes and are therefore not in a position by themselves to give rise to a new organism with a full complement of 46 chromosomes.[52] Sex cells are thus different from somatic cells (each of which has its full complement of 46 chromosomes) in an adult human being, but this difference does not affect the fact that they, like somatic cells, are *parts* of the adult human being.

When sperm and oocyte unite within the fallopian tube (or oviduct) close to the ovary (the ampullary region), the sperm penetrates an outer layer of the egg known as the zona pellucida. Once the sperm and egg cell membranes fuse, the danger of polyspermy must be avoided. Polyspermy would introduce another haploid cell into the egg membrane, which would yield, not the needed 46 total chromosomes, but an extra 23, resulting in 69 total chromosomes. This is nearly always fatal, and would result in an "inviable zygote that cannot develop into a normal individual."[53] Happily, the fusion of egg and sperm membranes first causes the zona pellucida to harden, preventing the fusion of any other sperm, and releasing any sperm that may have already become bound to the zona. This hardening also prevents the embryo from adhering to the oviduct's walls, which would result in an ectopic pregnancy, which we have mentioned above. The fusion of sperm and egg also releases calcium ions that "send a signal that triggers the completion of the egg's meiotic division, the synthesis of new DNA, and the resumption of protein synthesis. The zygote is now ready to proceed with cleavage and normal development."[54]

During its journey through the oviduct eventually into the uterus, the single-cell zygote divides into two cells, then four, then eight, and then sixteen (during days one through four of the newly fertilized zygote's life). The embryo then enters the uterus and implants in the uterine wall sometime around day seven of the embryo's life. It is worth noting that in order for all of this to occur, the zona pellucida played a very integral part in the survival of the newly fertilized egg. As part of the egg cell's own life and development, it needed to be permeable by a sperm. But once the sperm and egg membranes fused, the zona hardened to protect the newly fertilized egg from polyspermy. Its hardening also (hopefully) prevents an ectopic pregnancy during the embryo's journey to the uterus. But, just as the zona prevents adherence to the oviduct walls during days 1–4 (during the process of cleavage), it would prevent adherence to the uterine wall if, upon entry into the uterus, another enzyme were not released to open a hole in the zona through which the inner blastocyst can proceed, allowing it to adhere to the uterine wall and continue its development there. Clearly, the protection provided by the zona is important, but it is also important that that protection recede at precisely the right points.

Now, we need to note some things at this point. We are not looking for the embryo to reach a threshold upon which it can deploy a certain set of abilities. We don't need to see that it responds to visual stimuli, winks at us, or anything like that. We are not looking for it to *perform* anything in particular. We are also not looking for some moment of ensoulment, at least not for the purposes we have here. The only thing we might be looking for it to *do*, in a rough sense, is to attain enough organic integrity for it to be biologically continuous with the person reading this page. When might it become such an entity? One clear response to this is that it becomes a new entity when it is no longer a haploid cell. As a haploid cell with only 23 chromosomes, it is a sex cell of one of the biological parents. By the time it has 46 chromosomes, it is a diploid cell that is undergoing mitotic development and on a journey to the uterus. Such a cell is no longer simply a part of the mother or father, but a new entity that is developing more and more as an organism, each of whose newly divided cells has the new genome that never belonged as such to either of the parents, but belonged at first to the single-cell zygote formed from the union of sperm and egg cells. George and Tollefsen suggest an earlier answer as to when the embryo becomes an organism in its own right, namely, the point at which the sperm has united with the egg. At this point, the sperm, apart from its nucleus, essentially dissolves and the zona hardens to prevent polyspermy. George and Tollefsen write that this hardening "especially seems characteristic of a new organism, whose existence depends upon a structural barrier to outside forces."[55] Whether they are right in this contention or not, the assertion that organic unity and integrity begin no later than syngamy, or when the two pairs of 23 chromosomes line up to form the 46 chromosome complement, seems plausible to me.

We often hear that this is just a "clump of cells" or some such thing, but when we return to how Locke sees the unity of the animal (take Zoe the zebra) or the human being (not Locke's "person") through time, we remember that identity conditions for animals are not what they are for heaps of matter (the weekly dumpster load). Rather, there is a common life of which these materials partake. Here I think Locke is persuasive. Every organism is, after all, a clump of cells in one way, but in another way an organism is always *organized*, always sloughing off material just as it takes new material on. The real question, in regard to its organic unity, is whether that clump hangs together in a systematic way through time. In regard to the embryo, this happens at a very early stage, when the organism begins a new developmental trajectory that would not begin apart from the fusion of sperm and egg, and also begins to protect itself and the ensuing chain of development it has begun. As Kaczor writes "to claim that the zygote is not the same organism as the fetus, newborn, or child requires positing significant additional changes without need or cause."[56] Thus, I think it is right that human organic integrity is achieved no earlier than the fusion of sperm and egg that results in the hardening of the zona, and no later than syngamy.

Given that organic integrity sufficient for the human animal life to begin has been achieved at this point, then, the next major question is whether this animal can be said to be a person. It is worth remembering again here that the presumption in favor of a living human body counting as a person should be so strong that we should want quite an argument for an alternative view. Why? We have already seen that the view that a human person is a consciousness requires a strange, and unwarranted, metaphysical commitment with little payoff. But the idea that the human person is a living body requires no such challenge to our everyday experience. Every theory, as we have said, will have its surprises, but generally we want to do our explaining in public discourse with as little metaphysical furniture as possible. If two theories accord with most of our common judgments and part ways at matters of controversy, we should generally prefer the theory that does not require us to posit a new entity without good reason. The view that living human bodies (or animals) are persons does not require this.

When we look in the mirror, after all, it strikes us as requiring too much in the way of mental gymnastics to say "the person in some way associated with my body has just discovered a pimple on the face with which it is in some way associated." Rather, we just say "I have a pimple," or "do I have something in my teeth?" There could seem to be tension, since organisms have parts in a sense. Despite their being integrally connected to the animal life that persists through time, my teeth, my fingernails, and even my finger can be removed without destroying me, and in that way it can be a part. But this is just what Locke already knew about animals, namely, that parts come and go in connection with the common life in which they all partake. The view, called animalism,[57] that a human person just is a living human body (or animal) thus accords to a large extent with common sense and our experience. There is nothing "spooky" about it in terms of the entities it introduces and it would seem a good candidate for a view about the human person in a pluralistic society, since its concept of personhood requires nothing controversial beyond what we all experience.

Nor is it a problem, as Kaczor points out in response to Michael Tooley, that we would prefer to keep our upper brain even if the rest of our body were destroyed over the alternative of having the rest of our body with our brain destroyed. It may simply be that the "smallest possible reduction of a human being would be to the size of the upper brain," and that "if we moved the upper brain, it would still be a human organism that we move, albeit a radically impaired organism until implanted in another body."[58] None of this means that this is the *best* state of a human being, though. We are more complete as the organisms that we nevertheless are, if we are not missing limbs, or senses, or signature abilities, but this does not mean we are to be respected any less if we are missing those things. As George and Tollefsen, who also advocate animalism, write "Body-self dualists look only at the properties essential to human life, such as mental functioning and self-consciousness, as they exist at the height of their development. But where could such properties come from if they were not already rooted in the nature of the being that possesses them?"[59] Any property of this sort will always admit of varying degrees along the way, and some adults never fully develop them. Instead of saying, arbitrarily, that this point *must* be reached, and this capacity is the one that really matters, pro-lifers simply say that we should protect all human beings (who are all persons) at whatever stage of life.

At this point, before moving on to the next section of our work in this chapter, it may be worth spending some time with some customary objections to this view of the person. Many of these objections will have their roots in claims about embryonic development, so let us rehearse some other facts briefly. For the first eight weeks of its development, the human being is called an embryo. The "vast majority" of miscarriages occur during this period.[60] Even while it is still called an embryo, however, another important milestone is reached in the life of the early human being. This point is reached at day 14 of the newly fertilized egg and it is called gastrulation. Up until this point, the embryo has the remarkable ability to regenerate missing parts because its cells are pluripotent and can become many different types of things. Indeed, most stunning to those new to thinking about early embryogenesis is that the early blastomeres in the 2-, 4-, and 8-cell stages appear not just to be pluripotent, but to be totipotent. A totipotent blastomere can "twin" from the early embryo and itself form an entirely new organism. While fraternal (dizygotic) twins form from two eggs, "[i]dentical twins may be produced by the separation of early blastomeres, or even by the separation of the inner cell mass into two smaller clusters within the same blastocyst."[61] Thus, from a strictly scientific perspective, pro-lifers need to be careful about their claims that every human being is a person from the moment of conception, because, while it's true, and I hold, that every human being *who began her life at conception* is a person thenceforward, it is not strictly true that all human persons began at conception, for some identical (or monozygotic) twins did not. In the rest of this section, I want briefly to discuss the suggestion of implantation as the beginning of pregnancy, the significance of "twinning," the idea of "spontaneous abortion," and how to understand a difference between an abortion and contraception.

When it comes to the idea that a significant point is reached at implantation in the uterus with regard to the embryo's right to life, pro-lifers will find a surprising ally (of sorts) in David Boonin. While it is true that, at implantation, a hormone is secreted that is measured in pregnancy tests, this has nothing particularly to do with whether an embryo has reached the threshold (which it already has) of a new organic life. Boonin writes "the claim that implantation is 'the point at which pregnancy begins' is sometimes offered and accepted *with no justification at all*, particularly in the medical literature."[62] Boonin helpfully goes on to suggest that this is misleading when it is used to demarcate abortion from contraception, since any interventions that purport to be contraceptive but that nevertheless prevent implantation should not be understood as merely contraceptive, but as resulting in the death of the embryo.[63] All of this from a pro-choice advocate.

When it comes to the issue of twinning, it is truly remarkable that, in the early stages, the embryo can "twin." This is sometimes thought to cause problems for the view that the embryo, prior to gastrulation, might nevertheless be a person.[64] But in my view this is not a serious problem. If the embryo "twinned" prior to gastrulation, it would simply mean that, either we had one individual who effectively died, giving rise to two new individuals, or (what seems the more likely view), that the one individual who had been a person since conception, gave rise to another, quite a bit like itself. Agata Sagan and Peter Singer write that "The difficulty of identifying the individual at this early stage becomes even more acute if we consider splitting an embryo, then fusing the split parts with parts of other embryos, then splitting them again, and fusing them again, and so on."[65] Why that would be a sporting thing to do with human embryos is questionable, but as to whether the embryo in any case has attained the organic integrity important for the beginning of a new human life does not seem to be imperiled by these suggestions. Perhaps the question is deeper, though, and something more like this: "is the embryo, at an early stage of this process, identical with an embryo with which it is materially identical at the end of this process?" This question may plumb deeper metaphysical caverns, but the only ones that are interesting concern numerical sameness, and not moral status. That is, it might be an interesting question whether Toby the embryo is still the same Toby at the end of the process if he has all the same parts, but it doesn't introduce a *new* difficulty for our work here to ask whether $Toby_1$ and $Toby_2$ are human beings or not.

A related worry, full of twists and turns that we do not have the space for here, concerns issues of cloning. Sagan and Singer raise this worry when they suggest that if a pro-life view were taken of the embryo, then we could not use stem cells of any kind in research, whether from adults or umbilical-cord blood.[66] Somatic cells of adults can be extracted and then manipulated so that their specialization (as a skin cell, say) can be reversed, but as even Sagan and Singer admit, such cells will then need to be placed in an enucleated egg for them to develop in the way that an embryo would, which leads George and Tollefsen to argue that the enucleated egg is less like soil and more like a gamete, or a sperm or egg cell in the normal fertilization process.[67] In short, something needs to be *done* to somatic cells and even stem cells so as to make them the sorts of cells that have internal organic unity, that is, to make them embryos. Failing that intervention, we can continue to treat such cells as the parts of us that they are.

Some years ago, Toby Ord authored a provocative article titled "The Scourge: Moral Implications of Natural Embryo Loss," in which he argued that natural embryo loss (NEL) sometimes also – inaccurately, in my view – termed "spontaneous abortion," would, for pro-lifers, have to be reckoned as on a par with, or worse than, the worst plague-type scourges humanity has ever faced.[68] The reason for this comparison is that, since figures for NEL range from 45% to 75%, according to Ord, and, for example, a mother of three is likely to have had at least five "spontaneous abortions," we might estimate the yearly loss of human beings from NEL at over 200 million.[69] Ord alleges that the lack of interest in this issue suggests that those who claim to be pro-life must not seriously believe that embryos are persons.

Ord is aware of a first response that would suggest that perhaps a large proportion of embryos lost in NEL were never embryos to begin with, because they did not form completely, or had some other defects, such as an empty ovum. Because of this, Ord proposes to lower his number to 90 million embryos a year.[70] Certainly, the suggestion that not all apparent embryos lost in NEL are true embryos is important, but does not win the argument completely. Nevertheless, that suggestion does point up some important facts. First, as Ord recognizes, "Spontaneous abortion has not arrived suddenly; it has been with us since humanity arose."[71] A second, and related, point is that NEL's persistence points up the fact that the matter is not as if one simply takes a pill to ensure against NEL.[72] Life emerges in precarious circumstances, and there is little reason to think that will stop anytime soon. We know this on a societal level, and to some extent, we do care about it, since we counsel women who "are pregnant or may become pregnant" to talk to their doctors before taking new medication. Most pregnant women also avoid alcohol, nicotine, and other drugs, even down to caffeine, out of a concern for the life growing inside them and take positive measures for the health of their child, such as increasing their consumption of folic acid and other nutrients.

If one still persists that, by some measure, pro-lifers just don't care about NEL *enough*, then repentance is certainly an option. But if the concern is about pro-lifers' real *priorities*, the situation could at best be likened to cases where one needs to choose to save, say, either ten frozen embryos or a smaller number of grown children or adults.[73] The important thing to remember here is that abortion is, as we will go on to discuss, a direct action against the life of the embryo or fetus, and that is not at issue here. The extent to which fighting NEL is a priority for pro-lifers (as we've seen, it's not as if they don't care at all) will have to be assessed with multiple factors, and the action may not be easily determinable in the abstract. To name just a few, it might turn out that it matters, in a triage situation, that the grown would-be victim(s) could experience terrible pain and could be spared this. Sentience may be neither here nor there for whether embryos can be directly *killed*, but it might have something to say about whether embryos take priority over victims who would experience especially gruesome deaths in a decision about whom to *save*. Second, it might matter whether one has certain familial attachments to the grown would-be victims over against the (perhaps) random embryos.

To bring this long section to a close, we need to discuss a bit about the difference between abortion and contraception. While even Pope John Paul II, whose opposition to both is well known, knew there was a difference in that he saw abortion as a variety of killing, and contraception as a failure to respect the "full truth of the sexual act," he nevertheless saw a connection between the two in various ways.[74] An interesting case for discussion might be the case of a woman who undergoes tubal ligation as an elective procedure. While tubal ligation is meant to be a permanent form of sterilization, pregnancy can occur, and, when it does, the woman is at an increased risk of ectopic pregnancy, as even Planned Parenthood recognizes.[75] I offer it as a question how "pro-life" one could be while embracing a form of sterilization that significantly enhances the likelihood that any possible embryo would neither implant in the uterus nor make it to term because of the danger it would cause to mother and embryo alike.[76]

Other types of birth control, known as emergency contraception, if used as part of rape protocols in hospitals, could actually be pro-life measures to prevent fertilization by a sexual assailant if preventing conception is *all that they do*.[77] This was argued at length in regard to Plan B, or levonorgestrel emergency contraception (or LNG-EC), in an article from June 5, 2012 in the *New York Times* by Pam Belluck on the basis of existing medical data.[78] However, serious research since then urges us to be more cautious with the data.[79] The authors of this study argue for the modest conclusion that "the claim of moral certitude in regard to a non-abortifacient action of LNG-EC is not justifiable." The position that LNG-EC *never* operates in an abortifacient (abortion-causing) way requires a very strong basis of evidence. The position that, on the basis of the relevant data, *we are not certain whether* LNG-EC ever operates in an abortifacient way is a more cautious claim. In any case, each side should be looking at the data carefully. Indeed, each side has its own motivations, to be sure, but no one could be surprised at the idea that pro-life advocates wish to be very sure about the distinction between delaying ovulation or preventing fertilization on the one hand, and preventing implantation on the other.

Nor should there be surprise at the idea that pro-lifers are somewhat on alert about this, given increasing calls to develop "contragestive" technology to prevent implantation, sometimes partially to exploit loopholes in existing law.[80] As Sally Sheldon writes "this blurring of the received boundary between contraception and abortion might be seen as an advantage that would render the technology attractive to some in a context where abortion is a far more stigmatized treatment."[81] Nevertheless, while there may be debate concerning the action of LNG-EC, there is no debate that mifepristone, or RU-486, which is often taken after implantation, does disrupt implantation and thus cause an abortion. All of this merely shows how precarious the beginning stages of life are, and how those on either side of this difficult debate will attempt whatever progress they can muster, even if it is only to work within legal frameworks that need to be substantially altered. Both sides know this, and both sides do it. But presumably a better result would be to have society engaged in a deeper debate about when life begins and to avoid mischaracterizing each other's position.

In this section, we've come a long way in discussing why certain definitions of personhood favorable to pro-choice thinkers seem problematic. A Locke-inspired view of consciousness seems strange and unappealing given what it requires of us metaphysically. A performance-related view of personhood also seems problematic, because every time it attempts to account for those who cannot actualize the performance in the standard way, that explanation seems easy enough to tailor so that it would include fetuses. If we turn to an organic account of the person, however, which is not intrinsically faith-based, does not require positing any "spooky" entities like "consciousnesses" or "souls" in their own right, and accords with how we have thought of ourselves as rational animals for thousands of years and in common experience, we may be on firm ground. However, opting for this account of the person requires recognizing that, when the human animal has begun its developmental trajectory as a new organism, however small, it has attained the organic integrity sufficient for personhood. This means, as I have argued, that embryos and fetuses merit the moral status we assign to any person. Nor is this account susceptible to a range of objections having to do with the precarious state of the early human being, though it does call on pro-lifers to be vigilant (which is not the same as militant) in our pro-life convictions, and in our treatment of unborn human life. We're not done yet, though. What is perhaps a still more serious objection to pro-life convictions awaits us in the next section. This argument holds that, *even if* the intra-uterine human being is a person and has a right to life, that right does not extend so far as to require the pregnant woman to carry her pregnancy to term. It is to that argument we now turn.

4 Violinists, autonomy, and abortion

It is the task of this section to address a range of issues concerning abortion that do not bear directly on the personhood of the embryo or fetus.[82] In one way or another, the arguments treated here attempt to sidestep that question. Instead of answering the question of whether the fetus is a person, these types of arguments suggest that the crucial set of issues concern how far the fetus's rights extend *even if* the fetus is a person and has a right to life. The central pro-choice contention among this family of arguments is that even if the personhood issue is decided in favor of the personhood of the fetus, the abortion right stands because the fetus's rights do not entail that the fetus has the right to the assistance of the mother. I have the liberty of treating this issue philosophically, not juridically, and will not even attempt to summarize or critique the dizzying ways the United States Supreme Court, for example, has tried to transmit its inheritance of *Roe v. Wade* (1973). Happily, the court has sometimes given its own summaries. I don't offer any judgment on whether each of those has been consistent one with the other, but one of the brief discussions in *Planned Parenthood v. Casey* (1992) strikes me as worthy of mention. It reads:

> It must be stated at the outset and with clarity that *Roe*'s essential holding, the holding we reaffirm, has three parts. First is a recognition of the right of the woman to choose to have an abortion before viability and to obtain it without undue interference from the State. Before viability, the State's interests are not strong enough to support a prohibition of abortion or the imposition of a substantial obstacle to the woman's effective right to elect the procedure. Second is a confirmation of the State's power to restrict abortions after fetal viability if the law contains exceptions for pregnancies which endanger a

woman's life or health. And third is the principle that the State has legitimate interests from the outset of the pregnancy in protecting the health of the woman and the life of the fetus that may become a child. These principles do not contradict one another; and we adhere to each.[83]

Again, without offering a legal analysis of this summary, philosophically, it is worth noting a couple of things. Prior to viability, it is thought here, the woman has a right to terminate her pregnancy and the state's interest in the life of the fetus does not extend far enough to conflict with that. After viability, given the fact that the fetus can be separated from its biological mother without this resulting in its death, other things being equal, states can choose to restrict abortion. The state, accordingly, has *some* interest in both the life of the fetus or unborn child and in the life of the woman carrying the child, but the Court has set some limits to when those interests become strong enough for there to be restrictions on abortion access. It is important to note that viability here is not mentioned as something that makes the fetus intrinsically more worthy of respect, but because attaining viability makes the fetus no longer dependent on the caregiving role the mother has that no one else can assume. After viability, someone else can, in theory, assume this role, and the state's legitimate interest in regulating abortion access can, in theory, begin here.

This broad line of argument bears some relation to the now famous argument offered by Judith Jarvis Thomson in her 1971 article, "A Defense of Abortion." While we will have some time to discuss its descendants in this family of arguments, our analysis in this section should begin here. Two things are noteworthy about her article up front. The first is that, whether it maps onto US Supreme Court issues exactly (it doesn't), the main line of argument hangs on a woman's right to terminate a pregnancy, not on the personhood of the fetus. The second thing worthy of note is that, in the article, Thomson writes "I agree that the desire for the child's death is not one which anybody may gratify, should it turn out to be possible to detach the child alive."[84] That is, while a mother has the right to terminate a pregnancy even if it should result in the fetus's death, if the fetus should survive some manner of abortion, the mother has no right then to kill the child. These points will help frame some of the discussion, but now we turn to the article itself.

Thomson's logical argument begins a bit later than her first invocation of the most famous example from the article, namely, that of the unconscious violinist, which we will discuss below. Rather, if set out logically, Thomson wants first to combat an "extreme view" according to which "abortion is impermissible even to save the mother's life."[85] To do this, she asks you, the reader, to imagine yourself trapped in a tiny house with a rapidly expanding infant.[86] The child is growing so rapidly that you are pinned against the wall of the house and you will soon be crushed to death. However, the child is not imperiled by any of this. He will simply walk out of the house after its frame gives way, but you will have died. This, we should notice, clearly signals that the child is viable when it compares to abortion questions. Even so, Thomson thinks, you personally can only protect yourself in this situation, and so you may kill the rapidly expanding child in self-defense. Doing so is not wrong, and likewise aborting one's own child can be permissible if it is necessary to save one's own life.

Thomson's next step in the argument is to notice that, pregnancy being what it is, it's often not much of a serious option to abort one's fetus by one's own efforts. Thus, while one might have been tempted by a more moderate view according to which abortion is permissible to save the mother's life but not when performed by a third party, Thomson finds this modification wrongheaded. I mention this not because I find it independently plausible as a principle, but because in reply to it, Thomson invokes some interesting ideas of her own. She notes that in the case of the tiny house, it is relevant that the mother *owns* the house, since she likewise owns her body. Similarly, if Smith and Jones were at loggerheads in the bitter cold about whom should get the one remaining winter coat it is relevant to the dispute that Smith *owns* the coat.[87] A third party is capable of adjudicating the dispute in this way, and so a third party (e.g., a doctor) should be able to help a mother procure an abortion, says Thomson.

In an article packed with analogies, the analogy Thomson uses first in the article, the violinist analogy, is the most famous. This analogy is actually meant to respond to another view that would hold that abortion can only be performed if the mother's life is in jeopardy. In the violinist analogy, Thomson asks you, the reader, to imagine waking up to find yourself, quite by surprise, in bed with an unconscious violinist whose kidney ailment is fatal if not addressed, and whose fame is such that an entire society, the fictitious Society of Music Lovers, has kidnapped you, the reader, to supply the needed aid by being plugged in to his circulatory system. Now of course this was a rotten thing for the Society of Music Lovers to do, and the hospital staff recognizes it, but now it's been done, and you cannot safely be unplugged from the violinist without causing his death because, by hypothesis, "*you alone* have the right blood type to help."[88] Because of this, and the fact that the violinist has a "right to life," you must remain plugged in to the violinist for nine months, after which time, the violinist should have healed and the two of you can be separated. The analogy with pregnancy (especially the nine-month duration) should be clear. But surely, goes the argument, we cannot be *forced* to accede to this situation. In related fashion, surely women cannot be *forced* to give life-sustaining aid to the children growing inside them. I should note that I use the term "children" advisedly here because it is part of Thomson's argument that it *does not matter* whether the fetus is a person or not. Even if that is the case, the woman cannot be expected to gestate the fetus against her will.

Now the clearest parallel in the case of the violinist analogy is to pregnancy in the case of rape. Allowing abortion in the case of rape is an exception to a view that states that "having a right to life includes having a right to be given at least the bare minimum one needs for continued life."[89] This is because, in the violinist case, you were kidnapped and forced to give life-sustaining aid to the violinist, and denied the right to terminate that relationship of dependency. Nevertheless, you are the only one who can provide the "bare minimum" that the violinist needs, and so you must provide it. Thomson sets her sights a bit further than just the case of rape, though, and argues that the issue is not just about how the dependence relationship was entered, but about how much those who need aid can expect from those who can give it. She writes "If I am sick unto death, and the only thing that will save my life is the touch of Henry Fonda's cool hand on my fevered brow, then all the same, I have no right to be given [it]."[90] Again, just as in the case of the violinist, it might be generous and "frightfully nice" of Fonda to provide such aid, but the point is that he is not at burden to provide it. Presumably, though Thomson doesn't directly mention it, this is also meant to apply if Fonda does *voluntarily* fly out to wherever you might be (he died in 1982, but that's not the point), begin to touch your fevered brow, and, mid brow touching, decide to remove his hand. Doing this might even be *indecent* in some circumstances, but the question is whether he can be forced to continue this, and Thomson is convinced that neither Fonda nor you can be forced to touch anyone's brow or be forced to be plugged in to the violinist.

Thomson's article has spawned an enormous literature in response, both critical and defensive. It is certainly not possible to rehearse every aspect of that literature here. Instead, I will offer some brief responses to Thomson here and consider some new avenues that have been taken in the more recent literature. Later, I will consider what my views may commit us to in terms of what a well-ordered society needs to look like, both in regard to political matters (as opposed to merely moral matters) and in regard to the treatment of the vulnerable. Returning to Thomson, I will respond first to the house analogy, then to the coat analogy, and finally to the violinist and Fonda cases.

The trouble with the tiny house and the expanding child case is that the analogy is, for the most part, a bad fit for the case of pregnancy. The main problem is that the rapidly expanding child is clearly viable. It *can* survive; indeed it *will survive* outside of the mother. Now if the mother's life is threatened, either the fetus is viable or it is not. If the fetus were viable, we could induce an emergency delivery or perform a cesarean section.[91] Then we would care for the child in the best way possible once it had been delivered, and likewise for the mother. If the fetus were not viable (contrary to what Thomson says), the case is a better fit for an ectopic pregnancy, where the embryo is lodged in the fallopian tube. In an ectopic pregnancy, one procedure that all pro-life moralists, down to the most rigorous Catholic moralists, would permit one to consider, and in the right circumstances, apply, would be what is known as a salpingectomy, which we have noted earlier in passing would not even qualify as an abortion using the definition I offered earlier. This would be to remove the tube or a portion of it so that the threat to the mother's life would end. This would have the foreseen effect of ending the life of the embryo, but since the embryo is not yet viable, the mother needs to live to provide the embryo with life. Direct action is not taken against the embryo, rather, it is itself removed from one source of danger (the tube that cannot hold it), and it will unfortunately die as a result. This situation is a bit more like a mountaineer cutting a rope that is stretched beyond its capacity by holding two people. In this situation, the person nearer the top cuts the rope below her, saving herself, while knowing this will almost certainly result in the death of her partner. She may understandably experience a great deal of grief and anguish over this decision, but I hold that it would have been the right decision. It is a case governed by the principle known as "double effect."

One of the reasons the abortion issue is so perennially interesting to philosophers is that it engenders so many different conversations. It requires discussion of the metaphysics of personhood, moral principles of right and wrong, rights in a political context, feminist philosophical concerns, and more. My treatment of the abortion issue here requires a brief description of double effect, a very controversial philosophical principle. Nevertheless, it cannot detain us here for very long. The principle has many versions, but the core contention is an act can be performed that is in itself good, even if it has bad effects, so long as the bad effects are inseparable from the good end, and the act in question is the least harmful way to realize the good at issue.[92] This principle is often used to distinguish between terrorist bombing and tactical bombing. The former targets noncombatants, whereas the latter might target, say, a munitions factory in wartime (supposing the relevant war effort is just). As part of a tactical bombing campaign, there may be unavoidable harm to a small number of noncombatants, but if these civilian deaths are minimized as far as possible, and not directly intended but only foreseen, and the bombing campaign is an important piece of a just war effort, this campaign may be permitted.

We cannot be detained by the principle of double effect for long here. It has its defenders and detractors like every other significant principle. All I can say here is that I can scarcely imagine my life without it. Principally as a parent, there are many decisions we make for our children that we can easily foresee will cause them harm we would never directly intend. When I comb my young son's very curly hair, he screams and whimpers. I intend only that his hair be healthy and clean, but all he sees is the pain it causes him that I merely foresee. Parents do more serious things, of course. Parents in past generations willingly offered their children to the Allied effort against Nazi Germany, intending the good of contributing to the downfall of that terrible regime. Certainly they foresaw at minimum grave peril and the probability of a death they would never directly intend. Some actions do not admit of a sufficiently serious reason to pursue them, though. One might cauterize a wound by some salve that "stings" but one would hardly do it by the use of a blowtorch, as this would create a wound worse than the wound one wished to treat. The important matters in regard to double effect are that there is a serious reason to choose *only* this action and that the bad effect it engenders is not intended. Again, the principle of double effect cannot detain us here for long, but it plays an important role in discussions of abortion.

To return to Thomson, let us consider the coat analogy for a moment. This is supposed to show that a third party can adjudicate a dispute over whose rights trump whose, and to take the appropriate action. It is supposed to show that a third party can act on a woman's right to her body by performing an abortion for her. To do this, Thomson argues that, just as Smith owns the only available coat in the bitter cold, the woman owns her body. Indeed, Thomson dismisses suggestions (presumably ones she perceives as coming from theistic traditions) that the woman's body is merely "on loan" to her.[93] Both Thomson and Warren have been taken to task over this language of ownership, but even Warren admits that "it is probably inappropriate to describe a woman's body as her property."[94] This critique has taken an interesting turn in the recent literature. While the pro-life side of the debate would critique this view as containing a certain dualism about the person and her body (which *she* owns), the pro-choice side has also criticized some problems with the ownership paradigm. While both sides could find some agreement on the phenomenology of embodiment, some conclusions the pro-choice side might reach would be distressing for the pro-life side.

For example, Catriona Mackenzie has argued that this ownership model in regard to the body fails to grapple with the phenomenological reality of pregnancy. She argues that pregnancy "defies a sharp opposition between self and other" and that because of this, we cannot think of fetuses as merely occupying women's uteruses, because this "divorce[s] women's bodies from their subjectivities."[95] She is aware that the irony is that the pro-choice views she critiques do precisely this, and so run the risk of treating women as fetal containers – the very charge pro-choicers often level at pro-lifers.[96] But Mackenzie's view is also pro-choice, and instead of arguing that, say, the woman and child are "in this together" and that both should be protected, she instead argues that the fetus's life is so indistinguishable from the woman's that the woman's desire that *there be no future child* so intimately related to her is an expression of her lived reality that should be honored.[97] This leads her to a subtle critique of Thomson's and Christine Overall's (early) view that abortion should be about "evacuation" of the fetus and not about its death.

While Mackenzie stops short of advocating a right to kill a fetus that survives abortion, Soran Reader positively defends the "abortion-as-killing" paradigm. To pro-life readers, Reader's position seems extreme, almost a caricature of itself. Not only does she argue that killing the fetus, and not merely evacuating it is an appropriate discharge of maternal authority, she argues that adoption is "beyond the moral pale," suggests that aborting children conceived through rape may be "morally required," and embraces the idea that, at particular times, infanticide can be justified as the "final protection" of a dutiful mother.[98] Thankfully, Overall has the good sense to critique Reader for being over the top on some of these points.[99]

These thinkers have critiqued the ownership paradigm, which I, too, reject, but have they really escaped it? As much as Mackenzie wants to distance herself from the ownership model and to embrace an integrated lived reality for the pregnant woman, it is always the pregnant woman's reality of which the fetus, at least in its early stages, is not *even* a part. Rather, evacuating the fetus is merely another mode of expression for *her* lived reality. Mackenzie writes:

> Bodily autonomy in pregnancy and abortion thus cannot be construed simply as the right to bodily integrity. Rather it is a question of being able to shape *for*

oneself an integrated bodily perspective by means of which a woman can respond to the bodily processes which *she* experiences in a way with which *she* identifies, and which is consistent with the decision *she* makes concerning *her* future moral relationship with the fetus.[100]

Mackenzie may treasure the integrated lived reality of the mother, but it is always *hers*, and *not* the fetus's. If you accept that, keep in mind that at this point, I am not yet critiquing the ownership model as such, only suggesting that Mackenzie does not escape it. Reader claims that fetuses have significance, but argues that it is sometimes precisely an expression of this maternal lived reality to end one's child's life.[101] While there is a limited sense in which she is right that the fetus conceived as a result of rape "should not exist" because the sexual assault that gave rise to this fetus should never have occurred, she further claims that such fetuses have "negative moral status" and should be aborted.[102]

There are three things that I think should be said in response to Reader on this point. The first is that, even though there is a limited sense in which fetuses conceived through rape "should not exist" because the act that gave rise to them should not have occurred, this limited sense can be replicated too easily. While rape is a heinous violation of the person and belongs in a legal category of its own, the harms of patriarchy extend even to acts of intercourse that meet the definition of legal consent, as Robin West has shown.[103] If Reader is right that fetuses conceived through rape "should not exist" because the act that gave rise to them should not have occurred, how many people would be willed out of existence if the long harms of patriarchy were magically whisked away? Notwithstanding harms that attended their coming into existence, it is implausible to argue that all such fetuses born through unwanted (though legally consensual) sex have a "negative moral status," since some may be wanted even though sex as such (again, in a legally consensual sense) was not. Rape is a tremendously grievous harm, but if the fact that it should never have occurred is what gives the resulting fetus its "negative moral status" then all regrettable acts giving rise to pregnancy should confer such "negative moral status," but this seems implausible. Second, consider the grown adult, adopted earlier, whose conception as a result of rape is unknown to her, because of privacy policies in adoption. If she had "negative moral status" while in utero, when did she acquire the "positive moral status" that presumably she now enjoys? Either she still does not have it (which seems implausible), she acquired it at some point in utero, or she acquired it at birth or later. Suppose she acquired it in utero. Then Reader's discussion of moral status hangs on the question of intra-uterine personhood, but she clearly rejects this entailment. Suppose instead that our adult conceived through rape acquired positive moral status at birth or later. If so, Reader will need a threshold for when someone makes the transition from (not merely indifferent but) *negative* moral status to *positive* moral status, and it's not clear what would do this if not personhood criteria that we have considered and rejected above.

The third thing to notice is that it is true that, while ownership may be odd language for something as intimate as one's body, we must admit that sexual assault is a horrible attack on the sexual integrity of a person, and that, as Reader says, conception through rape *is*, in one way, another assault on her.[104] If this were not so, the United States Conference of Catholic Bishops would be wrong in saying that a woman raped may "defend herself" from potential conception through sperm incapacitation or delayed ovulation, but this seems right.[105] The question, however, is what happens when there is a new life inside the woman and how may it be treated? To answer this question, we should turn to the violinist and Fonda cases from Thomson's article.

The violinist case finds an analogue in the case of pregnancy through rape, since you, the reader, have been abducted and forced to give nine months of aid to the violinist. The Fonda case is intended to expand the argument about what kind of aid one can be compelled to give to another in need, and to suggest that one is neither morally nor legally required to give certain forms of aid. In response to cases like the Fonda case, a rather famous argument against Thomson has developed, usually called the "Responsibility Objection." The Responsibility Objection, in short, holds that women have a responsibility to care for their fetuses because they assumed this responsibility through engaging in an act (sexual intercourse) that foreseeably resulted in pregnancy, and now, because they knew this to be a foreseeable result of their action, they are responsible for the fetus's needs.[106]

My view here will be perceived as extreme by some folks usually thought of as conservative: I believe the Responsibility Objection is simply irrelevant to the abortion question. The first reason I think this is a practical one in regard to law. Cases of rape straightforwardly fail the test of responsibility, but not every case in which women give legal consent is a case in which the woman can be plausibly said voluntarily to assume all the possible repercussions of the intercourse. After all, men desert their female sexual partners after a pregnancy all the time. Both pro-choice and pro-life writers have remarked on how existing ways of construing the abortion right feed masculinist ideology and, in my view, laying too much emphasis on the Responsibility Objection may be one of them.[107] Certainly, aspects of current law may have a hand in the mischief,[108] but while such systems persist, so does the fetus, about whose life and rights we are currently asking. The second reason I think the Responsibility Objection is irrelevant is that again it permits a disanalogy in the case of rape. Many think abortion law could permit exceptions, for example in the case of rape or incest. As difficult as I believe such questions are, I nevertheless believe such views are mistaken. If the fetus's rights extend to a right to be given the care it needs for survival, then it merits such care in virtue of what it is or it does not merit such care at all. Reader's argument that the fetus conceived through rape has "negative moral status" has been seen to have serious problems. The properties the fetus has in virtue of which we accord it moral treatment are not properties that it loses or gains based on how it came into existence. The question, whether it is asked in reference to a fetus conceived through rape or through consensual intercourse, is whether the fetus has the right to be given the life-sustaining aid it needs from the mother. Indeed, it would be one thing if the fetus could safely be removed at any stage of pregnancy without killing it,[109] but as things are, the only way to remove a nonviable fetus is through killing it, and the common methods for removing even a viable fetus prematurely are ones that can place it in serious peril.[110] If the only way to end a pregnancy in this way is to take a positive action against the fetus, then this seems problematic.

Margaret Olivia Little, however, argues that things are not so simple. She argues that pro-life views "ride atop a problematic misconception of the act of aborting itself."[111] Rather than regarding the abortive act as a "discrete event," Little urges us to see the fetus as on a "downward trajectory" in that she would never have existed and would not exist now without the mother's aid.[112] Thus, Little argues, abortion is often a case of letting die rather than directly killing and is more about the ethics of gestation than the ethics of killing.[113] The problem, however, is that certain forms of letting die constitute negligent acts, even if there is not a discrete moment in which such acts are decided. In his famous discussion of active and passive euthanasia, James Rachels argued that the distinction between killing someone and letting her die dissolves through two cases he offered. In the first case, Smith stands to gain an inheritance from his six-year-old cousin's death. So he drowns the child in the bath and makes it look like an accident. In the second case, Jones still hopes to gain the inheritance, but before he does anything, the child slips, hits his head, and drowns. Jones merely stands idly by.[114] Astonishingly to pro-lifers, these cases were supposed to help show that if letting die in cases of euthanasia is permitted, then so are cases of active euthanasia. In a telling rebuttal, Thomas D. Sullivan argues that, of course, both of these lives should be saved. Thus, the key issue is not killing versus letting die, but rather when a medical intervention is *extraordinary* (as in another debilitating round of chemotherapy when one's death is imminent) and *ordinary* (as in providing food and water to a person).[115]

In response to Little's view of abortion, then, we must say a couple of things. First, the suggestion that for example, a suction curettage, a common method of abortion in which uterine contents are suctioned out, is not a discrete event is implausible. We can grant that pregnancy is not a purely *passive* process, but common methods of abortion are a violent disruption of a process that will likely continue without such acts. Of course, something involuntary could go wrong, but the question is whether it is permitted voluntarily to *make* something go wrong. A second point in response to Little is that even if we suppose that an abortion is a case of letting die, an assumption of which I am not really persuaded, we must ask whether the kind of letting die this might then be would be a negligent kind of letting die or an indifferent kind of letting die. It would be negligent for Smith to allow his cousin to die. Would it be negligent for Fonda not to place his hand on my fevered brow? Would it be negligent of me not to provide the violinist with life-sustaining aid? This turns into a larger question. To consider this question, I want to introduce two cases.

Let us suppose that, on a trans-Atlantic voyage of a sufficiently large vessel, because of emergent weather conditions, or operator misconduct, or both (think of the *Titanic*), crew and cabin alike are boarding the lifeboats. A man and a child are the last with a real chance at survival and yet it is clear the lifeboat will hold only one of them. The boat is going to sink, so "essential crew" are a nonissue, and in any case the crew acquitted itself valiantly and at great cost.[116] A decision is called for regarding who will survive, since either could survive but both cannot (unlike the mountain climbing case where the person at the high end of the rope is the only one whose survival can be really intended). Similarly, in our new case (call it the *Titanic* case), a decision is called for regarding who will survive, the child or the adult. Now every life, let us say, is of equal dignity, but some moral considerations tip the scales in various directions. I submit that most of our moral intuitions at this point regard it as strange to insist that the adult be given the seat on the lifeboat when, in consequence, a young child is left for dead in a chilling sea. Rather, it seems to me that the only thing to do is to allow the child the seat precisely because she or he is a *child*. What I think this case reminds us is that we typically do think that it matters which party is more vulnerable, and we think that, even in many life or death situations, the vulnerable be given preference, even if their aid requires significant sacrifices on our parts.[117]

A second case is often claimed to be similar to Thomson's violinist case. It can be found in *McFall v. Shimp* where David Shimp refused to undergo a bone marrow extraction to save the life of his cousin, Robert McFall, who died as a result. In these cases, it is said, one's bodily autonomy (understood as the right to refuse) is threatened.[118] The judge in the case, Judge John P. Flaherty, Jr., claimed that Shimp's refusal was "morally indefensible" but that his assent could not be legally compelled. He wrote as follows:

> For our law to *compel* defendant to submit to an intrusion of his body would change every concept and principle upon which our society is founded. To do so would defeat the sanctity of the individual, and would impose a rule which would know no limits, and one could not imagine where the line would be drawn. This request ... if granted, would require the forceable submission to the medical procedure. For a society which respects the rights of *one* individual, to sink its teeth into the jugular vein or neck of one of its members and suck from it sustenance for *another* member, is revolting to our hard-wrought concepts of jurisprudence. Forceable extraction of living body tissue causes revulsion to the judicial mind. Such would raise the spectre of the swastika and the Inquisition, reminiscent of the horrors this portends.[119]

The judge in this case clearly felt the need to use strong language, but in his fervor I think some things may have been missed. First of all, it's just not clear that ruling against Shimp would forthwith entail that one individual could "sink its teeth into the jugular vein or neck" of another member of society. Judge Flaherty himself admitted that Shimp's refusal was morally indefensible, but the sort of indefensibility involved is one that he thought the law could not touch. But this strikes me as hasty. It is fallacious to suggest that our only two options are strapping Shimp down for this procedure and having the law turn a blind eye. Rather, we could regard Shimp's refusal as criminally callous. Thus, we *can* imagine where a line might be drawn. After all, nations have drawn it frequently, for instance by insisting upon compulsory military service (indeed, some developed nations have an active program), but imposing sanctions on those who refuse. My point here is not to argue for one punishment or another, but rather to say that the law need not take a completely "hands-off" attitude toward such callousness.

In regard to a comparison with abortion, there are two things I will say about this. The first is that we should make a distinction between withholding the bone marrow that one needs to survive on the one hand, and acting directly against the bodily integrity of the fetus on the other.[120] In the case of Shimp and McFall, it is significant that, in Shimp's refusal, he does not make McFall worse off than he would have been by a direct action against him. Rather, even though his refusal to submit his bone marrow is callous, and the law should not regard this as a matter of indifference, it is more significant to take a positive action against a vulnerable party, and, *contra* Little, I do think that abortion is a positive action against a vulnerable party, an action of killing.

Second, while this is an important distinction, I am not persuaded that this strategy alone will do all the work that needs to be done, since I think that Thomson's violinist case is relevantly similar to pregnancy in the case of rape. After all, in that case, you *alone* are the person through whom the violinist can secure aid, and the idea is that, by terminating this relationship, the violinist will die. I am not persuaded that abortion in the case of rape is permissible, since it is still the direct targeting of a vulnerable party. I also believe that the rest of the pro-life scaffolding, which I think is correct, is imperiled by this admission. This necessitates a more radical, but not entirely original, turn in my view, namely, that Shimp should be legally *expected* to give his bone marrow, and that, if the case is tailored just so, there are circumstances in which it may be morally and legally expected that you remain plugged in to the violinist.

Under what circumstances might this be required? They would be very particular circumstances to be sure. They would require that the relationship of "being plugged into" the violinist had already been established, and that the relationship was such that its termination would *directly* result in the violinist's death. Such circumstances would also require that you are the *only person* (as Thomson says) who can now provide the aid in such a way that the violinist will die, once you are unplugged, and that no one else can be found in a reasonable space of time to relieve you before this happens. If there are other people, and they could be transferred *even if they also refuse*, your unplugging is more like Shimp's abstention than the pregnant woman's abortion. While I also think Shimp's abstention is bad even from the standpoint of just law, I reject its compulsion by force. Finally, it must also be the case, I maintain, that you are warranted in your belief that, while violence was done to you in plugging you in to the violinist in the first place, you will now be treated by qualified medical personnel without nefarious motives who are not party to the mischief. It may be hard to trust any such people, and if you have good reason not to do so, your unplugging may be fully justified. This may yield a difference between being plugged in to the violinist and being pregnant in that, while you would perhaps always need to take the attending medical personnel's word for it about how necessary your being plugged in was, as pregnancy continued, it would become clearer and clearer that you were really pregnant (even if you distrusted an early pregnancy test administered by dubious folks) and what it would take to terminate that pregnancy. Further, while unplugging yourself in these surpassingly unique circumstances may be morally and legally impermissible, if you choose to unplug out of a reaction to the violence done to you by the Society of Music Lovers, this action, while not fully permitted by law or morality, may be *understandable*. It may diminish your *culpability* in important ways.

Nevertheless, if you still find this view implausible, consider this. Kaczor imagines that we make one change to the violinist case, namely, that there is another person to whom the violinist would *like* to be plugged in, and that if he snips the cord connecting the two of you to make this switch, it would cause *your* death. While there are differences between this new case and the old one, Kaczor does not think they are morally relevant. Thus, here, Kaczor's verdict seems to be that "Since the violinist may not unplug himself from you at the cost of your life, you may not unplug yourself from him at the cost of his life."[121] While Kaczor's book concerns the morality and not legality of abortion, let us consider this on the level of a just law briefly. This view simply claims that, when people's needs are sufficiently grave and unique, others who can supply these needs are sometimes required to do so, and that society has an obligation to support both the patient in her suffering and the agent of healing in her own suffering and/or inconvenience.[122] In the language of Thomson, this view simply raises the level of decency a society has reason to expect from its citizens. While one should not be "strapped down" to offer one's bone marrow, the idea that society could legally expect such assistance for its members does not strike me as far-fetched. The suggestion by Judge Flaherty that such an expectation raises the "spectre of the swastika," needs to be seen as the overweening rhetoric that it is. As we've noted, compulsory military service, often for very long periods of time, is still practiced in some armed forces, and this, presumably, has everything to do with providing for the common good of society and the persons who are members of it.[123] If fetuses are persons (and I have argued that they are) then they might very well have a claim on the protection of society and, perhaps, those members of it who are uniquely poised to offer this protection.

Now you might think that this imposes a burden on women that men don't have to bear. You're right. I believe that pregnancy is simply a unique moral state, and it carries with it burdens that cannot be glimpsed without remainder in any other state of a human being. After all, as Rosalind Hursthouse has remarked, "nature bears harder on women than it does on men."[124] Further, even society has unconscionably borne harder on women than it has on men. Recently, as a means of showing this to my college community, a campus group offered a bake sale in which women were charged 75 cents for their treats and men were charged a full dollar. The idea was to offer a critique of the reality that, according to then current statistics in our state of Michigan, women made 72 cents on the dollar made by men in the workplace (75 cents works better for giving proper change after a purchase, though). My own view is that, however difficult it would be to *prove* to naysayers, Hursthouse's statement on this is simply accurate. Mackenzie, too, acknowledges that, in regard to pregnancy, things are "inescapably asymmetrical" between men and women.[125] One strategy to combat this asymmetry in regard to nature is abortion. It attempts to erase the asymmetrical burden of pregnancy. Yet Frederica Mathewes-Green has argued that abortion is exactly the strategy one should use if one wishes to continue living in a "man's world."[126] Another strategy would be the long, patient work of making society conform to the reality of pregnancy and motherhood, rather than making the reality of pregnancy and motherhood conform to society such as it is.

Now of course, there is the serious danger that this very goal will be pursued in a patriarchal way, and familiar pernicious social schemes have arisen for just this reason. Nevertheless, this strategy would have to include, to scratch the surface, things like a decent family leave policy, a more equitable share of parenting and caregiving duties between men and women, and, perhaps most of all, a deeply enculturated refusal to objectify and sexualize the female body at every turn. Doubtless Hursthouse and Mackenzie would have us avail ourselves of this strategy as well as the abortion right, but an important question is whether we're doing any better as a society as far as objectification is concerned when we regard a woman's direct action against the person inside her (who may be female, as well) to be a positive right. This is why I do not believe that the abortion right combats objectification. I believe that it exacerbates it.

5 What does all this mean?

While I hope I have made my views on the moral status of abortion clear, and I have claimed that the law itself should take a position on the matter, there remain a number of puzzles about the latter view. After all, many famous politicians have argued that they reject abortion on a moral level, but also believe that access to it should not be curtailed or that it should remain legal.[127] Could we remain personally, morally, opposed to abortion, but not to its legality in society?

David B. Hershenov and Rose Hershenov argue that this position is not coherent under all but the most implausible moral theories.[128] That is, it might be possible to be a subjectivist about morality and be personally opposed to abortion but not legally opposed, but subjectivism is riddled with problems in its own right. In even the more plausible cases there are problems, however. Recall that this position is different from Thomson's, in that people of this opinion are morally *opposed* to abortion, where Thomson regards carrying one's fetus to term in most cases as, at best, a supererogatory act, one that may be morally praiseworthy but not morally required. Thomson compares continuing an undesired act of pregnancy to being a Good Samaritan to someone in need of aid. It is not required, but it may be good or "frightfully nice." However, in this case, we are considering people who already hold that abortion is *morally wrong*. Can such people also regard abortion access as a legal right?

As the Hershenovs discuss, it cannot be that there is an outweighing harm in the cases of *other* pregnant women, because, by hypothesis, women in the "I'm personally opposed to abortion but…" (IPOB) camp already reject abortion as a *moral* wrong, and it makes no sense (unless one is a subjectivist) to claim that abortion is a moral wrong *just for me*; it must be that it is a moral wrong for anyone in like circumstances.[129] We can reserve judgment about culpability, but in terms of an act's being morally wrong, this is supposed to transfer across relevantly similar cases. One might also suggest that, because we just don't know enough about, say, the personhood of the fetus, then we can't justify confidence that others shouldn't be allowed abortions. But then what grounds the confidence possessed by these women (the Hershenovs restrict their attention to women) in the IPOB position in the first place? Even if they are uncertain, by hypothesis their uncertainty is enough to move them to reject abortion in their own case (or they would not be "personally opposed"). Thus, "Rather than tolerate women aborting because of some uncertainty about whether their own opposition is wrong, they should insist that such women join them in playing it safe and err on the side of caution."[130] The Hershenovs also consider the role Rawlsian public reason may play here, but I will reserve discussion of this until a little later in this section. The final argument they consider concerns autonomy. But since the women in the IPOB position, by hypothesis, believe that abortion is not a permissible use of autonomy, it is unclear why they would believe that to use autonomy in this way would be permissible if someone *else* chose abortion.[131]

To the Hershenovs' discussion of why moral opposition to abortion should translate into legal opposition I might like to add one other element. Suppose some woman, call her Millie, holds that abortion is morally impermissible both to procure and to perform, but that its access should be legally available. Moreover, suppose that Millie undertakes to defend her view in the public square, with the idea that everyone would do well to hold her view. Suppose, in some remote possible world, that Millie's arguments are thought to be so persuasive that everyone holds a view that is *at least as permissive* in regard to abortion as Millie's view. That is, suppose that there are no longer any citizens left who are morally *and* legally opposed to abortion. Because of Millie's arguments, everyone in this scenario who has a moral opposition at all does not believe that this can be developed into a law against abortion access. Now suppose that in this society there is a very small number of obstetricians or other abortion providers, and they all hold Millie's view, that abortion is morally impermissible to procure or perform, but should be legally accessible. Finally, suppose that another woman, call her Elizabeth, believes that abortion is morally permissible and seeks an abortion. There are (barely) enough obstetricians to go around, but none of them is willing to perform an abortion for Elizabeth because each regards the procedure as morally impermissible to procure and perform. The point in this highly fictional scenario is that, in it, eventually either the law allowing for abortion access means nothing or there will be pressure on obstetricians to violate their consciences.

I phrase this case in a fictional way because, while the issue of conscience clauses and what constitutes the sort of conscientious belief that can be protected by them is complex, the fact of *tension* between conscientious objection to abortion and legalized abortion access is simply a logical reality.[132] Indeed, at some point, those who practice medicine may begin to argue, as Julie D. Cantor has, that conscientious objection in medicine is ultimately a matter of the physician's self-interest trumping professionalism.[133] She further argues that aspiring professionals have an obligation not to enter fields that are "moral minefields" for them. She writes "Qualms about abortion, sterilization, and birth control? Do not practice women's health ... Conscience is a burden that belongs to the individual professional; patients should not have to shoulder it."[134] While the American College of Gynecologists and Obstetricians still allows for those with religious and moral objections to opt out of abortion training, it nevertheless works, on an organizational level, to fight restrictions on abortion access and funding and to integrate abortion training into medical curricula.[135] IPOB gynecologists and obstetricians, however, should be reminded that medical boards and associations inevitably reflect the convictions of those who actually take up the profession. All of this is simply to say that, if one wishes to leave one's vocational choices as open as possible, it may be important to push for legislation that reflects one's view of justice, and it's not always clear that carving out a conscience objection will be sufficient. While I do hold that there should be some real conscience protections in place for pro-life medical personnel, at some point, the reality of what is permissible in law will inevitably affect what is expected in medicine, and it is impossible that this will not affect professional opportunities.

Indeed, the pro-choice side will probably rejoin that the problem with laws against abortion, and in some less populated areas, even conscience clauses of a certain sort, is that they make what should be a legal right a privilege for the wealthy. If there are only so many obstetricians or abortion providers in your city or state, and they all attempt to take refuge in a conscience clause, procuring a legal abortion will become difficult. In his review of *Vera Drake*, famed movie critic Roger Ebert gave voice to a related sentiment. He wrote "No matter what the law says, then or now, in England or America, if you can afford a plane ticket and the medical bill you will always be able to obtain a competent abortion, so laws essentially make it illegal to be poor and seek an abortion."[136] Now this is, of course, true. But it will always be true of a great variety of other things that if money allows you to cast a wider net for, say, surgeons with fewer (or different) scruples, or geographical areas of less visibility to the law, then your opportunities are nearly limitless. If law were to provide opportunities consistent with what anyone with means could get away with, it is not an exaggeration to say that there would be no law at all. This merely underscores the point that the job of law is not to track every situation on the ground, provide a consequentialist assessment of what will keep people most out of trouble, and codify a law on that basis. Rather, the purpose of law is to protect the common good by doing things like protecting rights and promoting justice.

This may be a fair point at which to briefly note two possible criticisms that might suggest my view is objectionable in a liberal democratic state. First, it might be thought that my view on abortion and other ways in which we may need to lend aid to one another is an unjustifiable infringement upon individual liberty. You might think that either because you think (a) the principles I've used are illegitimate in the context of public reason, or you might think that because you think (b) it fails some criterion for when states can justifiably limit liberties. Second, you might think that I'm playing fast and loose with notions like "vulnerability" and that this threatens a kind of paternalism. Although these notions are quite a bit more political and I will not be offering a political theory here, it would behoove most of us in contemporary philosophy to show how our views are at least in conversation with forms of liberalism.

The first suggestion under (a) is that this kind of opposition is untenable in a pluralistic context where reasons can only be offered that are non-sectarian. I have already argued at some length about this in the second section above. I have pointed out that we simply need to know things about the personhood or non-personhood of the fetus, what rights it enjoys, and how far those rights extend in order to frame a just society. Nevertheless, you might think that these kinds of things are inadmissible in the context of John Rawls's famous, and influential, notion of public reason. While Rawls may have leaned toward this view,[137] I think this may be a hasty use of his own theory. Rawls rejects "comprehensive" doctrines in the use of public reason for political purposes, whether those are religious or secular, and we actually agreed, for strategic purposes, to operate with this view, or something very close to it, in response to Thomas W. Clark earlier. While we have helped ourselves to some metaphysical views and argued for their necessity, what we have argued they are necessary *for* is getting clear about matters of basic justice in regard to the unborn human person. This was not an appeal to a comprehensive religious or even metaphysical doctrine, though. It was a preference for one view of the person because it did the necessary work where other views failed. This is part of why we eschewed the rather "spooky" Lockean conception of personhood, since it introduces an unnecessary metaphysic without adequate justification when a competing view (animalism) seems preferable both because of its theoretical coherence and its parsimony.

Indeed, while Rawls himself was rather cagey about abortion, he signaled a very tentative preference for the view Judith Jarvis Thomson expressed in a 1995 paper.[138] But Thomson's article has come in for important criticism, not because the liberalism it espouses is wrong, but because it *begs the question* against abortion opponents.[139] In his tepid recommendation of Thomson's article, Rawls himself allows that if a pro-life argument could satisfy the demands of public reason, it could make its case therein, and he even cites an example of such an argument.[140] But we have now given such an argument that does not appeal to any *more* metaphysics than is necessary to answer the relevant political question, and that argument simply calls for assessment.

But maybe you think, as in (b), that my view that taking direct action against the fetus fails some criterion for when states can justifiably limit liberties. This, of course, is an enormous topic in political philosophy, but careful reflection on a variety of cases in which the state often limits liberties, whether justifiably or not, will show that the laws of any actual state at times seek the common good through both defending fundamental rights and promoting peace and public morality.[141] All one need do to see this is to consider whether the state should take action concerning matters as diverse as seat belts, motorcycle helmets, prescription drugs, illicit drugs, military conscription, blackmail, noise levels, dwarf tossing, pediatric medical care for children of Christian Scientists, minimum wage, state-sanctioned health insurance, contempt of court for witnesses who refuse to testify, gun control, blood donation for able-bodied citizens, the dissemination and consumption of pornography, and prostitution.[142] By no means do I equate the question of state policy on abortion with very many of these issues or any of them at all. My only point here is to remind the reader that any adequate theory of what constitutes an unjustifiable limit to state intervention in matters of liberty will have cases and principles by the plenty to consider. My view in the particular matter of abortion is that, in a just society, you are not morally or legally permitted to take direct action against the vulnerable life of the fetus, and that you may be morally and legally expected (though not physically compelled) to participate in varying ways in the care of other members of society, by donating, say, bone marrow in cases where yours is sufficiently unique or necessary.

But what shall we say qualifies someone as vulnerable in this way? If you can be expected to donate bone marrow can you be expected to donate a kidney? I do think some account of the relevant risks to the donors and their own varying degrees of vulnerability will need to be given. This will not be easy to give, but the fact that every society needs to draw *some* actual lines does not mean that actually drawing them will ever be easy. Indeed, some people may be vulnerable even while it is not realistically possible to save them. I do hold, though I cannot argue for it here, that the direct killing (euthanasia) of the elderly, even if they do not actually desire their futures, is wrong for the same reasons that I believe abortion is wrong. Even so, there are times when accepting imminent death with serenity rather than pursuing unnecessarily aggressive treatment is simply the course of wisdom. I also reject capital punishment in the vast majority of cases where the criminal can be safely restrained. One could argue for principles that could prevent the entailment from a pro-life view on abortion to what I regard as a pro-life view on euthanasia and capital punishment, to which I might then respond, but such arguments can be left for another time, though I briefly discuss this again in the fifth chapter.[143]

One might be worried that the views discussed thus far threaten an overly paternalistic sort of state, and that frequent invocations of the care for the most vulnerable suggest that the state means to take an overly paternalistic care of them. There are many definitions of paternalism, but Gerald Dworkin's seems useful for the present. He writes that "Paternalism is the interference of a state or an individual with another person, against their will, and defended or motivated by a claim that the person interfered with will be better off or protected from harm."[144] But in the case of the fetus, once we have argued that the fetus is a person, the fetus will be acted upon against its will in precisely those cases in which it is aborted. The suggestion, which is sometimes made, that abortion may be in the fetus's interest, is hardly going to be a help in this argument, since it confirms, rather than deflects, the *maternalism* that would be involved in abortion.[145] But of course, someone might object, parents *should be* parental, so perhaps they are caring for their vulnerable child in choosing abortion over other life possibilities for their child.

While vulnerability is a difficult concept in medical ethics, one worthy suggestion is that the vulnerable have a greater likelihood of being "denied adequate satisfaction of certain legitimate claims."[146] It is difficult to see how, if the fetus qualifies as a person and it lacks any ability to communicate its interests, how those interests are not significantly likely to be violated. Among the claims we might wish to include for anyone qualifying as vulnerable would be, at minimum, the negative requirement of physical integrity, that is, not to harm others and the expectation that one will not be (directly) harmed. Others might be the positive requirement to help others not to incur harm, along with clauses about autonomy, freedom, and even forms of social goods that are very basic.[147] Certainly pregnant women are often vulnerable in many ways, and, again, I think there is ultimately nothing quite like the unique burdens of pregnancy. But in terms of the gravity of moral wrongs, there is nothing quite like the direct targeting of the vulnerable. I have argued that this is what abortion is. Society, indeed, should be more active in helping pregnant women and in making society more welcoming to pregnant women and caregivers, but as far as having rights that should be ensured, it is difficult not to place the direct harming of another at the top of a range of claims the vulnerable have the right to make.

It is another thing entirely to apply anti-abortion laws in a deeply insensitive manner. Arresting women for "fetal homicide" on suspicion that their falling down the stairs was undertaken with this in view should be an obvious mistake, as would be prosecuting depressed women who attempt suicide while pregnant.[148] We certainly should work across the abortion spectrum to defend pregnant women, and anti-abortion legislation should be very careful on this matter. After all, a thing's being legally impermissible and being legally punishable in some particular way are quite different things. Culpability must factor in here as well. Perhaps every pregnant woman who has an abortion, or nearly every such woman, is coerced by other people or dire circumstances. There is also an important pragmatic consideration, namely, that even though abortion should not be legally tolerated as such, it is simply very difficult to enforce with the use of punishment all aspects of such laws (though some aspects more than others).[149] Nevertheless, pro-lifers should recognize, as we ourselves claim, that the loss of a child through abortion is a very significant loss and that women who experience miscarriages should be cared for in their grief in all charity, rather than punished in suspicion.

While abortion providers may fall into a different category, the reality is that abortion will remain, for the foreseeable future, the kind of complex issue on which people will in good faith disagree. Plato himself advocated infanticide and no one proposes burning his books.[150] That does not mean that Vera Drake, in the movie we considered at the outset of this chapter, should be allowed to provide undercover abortions with impunity. Such rings, however well-intentioned, would be seriously unjust to the unborn child. Vera's character is, in many respects, a deeply good person. Indeed, probably every decent person can think of laws in her own society with which she disagrees profoundly. But that cannot prevent a state from making just laws. Still, civil society can and must have better and more sympathetic dialogue on the abortion issue. While there can be reasoned disagreement, just laws must be made that recognize the life and rights of the unborn child.

6 Conclusion

I am pro-life. In this chapter, I have tried to explain why. While I believe that there are pitfalls that any pro-life movement should avoid, the injustice of directly targeting an innocent and vulnerable life in the womb is, I think, a serious wrong. I also think that a just society should care about this wrong, because the type of wrong it is qualifies as the kind of wrong to which the law dare not turn a blind eye. That does not mean that the law should be distrustful of pregnant women. On the contrary, women bear a surpassingly unique burden because of the reality, and even potential reality, that pregnancy represents in any woman's life. The law should care about the innocent life that the woman gestates as well as the woman herself, and even owes the woman a degree of methodological charity. But as to whether the woman can procure an abortion and thus target the vulnerable life inside her, I think this question must be answered in the negative. I think that an adequate defense of that answer requires our society to take a hard, radical, look in the mirror, and I am not confident we will like what we see. Nevertheless, progress on such issues is not made without sincere dialogue by people of good will, an effort in which I hope this book is a small installment.

Notes

1 Portions of this chapter appeared in, or are revised from, my "A Short Argument Against Abortion Rights," *Think*, 34 (2013): 57–68. My thanks to editor Stephen Law, *Think*, and The Royal Institute of Philosophy for permission to use the material.
2 There is much to commend in Charles C. Camosy's "Mother and Prenatal Child Protection Act" as an attempt to move forward in some respects (especially in legislative contexts where it is unlikely that either side will get everything it wants). See chapter 6 of Camosy, 2015, *Beyond the Abortion Wars: A Way Forward for a New Generation* (Grand Rapids, MI: Eerdmans).
3 See Kaczor, 2011, *The Ethics of Abortion* (London: Routledge), p. 79.
4 "Viability" is the point at which it is possible for the fetus to survive outside the womb. No embryo is viable.
5 Thus, it is possible to survive the act of abortion. Kaczor claims that "properly speaking, abortion is intentionally killing the human fetus" (*The Ethics of Abortion*, p. 8). Thus, he argues that if the fetus does not die, then the would-be abortion has failed. I think this is not quite right. The pro-life movement is not always conceptually consistent about this. Sometimes we hear "botched abortion" and sometimes we talk of "abortion survivors." I propose that feticide is what fails if the fetus does not die.

Considering abortion as incompatible with the survival of the fetus weds the process too closely to a voyage or mission, as Kaczor suggests, one that can only *fail* if the child is safely delivered. But some pregnant women might consider their purpose that of "aborting" or "terminating" their pregnant state without regard to whether the fetus lives or dies (this is often referred to as "abortion as evacuation"). For such women, an abortion will have succeeded in its purpose once they are no longer pregnant. The woman who takes RU-486 but whose pregnancy continues *attempted* an abortion. The fetus who survives an abortion late enough to be humanely cared for after doing so has *survived* an abortion. As another example, the United States Conference of Catholic Bishops, in their *Ethical and Religious Directives for Catholic Health Care*, fifth edition (Washington, D.C., United States Conference of Catholic Bishops, 2009), define an abortion as "the directly intended termination of pregnancy before viability or the directly intended destruction of a viable fetus." The only reservation I have about this as a matter of technical definition is that, because of changing technology, viability is a moving target. Thus, what might be perceived as a directly intended termination of a pregnancy before viability could, in theory, turn out to be the placing of a viable fetus in grave peril from which a rescue may be possible. This does not strike me as a "botched abortion" but a genuine abortion from which a fetus was rescued.

6 Even stridently pro-life Catholic moral theologians would recognize this kind of procedure, when necessary, as morally permissible. See William E. May, 2008, *Catholic Bioethics and the Gift of Human Life*, 2nd edition (Huntington, IN: Our Sunday Visitor), p. 200.

7 For a timely and thoughtful treatment of these issues, consider Naomi Zack's, 2015, *White Privilege and Black Rights: The Injustice of U.S. Police Racial Profiling and Homicide* (Lanham: Rowman and Littlefield).

8 In a controversial piece of legislation in the Wisconsin state legislature, abortions were effectively proscribed at or subsequent to 20 weeks of "probable postfertilization age." The argument was based on the idea that the unborn child in question would be capable of feeling pain. While there are doubts about this timeframe as a matter of embryology, I would no more work to reverse such or similar legislation (without something better in its place) than Manninen (my coauthor) would overturn *Roe* on the basis of what she admits is its flawed argumentation. See her treatment in her earlier chapter as well as the first chapter of her *Pro-life, Pro-choice: Shared Values in the Abortion Debate* (Nashville: Vanderbilt University Press, 2014). See the relevant law at Wisconsin State Legislature, 2015, http://docs.legis.wisconsin.gov/2015/related/proposals/sb179.

9 This issue has loomed large in many United States Supreme Court decisions related to abortion, beginning with *Belliotti v. Baird* (United States Supreme Court, 1976).

10 In some ways the "should" may have to be a weak "should," though. I would not advocate overturning poorly articulated laws that nevertheless execute some measure of justice until I had some assurance an equal or greater justice would be done by a different law.

11 Consider Charles Taylor's proposal for how some Buddhist visions of individual responsibility and non-violence might align with some western ideals of rights even though western ideas of individuality would seem problematic to many Buddhists. See Taylor, 2011, "Conditions of an Unforced Consensus on Human Rights," in *Applied Ethics: A Multicultural Approach*, fifth edition, Larry May, Kai Wong, and Jill Delston, eds. (Boston: Prentice Hall), pp. 126–139.

12 For the most part, the brief descriptions of the positions of various religions in Scott Gilbert, et al., 2005, *Bioethics and the New Embryology* (Sunderland, MA: Sinauer Associates, Inc.) are fairly helpful (see pp. 34–40). Some helpful clarification could be had on Buddhism in William R. LaFleur, 1990, "Contestation and Consensus: The Morality of Abortion in Japan," *Philosophy East and West*, 40: 529–542 and on Hinduism in Julius Lipner, 2011, "The Classical Hindu View on Abortion and the

Moral Status of the Unborn," in Larry May, et al., 2011, *Applied Ethics: A Multicultural Approach*, 5th edition (Boston: Prentice Hall), pp. 471–479. In regard to Catholic views, while the prohibition itself is clear, much of the careful discussion can be found in Pope John Paul II's 1995 encyclical *Evangelium Vitae* (see http://w2.vatican.va/content/john-paul-ii/en/encyclicals/documents/hf_jp-ii_enc_25031995_evangelium-vitae.html).

13 This does not mean that one cannot place restrictions on the types of appeals that would be legitimate, though.

14 Clark, 2007, "Faith in Hiding: Are There Secular Grounds for Banning Abortion?" *The Humanist*, 67: 27–31 at 28.

15 See George and Tollefsen, 2011, *Embryo: A Defense of Human Life* (Princeton: Witherspoon Institute), p. 20. See also p. 140. Their claim, like mine, is not that religious views are impermissible in the public square where it concerns questions of pre-natal morality, but that they are *unnecessary*.

16 See Manninen, 2014, *Pro-life, Pro-choice*, p. 19. On the pro-life side, Francis J. Beckwith (2007) argues that the abortion debate in general cannot be resolved without metaphysics, effectively critiquing those who disagree. See chapter 3 of his *Defending Life: A Moral and Legal Case Against Abortion Choice* (Cambridge: Cambridge University Press, 2007). It is worth noting that Justice Blackmun did not appear to see this when delivering the court's opinion in *Roe*. He wrote "We need not resolve the difficult question of when life begins" See *Roe v. Wade*, United States Supreme Court, 1973, p. 160 at https://www.law.cornell.edu/supremecourt/text/410/113#writing-USSC_CR_0410_0113_ZS)/.

17 One might cite Rawls's attempt to construct a political liberalism in this vein. I discuss this more later in the chapter.

18 This clause makes an appearance in Kai Nielsen, 2003, "Against Moral Conservatism," in Louis P. Pojman, ed., *Moral Philosophy: A Reader*, third edition (Indianapolis: Hackett), pp. 147–156 at 152.

19 A lot hangs on how words like "intentionally," "directly," and "vulnerable" are understood in this sentence. While the defense of the overarching moral claim goes beyond the scope of this chapter, some reflection on the principle of double effect will be required here, and I will discuss that briefly in the fourth section below.

20 Rawls, 1999, *A Theory of Justice*, revised edition (Cambridge, MA: Belknap Press), p. 13. Emphasis mine.

21 See Thomson, 1971, "A Defense of Abortion," *Philosophy and Public Affairs* 1: 47–66.

22 See Kaczor, 2011, *The Ethics of Abortion*, p. 93.

23 Locke, 1975, *An Essay Concerning Human Understanding*, Book II, chapter XXVII, §4, ed. Peter H. Nidditch (Oxford: Oxford University Press), p. 331.

24 Locke, *Essay*, II.XXVII.§4, p. 331.

25 Locke, *Essay*, II.XXVII.§6, p. 332, emphasis original.

26 Locke, *Essay*, II.XXVII.§19, p. 342, emphasis original.

27 Locke, *Essay*, II.XXVII.§9, p. 335.

28 Locke, *Essay*, II.XXVII.§23, p. 344.

29 Locke supposes that, in the cases where we have two persons in one body, and one person in two bodies, these would be taking turns "by Intervals" but he offers no reason for this restriction.

30 See Samuel C. Rickless, 2014, *Locke* (Oxford: Blackwell). He writes "it is possible to conceive (and hence, for Locke, it is possible) that X is the same person as Y despite the fact that X's living body is numerically distinct from Y's living body" (p. 116).

31 See Rickless, *Locke*, p. 119.

32 See Singer, 1999, *Practical Ethics*, second edition (Cambridge: Cambridge University Press), p. 87.

33 For a particularly clear and brief example, consider Galen Strawson's recent post in the *New York Times* blog *The Stone* on May 16, 2016 titled "Consciousness Isn't a Mystery. It's Matter." See http://www.nytimes.com/2016/05/16/opinion/consciousness-isnt-a-mystery-its-matter.html?_r=0.

34 This argument is not the same as David Boonin's, 2003, "Parsimony Argument" in his *A Defense of Abortion* (Cambridge: Cambridge University Press), because his parsimony argument relies on membership in the species *Homo sapiens* as the key to whether or not one bears a right to life (see pp. 20–23). Here I am merely arguing that positing consciousness as substance *sui generis* is not clearly warranted and so is not parsimonious.

35 Notably, at least on Rickless's reading, the potentiality to perform a conscious act (of memory), which is central to Rickless's defense of Locke against Thomas Reid's famous "brave officer" objection (see Rickless, *Locke*, p. 127).

36 See Warren, 1973, "The Moral and Legal Status of Abortion," *The Monist*, 57: 43–61. See esp. pp. 54–55.

37 Warren, "The Moral and Legal Status of Abortion," p. 56.

38 See Warren, 1993, "Abortion," in Peter Singer, ed., *A Companion to Ethics* (Oxford: Blackwell), pp. 303–314, esp. 311–312.

39 See Boonin, *A Defense of Abortion*, p. 127.

40 Marquis, 1989, "Why Abortion is Immoral," *Journal of Philosophy*, 86: 183–202.

41 Marquis, "Why Abortion is Immoral," p. 191.

42 Marquis, 1998, "A Future Like Ours and the Concept of a Person: A Reply to McInerney and Paske," in Louis P. Pojman and Francis J. Beckwith, eds., *The Abortion Controversy 25 Years After Roe v. Wade: A Reader*, second edition (Belmont: Wadsworth), pp. 372–386 at p. 373.

43 See Boonin, *A Defense of Abortion*, p. 57.

44 See Boonin, *A Defense of Abortion*, p. 68.

45 Boonin, *A Defense of Abortion*, pp. 74–75.

46 Boonin, *A Defense of Abortion*, pp. 78–85.

47 Boonin, *A Defense of Abortion*, p. 80.

48 George and Tollefsen, *Embryo*, p. 113.

49 Boonin, *A Defense of Abortion*, p. 81.

50 I say this despite my misgivings about Boonin's necessary conditions for "conscious desire." He writes "All that matters is that the individual have an attraction to a given subject that is associated with certain conscious states and is not merely behavioral in nature in the way that the thermostat's desires are" (*A Defense of Abortion*, p. 81). What, after all, is an attraction? Why does an inherent developmental course that ends in fully articulate adult desire not count? Thermostats don't have it. Besides, surely being "associated with certain conscious states" is too weak.

51 See Boonin, *A Defense of Abortion*, pp. 69 and 82.

52 I say this notwithstanding the possibility of parthenogenesis, which is still quite mysterious in other animals and in any case would involve a distinct change in the sex cell itself.

53 See Gilbert, et al., *Bioethics and the New Embryology*, p. 59. My brief discussion of embryology relies to a large extent on chapters 1 and 3 of this book.

54 Gilbert, et al., *Bioethics and the New Embryology*, p. 63.

55 George and Tollefsen, *Embryo*, p. 38.

56 Kaczor, *The Ethics of Abortion*, p. 104.

57 For an interesting view of animalism with which I mostly agree, consider Andrew M. Bailey, 2016, "You Are an Animal," *Res Philosophica*, 93: 205–218.

58 Kaczor, *The Ethics of Abortion*, p. 111.

59 George and Tollefsen, *Embryo*, p. 80.

60 Gilbert, et al., *Bioethics and the New Embryology*, p. 7.

61 Gilbert, et al., *Bioethics and the New Embryology*, p. 15.

62 Boonin, *A Defense of Abortion*, p. 93, emphasis mine.

63 Boonin, *A Defense of Abortion*, p. 93.

64 Consider Will Saletan's 2008 article in *Slate* (February 13), titled "The Machine of a New Soul: The Messy Biology of Human Embryos," accessed at: http://www.slate.com/articles/health_and_science/human_nature/2008/02/the_machine_of_a_new_soul.html.

This is also reprinted in the second edition Appendix to George and Tollefsen's *Embryo*.
65 Sagan and Singer, 2007, "The Moral Status of Stem Cells," in *Stem Cell Research: The Ethical Issues*, eds. Lori Gruen, Laura Grabel, and Peter Singer (Oxford: Blackwell), pp. 124–144 at p. 126.
66 Sagan and Singer, "The Moral Status of Stem Cells," p. 129.
67 See George and Tollefsen, *Embryo*, p. 159.
68 See Ord, 2008, "The Scourge: Moral Implication of Natural Embryo Loss," *American Journal of Bioethics*, 8: 12–19.
69 Ord, "The Scourge," pp. 16, 13, and 12.
70 See Ord, "The Scourge," p. 17 and George and Tollefsen, *Embryo*, pp. 134–136.
71 Ord, "The Scourge," p. 15.
72 Though, see Leonard M. Fleck, 1978, "Abortion, Deformed Fetuses, and the Omega Pill," *Philosophical Studies*, 36: 271–283.
73 See Kaczor, *The Ethics of Abortion*, pp. 89 and 139 and George and Tollefsen, *Embryo*, pp. 136–139.
74 See Pope John Paul II, *Evangelium Vitae*, 13.
75 See Planned Parenthood, 2017, https://www.plannedparenthood.org/learn/birth-control/sterilization-women, and William E. May, *Catholic Bioethics and the Gift of Human Life*, p. 148.
76 I suppose one could exercise a rigorous form of Natural Family Planning to avoid the possibility of more dangerous pregnancies, but this would seem surprising given one's likely motives for procuring a tubal ligation in the first place.
77 See Kaczor, *The Ethics of Abortion*, p. 136, and the United States Conference of Catholic Bishops' *Ethical and Religious Directives*, directive 36.
78 See Belluck, 2012, http://www.nytimes.com/2012/06/06/health/research/morning-after-pills-dont-block-implantation-science-suggests.html?_r=0.
79 See Chris Kahlenborn, Rebecca Peck, and Walter B. Severs, 2015, "Mechanism of Action of Levonorgestrel Emergency Contraception," *Linacre Quarterly*, 82: 18–33.
80 See Elizabeth Raymond, et al., 2013, "Embracing Post-fertilisation Methods of Family Planning: A Call to Action," *Journal of Family Planning and Reproductive Health Care*, 39: 244–246. See also Sally Sheldon, 2015, "The Regulatory Cliff Edge between Contraception and Abortion: The Legal and Moral Significance of Implantation," *Journal of Medical Ethics*, 41: 762–765 which discusses how a past decision in English law against "procured miscarriage" was subsequently interpreted to allow for preventing implantation on the ground that "carriage" had not yet begun.
81 Sheldon, "The Regulatory Cliff Edge between Contraception and Abortion: The Legal and Moral Significance of Implantation," p. 2.
82 The term "embryo" is used for the early human being in its first 8 weeks of gestational age. In this section, I will usually use the term "fetus" more broadly for any unborn human person.
83 See United States Supreme Court, 1992, *Planned Parenthood v. Casey*, p. 846 at https://www.law.cornell.edu/supremecourt/text/505/833#writing-USSC_CR_0505_0833_ZO.
84 Thomson, "A Defense of Abortion," p. 66.
85 Thomson, "A Defense of Abortion," p. 50.
86 Thomson, "A Defense of Abortion," p. 52.
87 Thomson, "A Defense of Abortion," p. 53.
88 Thomson, "A Defense of Abortion," p. 49, italics mine.
89 Thomson, "A Defense of Abortion," p. 55.
90 Thomson, "A Defense of Abortion," p. 55.
91 One might object by appealing to the issue of a craniotomy, on which, see Kaczor, *The Ethics of Abortion*, pp. 188–191.
92 See Thomas A. Cavanaugh, 1996, "The Intended/Foreseen Distinction's Ethical Relevance," *Philosophical Papers* 25: 179–188, at pp. 179–180.

93 Thomson, "A Defense of Abortion," p. 54.
94 Warren, "The Moral and Legal Status of Abortion," p. 44.
95 Mackenzie, 1992, "Abortion and Embodiment," *Australasian Journal of Philosophy*, 70: 136–155, at pp. 148 and 151.
96 See Mackenzie, "Abortion and Embodiment," p. 151.
97 Mackenzie, "Abortion and Embodiment," p. 152.
98 See Reader, 2008, "Abortion, Killing, and Maternal Moral Authority," *Hypatia*, 23: 132–149; see pp. 143, 141, 144, and 146.
99 See Christine Overall, 2015, "Rethinking Abortion, Ectogenesis, and Fetal Death," *Journal of Social Philosophy*, 46: 126–140, at pp. 132–133.
100 See Mackenzie, "Abortion and Embodiment," p. 151, emphasis mine.
101 Reader, "Abortion, Killing, and Maternal Moral Authority," p. 147.
102 Reader, "Abortion, Killing, and Maternal Moral Authority," p. 141.
103 See Robin West, 2008, "The Harms of Consensual Sex," in Alan Soble and Nicholas Power, eds., *The Philosophy of Sex*, fifth edition (Lanham: Rowman and Littlefield), pp. 317–324.
104 Reader, "Abortion, Killing, and Maternal Moral Authority," p. 141.
105 See the USCCB's *Ethical and Religious Directives*, directive 36.
106 See Boonin, *A Defense of Abortion*, p. 167 and Beckwith, *Defending Life*, pp. 184–189.
107 On the pro-choice side, consider Catharine MacKinnon, 1999, "*Roe v. Wade*: A Study in Male Ideology," in Pojman and Beckwith, eds., *The Abortion Controversy*, pp. 95–103. On the pro-life side, consider Frederica Mathewes-Green, 2013, "How Feminism Went Wrong: Abortion as the Price for Conformity with the Male Model," *Christian Bioethics*, 19: 130–132.
108 See Lois Pineau, 1989, "Date Rape: A Feminist Analysis," *Law and Philosophy*, 8: 217–243.
109 See Kaczor, *The Ethics of Abortion*, chapter 9.
110 See Beckwith, *Defending Life*, pp. 83–92 for more on abortion methods.
111 Little, 2005, "The Moral Permissibility of Abortion," in Andrew I. Cohen and Christopher Heath Wellman, eds., *Contemporary Debates in Applied Ethics* (Oxford: Blackwell), pp. 27–39.
112 Little, "The Moral Permissibility of Abortion," pp. 28 and 30.
113 Little, "The Moral Permissibility of Abortion," pp. 30–31.
114 See Rachels, 1994, "Active and Passive Euthanasia," in Bonnie Steinbock and Alastair Norcross, eds., *Killing and Letting Die*, second edition (New York: Fordham University Press), pp. 112–119, at p. 115.
115 Sullivan, 1994, "Active and Passive Euthanasia: An Impertinent Distinction?" in Steinbock and Norcross, eds., *Killing and Letting Die*, pp. 131–138 at pp. 134–135.
116 In *United States v. Holmes*, a guiding principle was that "passengers must always be saved in preference to seamen, except those indispensable for operating the boat." See "Seaman Holmes and the Longboat of William Brown," reported by John William Wallace (2011) in Louis P. Pojman and Lewis Vaughn, eds., *The Moral Life: An Introductory Reader in Ethics and Literature*, fourth edition (Oxford: Oxford University Press), pp. 220–221.
117 I am only making a general point about law and what it can require in regard to the vulnerable right now. Whether and how this would bear directly upon abortion in more concrete cases is complex even among people who identify as pro-life, and I note some of these complexities in my later response to Manninen in this book.
118 See Bertha Alvarez Manninen, *Pro-life, Pro-choice*, p. 20.
119 See Common Pleas Court of Allegheny County, Pennsylvania, 1978, *McFall v. Shimp*, 10 D. & C. 3d, 91–92 at: http://www.leagle.com/decision/197810010PaDampC3d90_189/McFALL%20v.%20SHIMP.
120 See Jason T. Eberl, 2010, "Fetuses are Neither Violinists nor Violators," *American Journal of Bioethics*, 10: 53–54.
121 Kaczor, *The Ethics of Abortion*, p. 156.
122 See Mulder, 2010, "Let's rethink Roe v. Wade – and overturn it," *American Journal of Bioethics*, 10: 65–66.

123 See Kaczor, *The Ethics of Abortion*, pp. 168–175 for a discussion of Alexander Pruss's comparison to military drafts.
124 See Hursthouse, 1991, "Virtue Theory and Abortion," *Philosophy and Public Affairs*, 20: 223–246 at p. 243.
125 Mackenzie, "Abortion and Embodiment," p. 143.
126 Mathewes-Green, "How Feminism Went Wrong," p. 132.
127 See, for example, Mario Cuomo's, 1996, "Religious Belief and Public Morality: A Catholic Governor's Perspective," in Lloyd Steffen, ed., *Abortion: A Reader* (Cleveland: Pilgrim Press), pp. 373–388.
128 See Hershenov and Hershenov, 2009, "The 'I'm Personally Opposed to Abortion But…' Argument," *Proceedings of the American Catholic Philosophical Association*, 83: 77–87.
129 Hershenov and Hershenov, "The 'I'm Personally Opposed to Abortion But…' Argument," pp. 79–80.
130 Hershenov and Hershenov, "The 'I'm Personally Opposed to Abortion But…' Argument," p. 81.
131 Hershenov and Hershenov, "The 'I'm Personally Opposed to Abortion But…' Argument," p. 84.
132 For a stridently pro-life perspective on this, consider M. Casey Mattox and Matthew S. Bowman, 2010, "Your Conscience, Your Right: A History of Efforts to Violate Pro-Life Medical Conscience, and the Laws that Stand in the Way," *Linacre Quarterly*, 77: 187–197.
133 See Cantor, 2009, "Conscientious Objection Gone Awry – Restoring Selfless Professionalism in Medicine," *New England Journal of Medicine*, 360: 1484–1485.
134 Cantor, "Conscientious Objection Gone Awry," p. 1485.
135 See the American College of Obstetricians and Gynecologists, 2014 statement at: https://www.acog.org/-/media/Committee-Opinions/Committee-on-Health-Care-for-Underserved-Women/co612.pdf?dmc=1&ts=20160616T1526313288.
136 See Ebert, 2004, at: http://www.rogerebert.com/reviews/vera-drake-2004.
137 See Rawls's 1997 paper, "The Idea of Public Reason Revisited," in John Rawls, *Collected Papers*, ed. Samuel Freeman (Cambridge, MA: Harvard University Press, 1999), pp. 573–615, esp. pp. 605–606 n. 80. Notably, this postdates both editions of *Political Liberalism*, and clarifies certain matters in regard to abortion therein.
138 See Thomson, 1995, "Abortion," *Boston Review*, 20. See: http://new.bostonreview.net/BR20.3/thomson.html.
139 See Beckwith, *Defending Life*, pp. 56–62.
140 See Rawls, "The Idea of Public Reason Revisited," p. 606 nn. 80 and 82, where, in the latter case Rawls explicitly mentions a pro-life argument from Cardinal Joseph Bernadin that he clearly states is admissible within public reason, even though he declines to assess the argument.
141 This claim comes from the (Catholic) Congregation for the Doctrine of Faith's 1987 letter *Donum Vitae*, chiefly concerning reproductive issues, but it is a defensible opinion anyone might have about the purpose of a state. It appears in the section titled "The Values and Moral Obligations that Civil Legislation Must Respect and Sanction in this Matter." See: http://www.vatican.va/roman_curia/congregations/cfaith/documents/rc_con_cfaith_doc_19870222_respect-for-human-life_en.html.
142 Many of these cases are found in Alan Wertheimer's, 2002, "Liberty, Coercion, and the Limits of the State," in Robert L. Simon, ed., *The Blackwell Companion to Social and Political Philosophy* (Oxford: Blackwell), pp. 38–59.
143 Kaczor argues against these entailments, though not against the moral positions they would entail. See Kaczor, *The Ethics of Abortion*, pp. 116–120.
144 Gerald Dworkin, 2014, "Paternalism," *The Stanford Encyclopedia of Philosophy* (Summer 2014 Edition), Edward N. Zalta (ed.), at: http://plato.stanford.edu/archives/sum2014/entries/paternalism/.

145 Soran Reader sometimes suggests that abortion could be in the fetus's interests, precisely because of maternal care and authority (see Reader, "Abortion, Killing, and Maternal Moral Authority").
146 See Nicholas Tavaglione, et al., 2015, "Fleshing Out Vulnerability," *Bioethics*, 29: 98–107, at p. 98.
147 Tavaglione, et al., "Fleshing Out Vulnerability," pp. 101–105.
148 See Lynne M. Paltrow and Jeanne Flavin, 2014, "Pregnant, and No Civil Rights," November 7, 2014, *New York Times*, at: http://www.nytimes.com/2014/11/08/opinion/pregnant-and-no-civil-rights.html?_r=0.
149 See Beckwith, *Defending Life*, pp. 108–111 and 170–171. See also philosopher Michael Pakaluk's 1990 presentation to the Augustine Club of Columbia University, NY, titled "Difficult Questions for Pro-Choice Persons," esp. Question 6 under the heading "Questions for pro-life people, and replies" at https://michaelpakaluk.files.wordpress.com/2012/03/difficult-questions-for-pro-choice-persons.pdf.
150 See Plato, 1992, *Republic*, 460c, trans. G.M.A. Grube, revised C.D.C. Reeve (Indianapolis: Hackett, 1992), p. 134.

References

American College of Obstetricians and Gynecologists. 2014. "Abortion Training and Education." *The American Congress of Obstetricians and Gynecologists*. See https://www.acog.org/-/media/Committee-Opinions/Committee-on-Health-Care-for-Underserved-Women/co612.pdf?dmc=1&ts=20160616T1526313288. Accessed September 12, 2017.

Bailey, Andrew M. 2016. "You Are an Animal." *Res Philosophica*, 93: 205–218.

Beckwith, Francis J. 2007. *Defending Life: A Moral and Legal Case Against Abortion Choice*. Cambridge: Cambridge University Press.

Belluck, Pam. 2012. "Abortion Qualms on Morning-After Pill May Be Unfounded." *New York Times*. June 5, 2012. http://www.nytimes.com/2012/06/06/health/research/morning-after-pills-dont-block-implantation-science-suggests.html?_r=0. Accessed September 11, 2017.

Boonin, David. 2003. *A Defense of Abortion*. Cambridge: Cambridge University Press.

Camosy, Charles. 2015. *Beyond the Abortion Wars: A Way Forward for a New Generation*. Grand Rapids, MI: Eerdmans.

Cantor, Julie D. 2009. "Conscientious Objection Gone Awry – Restoring Selfless Professionalism in Medicine." *New England Journal of Medicine*, 360: 1484–1485.

Cavanaugh, Thomas A. 1996. "The Intended/Foreseen Distinction's Ethical Relevance." *Philosophical Papers*, 25: 179–188.

Clark, Thomas W. 2007. "Faith in Hiding: Are There Secular Grounds for Banning Abortion?" *The Humanist*, 67: 27–31.

Common Pleas Court of Allegheny County, Pennsylvania. 1978. *McFall v. Shimp*. See https://www.leagle.com/decision/197810010padampc3d90189. Accessed September 12, 2017.

Congregation for the Doctrine of Faith. 1987. *Donum Vitae*. http://www.vatican.va/roman_curia/congregations/cfaith/documents/rc_con_cfaith_doc_19870222_respect-for-human-life_en.html. Accessed September 12, 2017.

Cuomo, Mario. 1996. "Religious Belief and Public Morality: A Catholic Governor's Perspective." In *Abortion: A Reader*. Ed. Steffen H. Lloyd. Cleveland: Pilgrim Press, pp. 373–388.

Dworkin, Gerald. 2014. "Paternalism." *The Stanford Encyclopedia of Philosophy*. Ed. Edward N. Zalta. http://plato.stanford.edu/archives/sum2014/entries/paternalism/. Accessed September 12, 2017.

Eberl, Jason T. 2010. "Fetuses are Neither Violinists nor Violators." *American Journal of Bioethics*, 10: 53–54.

Ebert, Roger. 2004. "Review of Vera Drake." http://www.rogerebert.com/reviews/vera-drake-2004. Accessed September 12, 2017.

Fleck, Leonard M. 1978. "Abortion, Deformed Fetuses, and the Omega Pill." *Philosophical Studies*, 36: 271–283.

George, Robert P. and Tollefsen, Christopher. 2011. *Embryo: A Defense of Human Life*. Princeton: Witherspoon Institute.

Gilbert, Scott, Tyler, Anna, and Zackin, Emily. 2005. *Bioethics and the New Embryology*. Sunderland, MA: Sinauer Associates, Inc.

Hershenov, David B. and Hershenov, Rose. 2009. "The 'I'm Personally Opposed to Abortion But…' Argument." *Proceedings of the American Catholic Philosophical Association*, 83: 77–87.

Hursthouse, Rosalind. 1991. "Virtue Theory and Abortion." *Philosophy and Public Affairs*, 20: 223–246

John Paul II, Pope. 1995. *Evangelium Vitae*. http://w2.vatican.va/content/john-paul-ii/en/encyclicals/documents/hf_jp-ii_enc_25031995_evangelium-vitae.html. Accessed September 10, 2017.

Kaczor, Christopher. 2011. *The Ethics of Abortion*. London: Routledge.

Kahlenborn, Chris, Peck, Rebecca, and Severs, Walter B. 2015. "Mechanism of Action of Levonorgestrel Emergency Contraception." *Linacre Quarterly*, 82: 18–33.

LaFleur, William R. 1990. "Contestation and Consensus: The Morality of Abortion in Japan." *Philosophy East and West*, 40: 529–542.

Lipner, Julius. 2011. "The Classical Hindu View on Abortion and the Moral Status of the Unborn." In May, Larry, Wong, Kai, and Delston, Jill, eds. *Applied Ethics: A Multicultural Approach*. 5th edition. Boston: Prentice Hall, pp. 471–479.

Little, Margaret Olivia. 2005. "The Moral Permissibility of Abortion." In Cohen, Andrew I. and Heath Wellman, Christopher, eds. *Contemporary Debates in Applied Ethics*. Oxford: Blackwell, pp. 27–39.

Locke, John. 1975. *An Essay Concerning Human Understanding*. Ed. Peter H. Nidditch. Oxford: Oxford University Press.

Mackenzie, Catriona. 1992. "Abortion and Embodiment." *Australasian Journal of Philosophy*, 70: 136–155.

MacKinnon, Catharine. 1999. "Roe v. Wade: A Study in Male Ideology," in Pojman, Louis P. and Beckwith, Francis J., eds. *The Abortion Controversy 25 Years After Roe v. Wade: A Reader*. 2nd edition. Belmont: Wadsworth, pp. 95–103.

Manninen, Bertha Alvarez. 2014. *Pro-life, Pro-choice: Shared Values in the Abortion Debate*. Nashville: Vanderbilt University Press.

Marquis, Don. 1998. "A Future Like Ours and the Concept of a Person: A Reply to McInerney and Paske." In Pojman, Louis P. and Beckwith, Francis J., eds. 1999. *The Abortion Controversy 25 Years After Roe v. Wade: A Reader*. 2nd edition. Belmont: Wadsworth, pp. 372–386.

Marquis, Don. 1989. "Why Abortion is Immoral." *Journal of Philosophy*, 86: 183–202.

Mathewes-Green, Frederica. 2013. "How Feminism Went Wrong: Abortion as the Price for Conformity with the Male Model." *Christian Bioethics*, 19: 130–132.

Mattox, M. Casey, and Bowman, Matthew S. 2010. "Your Conscience, Your Right: A History of Efforts to Violate Pro-Life Medical Conscience, and the Laws that Stand in the Way." *Linacre Quarterly*, 77: 187–197.

May, Larry, Wong, Kai, and Delston, Jill, eds. 2011. *Applied Ethics: A Multicultural Approach*. 5th edition. Boston: Prentice Hall.

May, William E. 2008. *Catholic Bioethics and the Gift of Human Life*. 2nd edition. Huntington, IN: Our Sunday Visitor.

Mulder Jr., Jack. 2010. "Let's rethink Roe v. Wade – and overturn it." *American Journal of Bioethics*, 10: 65–66.

Nielsen, Kai. 2003. "Against Moral Conservatism." In Louis P. Pojman, ed., *Moral Philosophy: A Reader*. 3rd edition. Indianapolis: Hackett, pp. 147–156.

Ord, Toby. 2008. "The Scourge: Moral Implication of Natural Embryo Loss." *American Journal of Bioethics*, 8: 12–19.

Overall, Christine. 2015. "Rethinking Abortion, Ectogenesis, and Fetal Death." *Journal of Social Philosophy*, 46: 126–140.

Pakaluk, Michael. 1990. "Difficult Questions for Pro-Choice Persons." https://michaelpakaluk.files.wordpress.com/2012/03/difficult-questions-for-pro-choice-persons.pdf. Accessed September 12, 2017.

Paltrow, Lynne M. and Flavin, Jeanne. 2014. "Pregnant, and No Civil Rights." *New York Times*. http://www.nytimes.com/2014/11/08/opinion/pregnant-and-no-civil-rights.html?_r=0. Accessed September 12, 2017.

Pineau, Lois. 1989. "Date Rape: A Feminist Analysis." *Law and Philosophy*, 8: 217–243.

Planned Parenthood. 2017. "How Safe Is Tubal Ligation." https://www.plannedparenthood.org/learn/birth-control/sterilization/how-safe-tubal-ligation. Accessed September 11, 2017.

Plato. 1992. *Republic*. Trans. G.M.A. Grube. Revised C.D.C. Reeve. Indianapolis: Hackett.

Rachels, James. 1994. "Active and Passive Euthanasia." In Steinbock, Bonnie and Norcross, Alastair, eds. *Killing and Letting Die*. 2nd edition. New York: Fordham University, pp. 112–119.

Rawls, John. 1999. *A Theory of Justice*. Revised edition. Cambridge, MA: Belknap Press.

Rawls, John. 1997. "The Idea of Public Reason Revisited." Reprinted in *John Rawls, Collected Papers*. 1999. Ed. Samuel Freeman. Cambridge, MA: Harvard University Press, pp. 573–615.

Raymond, Elizabeth, Coeytaux, Francine, Gemzell-Danielsson, Kristina, et al. 2013. "Embracing Post-fertilisation Methods of Family Planning: A Call to Action." *Journal of Family Planning and Reproductive Health Care*, 39: 244–246.

Reader, Soran. 2008. "Abortion, Killing, and Maternal Moral Authority." *Hypatia*, 23: 132–149.

Rickless, Samuel C. 2014. *Locke*. Oxford: Blackwell.

Sagan, Agata and Singer, Peter. 2007. "The Moral Status of Stem Cells." In *Stem Cell Research: The Ethical Issues*. Eds. Lori Gruen, Laura Grabel, and Peter Singer. Oxford: Blackwell, pp. 124–144.

Saletan, Will. 2008. "The Machine of a New Soul: The Messy Biology of Human Embryos." February 13, 2008. http://www.slate.com/articles/health_and_science/human_nature/2008/02/the_machine_of_a_new_soul.html. Accessed September 11, 2017.

Sheldon, Sally. 2015. "The Regulatory Cliff Edge between Contraception and Abortion: The Legal and Moral Significance of Implantation." *Journal of Medical Ethics*, 41: 762–765.

Singer, Peter. 1999. *Practical Ethics*. 2nd edition. Cambridge: Cambridge University Press.

Strawson, Galen. 2016. "Consciousness Isn't a Mystery: It's Matter." *The Stone* (New York Times Blog). May 16, 2016. http://www.nytimes.com/2016/05/16/opinion/consciousness-isnt-a-mystery-its-matter.html?_r=0.

Sullivan, Thomas D. 1994. "Active and Passive Euthanasia: An Impertinent Distinction?" In Steinbock, Bonnie and Norcross, Alastair, eds. *Killing and Letting Die*. 2nd edition. New York: Fordham University Press, pp. 131–138.

Tavaglione, Nicholas, Martin, Angela, Mezger, Nathalie, et al. 2015. "Fleshing Out Vulnerability." *Bioethics*, 29: 98–107.

Taylor, Charles. 2011. "Conditions of an Unforced Consensus on Human Rights." In May, Larry, Wong, Kai, and Delston, Jill, eds. *Applied Ethics: A Multicultural Approach*. 5th edition. Boston: Prentice Hall, pp. 126–139.

Thomson, Judith Jarvis. 1995. "Abortion." *Boston Review*, 20. See: http://new.bostonreview.net/BR20.3/thomson.html.

Thomson, Judith Jarvis. 1971. "A Defense of Abortion." *Philosophy and Public Affairs*, 1: 47–66.

United States Conference of Catholic Bishops. 2009. *Ethical and Religious Directives for Catholic Health Care*. 5th edition. Washington, D.C.: United States Conference of Catholic Bishops.

United States Supreme Court. 1976. Belliotti v. Baird. https://www.law.cornell.edu/supremecourt/text/428/132. Accessed September 10, 2017.

United States Supreme Court. 1973. Roe v. Wade. https://www.law.cornell.edu/supremecourt/text/410/113#writing-USSC_CR_0410_0113_ZS/. Accessed September 10, 2017.

United States Supreme Court. 1992. Planned Parenthood v. Casey. https://www.law.cornell.edu/supremecourt/text/505/833#writing-USSC_CR_0505_0833_ZO. Accessed September 10, 2017.

Wallace, John William. 2011. "Seaman Holmes and the Longboat of William Brown." In *The Moral Life: An Introductory Reader in Ethics and Literature*. Eds. Louis P. Pojman and Lewis Vaughn. 4th edition. Oxford: Oxford University Press, pp. 220–221.

Warren, Mary Anne. 1993. "Abortion." In Peter Singer, ed., *A Companion to Ethics*. Oxford: Blackwell, pp. 303–314.

Warren, Mary Anne. 1973. "The Moral and Legal Status of Abortion." *The Monist*, 57: 43–61.

Wertheimer, Alan. 2002. "Liberty, Coercion, and the Limits of the State." In *The Blackwell Companion to Social and Political Philosophy*. Ed. Robert L. Simon. Oxford: Blackwell, pp. 38–59.

West, Robin. 2008. "The Harms of Consensual Sex." In Alan Soble and Nicholas Power, eds. *The Philosophy of Sex*. 5th edition. Lanham: Rowman and Littlefield, pp. 317–324.

Wisconsin State Legislature. 2015. 2015 Senate Bill 179. http://docs.legis.wisconsin.gov/2015/related/proposals/sb179#d_assembly. Accessed September 10, 2017.

Zack, Naomi. 2015. *White Privilege and Black Rights: The Injustice of U.S. Police Racial Profiling and Homicide*. Lanham: Rowman and Littlefield.

3

A RESPONSE TO MULDER

Bertha Alvarez Manninen

I thoroughly enjoyed reading Mulder's chapter, and found myself quite sympathetic to much of what he has to say, particularly in reference to his analysis of Thomson's argument. I also think he brings up three peripheral, but nevertheless really important, issues: the *prima facie* moral impermissibility of late-term abortions, whether birth control measures such as the "morning-after pill" are actual abortifacients, and whether pro-life advocates are inconsistent in not really seeming to care about natural embryo loss. I will discuss these towards the end of the chapter. While I am not able to touch upon every single argument he proffers, I will address what appear to me to be his most formidable and relevant ones. First, I would like to address his arguments in favor of animalism and person essentialism. Second, I will address his arguments against Judith Jarvis Thomson's pro-choice stance, which I heavily endorsed in my chapter and for which Mulder's responses have served to give me great pause.

I. Animalism and person essentialism

I agree with Mulder that pro-life advocates should avoid "the error of couching its rhetoric too heavily in religious language when speaking in a public forum" (p. 68) Oftentimes I have heard the pro-life position derided as being "merely religious," the assumption being that pro-life advocacy has no viable leg to stand on outside of religious premises. Therefore, it is reasoned, no one who is not religious has any reason to even consider their views, rendering the pro-life position easily dismissible. This is unfortunate since I, like Mulder, do believe that there are some legitimate issues raised by pro-lifers to which pro-choicers should pay serious attention. Moreover, adopting a dismissive attitude toward others because they differ from one's ethical or religious beliefs is no way to foster a community of rational dialogue in a pluralistic society. I appreciate that Mulder has approached his pro-life defense in this way, and while I do, ultimately, think that some of the arguments he proffers here are problematic, they are certainly philosophically respectable ones.

As I noted in Chapter 1, a secular defense of a pro-life perspective that employs personal identity considerations would likely have to appeal to some version of animalism. Don Marquis' famous secular pro-life argument does this, and Mulder also appeals to animalism in defending the claim that moral status for human beings begins at conception. As Mulder writes, he believes this because it is at conception, when the male and female gametes have thoroughly fused to form a new distinct organism, that we have a being that "has attained the organic integrity important for the beginning of a new human life" (p. 81). Mulder argues that a newly conceived embryo is continuous with the future human being the embryo becomes because they share the same organism. That is, if human beings are essentially living organisms, then each one of us began to exist whenever our organism first began to exist, and this, he argues, occurs at conception. Mulder rejects what he calls the "performance" account of personhood, which maintains that a human being is a person if and only if she functions at a certain cognitive level. Mulder rejects Warren's cognitive account of personhood (as do I) and also David Boonin's arguments concerning the role the capacity to desire one's life plays in rendering a human being a human person.

Instead, Mulder supports Christopher Kaczor's "endowment view" of personhood, which states that "each human being has inherent, moral worth simply by virtue of the kind of being it is."[1] Kaczor describes the "endowment view" as inclusive in that "all human beings regardless of any consideration whatsoever have fundamental dignity and are therefore owed respect."[2] This respect is owed regardless of a particular human being's physical or cognitive capacities. Rather, the genesis of this respect comes solely as a result of species membership. The human species is an inherently rational species, and every single member of that species can, according to Kaczor (and, I assume, Mulder as well, since he endorses Kaczor's view) be properly called a rational animal even if she is not exercising her rational capacities at any given time (e.g., because she is an embryo, or cognitively disabled, or senile). This view is endorsed by other philosophers as well, including Francis Beckwith (whose arguments will be further explored below) and Russell DiSilvestro, who argues that "all human organisms have serious moral status, which includes a strong moral presumption against being killed, and that all human organisms have this serious moral status because they have a set of typical human capacities."[3] You, as a human being, are always a member of that species from the very moment you begin to exist, as an embryo, and so you are a person from the time you were that embryo. So there are actually two different claims that are being made here that need to be teased out and analyzed separately: one is an identity claim (animalism), and the other a claim about what essential properties (in this case, personhood) you possess throughout your existence.

1. Animalism: A human being begins to exist whenever her living human organism first begins to exist.

2. Person Essentialism: A human being is a person throughout all stages of her existence because she is a member of a certain kind of being that is biologically constituted towards possessing rational capacities. This holds true regardless of whether she is actually capable of exercising those rational capacities at any given time.

Mulder additionally defends a third premise relating to animalism, arguing that the human organism begins to exist at conception (this premise will also be explored below). The three premises together yield the conclusion that a human embryo is a human person: we are persons essentially whenever it is that we begin to exist and since we begin to exist at conception, we are persons since conception.

The reason I think it is important to distinguish between 1 and 2 is because it is quite possible to hold one and reject the other, and doing so would render very different outcomes for the abortion issue. For example, let's revisit my argument in favor of the interest view of moral status and the embodied mind account of identity. The two in conjunction lead to a kind of moral person essentialism.[4] Remember I argued that there is good reason to think that personal identity begins at the "birth" of the human mind, when the brain develops the capacity for sentience and consciousness, and that these are also the necessary and sufficient conditions that any being (human or not human) must meet in order to be a person in the moral sense of the term. That is, my personal identity and my moral status begin *at the same time* and *because of the same reason*. Moreover, my personal identity and moral status persist over time, again, so long as the same criteria are met: that I continue to possess the capacity for conscious awareness. I do not cash out the importance of consciousness as Boonin does – it is not about having desires either in the occurrent, ideal, or dispositional sense (this is why I will not be devoting any time here to addressing Mulder's objections to Boonin, although I do believe he brings up some very good points). Rather it is because it is at the onset of consciousness that we have the beginning of a phenomenology, or a biographical, versus merely a biological, life. My view can also be construed as a kind of person essentialism because it leads to the conclusion that I am a (moral) person at all stages of my existence. But because my view of identity is different, because I do not believe I begin to exist when my organism begins to exist, this has a radically different outcome for the moral status of the human fetus (since, as I argued, consciousness does not begin until mid-gestation). Person essentialism, therefore, is not, by itself, sufficient to argue in favor of a pro-life perspective.

Mulder ends his criticism of Boonin by arguing that Boonin has given no good reason in favor of why we should treat a patient in a temporary comatose state (who is not actually sentient or conscious at the time) as a person, but not extend the same treatment to a pre-conscious fetus. Boonin maintains that a temporarily comatose person has "actual dispositional desires that he has developed under actual conditions" (p. 76), but that a fetus does not, and as such the former should still be treated as a being with moral status while the latter, the fetus, has no similar claim.

Mulder rejects Boonin's distinction here, maintaining that whatever exception Boonin makes for the temporarily comatose individual's claim to personhood could easily apply to the fetus: "a performance-related view of personhood also seems problematic, because every time it attempts to account for those who cannot actualize the performance in the standard way, that explanation seems easy enough to tailor so that it would include fetuses" (p. 83). But, for those who support the embodied mind account of identity, there is one distinction between pre-conscious fetuses and individuals in temporary comas that, I think, makes a significant difference: an individual in a *temporary* coma (not a permanent one) will experience a *continuation* of his personal identity upon re-awakening, similar to someone who wakes up after a deep sleep. Or, as DiSilvestro puts it, there are no "temporal gaps" when it comes to personal identity in these cases; it isn't the case that a person in a temporary coma ceases to exist whilst in the coma, and then just begins to exist again. While sometimes there may be lapses in the patient's memory or cognitive abilities, he retains the *capacity* for consciousness throughout, and typically some of his mental contents will "pick up" right where they "left off." As Jeff McMahan puts it:

> In deep coma, there is physical, functional, and organizational continuity of the areas of the brain in which consciousness and mental activity are realized ... all aspects of the mind are preserved intact in the tissues of his cerebral hemispheres, but their arousal is impeded by a defect in a critical support system.[5]

In other words, there was never an eradication of a human some*one* during a temporary coma, the some*one* only laid dormant. A pre-conscious fetus, however, is not yet a human some*one*, there is no personal identity that has yet commenced until the cerebral cortex is sufficiently developed towards mid-gestation. We preserve the life of an individual in a temporary comatose state for the same reason we preserve the lives of fully conscious people: he has a life, a future, that is properly *his* and will continue upon reawakening, and he therefore retains an interest in that existence. A pre-conscious fetus has no personal life *yet* that can be properly claimed as its own, and as such there is nothing *yet* to lose (the fetus is indeed a potential person in this respect, it *will* have a conscious life once its brain sufficiently develops, but unless we are under obligation to bring potential persons into existence, this alone is not sufficient for ascribing onto it an interest in continued existence).

Of course, for someone who rejects mentalist accounts of identity altogether, as Mulder does, this difference may not be very significant at all. Given that Mulder's argument in favor of fetal personhood from conception onwards vitally relies on animalism, let's explore the theory a bit further.

A discussion about animalism

In Chapter1, I wrote that pro-life advocates "have to think about metaphysical issues in a way that they were perhaps not anticipating" (p. 25) and Mulder has clearly risen to that challenge. While I anticipated that a pro-life argument would have to make some appeal to animalism, I did not detail in Chapter 1 why I find the view problematic (though still philosophically formidable). I will do so here.

Why think that having a phenomenology, a mental and biographical life, is necessary for personal identity to exist and subsist over time? Mulder maintains, in reference to animalism, that "generally we want to do our explaining in public discourse with as little metaphysical furniture as possible. If two theories accord with most of our common judgments and part ways at matters of controversy, we should generally prefer the theory that does not require us to posit a new entity without good reason. The view that living human bodies (or animals) are persons does not require this" (p. 79). However, I *don't* think that animalism accords with "most of our common judgements" about identity. Let's test these judgments and intuitions by first appealing to a fictional scenario. In the *Harry Potter* books, the students of Hogwarts learn to apparate and disapparate, a method of teleportation, when they turn 17. One reason why they must be older teenagers is because such a method of transportation, when not done correctly, can have harmful effects. If the mind of the traveler is not sufficiently concentrated on their destination, random body parts can be separated from the rest of the body, a process known as splinching. In Book 7 of the series, Ron Weasley leaves behind his lower arm when he disapparated from the Ministry of Magic into the woods, and almost bled to death from his left shoulder.

Now, suppose it had been Ron's head that had been splinched – his body lying in the woods while his head was left behind in the Ministry of Magic. In that situation, *where is Ron*? As many science fiction scenarios illustrate, we seem to believe we go where our heads go, and so many would likely say that Ron, the person, remained at the Ministry. Suppose the splinching had an even worse affect – Ron's whole body, head and all, appeared in the woods while his brain apparated into a new organism that had perished in a Death Eater attack. That new organism now had all of Ron's thoughts, personality traits, and memories. Where is Ron now? Again, I think many people would say that Ron is now residing in this new organism. And the reason we think this seems to be because we are following Ron's mind – Ron goes wherever his mind does.

Philosophers have been discussing the issue of head transplants in their writings on personal identity for decades. It may be the case very soon that this will no longer be a science-fiction scenario. In 2013, Dr. Sergio Canavero, an Italian neurosurgeon, announced that he was close to being able to perform the world's first head transplant using two procedures: a head anastomosis venture and a spinal cord fusion.[6] The patient whose head will be transplanted is 31-year-old Valery Spiridonov, who suffers from Werdnig-Hoffman disease, a muscle degeneration disease, and feels that this surgery is his only hope for gaining a functional body. While explaining how the surgery proceeds, notice the language used by the author:

> In a specially equipped hospital suite, two surgical teams will work simultaneously – one focused on Spiridonov and the other on the donor's body, selected from a

brain-dead patient and matched with the Russian for height, build and immunotype. Both patients – anesthetized and outfitted with breathing tubes – will have their heads locked using metal pins and clamps, and electrodes will be attached to their bodies to monitor brain and heart activity. Next, Spiridonov's head will be nearly frozen, ultimately reaching 12 to 15 degrees Celsius, which will make him temporarily brain-dead. ... Under an operating microscope, doctors will cleanly chop through both spinal cords ... so thin that it is measured in angstroms, provided by the University of Texas. Then the rush is on: Once sliced, Spiridonov's head will have to be attached to the donor's body and connected to the blood flow within an hour. (When the head is transferred, the main vessels will be clamped to prevent air from causing a blockage.) Surgeons will quickly sew the arteries and veins of Spiridonov's head to those of his new body. The donor's blood flow will then, in theory, re-warm Spiridonov's head to normal temperatures within minutes ... Once he awakens, Spiridonov will start his rehabilitation, including virtual reality training. Canavero predicts his patient will be able to walk three to six months after surgery.[7]

The only reason Spiridonov would put himself through this ordeal, knowing that he may die, is because he thinks there is a possibility that *he* will survive the surgery. It is *Spiridonov* who will emerge from the operating table, not the donor body. It is *he* who will have to go through physical therapy, it is *he* that has to learn to walk again. Because it is Spiridonov's head that will (hopefully) survive, it is Spiridonov himself who will survive. And if we ask why it is Spiridonov who we think will survive, it is likely because we feel that Spiridonov goes where his brain goes, because it is his brain that is responsible for all the aspects of his mind that form his personal identity. This is the same belief that fueled the respective families of Terri Schiavo and Nancy Beth Cruzan to inscribe two death dates on their loved one's tombstone – the tacit implication is that the person dies when the mind does, and that this can be a separate death than the death of the body.

In response to the issue of brain transplants (or splinching), which appears to highlight the significance of our conscious life for our personal identity, animalists like Eric Olson and Christopher Kaczor would simply argue that our respective brain, most importantly the upper brain, is part of the human animal, and moving it to another body would just mean moving parts of that animal into another part of another animal. Mulder cites Kaczor here, and so I will quote him in full:

> ... we can grant the intuition that "we" go with our brains so to speak, but still maintain that we are rational animals, albeit in the transplant case radically mutilated animals missing most of our bodies. In other words, if we were to assume that the smallest possible reduction of a human being would be to the size of the upper brain, then if we moved the upper brain, then it would still be a human organism that we moved, albeit a radically impaired organism until implanted in another body whose organs would then take over the functions formerly exercised by the previous body.[8]

Because neither Mulder nor I are assuming that there exists any non-physical component to our identities, I have no problems with the stance that our conscious mind is reducible to a physical component – a functioning cerebral cortex. But the cerebral cortex only matters because of what the cerebral cortex *can do* – sustain our conscious life. If, for whatever reason, we evolved into the kinds of beings whose conscious life originates and is sustained at our left pinky finger, then we'd go where our left pinky finger goes, and Spiridonov would be searching for a pinky finger, rather than a brain, transplant. What makes our upper brain valuable is that it sustains our consciousness – if any other part of our organism did this instead, we'd be focusing on it for this conversation. This shows that what we are really after isn't so much a particular body part, but a body part that performs the function of sustaining our consciousness; *it is our consciousness that matters.*

Suppose, in a clearly science-fiction scenario, that neuroscientists determine that human consciousness is derived solely through three specific neurons in the cerebral cortex and that those three neurons can be removed and transplanted into a wholly new organism and new brain. A person who undergoes this procedure awakens in the new body as if she just woke up from a slumber – she is mentally continuous with herself before her transplant. Could Kaczor (and other animalists) support the claim that a human organism can be reduced to those three neurons? This seems to be stretching any plausible definition of "organism" from my perspective. And, going along with Kaczor (and Mulder) here, suppose I grant that the human organism could just be reduced to a functioning upper brain. In *this* scenario, a human fetus wouldn't have a functioning organism, necessary to create and sustain its particular personal identity, until *that* aspect of its organism, its upper brain, began to exist and function – and that does not occur at conception, or even early pregnancy.

Now clearly Mulder is right when he writes that, in our ordinary language, we don't say "'the person in some way associated with my body has just discovered a pimple on the face with which it is in some way associated.' Rather, we just say 'I have a pimple,' or 'do I have something in my teeth?'" (p. 79). Kaczor also argues that "if we were nothing but our brains, then we never see persons ... we could not normally distinguish one person from another by appearance even if we did see persons. And we never kiss or have been kissed by a person."[9] But this seems to me, again, reaching a bit. No one is denying that human beings are intimately related to their bodies and, because we identify each other visually, of course we will distinguish each other by looking at our organisms. And it is also true that I say "I have a pimple" and not the mouthful Mulder mentions. But in our common language, we also make distinctions between our bodies and our selves, as was evident in Cruzan's and Schiavo's tombstones. When discussing ethical issues for patients in persistent vegetative states, many of my students will say things like: "If I am ever in a permanent coma, then I have already died." All this shows is that our everyday language seems to endorse conflicting metaphysical claims. And if my husband's brain were transplanted into a wholly new body, while I admit it would take some time getting used to, I would still say that it remains my husband who kisses me.

Now, I do not deny that there is some metaphysical baggage that comes with the embodied mind account – it seems like I am committed to saying that there are two substances occupying the space where I currently reside: my organism and my mind. This does seem like I am multiplying substances (though I do not think needlessly), and so not as metaphysically parsimonious as Mulder prefers. Animalism, however, is not immune from thorny metaphysical issues in its own right. Lynn Rudder Baker, for example, argues that Olson's view of animalism is subject to what she calls the "corpse problem." She writes:

> To see that [Olson] has a "corpse problem", ask: On Olson's view, what happens to the organism after death? Does it still exist as a corpse? On the one hand, if Olson says yes, then he must abandon his view that an animal "persists just in case its capacity to direct those vital functions that keep it biologically alive is not disrupted." But this view is central to Olson's entire program. On the other hand, if Olson says no (on pain of undermining his whole view), then what happens to the animal, and where does the corpse come from? I charge Olson is the one who has no answers to the parallel question about corpses.[10]

In other words, if Olson, and other animalists, maintain that human beings cease to exist when the organism ceases functioning, it seems that we have a wholly new substance, a corpse, who has now taken the place of the former substance, the living organism to which I was identical (since I am not identical to this corpse). But that seems odd to contend given that the corpse is clearly biologically continuous with the living organism. I will not devote any more time here to parsing out these metaphysical difficulties for either view; I write this simply to call into doubt Mulder's claim that animalism has less "metaphysical furniture," so to speak, than mentalist accounts of identity.

But suppose we grant that animalism is indeed the way to go when it comes to understanding our personal identity. There is still a case to be made that early embryos (called zygotes, which span from conception to implantation, at about two weeks post-fertilization) are not biologically continuous with our later organism because of the embryos' inherent capacity to twin into two or more distinct embryos. Indeed, early embryos are so versatile that not only can one give rise to identical multiples, but also the reverse of twinning can occur: a process called "chimera," when two zygotes "derived from the independent fertilization of two eggs fuse ... [and] one individual [results] from two fertilization events."[11] Given that the cells in a zygote are totipotent up until the blastocyst stage (meaning that each cell in the zygote can give rise to every single type of human cell), and pluripotent after that (meaning that each cell in the zygote can give rise to every single cell in the human organism, but not to the extra-embryonic tissue), each particular cell is capable of giving rise to a particular embryo up until approximately 14 days after fertilization. The single zygote, thus, can give rise to a multitude of beings, and so the zygote, if this occurs, would not be numerically identical or continuous to the later embryos.

Mulder is aware of this alleged difficulty. His main response here is that "if the embryo 'twinned' prior to gastrulation, it would simply mean that, either we had one individual who effectively died, giving rise to two new individuals, or (what seems the more likely view), that the one individual who had been a person since conception, gave rise to another, quite a bit like itself" (p. 81). But from my perspective, this is not the imperative point about a zygote's capacity to divide into one or more distinct organisms, or to fuse together into a single embryo. Regardless of whether the zygote actually does divide, the point is that they all have the *capacity* to divide, and that this capacity is part of the *essence* of what a zygote *is* given the totipotency of its cells. Since our concern here is the implications for identity, the important point here is that zygotes possess an essential capacity that an individual human organism does not essentially possess. Human beings are *essentially* individuals. Human zygotes are *not essentially* individuals. They cannot, therefore, be identical entities.[12]

Consider another point. At the very onset of fertilization, some of the cells in a zygote will go on to form the embryo proper (which will indeed be biologically continuous with a human organism) and some will form the embryonic auxiliary tissue (for example, the placenta). Given this, neither the embryo nor the extra-embryonic tissue can be identical to the zygote, unless they are identical to each other, which obviously they are not. That is, the whole zygote *does not* become the embryo or the resulting fetus; some parts of the zygote become the embryo and some parts of the zygote become the auxiliary tissue. Since the embryo proper is not identical to this tissue, it cannot be identical to the zygote, since the zygote consists of totipotent cells that have not yet differentiated into what will be the embryo and what will be its protective features. Therefore, as Norman Ford puts it, "it is very difficult to sustain that the human embryo could be a human individual prior to the blastocyst stage when it differentiates into that which will develop into the embryo, fetus, and adult human ... how could the cluster of cells of the early embryo be an actual ontological human individual if it has not yet differentiated into the cells and tissues which will constitute the embryo proper?"[13] A zygote can best be construed as a collection of cells, the "stuff" or material, that will give rise to a single human biological organism (or perhaps more than one), and also to the extra-embryonic tissues. Given this, the embryo, fetus, or later individual doesn't even share the same organism as the zygote. The individual organism, whether a single one or multiple ones, does not begin to exist until the post-segmentation period, when the primitive streak appears and gastrulation begins to occur, at approximately 14 days post-fertilization.

Now, to be sure, this has little relevance for the ethics of abortion. By the time a woman discovers she is pregnant, this 14 day period has passed, and we certainly have an individual human organism growing in her womb. However, whether or not a newly conceived zygote is an individual may indeed be relevant when it comes to other issues. For example, there is debate concerning whether it is permissible to destroy extra-uterine zygotes either for research purposes or simply because they were leftover from successful fertility treatments. If pre-14-day-old zygotes are not yet human individuals, then not even an animalist should hold that we are destroying a nascent human being. Along the same vein, the debate concerning emergency contraception, also known as the "morning-after pill," would vanish if the early embryo were not yet an organism, since, even if the pill were to function as an abortifacient, it wouldn't be destroying an individual human being yet (this latter issue is a topic I will take up toward the end of this chapter).

To be clear, the purpose of this section is not to offer a definitive case against animalism, nor even a definitive case in favor of the embodied mind account of identity. However, I do think that animalism has some formidable issues with which to contend, and my sole concern here is to highlight these difficulties. I am simply not convinced that a human being's personal identity has its genesis at the onset of her biological organism. If we were to grow a fully functioning human organism in a laboratory with all of its parts intact *except* the cerebral cortex, so that it lacks any and all capacity to generate conscious awareness, I would not say that this otherwise functioning human organism has any *personal* identity, and I certainly would not morally equate this functioning human organism with you, or me, or any other human being with the capacity for consciousness. Perhaps creating such a human being would not be, as Mulder puts it, a "sporting thing to do" (p. 81), but for whatever reason it wouldn't be, it's not because we are harming a person in any significant sense of the term. A human being who enters a permanent unconscious state is no longer a moral subject in her own right. We may still care for the remaining body out of respect for the loved ones left behind, or for the person she used to be (depending on her wishes), but once consciousness is irrevocably eradicated, there is no longer anyone there who can be harmed or benefitted. As Jeff McMahan puts it, what distinguishes a some*thing* from a some*one* is the capacity for a biographical, conscious, life. All human some*ones*, I contend, are definitely moral subjects (which includes post-conscious fetuses, infants, the senile, and humans of all races, creeds, and religions). I am not convinced some*things*, even human ones, are.

A discussion about (metaphysical and moral) person essentialism

Traditionally, philosophers have defined the term "person" in two different ways. A metaphysical person is a being that possesses robust cognitive capacities: self-consciousness, rationality, moral agency, amongst others. A moral person, on the other hand, is any being that has moral status and moral rights, and also legal rights that protect that moral status, including a right to life. My main criticism of Warren, Tooley, and Singer is that they, essentially, almost collapse these distinctions, or that they hold that being a metaphysical person is necessary for being a moral person (at least when it comes to having a right to life). I have already argued that this is morally problematic, as post-conscious fetuses, infants, young toddlers, the very elderly and senile, and the severely mentally disabled do not meet the metaphysical definition of personhood, but I am not willing to deny them moral personhood as a result. At the same time, there are many non-human animals who approximate metaphysical personhood and are routinely denied moral personhood in our society. An adult gorilla more closely approximates a metaphysical person than a human infant, yet the latter is given the status of moral personhood while the former typically is not. If we are to be consistent that metaphysical personhood should be sufficient (though not necessary) for moral personhood, then any being that possesses some of the cognitive traits of metaphysical personhood should be treated at the appropriate level of moral personhood (meaning that a gorilla has some moral status, but not necessarily equal to that of an adult human being).

From an identity perspective, essential properties are any properties that, were I to lose them, would result in my personal identity being compromised. This is different from what philosophers call accidental properties – properties that I possess, but whose loss or change would have no effect on my identity at all. The fact that my hair is brown is an accidental property of mine; I can easily change my hair color and I would still be me. The same goes for my eye color, or weight, or skin complexion. Whatever counts as an essential property depends largely on one's view of personal identity. For someone like me, who endorses the embodied mind account of identity, the capacity for conscious awareness is an essential property – without that capacity, my identity would be lost. Because I also believe that the same properties that underlie my personal identity also make me a moral person, I also believe I am essentially a moral person – at all stages of my existence, I believe I have moral status. However, I do not think I am essentially a metaphysical person because I believe that my identity persists even if I lack the robust mental capacities that comprise a metaphysical person – I would still be me even in the advanced stages of dementia, and I was once a baby who lacked all such robust cognitive capacities. I think it is important, therefore, when discussing person essentialism, to distinguish between the two (and this is not often done): one can believe in moral-person essentialism without believing in metaphysical-person essentialism. Mulder and I are both moral-person essentialists: we believe that moral personhood begins for a human being *whenever* that human being comes into existence (though we disagree when that is).

By invoking Kaczor's endowment view of personhood, Mulder seems to be endorsing not just animalism, but also metaphysical-person essentialism, from which moral-person essentialism seems to follow, according to the argument. Here is what Kaczor says that makes me think he endorses metaphysical-person essentialism:

> Many individual human beings do not function rationally, including the human embryo, the human fetus, the senile, the sleeping, the temporarily comatose, and the mentally handicapped ... However, every single human being is nevertheless properly described as a rational being. Not a *potentially* rational being, but a currently existing *actual* rational being ... obviously, not all human beings function rationally at any given time, but every human being is a member of a kind of being (namely human beings) who can, in certain circumstances, perform actions specifically defined as rational ... to say that the

human being in utero is not a rational being because he or she is not functioning rationally makes as much sense as saying that a human being is not gendered male or female unless in the act of successfully reproducing.[14]

Here, Kaczor is specifically talking about rational, cognitive capacities – the capacities that make anyone who has them a metaphysical person. He acknowledges that not all human beings function at this capacity at all times, but this is irrelevant to him. All human beings are members of a kind of species that is biologically geared toward possessing these cognitive capacities, and that, he argues, *is sufficient for ascribing the status of metaphysical person onto all stages of that being's existence.* This is true even if the human being in question is so cognitively disabled that they cannot ever function as a rational animal – they nevertheless remain part of our species, of our kind. According to Kaczor, to say they are not persons because they do not possess the cognitive capacities of persons is like saying that reproductive organs that are incapable of functioning in a reproductive manner (say because of infertility) have any less claim to being reproductive organs. And because all human beings are metaphysical persons regardless of their actual capacities, they are moral persons as well: "the endowment account holds that each human being has inherent, moral worth simply by virtue of the kind of being it is."[15] Given his reliance on Kaczor here, I will assume that Mulder holds all these views as well.

This conjunction of animalism with metaphysical- and moral-person essentialism is common amongst pro-life philosophers' arguments. Francis Beckwith proffers a similar argument, but he calls it the "substance view of persons":

> According to the substance view, a human being is intrinsically valuable because of the sort of thing it is and the human being remains that sort of thing as long as it exists. What sort of thing is it? The human being is a particular type of substance – a rational moral agent – that remains identical to itself as long as it exists, even if it is not presently exhibiting the functions, behaving in ways, or currently able to immediately exercise these activities that we typically attribute to active and mature rational moral agents.[16]

Again, the argument appears to be something like this: human beings exhibit the cognitive capacity of persons throughout most of their existence because they are biologically geared to do so. Therefore, they should be considered metaphysical persons throughout *all* stages of their existence because at all times they are members of a species-kind that possesses that biological constitution. And, because all metaphysical persons are also moral persons, humans are also moral persons throughout the entirety of their existence (from conception onwards, given animalism).

But here's the rub: granted that mostly all (healthy) human beings attain metaphysical personhood, and that being a metaphysical person encompasses the vast majority of their lives (from childhood to old age), but why should this mean that we should *also* regard them as metaphysical persons during those stages of existence when they are *not* capable of these cognitive capacities (like embryo-hood, or in a persistent vegetative state)? Kaczor's defense of the "endowment view" appears to place a lot of stock on the genetic basis that underlies our capacities.[17] Mulder also highlights Robert George and Christopher Tollefsen's claim that a human person's cognitive capacities are "already rooted [from conception] in the nature of the being that possesses them" (p. 80). Because our biological constitution is what causes our metaphysical personhood, and because we always possess that biological constitution throughout all our existence, we are always metaphysical persons. But this is a highly contentious premise (as I said in Chapter1, I have never been clear how a biological fact, species membership, translates into a moral fact). If it is *rational capacities* that ultimately matter, why not withhold metaphysical personhood until those rational capacities actually manifest themselves? Why should possessing the biological constitution that underlies those rational capacities be sufficient in cases where there is no actual rationality? I don't see where Mulder (or Kaczor or Beckwith) defends this very important aspect of his argument; rather the substance view/endowment view just seems to assert, rather than argue, that being a metaphysical person at one stage of your life ought to translate to being considered a metaphysical person at all stages of your life because at all points in your existence, you possess the same biological constitution that generates metaphysical personhood. Philosopher Nathan Nobis offers just this criticism, and essentially charges that these views beg the question by assuming the key premise they should be defending:

> One could assert that at all times and stages biologically human organisms are prima facie wrong to kill or that they are "essentially" wrong to kill or that they essentially have the properties that make them so. But ... we are seeking a reason to accept [this view]. *The Substance View does not provide such a reason since it appears that it just is that view.*[18]

To be fair, Kaczor's main concern seems to be that by denying metaphysical personhood, we also deny moral personhood, and he is quite right that denying human beings moral status has an ugly past that we should strive never to relive. It is also true that making metaphysical personhood a prerequisite for moral personhood, and also holding that we are only metaphysical persons throughout some of our lives, leaves out not only embryos and fetuses, but infants, the disabled, the senile; as I pointed out in Chapter 1 this is certainly something we must avoid. But we can get around this by focusing on *other* properties as being necessary and sufficient for moral status, as I did by arguing in favor of sentience and consciousness being those properties, and this covers mostly every single human being regardless of race, ethnicity, disability, and mental impairment (and many non-human beings as well). Yes, it leaves out zygotes, embryos, early fetuses, and humans in persistent vegetative states, but we can offer an argument as to why it is appropriate to leave out such beings (because a lack of a phenomenological life means such beings lack the capacity for being harmed or benefitted). This also does not necessarily mean these kinds of humans can be treated in an undignified manner, since we can argue that there are other reasons to treat them with respect that aren't dependent on them possessing intrinsic moral status.

Philosopher David DeGrazia is also an animalist in terms of identity; he writes: "we human persons – and, for that matter, human beings who are not persons – are essentially human *animals*, members of the species *Homo sapiens*."[19] However, DeGrazia also holds that the term "person" should not be understood "as a basic kind," but rather "as comprising a set of capacities that things of different basic kinds might achieve. On this view, personhood represents merely a phase of our existence."[20] According to DeGrazia, metaphysical personhood constitutes a segment in our existence, for most of us our longest phase, but it is not part of what we essentially are. And, moreover, there is no justification in applying metaphysical personhood retroactively – just because you are a metaphysical person now does not mean you always were.

One important reason why I think it behooves Mulder to address this kind of disagreement amongst animalists when it comes to person essentialism is because it deeply influences one's stance on abortion. DeGrazia does not associate the commencement of a being's personal identity with a simultaneous commencement of an interest in continued existence, at least not an interest strong enough to justify a right to life. While DeGrazia does argue that a human being begins to exist in an embryonic stage (though not at the zygotic stage – DeGrazia agrees with the view that a zygote's capacity to divide and form new zygotes precludes it from being an individual human organism), when the organism first begins to exist, this does not mean that it possesses a right to life at that time. DeGrazia specifically responds to Don Marquis' argument, since they both hold to the same theory of identity, but have different conclusions about the moral permissibility of abortion. DeGrazia argues that the loss of life a fetus suffers as a result of an abortion is not that great of a loss because the fetus is simply too mentally removed from its future to have a real stake in it. Note, it's not that he denies that the fetus loses its life and future in an abortion, he just denies that this loss is a significant one for a being that has no mental connections at all with that future life. He writes:

> The degree of psychological unity in a life, or over a stretch of a time, is a function of the richness, complexity, and coherence of the mental life that is carried forward over time. When the psychological unity that would have bound an individual at the time of death to himself in the future, had he lived, is weak, death matters less prudentially – for that individual – at that time.[21]

In other words, the actual stake you have in your continued life and future is contingent upon the degree of mental connections you have with that continued life and that future. Death means nothing for a pre-conscious fetus because there is no mental connection with that fetus and its future life. Death means a little more for a post-conscious fetus, but still not much more, since the mental connections that exist are still relatively weak ones. For an infant, death matters a bit more for him because the mental connections with his future self are slightly more robust than from when he was a fetus, but still, it is not equivalent to the loss of life suffered by a metaphysical person: "the harm of death of any infant seems intermediate between the harm of death for a person and the loss of value of someone's never coming into existence."[22] When it comes to abortion, then:

> the killing of presentient fetuses [does kill] a human organism with a valuable future. This is what is right about [Marquis' argument]. *But the utter lack of psychological unity between the presentient fetus and the later minded being it could become justifies a radical discounting of the harm of the fetus' death* ... if the presentient fetus has an interest in remaining alive, it would be too weak to ground a right to life, so the interests of the pregnant woman or her family could easily justify abortion.[23]

Metaphysical persons have the greatest stake in their continued existence, and so suffer the most from their deaths, according to DeGrazia, because their robust day-to-day mental connections, and their mental connections to their future selves, ground a much stronger interest in realizing that future. When it comes to moral personhood, in particular the right to life, metaphysical persons have the strongest claim to that right. Because DeGrazia rejects person essentialism, we are only metaphysical persons when we actually possess those cognitive capacities and robust mental connections with our day-to-day, and future, selves. Our biological constitution alone is insufficient for rendering one a metaphysical or moral person. In that sense, DeGrazia's view more closely approximates the "performance view" of personhood, but for reasons that are different than Boonin's.

I for one, reject DeGrazia's claim that the strength of an individual's interest in his life and future is positively correlated with the extent to which he is psychologically connected to that life and future because I believe his position leads to odd consequences. As I mentioned in Chapter 1, robust cognitive capacities may indeed be needed to *take* an interest in your future life, but not to actually *have* an interest in your future life. Because of my father's dementia, he had a limited mental connection to his day-to-day and future life. DeGrazia's position would lead to the conclusion that his interest in his continued life is correspondingly weak (as would be any means taken to sustain that life, e.g., his insulin shots). I think this is mistaken. Suppose I had a vision where I saw myself as a 95-year-old woman suffering from advanced dementia, neglect, and abandonment. No one would fault me for being horrified that this is how my life would end. It matters not to me that my psychological connection to myself at that point will be extremely weak. Indeed, this is *part* of the tragedy of dementia, not an aspect that mitigates its harm. It is still *my* life that ends horribly. Similarly, say I discovered that I had a trust fund set up when I was a baby that would have sustained me financially for the rest of my life, but that one of my guardians decided to take all the money and gamble it away. It would be a poor excuse for him to defend his actions by saying: "Look, you really have no reason to be upset. That happened when you were a baby, and you are so psychologically removed from yourself at that point in your life that you have a negligibly weak interest in anything that happened back then." This, also, seems absurd.

For these reasons, I reject DeGrazia's contention that the strength of my interest in my life at any point in time is positively correlated to the strength of my psychological capacities. If it can properly be said to be *my* life and future, then I have an interest in realizing that life and future, and to deprive me of that opportunity harms me as much as it harms anyone. I suspect Mulder would agree with me on this point as well, still because of our differing views on identity we would come to different conclusions on abortion (for me, the interest in continued existence begins around mid-gestation, when the fetus gains the capacity for conscious awareness; for Mulder, it begins at conception). But, because he and DeGrazia hold the same view on identity, it would strengthen Mulder's argument to address DeGrazia on this issue and argue why, if you are an animalist, you should hold that a human being's interest in its continued existence begins fairly early in a fetus' life (at least two weeks after fertilization, if you believe a zygote's potential to divide compromises its individuality, but even earlier, at conception, if you don't believe this, as Mulder does not).

I am actually quite sympathetic to Mulder's claim that vulnerable human beings in our society are the ones in most need of our protection and care. Where Mulder and I disagree, at least for now, is when that vulnerable human being comes into existence, which is a metaphysical disagreement about identity, not a moral disagreement about denying moral status and protection to existing human beings. I want to stress this because I want the reader to see that our disagreement here has its roots in philosophical conversation not often taken up in our society. But having these disagreements do not render us bad people; it just illustrates the importance of philosophical education and conversation when it comes to policy and ethical discussions. We often neglect philosophy in our society, dismissing it as inconsequential to the "real world." Nothing could be further from the truth.

II. Thomson's argument

What I appreciated the most about Mulder's response to Thomson is that I often found myself nodding along with a lot of what he wrote, and while that may have sent many people into a panic (as in: oh no! I actually agree with my opponent), philosophy has taught me to take those experiences as opportunities for growth. Mulder's argument challenged me to think deeply about my allegiance to Thomson's argument, and I am grateful for that challenge.

Mulder spends some time discussing the "ownership" language taken up by Thomson in her defense of abortion. As I have argued in Chapter 1, I also reject such a language because I think the relationship between a woman and her body is deeper, more significant, and far more affecting than whatever relationship she may have with anything that can constitute her property. While I am not an animalist, I cannot deny that, no matter how we flesh out the exact relationship between a human being's mind and her body, what happens to our bodies has a profound effect on what happens to our minds, and therefore what happens to us. A fetus does not occupy a body as a person occupies a room for rent – a fetus occupies a *person*. Both Mulder and I criticize Catriona Mackenzie's argument (and, by extension, Soran Reader's rather concerning arguments) in favor of viewing abortion as a right to fetal destruction rather than a woman's right to remove aid from the fetus; like Thomson and Christine Overall, I also view a right to an abortion as a right to "evacuate" the fetus from a woman's body, not a right to kill it. If a fetus survives an abortion for whatever reason, that fetus should be treated as any other patient in need of care. The intimate embodiment of pregnancy, which I do believe underscores the permissibility of the abortion right, does not extend to when the fetus can survive outside the womb.

Mulder argues against Reader's contention that a fetus that results from rape can be permissibly aborted because such a fetus "should not exist." I must admit that I had never considered the counter-argument he proffers:

> Rape is a tremendously grievous harm, but if the fact that it should never have occurred is what gives the resulting fetus its "negative moral status" then all regrettable acts giving rise to pregnancy should confer such "negative moral status," but this seems implausible. Second, consider the grown adult, adopted earlier, whose conception as a result of rape is unknown to her, because of privacy policies in adoption. If she had "negative moral status" while in utero, when did she acquire the "positive moral status" that presumably she now enjoys? Either she still does not have it (which seems implausible), she acquired it at some point in utero, or she acquired it at birth or later. Suppose she acquired it in utero. Then Reader's discussion of moral status hangs on the question of intra-uterine personhood, but she clearly rejects this entailment. Suppose instead that our adult conceived through rape acquired positive moral status at birth or later. If so, Reader will need a threshold for when someone makes the transition from (not merely indifferent but) *negative* moral status to *positive* moral status, and it's not clear what would do this if not personhood criteria.
>
> (p. 90)

I can't see where Mulder goes wrong here. In general, I am wary of assigning a negative moral status to any being solely based on the circumstances of its genesis. There are many possible regrettable circumstances, outside of rape, where a fetus could have been conceived, and yet this alone seems like a very weak reason to deny it moral status. One could argue that a fetus conceived as a result of infidelity "should not exist" because the circumstances of its creation were regrettable – yet this alone would be a poor reason to deny a fetus moral status.

But Mulder's conversation here serves a greater purpose – to come right out and say something I always tell my students when we discuss the ethics of abortion: if you really believe that a fetus is a *full-fledged* member of the moral community – that it has the *same* moral rights and status as any other human being – then there is no justification for permitting abortion in cases of rape (or incest), even though this seems to be one of the few exceptions pro-lifers constantly make to the permissibility of abortion. In 2012, then vice-presidential nominee Paul Ryan came under fire for saying, in regards to his opposition of legal abortion even in cases of rape, that "the method of conception doesn't change the definition of life." But even back then, I found this criticism surprising – it is exactly what logically follows from any pro-life position that assumes the equal humanity of the fetus from the time of conception. I present the following as an inconsistent triune to my students.

1. From the time of conception, a fetus has equal moral status to any living person.
2. It is impermissible to kill an infant or a child were it to be discovered after his/her birth that (s)he was conceived via rape.
3. It is permissible to kill a fetus if it is a product of rape.

Many pro-lifers want to hold to all three of these principles – they cannot consistently do so. One of them has to be given up, and I do hope that no one wants to give up two. Therefore, either one or three has to go. If, as a pro-life advocate, you are committed to 1, then you should reject 3, as Mulder does.

Thomson herself acknowledges this; she notes that the violinist example may be more analogous to pregnancy due to rape as opposed to pregnancy due to consensual sex, yet she notes that, from a pro-life perspective, this difference should not be morally significant:

> Can those who oppose abortion on the ground I mentioned make an exception for pregnancy due to rape? Certainly. They can say that persons have a right to life only if they didn't come into existence because of rape; or they can say that all persons have a right to life, but that some have less of a right to life than others, in particular, that those who came into existence because of rape have less. But these statements have a rather unpleasant sound. Surely the question of whether you have a right to life at all, or how much of it you have, shouldn't turn on the question of whether or not you are the product of rape.[24]

On this point Thomson agrees with many pro-life philosophers. In addition to Mulder, who writes that "if the fetus's rights extend to a right to be given the care it needs for survival, then it merits such care in virtue of what it is or it does not merit such care at all … the properties the fetus has in virtue of which we accord it moral treatment are not properties that it loses or gains based on how it came into existence" (p. 91), Kaczor notes that "the circumstances of one's conception, even if conception takes place because of rape, do not seem to make any difference in terms of personhood."[25] Francis Beckwith likewise argues (with a particularly passive-aggressive statement against working women) that "we must not forget that the same innocent unborn entity that the career-oriented woman will abort to avoid interference with a job promotion is biologically and morally indistinguishable from the unborn entity that results from an act of rape or incest."[26] In other words, if the main reason fueling someone's pro-life stance is because they believe that the fetus is fully a moral person from conception onwards, there is no justification for not extending that moral status onto a fetus generated from rape. As Mulder rightly points out, the origins of your genesis should not translate into having a "negative moral status." This is something I impress upon my students: if you are pro-life, then this should be your conclusion. If you are horrified by this conclusion (and many of my students are), then you have to go back and re-think your commitment to the premise that the fetus is a full-fledged member of the moral community.

As a consequence of bringing this up in my class, the conversation typically shifts to what a woman allegedly "owes" a fetus in an effort to maintain that rape provides a justification for abortion even though the fetus is a full human person. According to many of my pro-life students, a woman who conceives due to rape owes little, if anything, to the fetus because she did nothing to contribute to its creation. It appears to me, then, that it boils down to, essentially, making women "pay" for the results of their sexual choices. (Note, I am not saying that this is what Mulder is doing – Mulder, like Kaczor and Beckwith, clearly is pro-life because he sincerely believes in the fetus' equal humanity. He is, therefore, being consistent when he holds the view that abortions even in cases of rape are impermissible. This is meant to target pro-lifers who want to make such exceptions.) This is perhaps a crude version of the "Responsibility Objection," and in Chapter 1, I offered some reasons why I do not think the objection works. Yet it does not matter for the purposes of responding to Mulder, for he honestly admits that "the Responsibility Objection is simply irrelevant to the abortion question" (p. 91). His focus remains on the fetus' humanity, and what is owed to the fetus in virtue of that humanity, regardless of how it began to exist.

So now, let me focus precisely on Mulder's treatment of Thomson's argument and the *McFall v. Shimp* case, both of which played a prominent role in my defense of the pro-choice perspective. In reference to the latter, Mulder offers a peculiar rebuttal of Judge Flaherty's arguments in opposition to forcing Shimp to donate bone marrow to McFall. Mulder accuses Flaherty of being hyperbolic when he states that he cannot, essentially, forcibly tie Shimp down and extract his bone marrow.

> It is fallacious to suggest that our only two options are strapping Shimp down for this procedure and having the law turn a blind eye. Rather, we could regard Shimp's refusal as criminally callous. Thus, we *can* imagine where a line might be drawn. After all, nations have drawn it frequently, for instance by insisting upon compulsory military service (indeed, some developed nations have an active program), but imposing sanctions on those who refuse. My point here is not to argue for one punishment or another, but rather to say that the law need not take a completely "hands-off" attitude toward such callousness.
>
> (p. 93)

But in the context of this case, there was no false dichotomy – the judges were literally being asked to decide whether Shimp could be forced to give his bone marrow over to McFall to save the latter's life. The case was not about whether someone who could have saved someone else's life should be held legally liable in any way for refusing to do so – this case was clearly about a clash between one person's right to life and another person's right to bodily integrity. To have upheld McFall's right to life over Shimp's right to his body would have resulted in nothing short of "strapping Shimp down for this procedure."

When it comes to abortion, Mulder argues that there is an important difference between Shimp's refusal to donate bone marrow and a woman's decision to abort, in that the former just "withholds" a life-saving resource, whereas a woman who aborts is "acting directly against the bodily integrity of the fetus" (p. 94). As I mentioned in Chapter 1, I am not convinced that there is a significant moral difference between actions of commission and omission, when both clearly and knowingly lead to the same result. Consequently, I am not convinced that Shimp's action does not amount to a kind of "direct action" against McFall. If there is someone on the floor having a heart attack and reaching out to me for help, stepping over him and walking away seems to me to be a direct action of some sort against him.

Moreover, I am not convinced that pro-lifers are as dedicated to this distinction as Mulder indicates. As I noted in Chapter 1, if we could devise a way to abort using more "passive" means, for example by removing the pre-viable fetus fully intact and just placing it on a table to die, without taking any further direct action to injure it, I doubt that this alone will all of a sudden render abortion permissible from a pro-life standpoint. I also think Mulder's use of the doctrine of double effect to draw a distinction between Shimp's action and abortion could be problematic, since adjudicating between a permissible and impermissible action using double effect seems to largely come down to the agent's intentions. Mulder doesn't intend to make his son scream and whimper when he brushes his hair, even though he knows his son will do so, because his real intention is to make sure his son's hair is nice and clean. This renders his action a very different kind than if someone were meaning to deliberately torture his son by pulling his hair. But couldn't the doctrine of double effect easily apply to abortion? If a woman is experiencing severe pre-eclampsia, suffering from blood pressure so high that she will likely experience a stroke and die, and the only way to save her is to end the pregnancy, one could argue that the intent isn't to kill the fetus, but to save the woman. A woman who aborts to avoid further trauma after a sexual assault could argue that the intent isn't to kill the fetus, but to end her pain. And a woman who aborts in order to continue her education or her career path could argue that her real intention is to resume the pathway her life was on, and killing the fetus is simply a foreseeable, but unintended, consequence. Mulder may likely claim that this latter example (and maybe the other two as well) stretches the boundaries of the doctrine of double effect into absurdity, but, as he acknowledged, the doctrine of double effect is a controversial principle that is not too expanded upon in these pages.

But here is where Mulder's argument takes a surprising, and admittedly bold, turn. He asks us to challenge the most basic premise that is assumed by Thomson and by the judges who decided *McFall v. Shimp*. Thomson appears to take for granted that *of course* you are not obligated to consent to using your body to sustain the violinist, and the judges argued that *of course* Shimp could not be obligated to donate bone marrow for McFall (and, by analogy, that a woman cannot be obligated to sustain the life of the fetus). But perhaps we shouldn't be so quick to draw this conclusion. Mulder argues that perhaps we *do* have a moral obligation, one that can be legally enforced, to sustain the life of another human being via the use of our body, especially in cases (as is the case in the violinist example and pregnancy), where the vulnerable human being has no other recourse to preserve her life. Mulder lists the following conditions that, if they were met, may lead to this conclusion:

1. The relationship of "being plugged into" the violinist has already been established (or, for discussing abortion, that the women were already pregnant).
2. Terminating that relationship results in the death of a person.
3. You are the *only* person who can provide that aid.
4. Your health would be safeguarded by medical professionals without nefarious intentions.

Let's discuss these conditions in turn, particularly in reference to abortion, which is the real reason we are here. The only one I will not discuss is 2, since no one is contesting that abortion leads to fetal death.

Because Shimp fails to meet condition 3 – in that another bone marrow donor *could* have been found, meaning the Shimp was not the *only* person who could have saved McFall's life – Mulder maintains that, while "Shimp's abstention is bad even from the standpoint of just law, I reject its compulsion by force" (p. 94). According to Mulder, if you fail to meet condition 3, if someone else *could* sustain the life of the vulnerable person in question (regardless of whether or not they actually *do*), then you cannot be forced to do it yourself. So we must ask ourselves what the meaning of "could" is in this context. For all practical purposes, no one else could have provided McFall the bone marrow he needed to survive. Bone marrow matching is notoriously difficult and time consuming. Given that McFall had very little time left (indeed, he died two weeks after the case was decided), for all intents and purposes, there really was not anyone else who *could* have saved McFall's life – practically speaking, Shimp *was* the only person who could have provided that aid. Perhaps what Mulder means is that you are let off the hook, so to speak, in your obligation to provide aid to someone else simply if it is *possible* for someone else to assume that charge. But now we have to be clear on what we mean by "possible."

It is certainly *theoretically* possible that someone else may have been a match for McFall. If the theoretical possibility of there being another donor is sufficient to release Shimp from his obligation to donate his bone marrow – in that he could not be legally compelled to do so – then this presents a problem for Mulder's argument when it comes to a pregnant woman's alleged obligation to sustain a fetus, since we can bring in what is theoretically possible in the science of pregnancy and gestation. In 2016, a 26-year-old woman at the Cleveland Clinic was the recipient of the first ever successful uterine transplant in the United States.[27] In 2014, a woman in Sweden gave birth to a baby boy two years after her uterine transplant.[28] Some medical professionals are hopeful that one day transgender women may be able to experience pregnancy through uterine transplants.[29] As of yet, there has not been a case of a pregnant uterus being successfully transplanted into a different woman, but medical technology can, and has, achieved marvelous things. Moreover, there have been advancements in the field of ectogenesis – gestation outside the womb – so that one day it may be possible for a woman to extract an embryo or fetus from her body and have it be gestated in a fully artificial environment. Suppose that, one day, these scenarios were to come into fruition, making it theoretically possible for another woman, other than the biological mother, to gestate an unwanted fetus. Would this absolve the biological mother from her alleged moral obligations to the fetus, so that she can no longer be legally compelled, from Mulder's perspective, to remain pregnant? In other words, it seems to follow from Mulder's argument that if, theoretically, another woman could gestate this particular fetus, then the woman who is actually pregnant is under no moral obligation to continue to sustain that fetus. She may then permissibly abort after all.

But let's shift away from the realm of mere possibility to a world of practicality. Practically speaking, given the particulars of the case, no one except Shimp could have saved McFall, just as, practically speaking, no one other than a particular pregnant woman could gestate a particular fetus. But if practical possibility is insufficient for rendering Shimp a candidate for legal compulsion in giving up his body to save another person, it should be equally insufficient for a pregnant woman.

Now perhaps Mulder could argue that pregnant women fail to meet condition 1, whereas Shimp clearly meets it – Shimp was never "plugged into" McFall, so to speak, whereas a pregnant woman already is "plugged into" the fetus. As it stands, however, I am failing to see the relevance of this condition. Consider this: if condition 1 (and 3) must be met in order for any human being to be a candidate for forcible intrusion of their body to save another human being, then Mulder loses any possible grounds for arguing that surplus embryos in fertility clinics should be implanted in women, and allowed the chance of gestation and birth. After all, when it comes to surplus embryos, no particular woman has yet been "plugged into" any particular embryo, and for any given extra-uterine embryo, there are many women who could choose to be its gestational mother. Would Mulder assent to the conclusion that these embryos may be permissibly destroyed, even though they are fully-fledged persons, according to his arguments? Why is the fact that no one has started aiding a person who is dying sufficient reason for arguing that no one is required to start that aid? Mulder needs to provide a better defense of condition 1 here – why may forcible bodily intrusion to save another person be compelled when the bodily relationship has already commenced, but it may not be equally compelled in order to begin the life-saving intrusion in the first place?

But it is condition 4 that I think is the one most worthy of discussion, because it is here where the crux of my pro-choice argument lies. Mulder admits that, if I had reason not to trust the intentions and qualifications of the medical professionals who are treating me "your unplugging may be fully justified." But there's the rub – it's not about being unable to trust the medical professionals who are caring for you as a pregnant woman, it's that pregnancy *itself* is an intrinsically precarious physical state of affairs. As I detailed in Chapter 1, almost all pregnancies result in physical sacrifices of varying degrees, and even if a woman is being meticulously cared for during her pregnancy, things can go horrible awry in even the best situations. And even if nothing goes horribly wrong – the adverse effects of pregnancy can be lasting, or permanent. I survived two pregnancies with two beautiful healthy children, but I still had to undergo invasive abdominal surgery in order to have them (where my chances of profuse bleeding increased). I now have permanent chronic back issues because of my first pregnancy, and an increased chance of becoming a type two diabetic because of my second pregnancy. Condition 4, therefore, can never really be met – for a woman's health can never be fully safeguarded in pregnancy. And that's a chance many women embrace in order to have their babies – but they do so *willfully*, because no one should be able to make that decision about their bodies and health but them.

Mulder cites Kaczor's thought experiment where he asks us to imagine that the violinist, being fully conscious of who he is plugged into, wishes instead to be plugged into someone else, but that doing so would result in *your* death instead. Because it would be wrong, Kaczor argues, for the violinist to unplug himself from you, costing you your life, it is equally impermissible for you to unplug yourself from the violinist (and therefore, by analogy, it is equally impermissible for a woman to "unplug" herself from her fetus). Kaczor writes:

> let's consider the scenario from the violinist's perspective. It is true that you didn't choose to be hooked up to him, but it is equally true that he didn't choose to be hooked up to you. Let's imagine that the violinist does not like being hooked up to you. Suppose further that he has spotted another person, who also could support him, a person he finds extremely attractive and charming. In ways too numerous to list, he finds her exciting to be near and, frankly, he has grown weary of being plugged into you … would it be morally permissible for him to detach himself from you, if the only way to do so would involve your death? After all, if *you* may unplug yourself from the violinist, causing his death, then he should be able to unplug himself from you, causing your death.[30]

Let's unpack this example a bit. Kaczor assumes a parity in circumstance here between a violinist wanting to unplug himself from you for clearly superficial reasons and a woman wanting to "unplug" herself from the fetus, but this example simply fails to appreciate the physically and psychologically precarious nature of pregnancy. Is the violinist's connection to my body potentially dangerous to him in some way? Does it intrude in his everyday activities? Can it possibly have permanent effects on his health? Will the unplugging process at the end of my recovery period entail an extremely painful experience for him, possibly leading to invasive surgery, that may result in heavy bleeding, or an injury to his genitals? If someone told the violinist that being "hooked up" to me may mean taking all these chances, as much as I would wish that he would *voluntarily* choose to stay "hooked up" to me, I would defend his right to make that decision for himself, as much as I would defend an individual's right to choose for herself whether she will donate her bone marrow or blood if I needed it for my life to be saved (and if in a fit of panic I somehow force the violinist to stay hooked up to me, I would never say it is because he had an obligation to do so, or because my right to life warrants his submission).

But Kaczor's example has a tacit implication that I have found present in many pro-life advocates' arguments (though not Mulder's in his chapter), and it's one that I think necessitates a response. Many of my students argue that, unless a woman's life is at stake (or in the cases of rape or incest, as abovementioned), any other abortion is an act of pure "convenience" and superficiality. Kaczor's example (perhaps unwittingly) enforces this stereotype. Women do not willy-nilly unplug themselves from one fetus because they "prefer" to be "hooked up" to another fetus, or because they find another fetus more attractive or charming; to compel women to stay "hooked up" to a fetus is not a matter of frustrating some extremely superficial preferences. As we will see in Chapter 5, the reasons women choose abortions are many and various, but the vast majority of reasons reflect some very legitimate concerns. Yes, there are indeed women who abort for reasons that can be described as superficial. One woman I know aborted a fetus because she had a sexual affair with an African-American man and didn't want to be "saddled with a mixed baby." No doubt that was a horribly racist sentiment, and a poor reason to take a nascent human life. But we are not here to judge the reasons women have abortion (that is a whole other conversation).

The reason the violinist chooses to unplug himself from me (or me from him) has little bearing on whether he has a right to do so, and this applies equally to pregnancy and a woman's right to abort. There are many women who choose abortion because the pregnancy has compromised their health in significant ways (for example, because they are suffering from pre-eclampsia), but I will concede that these are probably not the majority of cases. Rather, if asked why they are seeking abortions, women usually refer to some undesirable aspect of life after the birth of the infant. Steven Ross summarizes the reason most women seek abortions as follows:

> If upon entering a clinic women were told, "We can take the fetus out your womb without any harm to you or it, keep it alive elsewhere for nine months,

and then see it placed in a good home," many would, understandably, be quite unsatisfied. What they want is not to be saved from the "inconvenience of pregnancy" or "the task of raising a certain (existing) child"; what they want is *not to be parents*, that is, they do not want there to *be* a child they fail or succeed in raising … They cannot be satisfied *unless* the fetus is killed; nothing else will do.[31]

Ross is right that women typically seek abortions in order to avoid the existence of a child whom they later have to raise unprepared or hand over for others to raise. However, there is a conceptual distinction between what interest a particular right is meant to protect and how the right ends up being used in practice. Just because some, or even most, women may *use* the right to an abortion as a mechanism to relieve themselves from the future duties of parenthood (and even in the superficial ways Kaczor implies in his example), this does not entail that this is the purpose of the abortion right. Consider, once again, the *McFall v. Shimp* case. Suppose that the *reason* Shimp denied McFall bone marrow is because he always wanted to see McFall die a painful death, and his illness provided Shimp with the golden opportunity to see this occur. Here, Shimp invokes his right to bodily autonomy as a mechanism to ensure McFall's death, but whatever the reasons he had for choosing how he did, this in no way mitigates his right to choose whether he wants to use his body in this way – he still cannot be forced to donate bodily fluids to save someone else, regardless of *why* is he choosing to exercise his right in this way.

In the end, the upshot of Mulder's argument against Thomsonian-like defenses of abortion is to call into doubt the alleged obviousness that you do not have to stay "hooked up" to the violinist (and, by extension, that a woman does not have to stay "hooked up" to the fetus). On the contrary, Mulder argues, perhaps it is the case that "when people's needs are sufficiently grave and unique, others who can supply these needs are sometimes required to do so … if fetuses are persons (and I have argued that they are) then they might very well have a claim on the protection of society and, perhaps, those members of it who are uniquely poised to offer this protection" (p. 95). And this is the point that most gave me pause, because, *prima facie*, I don't disagree with him here. I *do* believe that some people's needs are so vital that they morally require other people to "step up to the plate," so to speak, to see that those needs are met. For example, I agree with Peter Singer in his article "Famine, Affluence, and Morality" that those of us with money to spend on luxury items have a moral obligation to re-direct that money to help others attain necessities like food, water, and basic medical treatment.[32] In my personal and political life, I favor a social welfare state that provides for its citizens a basic standard of living, so that no one dies from homelessness, hunger, thirst, or lack of medical care. I have discussed this at length elsewhere, where I concede that there are indeed positive rights – a right to be provided with something, which, in turn, creates an obligation for others to provide that thing – especially when that right involves protecting your most basic interests.[33] And here is where Mulder's point most challenged me: how can I be in favor of positive rights for human beings in order to secure their most basic welfare, but I do not grant human embryos and fetuses (who we are assuming are persons for the sake of argument) the positive right to be gestated by the woman, when it is the *only* thing they need for survival? Isn't this gravely inconsistent on my part?

After a long time of contemplating this question, the answer I came up with is simply that there are limits to all rights, including positive ones, and that one of those limits has to be that whatever your positive rights are, they cannot entail subjugating another human being and treating *her* (not just her property) as a mere means to even noble ends. Kant's formula of humanity serves as an ultimate guide here. Again, here is where I think Thomson's argument may be stronger than she herself regards it. I may concede that one person's right to life trumps another person's property rights so that, for example, if one human being is dying of thirst in front of someone who owns all the water sources in the city, it may be permissible to forcibly take water from the latter to save the former's life. But the reason I cannot expand this to the pregnant woman/fetus relationship is because, for all the reasons I detailed in Chapter 1, to violate bodily integrity is *not* akin to violating a property right – it is akin to violating the human being herself. To force a woman to gestate forces her into a state of bodily and mental intrusion that, as Mulder himself admits, is simply unparalleled in any other aspect of our biology. It would be morally and legally inconsistent to live in a society that does not compel human beings to donate blood or bone marrow to save other human beings, but would have no problems compelling women to submit to an even more precarious physical state, one that could have damaging psychological consequences as well, in order to save human fetuses.

Even Mulder admits that, although you may be "morally and legally expected" to donate blood or bone marrow, you cannot be physically compelled to do so (p. 100) – that is, even he recognizes that taking the step toward physical compulsion is incredibly significant. For Kantian reasons, it is not one I can take in regards to pregnant woman. As I admitted in Chapter 1, it may be the case that when it comes to aborting a pregnancy, there are no winners here – inevitably someone, either the woman or the fetus, will be treated as a mere means to the ends of the other. Mulder actually puts this dilemma in a powerful way on page 101: "Certainly pregnant women are often vulnerable in many ways, and, again, I think there is ultimately nothing quite like the unique burdens of pregnancy. But in terms of the gravity of moral wrongs, there is nothing quite like the direct targeting of the vulnerable."

I choose the woman as the "winner" mostly due to consistency issues – as I already noted, in similar cases, it is always the "Samaritan" who has the final say over what he is willing to do with his body in order to save another human being. It also appears to me that it is the woman who suffers more, since her phenomenology is adversely effected in a way the fetus' is not, simply because it lacks such a phenomenology (at least early in pregnancy, when 96.8% of abortions take place[34]). There are also utilitarian reasons I am pro-choice, which will be detailed more later in the book. In the end, however, from a Kantian standpoint, I simply demand consistency when it comes to how pregnant women are treated.[35] No human being – no man, no non-pregnant woman – can be forced into a state of bodily and mental compulsion to save another human being's life. Pregnant women cannot – should not – be treated differently in this regard.

III. Concluding thoughts: Three peripheral, but important, issues

Because it is not possible for me to address every aspect of Mulder's arguments, I have chosen to carefully analyze the ones that clearly counter my own arguments in Chapter 1. Nevertheless, there are some important issues that Mulder mentions that I believe warrant further discussion, even if they are not directly related to either of our respective arguments. I will briefly attend to three of these issues.

Late-term abortions

Mulder notes on page 66 that "I think that many who are not already in the grip of a theory would find quite a number of late-term abortions, however rare they may be, to be morally problematic, on a purely intuitive level." I don't disagree with him here – on an intuitive level, the idea of destroying an almost fully-formed, full-term, viable fetus is revolting, and morally on a par with infanticide. Many pro-life advocates rely on this intuition in order to advance their position – oftentimes, when pro-lifers protest or picket an abortion clinic, they will showcase many pictures of alleged late-term abortions (although to the discerning eye, it is clear that many of these pictures are actually of late-term miscarriages or stillbirths). But if we actually took some time to look into the practice of late-term abortions, perhaps we may come to rethink our initial moral revulsion.

I agree with Mulder that non-therapeutic late-term abortions are *prima facie* morally problematic. In fact, I defended this contention in my book.[36] It is precisely because I would find such "elective" late-term abortions difficult that I advocate for almost unfettered access to early-term abortions. Indeed, one of the reasons women sometimes wait until later in pregnancy to obtain an abortion is because they had difficulties obtaining one earlier. Nevertheless, abortions of this kind are *exceedingly* rare. Only 1.5% of all abortions take place after 20 weeks gestational age.[37] Out of those, many late-term abortions occur due to health complications for either the woman or the fetus. Here are, as examples, some cases of women who chose late-term abortions for extremely difficult reasons.

> Sometime early in the 8th month my wife, an RN who at the time was working in an infertility clinic asked the Dr. she was working for what he thought of her discomfort. He examined her and said that he couldn't be certain but thought that she might be having twins. We were thrilled and couldn't wait to get a new sonogram that hopefully would confirm his thoughts. Two days later our joy was turned to unspeakable sadness when the new sonogram showed conjoined twins. Conjoined twins alone is not what

was so difficult but the way they were joined meant that at best only one child would survive the surgery to separate them and the survivor would more than likely live a brief and painful life filled with surgery and organ transplants. We were advised that our options were to deliver into the world a child who's [sic] life would be filled with horrible pain and suffering or fly out to Wichita Kansas and to terminate the pregnancy under the direction of Dr. George Tiller.[38]

As we sat there, she said that the ultrasound indicated that the fetus had an open neural tube defect, meaning that the spinal column had not closed properly. It was a term I remembered skipping right over in my pregnancy book, along with all the other fetal anomalies and birth defects that I thought referred to other people's babies, not mine ... Instead of cinnamon and spice, our child came with technical terms like hydrocephalus and spina bifida. The spine, she said, had not closed properly, and because of the location of the opening, it was as bad as it got. What they knew – that the baby would certainly be paralyzed and incontinent, that the baby's brain was being tugged against the opening in the base of the skull and the cranium was full of fluid – was awful. What they didn't know – whether the baby would live at all, and if so, with what sort of mental and developmental defects – was devastating. Countless surgeries would be required if the baby did live. None of them would repair the damage that was already done ... We met with a genetic counselor, but given the known as well as the unknown, we both knew what we needed to do. Though the baby might live, it was not a life that we would choose for our child, a child that we already loved. We decided to terminate the pregnancy. It was our last parental decision.[39]

Her brain wasn't fully formed and there was also something wrong with her heart. As the doctor explained, I stayed solid. I asked questions – clinical, doctor's kid questions – and then my voice started to shake as I asked, "So, there is no chance that this baby is healthy?" Then I apologized for getting upset. Ridiculous. In true doctor speak he replied, "Well, there is always a chance – but if I had to make the call, I'd say this development is not normal." We left the doctor's office in a haze. Within hours, I was surrounded by my family, and I had spoken to my OB/GYN, my father, and a neonatal neurologist. All of these people had looked at my ultrasound images and the consensus was nothing good. No one could or would give me details, but everyone kept saying that my baby – the baby I could literally feel moving in my belly – would not be anywhere near okay. Together, Randy and I made the decision to not bring our daughter into the world.[40]

In a particularly heart-wrenching essay, Emily Rapp discusses life with her son Ronan, who suffered from Tay-Sachs disease before he died. Rapp reveals that had she known about her son's Tay-Sachs diagnoses while pregnant, she would have chosen to abort him.

If I had known Ronan had Tay-Sachs ... I would have found out what the disease meant for my then unborn child; I would have talked to parents who are raising (and burying) children with this disease, and then I would have had an abortion. Without question and without regret, although this would have been a different kind of loss to mourn and would by no means have been a cavalier or uncomplicated, heartless decision. I'm so grateful that Ronan is my child. I also wish he'd never been born; no person should suffer in this way – daily seizures, blindness, lack of movement, inability to swallow, a devastated brain – with no hope for a cure. Both of these statements are categorically true; neither one is mutually exclusive.[41]

Not only does Rapp manifest love and care for her child – and appeals to those same emotions to justify the abortion had she been aware of his condition – she also conveys the difficulties and nuances that make abortion such a morally complex topic. Here is a woman who loves her son, and feels that "his life is of utmost value to me." She writes that she doesn't "regret a single minute of this parenting journey, even though I wake up every morning with my heart breaking, feeling the impending dread of his imminent death." And yet, she also admits that had she known this was her son's reality, she would have sought an abortion to spare him a brief lifetime of suffering; that, for him, it would have been better not to have been born. Ronan's death here would have been more akin to euthanasia than to abortion.

I write this not to go into a deep analysis about the prevalence of late-term abortion, but to qualify Mulder's claim that late-term abortions are intuitively problematic. They are – but instead of relying solely on that intuition, let us keep in mind the relative rarity of such abortions, and the context in which many of them occur. Very few women will carry a fetus in her womb, feel it grow and move, and then seek an abortion wantonly. Many are suffering a horrible, terrible, gut-wrenching decision, and we should keep our moral compass tuned-in with that suffering instead of relying on our immediate intuitions.

The morning-after pill

I am grateful to Mulder for making the distinction between RU-486, also known as mifepristone, and the "morning-after pill." Because both are pills, they are often used interchangeably. RU-486 causes abortions by disrupting the hormone progesterone, which is necessary to continue the pregnancy. Because it is often taken for its abortifacient effects, clearly it does more than delay ovulation or prevent the implantation of an already-fertilized egg. As Mulder noted, for someone who believes that an embryo is a person from conception onwards, the latter function is as morally problematic as an actual abortion. Any drug that functions to prevent implantation destroys a fertilized egg in the process. It is this latter function that many pro-life advocates find troubling when it comes to the "morning-after pill," also known as the levonorgestrel emergency contraception pill (LNG ECP).

In 2014, the United States Supreme Court adjudicated *Burwell v. Hobby Lobby* and sided with the owners of the Hobby Lobby company when they challenged the Affordable Care Act's requirement that they cover contraceptive services for their employees in their medical insurance programs. The owners cited their religious belief that "life begins at conception" and therefore they refused to cover four kinds of contraceptives that they perceived as being abortifacients: two forms of the Intrauterine Device (IUDs) and two forms of LNG ECP. When it comes to the latter, the current scientific evidence simply does not support the view that LNG ECP prevents implantation of fertilized eggs. Several studies have indicated that the pill primarily functions to suppress ovulation. A 2007 study notes that the "data are supportive of the concept that the LNG ECP has little or no effect on postovulation events but is highly effective when taken before ovulation."[42] A 2010 study concluded that "LNG-EC prevents pregnancy only when taken before fertilization of the ovum has occurred."[43] In 2008, the International Consortium for Emergency Contraception and the International Federation of Gynecology and Obstetrics issued a statement that LNC ECP functioned to "inhibit or delay an egg from being released from the ovary when taken before ovulation [and to] possibly prevent the sperm and the egg from meeting by affecting the cervical mucus or the ability of sperm to bind to the egg." In reference to the specific concern that the pill functions to prevent the implantation of a fertilized egg, they highlight a number of studies that provide evidence in the negative:

- One study has estimated effectiveness of LNG ECPs by confirming the cycle day by hormonal analysis (other studies used women's self-reported cycle date). In this study, pregnancies occurred only in women who took ECPs on or after the day of ovulation, while no pregnancies occurred in the women who took ECPs before ovulation, providing evidence that ECPs were unable to prevent implantation.
- A number of studies have evaluated whether ECPs produce changes in the histological and biochemical characteristics of the endometrium. Most studies show that LNG ECPs have no such effect on the endometrium, indicating that they have no mechanism to prevent implantation.
- One study found a single altered endometrial parameter only when LNG was administered prior to the LH surge, at a time when ECPs inhibit ovulation.
- One study showed that levonorgestrel did not prevent the attachment of human embryos to a simulated (in vitro) endometrial environment.
- Animal studies demonstrated that LNG ECPs did not prevent implantation of the fertilized egg in the endometrium.
- Review of the evidence suggests that LNG ECPs cannot prevent implantation of a fertilized egg. Language on implantation should not be included in LNG ECP product labeling.[44]

I bring this up because, contrary to what the Supreme Court Justices wrote in their majority opinion for *Burwell v. Hobby Lobby*, facts do matter. Justice Samuel Alito wrote that "it is not for the Court to say that the religious beliefs of the plaintiffs are mistaken or unreasonable ... [what matters is] whether the plaintiffs' asserted religious belief reflects 'an honest conviction.'"[45] But certainly we *ought* to try to align our "honest convictions" with what evidence suggests, especially when those "honest convictions" affect other people. I have issues with the *Hobby Lobby* case that extend outside our immediate concerns – in general, I worry that it sets a precedent allowing employers to deny more basic healthcare services to their employees due to religious reasons (imagine that the owner of your company was a devout Jehovah's Witness and refused to cover even life-saving blood transfusions, or a Christian Scientist who eschewed medical technology altogether). For our purposes, however, I do understand a pro-life advocate's concerns over contraception that may function to prevent implantation and destroy a fertilized embryo. For someone like Mulder who believes personhood begins at conception, this moral stance is expected and consistent. But I do think we have plenty of evidence to conclude that the "morning-after pill" does not function in this way.

Natural embryo loss and other consistency concerns

On page 82, Mulder discusses the issue of natural embryo loss, and responds to Toby Ord's condemnation that pro-life advocates don't seem to care as much for such instances of loss as they should, given that approximately "90 million embryos a year" (p. 82) either never implant due to natural causes, or are lost early in pregnancy. According to Ord, the fact that so many pro-lifers have such a nonchalant attitude towards these losses calls into question whether they seriously believe embryos are persons.

Mulder first argues that we do indeed take the health of early embryos into account, as women are counseled to care for themselves and take vitamins to nourish the growing embryo. But this is not a good counter-reply – women are advised to do this in order to benefit the resulting infant; if she experiences an early miscarriage we mourn for what that life could have been, for all of the *possibilities* that were lost, not necessarily for the embryo itself. Why think this is the case? Well, imagine this: suppose that there was some natural disease that has been around "since humanity arose" (p. 82) and was responsible for killing 90 million infants and children per year. I do not think it is unreasonable to say that we, as a society, would be experiencing a major panic attack and we would commit to finding a cause and a cure for this disease. But this does not happen when it comes to spontaneous miscarriages or abortion. A recent personal experience really drove this point home to me. While talking with a self-proclaimed pro-life fertility specialist, we discussed why a woman would fail to get pregnant if she was routinely having sexual intercourse around her most fertile days. Many possibilities were brought up, but one thing he said was: "It could be that she is actually conceiving every month, and for whatever reason the embryos are not attaching to the uterine wall." What struck me was how casually he made such a statement – if he really believed that the life of a newly fertilized egg has the same moral status and significance as the life of an infant or child, I would expect that the possibilities that so many "children" were dying in the womb to be much more distressing. I cannot help but conclude that the reason there is no such reaction is because even the most committed pro-life advocate does not *really* believe that the loss of early embryonic life is *as tragic* as the loss of an infant's or child's life.

Mulder, of course, denies that this is the conclusion that should be drawn. Instead, he offers the following possible interpretation:

> The extent to which fighting NEL is a priority for pro-lifers (as we've seen, it's not as if they don't care at all), will have to be assessed with multiple factors, and the action may not be easily determinable in the abstract. To name just a few, it might turn out that it matters, in a triage situation, that the grown would-be victim(s) could experience terrible pain and could be spared this. Sentience may be neither here nor there for whether embryos can be directly *killed*, but it might have something to say about whether embryos take priority over victims who would experience especially gruesome deaths in a decision about whom to *save*. Second, it might matter whether one has certain familial attachments to the grown would-be victims over against the (perhaps) random embryos.
>
> (p. 82)

But I think this response misses the point. The issue isn't that we are called to choose between embryonic life and the life of other, more developed, persons. The issue at hand is that we *know* that approximately 90 million embryos a year die from "natural causes", many times a woman isn't even aware of her pregnancy when it happens, and we are unmotivated to do a thing about it. There is no March of Dimes equivalent for early natural embryo loss. It is just not a priority for our society, nor is there any call from pro-life advocates to make it a priority.

Again, we need to remember what follows from the premise that embryos are full-fledged members of the moral community: they are entitled to the *exact same moral rights, legal rights, and treatment as every other person*. That means that preventing the loss of 90 million embryos a year should be as much of a priority for us as cancer research (if not more so, since about 8 million people die of cancer every year in comparison). If one truly believes that embryos are persons, I am also not convinced by Mulder's contention that certain applications of anti-abortion laws, such as the kinds of laws that landed Carmen Aldana in prison, shouldn't be done on the basis on insensitivity. From a pro-life perspective, abortion doesn't just constitute the "loss of a child" – it can be nothing short of first degree murder. I don't see how a call to sensitivity would follow from this anymore than it should follow if a woman deliberately takes steps to kill her infant or children. Let me be clear here: I am not saying that abortion *is* tantamount to first degree murder (since I am not pro-life). What I *am* saying is that this is what *logically follows* from the premise that embryos and fetuses have a parity in moral status and legal rights to born infants and children. I also do not believe that, in general, pro-life advocates desire to punish pregnant women for abortions; I think Mulder's call for sensitivity and compassion for women who abort is not only admirable and kind, but also what I think most pro-choice advocates would promote. But while I appreciate the call for sensitivity, I just don't see how it can be any more consistently defended from a pro-life perspective than a rape exception could be (and Mulder admits the latter).

One final note. Because I do believe that fetal life has value, I take seriously Mulder's critique that, in my attempts to highlight the significance of a woman's pregnant embodiment when it comes to her decision whether to continue that embodiment, I may have, like Mackenzie, ignored the fetus' own embodiment and own lived reality. This bothers me. I don't want to be guilty of doing this. I will never again justify my pro-choice advocacy by dismissing fetal life as just a "clump of cells." Human life matters to me, and as such fetal life matters to me. But I simply do not regard forced gestation as a way to respect this value. Rather, I am interested in creating a society where we can do more to protect women from sexual assault and prevent unplanned pregnancies from occurring. But, when they do occur, we should strive to foster an actual pro-natalist society, where a woman (and her partner) who wants to parent is able to do so without fear of poverty, of losing her job, or of having to compromise her education and future prospects. These are the kinds of policies, not prohibiting abortions, that stand to make an actual difference. These are the policies that respect women *and* nascent human life.

Notes

1 Christopher Kaczor. 2011. *The Ethics of Abortion*. London: Routledge, p. 93.
2 Kaczor, 2011, p. 93.
3 Russell DiSilvestro. 2010. *Human Capacities and Moral Status*. New York: Springer, p. 14. It is important to note that while DiSilvestro being a member of the human species is sufficient for moral status, he does not mean to argue that *only* human beings have moral status. DiSilvestro acknowledges that non-human organisms may also have moral status given their possession of certain capacities common to *their* species ("perhaps the set of typical dog capacities generates serious moral status for anything that possesses it" (p. 164)). And, if it were possible for a non-human organism to acquire human capacities, then that organism, too, would have "serious moral status." Much of DiSilvestro's book also contains excellent discussions concerning the different ways we can understand the term "capacity" within the context of human abilities and moral status that, while taking us a bit beyond the scope of our current conversation, is relevant to the larger conversation concerning the issues discussed in this chapter.
4 I will offer a more detailed explanation of the difference between moral person essentialism and metaphysical person essentialism below.
5 Jeff McMahan. 2002. *The Ethics of Killing: Problems at the Margins of Life*. New York, NY: Oxford University Press, p. 449.
6 Ross Kenneth Urken. 2016. "Doctor Ready to Perform First Human Head Transplant." *Newsweek*, April 26. Available at: http://www.newsweek.com/2016/05/06/first-human-head-transplant-452240.html
7 Urken, 2016.
8 Kaczor, 2011, p. 111.
9 Kaczor, 2011, p. 112.
10 Lynn Rudder Baker. 2000. *Persons and Bodies: A Constitution View*. New York: Cambridge University Press, p. 207

11 Karen Dawson. 1987. "Fertilization and Moral Status: A Scientific Perspective." *Journal of Medical Ethics*, 13, p. 176.
12 DiSilvestro offers an objection to this argument in chapter 2 of *Human Capacities and Moral Status*: "Even if it is possible for me to undergo fission right now, this possibility of fission does not undercut the claim that I am an individual right now" (p. 55). I would argue that the capacity to undergo division (fission) undercuts one's claim to be *essentially* an individual. It seems that DiSilvestro would have to hold that being an individual is an accidental, rather than essential property, of human identity.
13 Norman Ford. 1988. *When Did I Begin?: Conception of the Human Individual in History, Philosophy, and Science*. Cambridge: Cambridge University Press, p. 156.
14 Kaczor, 2011, pp. 97–98.
15 Kaczor, 2011, p. 93.
16 Francis Beckwith. 2007. *Defending Life: A Moral and Legal Case Against Abortion Choice*. New York: Cambridge University Press, p. 132.
17 Kaczor, 2011, p. 97.
18 Nathan Nobis. 2011. "Abortion, Metaphysics, and Morality: A Review of Francis Beckwith's *Defending Life: A Moral and Legal Case Against Abortion Choice*." *Journal of Medicine and Philosophy*, 36, p. 264; emphasis added.
19 David DeGrazia. 2005. *Human Identity and Bioethics*. New York: Cambridge University Press, p. 48.
20 DeGrazia, 2005, p. 49.
21 DeGrazia, 2005, p. 287.
22 DeGrazia, 2005, p. 287.
23 DeGrazia, 2005, p. 288.
24 Judith Jarvis Thomson. 1971. "A Defense of Abortion." *Philosophy and Public Affairs*, 1.1: 47–66, at p. 49.
25 Kaczor, 2011, p. 183.
26 Beckwith, 2007, p. 106.
27 Fiona Ortiz. 2010. "First U.S. Woman with Uterus Transplant Looks Forward to Pregnancy." Available at: http://www.scientificamerican.com/article/first-u-s-woman-with-uterus-transplant-looks-forward-to-pregnancy/
28 Bill Chappell. 2014. "A First: Uterus Transplant Gives Parents a Healthy Baby." Available at: http://www.npr.org/sections/thetwo-way/2014/10/04/353691555/a-first-uterus-transplant-gives-parents-a-healthy-baby
29 Leah Samuel. 2016. "With Womb Transplants a Reality, Transgender Women Dare to Dream of Pregnancies." Available at: https://www.statnews.com/2016/03/07/uterine-transplant-transgender/
30 Kaczor, 2011, p. 154.
31 Steven Ross. 1982. "Abortion and the Death of the Fetus." *Philosophy and Public Affairs*, 11.3: 232–245, at p. 238.
32 Peter Singer. 1972. "Famine, Affluence, and Morality." *Philosophy and Public Affairs*, 1.1: 229–243.
33 Bertha Alvarez Manninen. 2014. *Pro-Life, Pro-Choice: Shared Values in the Abortion Debate*. Nashville: Vanderbilt University Press.
34 Guttmacher Institute. 2016. "Facts on Induced Abortion." Available at: https://www.guttmacher.org/fact-sheet/induced-abortion-united-states
35 See: Lina Papadaki. 2012. "Abortion and Kant's Formula of Humanity." *Humana Mente Journal of Philosophical Studies*, 22: 145–166 and also Allen Wood. 1998. "Kant on Duties Regarding Nonrational Nature." *Supplemental Proceedings of the Aristotelian Society*, 72.1: 189–210, for two excellent essays on the application of Kantian deontology to abortion.
36 Manninen, 2014, pp. 34–45.
37 Guttmacher Institute. 2016. "Facts on Induced Abortion." Available at: https://www.guttmacher.org/fact-sheet/induced-abortion-united-states

38 A letter in defense of Dr. George Tiller, who was murdered in 2009 for his late-term abortion practices (Hilzoy, 2009). Available at: http://washingtonmonthly.com/2009/06/01/dr-george-tiller/
39 Gretchen Voss. 2011. "My Late Term Abortion." Available at: http://www.ourbodiesourselves.org/stories/my-late-term-abortion/
40 Lindsey Averill. 2015. "This Is What It's Really Like to Have a Late-term Abortion." Available at: http://www.huffingtonpost.com/xojane-/this-is-what-its-really-like-to-have-a-late-term-abortion_b_8264562.html
41 Emily Rapp. 2012. "Rick Santorum, Meet My Son." Available at: http://www.slate.com/articles/double_x/doublex/2012/02/rick_santorum_and_prenatal_testing_i_would_have_saved_my_son_from_his_suffering_.html
42 N. Novikova, et al. 2007. "Effectiveness of Levonorgestrel Emergency Contraception Given Before or After Ovulation – A Pilot Study." *Contraception*, 75.2: 112–118.
43 G. Noe, et al. 2010. "Contraceptive Efficacy of Emergency Contraception with Levonorgestrel Given Before or After Ovulation." *Contraception*, 81.5: 414–420, at p. 414.
44 International Consortium for Emergency Contraception and the International Federation of Gynecology and Obstetrics. 2008. "How Do Levonorgestrel-only Emergency Contraceptive Pills (LNG ECPs) Prevent Pregnancy?" Available at: http://www.cngof.asso.fr/D_TELE/081022FIGO.pdf
45 United States Supreme Court. 2014. *Burwell v. Hobby Lobby*. Available at: http://www.supremecourt.gov/opinions/13pdf/13-354_olp1.pdf

References

Averill, Lindsey. 2015. "This Is What It's Really Like to Have a Late-term Abortion." Available at: http://www.huffingtonpost.com/xojane-/this-is-what-its-really-like-to-have-a-late-term-abortion_b_8264562.html

Baker, Lynn Rudder. 2000. *Persons and Bodies: A Constitution View*. New York: Cambridge University Press.

Beckwith, Francis. 2007. *Defending Life: A Moral and Legal Case Against Abortion Choice*. New York: Cambridge University Press.

Chappell, Bill. 2014. "A First: Uterus Transplant Gives Parents a Healthy Baby." Available at: http://www.npr.org/sections/thetwo-way/2014/10/04/353691555/a-first-uterus-transplant-gives-parents-a-healthy-baby

Dawson, Karen. 1987. "Fertilization and Moral Status: A Scientific Perspective." *Journal of Medical Ethics*, 13: 173–177.

DeGrazia, David. 2005. *Human Identity and Bioethics*. New York: Cambridge University Press.

DiSilvestro, Russell. 2010. *Human Capacities and Moral Status*. New York: Springer Publishers.

Ford, Norman. 1988. *When Did I Begin?: Conception of the Human Individual in History, Philosophy, and Science*. Cambridge: Cambridge University Press.

Guttmacher Institute. 2016. "Facts on Induced Abortion." Available at: https://www.guttmacher.org/fact-sheet/induced-abortion-united-states

Hilzoy. June 1, 2009. "A letter in defense of Dr. George Tiller, who was murdered in 2009 for his late-term abortion practices." Available at: http://washingtonmonthly.com/2009/06/01/dr-george-tiller/

International Consortium for Emergency Contraception and the International Federation of Gynecology and Obstetrics. 2008. "How Do Levonorgestrel-only Emergency Contraceptive Pills (LNG ECPs) Prevent Pregnancy?" Available at: http://www.cngof.asso.fr/D_TELE/081022FIGO.pdf

Kaczor, Christopher. 2011. *The Ethics of Abortion*. London: Routledge.
Manninen, Bertha Alvarez. 2014. *Pro-Life, Pro-Choice: Shared Values in the Abortion Debate*. Nashville: Vanderbilt University Press.
McMahan, Jeff. 2002. *The Ethics of Killing: Problems at the Margins of Life*. New York: Oxford University Press.
Nobis, Nathan. 2011. "Abortion, Metaphysics, and Morality: A Review of Francis Beckwith's *Defending Life: A Moral and Legal Case Against Abortion Choice*." *Journal of Medicine and Philosophy*, 36: 261–273.
Noe, G., H.B. Croxatto, A.M. Salvatierra, V. Reyes, C. Villarroel, C. Munoz, G. Morales, and A. Retamales. 2010. "Contraceptive Efficacy of Emergency Contraception with Levonorgestrel Given Before or After Ovulation." *Contraception*, 81. 5: 414–420.
Novikova, N., E. Weisberg, F.Z. Stanczyk, H.B. Croxatto, and I.S. Fraser. 2007. "Effectiveness of Levonorgestrel Emergency Contraception Given Before or After Ovulation – A Pilot Study." *Contraception*, 75. 2: 112–118.
Ortiz, Fiona. 2010. "First U.S. Woman with Uterus Transplant Looks Forward to Pregnancy." Available at: http://www.scientificamerican.com/article/first-u-s-woman-with-uterus-transplant-looks-forward-to-pregnancy/
Papadaki, Lina. 2012. "Abortion and Kant's Formula of Humanity." *Humana Mente Journal of Philosophical Studies*, 22: 145–166.
Rapp, Emily. 2012. "Rick Santorum, Meet My Son." Available at: http://www.slate.com/articles/double_x/doublex/2012/02/rick_santorum_and_prenatal_testing_i_would_have_saved_my_son_from_his_suffering_.html
Ross, Steven. 1982. "Abortion and the Death of the Fetus." *Philosophy and Public Affairs*, 11. 3: 232–245.
Samuel, Leah. 2016. "With Womb Transplants a Reality, Transgender Women Dare to Dream of Pregnancies." Available at: https://www.statnews.com/2016/03/07/uterine-transplant-transgender/
Singer, Peter. 1972. "Famine, Affluence, and Morality." *Philosophy and Public Affairs*, 1. 1: 229–243.
Thomson, Judith Jarvis. 1971. "A Defense of Abortion." *Philosophy and Public Affairs*, 1. 1: 47–66.
United States Supreme Court. 2014. Burwell v. Hobby Lobby. Available at: http://www.supremecourt.gov/opinions/13pdf/13-354_olp1.pdf
Urken, Ross Kenneth. April 26, 2016. "Doctor Ready to Perform First Human Head Transplant." *Newsweek*. Available at: http://www.newsweek.com/2016/05/06/first-human-head-transplant-452240.html
Voss, Gretchen. 2011. "My Late Term Abortion." Available at: http://www.ourbodiesourselves.org/stories/my-late-term-abortion/
Wood, Allen. 1998. "Kant on Duties Regarding Nonrational Nature." *Supplemental Proceedings of the Aristotelian Society*, 72. 1: 189–210.

4

A RESPONSE TO MANNINEN

Jack Mulder, Jr.

I am grateful for the opportunity to respond to Bertha Alvarez Manninen. I am also grateful for her thoughtful manner of proceeding on the issue of abortion. Both sides on the abortion issue are guilty of mischaracterization, and while it may be very difficult to cut through such mischaracterization, Manninen and I are driven by some similar concerns. She and I both share a concern about the most vulnerable, and hold that this can have an impact on one's morality across a wide range of cases. To be clear, while I do hold that vulnerability is an important consideration in establishing a just society, I do not hold that being more vulnerable means that one possesses *more* of a "right to life." The real reason one should not procure or perform an abortion, in my view, is that (non-consequentially) one should not carry out a direct act against the life of another human being, and this is what abortion does. The fact that the fetus is especially vulnerable should, I think, help reinforce our moral sensibilities about the act, but I do not hold that the mother has *less* of a right to life than the life inside her. I do, however, hold that forming a society in which the vulnerable are given special solicitude will, or at least should, serve to heighten our awareness of the serious wrong involved in abortion.

I should note also that I have always been grateful for Manninen's willingness to understand the pro-life viewpoint from within. Indeed, I have often been frustrated with other pro-choice friends who seem somehow unable to grasp the outrage that those of us who are pro-life feel about the tragedy of abortion. While I want to make it very clear that I absolutely reject any acts of violence that have been perpetrated against those who provide abortions, I do want to urge that we will continue to have bad polarizing debates on abortion so long as those on one side do not grant that the other side can be rationally defended. In this response chapter, I will offer a response to Manninen on several issues in her initial chapter to this book where there remain some significant differences in our viewpoints.

1 On "used" and "unused" embryos

Manninen is no enemy to me, but because she is at such pains to understand the pro-life perspective as well as her own, from the perspective of dialectical engagement, one is tempted to invert the famous dictum and say "with enemies like these, who needs friends?" We certainly take up different sides of the issue, but we have for years done so as friends. Nevertheless, as Aristotle famously observed, we must love our friends and truth, but truth first.[1] While I find Manninen to be a thoughtful interlocutor, as I hope she can say of me, I will need to respond to some of her arguments in this chapter, and this will include some critique both of the premises she uses to defend her arguments and some critique of how much purchase she takes her arguments to have. One example of the latter type of response I will offer is in regard to the question of "unused" embryos. Manninen suggests, in her discussion of *Davis v. Davis*, that the destruction of frozen embryos would amount to homicide.[2] Now homicide is primarily a forensic term. A coroner can give the verdict that one's death was caused by homicide without any knowledge of factors having to do with motive, aggravating circumstances, pre-meditation, or provocation. For this reason, I must assent to Manninen's claim that the destruction of embryos would constitute homicide. I have already said in the introduction, however, why I prefer not to use the term "murder" or "manslaughter" or other terms that would imply culpability or agency in legal or moral senses, which senses "homicide" does not necessarily transmit.

So, of course, yes, destruction of embryos would constitute homicide on a pro-life view. But other things that Manninen takes this line of argument to establish are not quite so easily gotten. Manninen next analyzes the decision in *Davis v. Davis*, where the crucial line she quotes (and italicizes) is "Ordinarily, the party wishing to *avoid procreation* should prevail."[3] The phrase I've italicized, however, makes it clear that this argument by the court assumes that an embryo is *not* a full person (since procreation is still something that can be *avoided*) but rather something like the amalgam of two people's gametes so that, by virtue of one gamete's being *his* and one gamete's being *hers*, both individuals from whom the gametes originated have some kind of legal claim to the embryo as property. But this is false. As I have argued in my earlier chapter (as have many others), the embryo is a new organism that results from two gametes and important changes that occur upon their uniting. Once this has happened, the gametes, which were sex cells belonging to the adults, no longer exist as sex cells but have joined to form a new organism. On the metaphysical view of persons that I have espoused, this new organism constitutes a person with moral rights that should have legal corollaries in a just society. Procreation can no longer be avoided. It has occurred. Thus, the only legal or moral *claims* one could assert in regard to the embryo are claims of custody or parenthood, and these relationships do not include, contra Soran Reader, the right directly to end one's child's life.[4]

When Manninen glosses the claim by the court that the party wishing to avoid procreation should ordinarily prevail, she writes:

If embryos were considered persons, with all the full rights therein, this decision would have been exactly the opposite – the party wishing to keep the embryos and bring them to term would always win, since this is the best way to ensure that they won't be destroyed. Now turn the tables and suppose that the party wanting the embryos to be gestated is the man, whereas the woman is the one refusing. It would seem to follow that the woman can be compelled into implanting the embryos and gestating them, since considerations of bodily autonomy are outweighed by the embryos' right to life (according to those who support Personhood Amendments as a way to ban abortions).[5]

I am sorry to say that this just doesn't follow at all. In fact, there are two moves that do not follow. First, it is not that just *any* party wishing to bring the embryos to term would *always* win, because the man, lacking a uterus, has no capability to gestate them, and he cannot force a woman to do so. A woman, especially the biological mother to the embryo, could always win this dispute (supposing any relevant conditions of competence are met), since the man, even if he is the biological father to the embryo, has no right to kill his biological child or even to stunt his or her development. He is at best the custodial parent, and not the owner of this *person*. Although the woman is not the owner, either, she can give the embryo the environment and nourishment it needs to grow, and she can exercise that as a right.[6] It is entirely true that pro-lifers hold that pregnant women have unique obligations that men, lacking uteruses, do not have. But it is therefore also true that women, in these sorts of circumstances, can assert rights that men do not have.[7] We cannot expect that all obligations and rights will (or could) be balanced out in some kind of perfect zero-sum alignment across the sexes, but it is not unreasonable to expect that a unique set of obligations might carry some unique prerogatives along with it.

Although I've spared the reader the theoretical details for my non-consequentialism in ethics, being a non-consequentialist means that consequences never make an act right that would intrinsically be wrong. Now I hold that forced gestation is akin to rape; thus it is a grave moral wrong. Indeed, it is a grave moral wrong no matter what we stand to gain by it. So I think the second move that fails in Manninen's earlier argument is that people who wish to bring embryos to term are not thereby licensed effectively to rape women by compelling them to gestate. It is actually not quite right to say, even from a pro-life perspective, that "considerations of bodily autonomy are outweighed by the embryos' right to life."[8] It is rather that a grievous, and direct, violation of an unborn human person's *autonomy* occurs in abortion, and this is not permissible any more than it would be permissible to force women to gestate. One might object that, at least in the case of rape (which would already be to restrict our inquiry significantly) women have already been violated. All too right, but this violation has occurred, and to introduce a new violation of the person within her (supposing any licit emergency contraception in rape protocols has failed) is to add a wrong to a wrong in the hope that it will make a right.

Manninen sets a lot of store by this point of forced gestation, but I, too, reject forced gestation in every case where we are dealing with a discrete act of legal compulsion. Indeed, theoretically, if a woman were able to terminate a pregnancy without putting the life within her or its developmental wellbeing in serious medically indicated jeopardy, then she should be legally allowed to do that (though I offer no verdict here on whether that would be *morally* right).[9] More importantly, though, I simply reject the claim that the state or any other agent is *compelling* a woman to gestate by denying her an abortion. I have defined an abortion as an act that by its own nature constitutes a grave threat to an unborn human person and I offer no legal argument against non-abortifacient contraception; women (and men) are legally free to prevent conception. Indeed, to force a woman to *initiate* gestation would be, I think, an act of violence on an analogy with rape. But when a woman is *already gestating* it is not compulsion to insist that a woman not give way to the desire to end the life within her even if that is the only way she can end her gestation until she delivers.

An analogy may help. Suppose you are on a seaworthy sailboat several miles from shore. For whatever reason, it becomes clear that you have a stowaway. A small child of 8 months is sleeping soundly in her car seat having somehow been deposited in one of the berths of your sailboat, perhaps snuck down there during your last stop at the marina. The law certainly expects that, miles from shore, you not toss the youngster to a watery grave no matter how much you wish to offload this particular passenger. It is not legal compulsion in any novel sense to expect that you refrain from this. It would be compulsion to expect you to adopt this young child upon disembarking.[10] It would also be compulsion to expect you to continue to harbor the child in your vessel indefinitely even once you were in reach of a civil authority to whom the child could be safely delivered.[11] But when the only option for ridding yourself of this passenger is to kill her or place her directly in grave peril (that is, don't just leave her unattended and helplessly bobbing in your dinghy, either), then you have no choice but to bring the child along with you to safety. Your choices are doing violence to the defenseless or going some distance to help the defenseless. Sometimes life is like that. But to call it *legal* compulsion seems to me a strange use of language. You are merely the only one who can help and until and unless someone else can, you must, not because you are a state functionary but because you are a human being.[12]

It is a fair question at this point to ask what we are going to do with all of the "unused" embryos we have. At the present time, the United States Department of Health and Human Services' Office of Population Affairs reports that there are likely to be around 600,000 frozen embryos in the United States alone.[13] While typically 90% of this number is considered (at least nominally) "in use," approximately 60,000 remain available for "embryo adoption." The trouble, however, is that "We find ourselves faced with the unusual situation of asking moral questions dealing with a human embryo in a setting in which it does not really belong."[14] Even if, as I am inclined to do, we accept the moral permissibility, even commendability, of human embryo adoption,[15] we cannot lose sight of the serious wrong involved in coercing a woman to gestate an embryo. At the present time, this is simply not a problem anyone can solve by force of will. Unless you are a woman who is non-coercively moved to gestate one of the very many frozen embryos that could be adopted (assuming that doing so is morally permissible), there is nothing good to do about this situation.[16]

It might behoove pro-choice thinkers to contemplate, for at least a passing moment, just how bad this situation is from a pro-life standpoint. This situation has arisen from treating human embryos not as persons but as items to be used or discarded. It has arisen from treating human embryos as the kinds of things one should make more of so as to ensure that at least one implants, and as the kinds of things one is likely simply to eliminate if whatever consulting physicians regard as too many implant and begin to grow in the uterus. This has now happened millions of times over. In our current, and foreseeable, state of technology, one can expect no grand societal plan as to how to undo this enormous wrong. All we can really do is refrain from coercing women to gestate and refrain from positively destroying the embryos that have been created, even as the conditions that preserve them slowly deteriorate. It is that bad.

2 On personhood

This is probably a good place to rehearse some of the reasons why I hold that embryos are not the sorts of things (or the sorts of persons) one should treat in the way just mentioned. Doing this affords me an opportunity to discuss some of the arguments Manninen gives on the issue of personhood. I have offered a version of a view known as animalism, according to which we human organisms or animals just are human persons. On that view, we needn't ask whether a human organism has yet developed a certain capacity for consciousness or anything else, because the dignity and rights that ought to be afforded human persons do not flow from only those capacities they can immediately activate or could have activated in the past. Rather, the dignity and rights that ought to be afforded human persons flow from what they *are*.[17]

Now this view is different from what Manninen identifies as the genetic view. By contrast, animalism, she agrees, is a "philosophically respectable position to hold."[18] I agree with her that holding to animalism needn't entail that one is also pro-life, but it is the kind of view one might coherently hold while being pro-life. In her initial chapter, Manninen suggests that pro-life advocates tend to slide from the (indefensible) genetic view to the (more defensible but less uniformly pro-life) view of animalism. In earlier work, she is perhaps a touch clearer on the distinction. In a 2009 paper, Manninen claims that "According to the genetic account, each one of us persists over time as long as our unique genetic code persists over time."[19] In the same paper, Manninen claims that "According to [animalism], a human being persists over time as long as her numerically distinct organism persists in a functional state."[20] I agree that pro-life advocates (and indeed pro-choice advocates) are often more to be admired for zeal than rigor. I also agree that sliding into a genetic account would be bad, and sliding into an animalist account would be more defensible for a pro-life view. I am a little concerned that Manninen has yet to locate a genuine proponent of the genetic view, since no pro-life scholar of which I'm aware (including Pope John Paul II) seriously holds that mere possession of a certain genetic code entails moral status of a certain sort.[21] After all, my somatic cells include my genetic code, but it would be absurd to hold a memorial service at the site of my skinned knee. Indeed, I agree with Manninen that mere belonging to a certain species without consideration of the unique potentialities of the members of that species (and the organism to which all of these would belong) is morally irrelevant. Peter Singer's famous concern with speciesism may be showing the wear of some decades, but there is something right about the contention that mere species identity is not sufficient to generate moral status.[22]

So I agree that any "genetic view" according to which the presence of a certain genetic code, of itself, generates moral status would be absurd. Rather, it is the organism, or animal, that possesses a genetic code that should be examined. Now there are a range of capacities that have been discussed that are supposed to help generate the privileged moral status that most of us think human beings enjoy. Whatever that capacity (or set of capacities) is, it could of course be shared by species with which we are unacquainted. Perhaps there are extra-terrestrials in a far-flung solar system or galaxy who have the same complement of capacities that human beings have, or a similar set that would be sufficient to generate a moral status at least as privileged. Perhaps the capacities humans possess exist on a continuum where, at the present time, we tend to see human beings at the farthest known end, but other animals possess some share of the relevant capacity and so are accorded greater or lesser moral status on such a basis. All of this is perfectly consistent with the animalist view I hold.

So there is no obvious reason to think my view, or the view of any defensibly pro-life thinker, need be "speciesist." Rather, both the "performance" views I criticized in my initial chapter, under the heading of which I would include both Manninen's cognitive and (preferred) embodied mind accounts of personal identity, as well as animalism, all focus upon signature capacities of human beings. These signature capacities are the kinds of capacities one might in principle share with, say, extra-terrestrials with whom we are unacquainted, but to whom we might owe moral treatment upon encountering. George and Tollefsen, for instance, agree that certain signature capacities, such as being a rational and moral agent, contribute to being a person. They simply argue that one needn't be in a position *immediately* to exercise those capacities to have the moral status human persons enjoy. Root, or radical, capacity is enough.[23] Accordingly, "endowment" and "performance" views can both agree that speciesism should be avoided. Where they would (and where Manninen and I do) part ways is in the assessment of what *kind* of capacity counts for moral treatment.

Manninen has argued against the genetic account of personhood, at times suggesting that my preferred form of animalism shares some of the same problems. I have responded to some of those allegations in the above section on embryos and will say more in a later section. Manninen has also argued against the "cognitive" account of personhood in favor of what she terms the "embodied mind account of personal identity" (EMAPI). According to EMAPI, one needn't have developed robust mental capacities, but some mental life is still relevant for moral status. Manninen gives a range between 20 and 35 weeks gestational age for the development of rudimentary conscious awareness.[24] Manninen holds, along with others, that one must be the sort of being with interests in order to possess moral status, and, on her view, one simply cannot have interests unless one has a mental life. Accordingly, Manninen suggests that her account is a phenomenological one.[25] Here she cites Joel Feinberg to the effect that one has an interest in all and only those things in which one has a stake, and that (post-natal) infants and dementia patients do, while cell phones and chairs do not, have an interest in their continued life.[26]

I certainly agree that infants and dementia patients have what we fittingly call an interest in their continued life while cell phones and chairs do not. But Feinberg's picture is used by others in ways that I think complicate the matter. For instance, consider David Archard's use of Feinberg's scheme in discussing the wrong of rape.[27] Archard, following Feinberg, uses "harm" for a "setback to another's interests" and "wrong" for "an *indefensible* setback to another's interests." Alongside this, he introduces "hurt" for "experienced pain, displeasure, or discomfort."[28] Accordingly, as Archard details, a bank robber could be *hurt* by a do-gooder during his attempted robbery. Perhaps she (our do-gooder) deals him (the bank robber) a concussive blow to the head in a manner that qualifies as self-defense. The bank robber's interests are set back by this blow. Perhaps he spends some time in a hospital, and in any case his robbery is thwarted. His interests are set back, and so he may be harmed by this, as when we might say "three were harmed in the fire, including the arsonist himself." But our bank robber is not *wronged* by our do-gooder's intervening blow, because he has no *legitimate* interest in robbing the bank.

This scheme allows Archard to dispute the concept of a "harmless rape," while admitting the theoretical possibility of a "hurtless rape,"[29] which might be visited upon a woman who has an interest (as presumably all of us do) in her own sexual integrity, but was unconscious during the perpetrator's act, is never told of it, and so never experiences the painful event of the rape in the same *direct* way that another victim might have. Archard argues that clearly she is harmed by this rape, and grievously wronged, but, he thinks, not *hurt* in this technical sense, or at least not hurt in the same *phenomenological* way that other victims might be. While my purpose here is not to defend Archard's claim, I do want to discuss how this scheme might apply to the abortion issue.

For Manninen, having a mental life in which sentience, the very basic capacity to experience pain, seems important. While Manninen says that she wants to move away from sentience *simpliciter* and toward the possession of a mental life as a key criterion for moral status, she never fully severs the possession of interests from having a mental life.[30] Nor is it clear from her theory why she would want to do this.[31] For while an EMAPI view might hold that the entity that *could* possess moral status had begun its life narrative upon the initiation of its mental life, it's not clear why it *would* possess moral status until it had interests. Further, it's not clear why an EMAPI theorist would think an entity rounded a significant personal-identity-related bend in the road unless that bend had to do with the acquisition of interests. But what would be the link between the possession of interests and the onset of a mental life except sentience, the capacity to feel pain? Why think a mental life would be important unless the experiential, the phenomenological, dimension of mental life could at that point, and not until it, be set back? In short, why believe sentience could be decoupled from the interest view of moral status for EMAPI theorists?

Here's why this question is important. Suppose, as I mean to allege, that sentience *cannot* be decoupled from the interest view of moral status for EMAPI theorists like Manninen. Now further suppose that categories other than experiential or phenomenological pain are still morally relevant to one's possession of interests. That is, we still care about the wrong of rape even if the victim never directly experiences it phenomenologically. Then it remains very unclear why the EMAPI theorist is allowed to say that someone is harmed who cannot have experienced the relevant wrong phenomenologically. To put it yet another way, if the forgoing is right, it is difficult for the EMAPI theorist to explain why harm is not reducible to hurt. I know that Manninen does not *want* harm to be reducible to hurt, but I'm unpersuaded that her account can pull it off.

To give a little bit more treatment of this point, suppose that the EMAPI theorist rejoins that, of course, the patient in a temporary coma is dealt a significant blow to her interests if, say, she is sexually assaulted during her treatment and no one other than her assailant ever becomes aware of the incident. Of course I hold that this is true, but how will the EMAPI theorist argue this? Perhaps the claim is that the patient in this temporary coma, upon resuming her phenomenological life, *would wish for this assault not to have occurred because things are worse for her as a result of its having occurred.*[32] But this is far too broad to get the EMAPI theorist all and only what she wants. After all, consider the water crisis still going on in Flint, Michigan as I write this. Clearly the lead poisoning of the water in Flint will affect the city's inhabitants for generations to come. Suppose now that we consider that at the time the key decisions are made that precipitated the water crisis, some fetus is at a mere seven weeks gestational age, having been conceived by a woman in Flint, who for socioeconomic reasons is highly unlikely to vacate the area. Is it really plausible to suggest that this fetus's interests are *not* set back by the water crisis? Pregnant women, as we've often remarked, go to considerable trouble to protect their unborn children, and maybe they do it because *they* want a healthy baby, but I suspect it makes a good deal more sense to many of them to say they're doing it *for* their baby.[33]

Accordingly, it makes more sense to me to suggest that unborn children have an interest in not being aborted. Remember that Boonin had to take refuge in the concept of an *ideal* desire to argue that the adulterer's wife still has a desire that her husband be faithful to her even while she is unable to attend to that desire because of her preoccupation with her son's failing health.[34] Now, does the future mature adult of 35 years of age have an ideal desire that the fetus to which her organic life corresponds not be aborted some 35-plus years ago? I think the EMAPI theorist must answer yes to this, and perhaps she can, with some of the right adjustments to her theory.³⁵ But even then we would be granting that a person's interests can be significantly set back not just when there is no phenomenological remembering of a harm, but even when it is *not possible* for there to be any phenomenological remembering of this harm. If there are cases in which it is not possible for there to be any phenomenological remembering of a harm that nevertheless is a harm, isn't it arbitrary to suggest that you *must* reach a phenomenological threshold before you have any interests that can be set back, that is, before you can be harmed at all?

Manninen has given an argument for the claim that our fetus of seven weeks gestational age is not a person, but I think her argument lets too much through the cracks. This is because I think her account will do one of two things. Either it will fail to explain why people who lack sentience have interests or it will fail to explain why fetuses lack them. It will fail to explain why people who lack sentience have interests because her EMAPI view cannot finally be severed from sentience and the capacity to feel pain, and yet clearly grievous wrongs can be visited upon people who lack sentience. If the reply is that their capacity for sentience has been initiated and so they have a dispositional capacity for it, I ask what this disposition means other than the ability to resume a phenomenological course of life, and why such a capacity to *resume* a course of life is morally different from the ability to *begin* it. There will always be a moment ten minutes (or some other arbitrary length of time) prior to the initiation of consciousness, just as there will be a moment ten minutes prior to the resumption of consciousness. I see no relevant reason why the two moments are morally different from one another. Thus as soon as Manninen gives a satisfying answer to why people who lack sentience have interests she will fail to give a satisfying answer to why fetuses lack them.

But why think that a root, or radical, capacity for rational and moral life is enough? What positive argument is there to hold that the fetus is an *actual* person? My only answer, which I have given at greater length in my initial chapter, is that this animalist picture of personhood does all the non-ad-hoc work we need it to do and the relevant alternatives that depend on phenomenological states seem to do only some of the work at too high a cost. I think that performance accounts of personhood end up unable to explain why phenomenologically inactive people bear moral rights, while multiplying rather peculiar entities like consciousnesses without explanatory necessity. George and Tollefsen write "there is little mystery in how an embryonic, fetal, or infant human being, incapable of exercising his or her mental capacities, is nevertheless a person: A human being does, by its nature, have the radical capacity for such mental acts and is by a self-directed process developing that capacity to the point where it is immediately exercisable."³⁶ Aren't temporarily comatose patients also developing (in the manner of healing) that capacity to the point where it will be immediately exercisable? Why is the fact that the latter has begun her mental life and the fetus has not yet done so morally relevant? The fetus can grow and the comatose patient can heal because of a combination of what each is and the sustenance or treatment each needs. That is how organisms work. When organismal integrity is working normally in human beings, it will help make conscious awareness possible. Sometimes an organism is growing or healing and cannot immediately exercise the most impressive capacities it has by nature. But neither state gives us a reason to treat an organism with any less dignity than it has at the peak of its development.

3 Precarious cases and questionable comparisons

In this section, I want to respond to Manninen about some vivid cases and questions she poses that concern the application of a pro-life viewpoint. Manninen's discussion of the tragedy that befell Dr. Savita Halappanavar, I think, suggests that pro-life principles and laws *themselves* and not merely their (perhaps wrongful) application were directly to blame for Dr. Halappanavar's death. This is not clear. While this is a philosophical treatment of the issue of abortion, seeing that the Catholic Church is the largest international organization with an avowedly pro-life view, it is not irrelevant to consider what the Irish Catholic Bishops' Conference said about this very case in their statement of 19 November 2012.[37] Anyone familiar with these types of statements will understand that we cannot expect from it detailed analysis of private medical information, but the principles it chooses to emphasize are telling. While first the statement of course expresses sympathy for this "devastating personal tragedy" and how it has "stunned our country," the document goes on to reaffirm some basic principles whose relevance in this context is fairly clear. The first is that "The Catholic Church has never taught that the life of a child in the womb should be preferred to that of a mother. By virtue of their common humanity, a mother and her unborn baby are both sacred with an equal right to life." The second principle asserts that "Where a seriously ill pregnant woman needs medical treatment which may put the life of her baby at risk, such treatments are ethically permissible provided every effort has been made to save the life of both the mother and her baby."

Certainly philosophers needn't take all their cues from a religious entity, but the point here is not to render slavish obedience; rather it is to illustrate that certain paths in the case of Dr. Halappanavar may have been available and morally licit (on pro-life principles) but were either not taken at all or not taken appropriately. It is true that I think in certain contexts the vulnerable have a special claim upon us, and in some cases (I've discussed a shipwreck) that may result in the practical (not intrinsic) preference for the very young or very old. But I have also indicated that certain cases in which the fetus or embryo might die as an unintended but foreseen consequence of medical intervention designed to save the life of the mother can be permissible.[38] Here are two of the clearest cases. On the one hand, we have salpingectomies designed to heal a mother with an ectopic pregnancy by removing the tube that is likely to rupture and kill both the mother and embryo. The other is the case of a hysterectomy performed on a woman with a cancerous uterus, which can be treated even while this treatment results in the death of the fetus or embryo.[39] As long as "every effort has been made to save the life of both the mother and her baby" then, especially when faced with a case where both will die, it may be not just permissible but obligatory to act in ways that save the mother and, as an unintended but foreseen consequence, lead to the death of the embryo or fetus.

Pro-choice thinkers will no doubt argue that the "every effort" clause could endanger the lives of pregnant mothers whose condition could be more easily alleviated simply by the administration of an abortion as opposed to making considerable efforts to save both the mother and child. To this it can only be said that of course there are cases in which abortion is simpler. Further, no amount of arguing is going to make an obstetrician's job easy, though certainly we rightly hold qualified physicians to high standards of competence. Healing the woman's pathology can be desperately important for both mother and unborn child, and when there is no other way to heal either, steps can be taken to heal the mother even when those steps will unfortunately result in harm or even death to the child. Nevertheless, the addition of another person into the equation whose care is not reducible to the care of the mother will always make things more difficult. Ask the nearest parent (two are writing this book). But this added difficulty does not mean we can regard the embryo or fetus as dispensable. If we are pro-life, can we avoid treating pregnancy as a state that is more precarious than others? No. Can we nevertheless treat a woman's serious pathology, when it endangers both her life and the life of the child within her, even when treating the pathology endangers the fetus's life? Yes, and there are circumstances in which this is permissible and important.

A second case that Manninen discusses is that of Carmen Guadalupe Vasquez Aldana, who was effectively imprisoned for a miscarriage.[40] Manninen writes that this is the kind of case that is likely to continue appearing if embryos and fetuses are awarded legal personhood. Manninen writes,

> while miscarriage *per se* would not be subject to criminalization any more than the accidental death of persons would render someone legally liable (fetuses often die in the womb for reasons unrelated to anyone's actions), determining whether the death of an embryo or fetus was indeed accidental means that women, in the midst of grieving their loss, would be subject to some degree of investigation.[41]

Manninen then goes on to argue against Francis Beckwith, who argues that we "do not ask those closest to the deceased to prove that they did not commit a murder."[42] Manninen responds that certainly people around those who die when the cause of death is not immediately clear must undergo an investigation. She further notes that "Given the fetus' location in a woman's body, and given the affects her action may have on it, even a cursory investigation of the circumstances of its death will involve probing a woman's body and any actions she took that may have affected the fetus."[43] I think that this conclusion can be walked back a bit. In just about every case I can imagine, it would be a genuine violation of a woman to compel an invasive examination of her body. If the reports on the Aldana case and other cases like hers are true, it hardly seems that principles of due process were respected.[44] Indeed, there are several ways to explain why we needn't punish women merely on suspicion of malfeasance related to a miscarriage. Michael Pakaluk has suggested, for instance, that perhaps an abortion carries with it its own penalty, and that those who perform abortions and support this choice might be susceptible to prosecution but the women themselves need not be.[45]

A related point I might wish to make in connection with the issue of wrongful prosecutorial steps taken in regard to miscarriage is that, while I have argued in my earlier chapter that authors like Catriona Mackenzie have not succeeded in escaping the ownership paradigm in mother-fetus relations, Mackenzie's work is genuinely helpful in getting us to consider the tight phenomenological connection that exists between mother and (unborn) child.[46] What this should point up is the fact that the action of abortion, at least if Mackenzie's phenomenology is right, can be the first choice of no one. There are of course important differences in the cases, but just as we normally presume that a person considering suicide is likely suffering some serious emotional or psychological trauma rather than imputing to him a willful murderous desire turned toward himself, so we should presume that those intent upon abortion are driven to consider this through very dire circumstances (though I would also insist that the cultural trivialization of abortion has now had time to impact the perceived gravity of the considerations). Abortion is a serious matter, *especially* if those urging respect for the phenomenology of pregnancy are right (and I suspect much of their phenomenology holds). This does make rape an especially grievous crime and a very deep violation of one's agency, but it also means that to undertake an abortion may very well involve some amount of coercion or entrapment and this can mitigate the responsibility and culpability involved considerably.[47]

To bring the point back to the Aldana case, I would urge that the law's job in this issue is not to invade a woman's uterus as if it were a crime scene. A law that reflects justice should not turn a blind eye to abortion, but that does not mean it needs to suspect an abortion anytime a tragedy occurs and to seek to punish it. Ultimately, the law can only investigate crimes there is a credible reason to suspect actually occurred. There are limits to physician-patient confidentiality, of course, as when a doctor has good faith reason to believe that her patient constitutes a serious and imminent threat to herself or others,[48] but without a credible, and lawfully obtained, medical (and not merely speculative) reason to suspect grave malfeasance, one has no reason criminally to investigate the death of an unborn child. Indeed, as I will go on to note below, even with such reason there are likely to be better reasons for the law to take no further action. Just as I hold that a woman cannot be forced to gestate embryos no matter how precarious the embryo's disposition, so I hold that a woman cannot be (physically) forced to submit to an examination of this sort no matter how much a law desires to protect the unborn. We cannot return a miscarriage of life with a miscarriage of justice. Does this mean that the clear way around the reach of abortion law in my ideal society is simply to use, for example, freely available and less detectable oral abortifacients with impunity? No, because in what I and others regard as a just society, such medications would not be on offer for abortions.[49]

If, in another case, a woman tearfully confides to her physician that she procured an abortion sometime after this had occurred, then should the law take an interest in this case? The first thing we need to do to answer this question is remember that most of the readers of this book live in a society in which abortion is legal. So, as things now stand, this is harder for many of them to square with because however much the woman may (or may not) regard this as a regrettable matter, most of our laws do not regard this situation as an infraction. Now what if the world for most of the readers of this book were different, and the law did regard an abortion as a legal infraction? Perhaps it's theoretically possible that some abortion is especially wanton or objectionable for some other reason, but in the main, I think Pakaluk's proposal is right. This strikes me as a case where the abortion is its own punishment. Still, when the law prohibits the provision of abortions out of consideration of the grave injustice involved (as I think it should), there could be reason to act on credible information exposing those who *provide* abortions. But even then, as Robert P. George and Ramesh Pannuru argue, at the moment most western cultures suffer from a legally and morally significant inability to appreciate the gravity of abortion. They write,

> What may be most important is that in our society, both the mothers and the abortionists have had their understandings of abortion shaped by a culture that does not communicate the truth about abortion and unborn children – a culture that includes laws that do not treat abortion as a crime or wrong at all, and that deny the very humanity of unborn children. In this way, our law and culture lead people into serious moral error. A reformed law and culture need to take account both of the seriousness of that error and of the way that our culture has diminished people's culpability for it.[50]

As we have often had occasion to notice, culpability and moral wrongness are different things, and many of us in the West currently live in a cultural environment in which the grievous wrong of abortion is not recognized as such. This certainly mitigates the culpability of pregnant women who procure abortions, but it can also mitigate the culpability of those who provide them, even though eventually a legal change toward proscribing abortion would need to impose some penalties on those who provide abortions (George and Pannuru suggest the loss of a medical license and fines for those physicians who continue the practice in such a reformed culture).

Manninen also discusses the topic of savior siblings, glossing Jodi Picoult's *My Sister's Keeper*. This discussion is actually embedded in a discussion of the "Special Relationship Objection," which I, unlike some other pro-life thinkers, do not find to be an especially telling objection to Manninen's more central concerns about autonomy. So while I don't feel my views are particularly in the crosshairs of Manninen's argument at the relevant point in the text, the concern she raises there might very well be a concern she might raise for my views in a slightly different context, so it may bear some comment. In the novel, Anna is a 13-year-old girl who is a "savior sibling," a girl conceived to be a donor match for her 16-year-old sister Kate's medical needs related to the latter's leukemia treatment. Manninen's point here is that Anna cannot be forced to donate a kidney to Kate, and I think there's a fair bit going for that conclusion. Still, a bit more of the context helps. While Anna makes an impassioned plea that she not be forced to donate her kidney (in the film version this is delivered by Abigail Breslin), we find out later that she is actually playing this part quite reluctantly so that Kate will be allowed to die as she wishes. This changes the circumstances a bit, since if Kate were legally an adult, Anna might not have needed to make her passionate plea for her sister's wishes under the guise of her own medical emancipation. But Manninen also brings in the *McFall v. Shimp* case to raise the issue of whether one is free to give or refrain from giving one's bone marrow. In my earlier chapter, I argued that the idea that one could be legally required (though not physically forced) to offer one's bone marrow (under very specific circumstances) is not so laughable or specter-raising as some seem to fear. Still, I think that there are limits to this kind of expectation, and the kinds of organ donation (a) where the organs are sufficiently unique (i.e., one only has two kidneys), (b) where sufficiently difficult and invasive surgical measures are required, and (c) the procedure itself could plausibly result in serious long-term diminution to the donor's quality of life going forward, then these cases strike me as ones in which a legal requirement to donate is likely to be misguided.

But what about savior siblings? Well, I don't think Manninen or I have any new problems in store for one another on this one. I don't think either of us wants to deny people's ability freely to reproduce, even if their motives are less than ideal. Certainly a savior sibling who didn't want to donate an organ could file for medical emancipation, but not all savior siblings will have reached an age at which they could assess whether or not to do so with the kind of clarity of mind that might be required to gain medical emancipation. The truth is, having two young children myself, I have enough difficulty figuring out when a parent needs to make it clear what's to be done come hell or high water, and when it's better to let children bump into the untoward consequences of their own bad decisions. But I don't think I need to get to the bottom of that one for the sake of my dispute with Manninen because it's not clear to me that either of us see savior siblings significantly differently from one another. If savior siblings can successfully apply for medical emancipation, then they can utilize whatever rights travel with that emancipation, even if they might otherwise have had certain things urged upon them by their parents. I'm a little more willing to countenance the idea that a just law could require a very unique donor to donate, say, bone marrow, to a very unique donee than Manninen is, but that doesn't mean Manninen and I are going to disagree about anything new or germane to this dispute when it comes to savior siblings.

Kate's case, however, might put one in mind of those who wish to die, and the question of euthanasia often travels with the question of abortion in significant ways. While I discussed euthanasia briefly in my initial chapter, Manninen used parallels between abortion and euthanasia in her initial chapter, and so I will offer some brief responses here. After mentioning the idea that abortion would be more akin to active euthanasia (as opposed to merely passive euthanasia – merely letting someone die), Manninen discusses how she thinks the distinction is irrelevant. She writes "I sincerely doubt that if we could devise a way to 'unplug' the fetus from a woman in a way more akin to passive euthanasia, pro-life advocates would all of a sudden find abortion permissible."[51] To be sure, she's right about that. But consider two points we have mentioned before. The case of the salpingectomy in the context of an ectopic pregnancy is significantly like "unplugging" the embryo from the mother (granted, there's more to it than that, but the parallel is morally relevant). The other case is the theoretical case Kaczor mentions of artificial wombs.[52] Nothing that I've said in this book militates against the use of a salpingectomy in the context of an ectopic pregnancy, if every effort has been made to save both mother and child. Likewise, nothing I've said in this book militates against the use of artificial wombs if, in some future state of technology, they allowed us artificially to gestate embryos and fetuses conceived elsewhere. Now if "abortion" were merely evacuation (which is not my definition), and evacuation could be medically procured safely, then at least Kaczor and I would presumably find the use of such artificial wombs permissible. I don't hold that abortion is merely evacuation because I believe that the kinds of procedures we have in mind when we think of abortions are those that put the unborn child in the line of grave harm by reason of the acts themselves. Without that, we're just talking about induction. But since abortion does involve an act that, things being what they are, places an unborn child in the line of grave harm, it is impermissible for the same reasons that other acts that do this are impermissible.

Manninen is clearly right that the distinction between (actively) killing and (passively) letting die is a vexed distinction that has been debated by bioethicists for decades. Indeed, she is right to say that "a pro-life advocate who wants to implement this distinction … has to contend with the plethora of philosophical literature that denies the moral relevance of the omission versus commission distinction."[53] Fair enough, but as for engaging topics that have seen a plethora of literature devoted to them, it seems this is the very item on our agenda in this book. As I mentioned in my initial chapter, as it concerns euthanasia, much of the time the key distinction may be less about active as opposed to passive euthanasia and more about ordinary as opposed to extraordinary measures one takes to save the life in question. As Thomas D. Sullivan pointed out in response to James Rachels's famous cases, both the active and passive cases are morally objectionable.[54] The real question is *not* whether you can take a life directly (because the answer is no), but whether, if all other options were exhausted, you could do something active to *prevent* someone else's life from being lost. This is where I find the endless proliferation of "trolley cases" often enough to be missing the big picture. Some of the more fine-grained cases get at other issues, but in Philippa Foot's original case of the tram heading toward five people that can be redirected toward only one person, I think this can be plausibly described the way any conductor acting in good faith would describe it to herself, namely, that she is steering the tram *away* from the five people.[55]

In my experience all too often pro-choice advocates pick a particularly thorny trolley-style case and imagine this objection to have won the day for the entire pro-choice side, as if pro-life thinkers were all of a piece and had no disagreements about which cases constituted appropriate applications of, say, the principle of double effect. Happily, Manninen does not make this assumption. Does the Phoenix case of a putative abortion in which the placenta was targeted constitute a direct abortion? That's a difficult issue with rigorous pro-life thinkers on either side.[56] Is the use of methotrexate to target the trophoblast of an embryo in the context of an ectopic pregnancy on a moral par with a salpingectomy, or does the use of methotrexate here constitute an act against the embryo itself? Here again, we find rigorous pro-life thinkers disagreeing among themselves.[57] The reality is that pro-life thinkers themselves do not agree about all cases, and this is to be expected. We've been thinking about this for a long time, too (even if it's not always practical to engage these disagreements in entirely secular fora). Granted, one's hospital and governing boards are still going to have to come to a decision, and it won't be easy. But the cases on which consistent pro-life thinkers disagree are about a very small number of cases relative to the number of abortions worldwide, and while this is not much consolation to the theorist, it may at least help us frame the debate Manninen and I are having.

4 Conclusion

Manninen and I certainly have some disagreements. In some cases, our intellectual commitments probably have something to do with our moral sensibilities, too. Manninen can describe the case of a woman reaching out to touch the cheek of her newly aborted child and saying "I'm sorry, baby" as "touching."[58] My emotions are stirred by this case, too. If you're checking, I feel no anger in regard to it. Manninen and I presumably both feel sadness upon considering it. But she must say that her sadness is based on the abortion's being at worst a necessary or permissible evil. As for me, all I can feel is grief. Grief for the woman forced into this terrible circumstance? Of course. Grief for the poor and marginalized who experience these terrible circumstances disproportionately? Certainly. But in addition to all of this, there is, for me, at bottom, and most fundamentally, a grief over the loss of this child.

I am aware that one's emotions are harder to stir at the level of the embryo, but I cannot regard others' emotions as determinative of very much in that regard. We still need consistency of thought in regard to what counts as the human person whose loss all of us would grieve if we could only agree on who is a person. I believe, along with many others, that embryos have the requisite organismal integrity to count as persons and should be respected in that way morally and legally. None of this changes the fact that women must be respected (and a great deal more than they are), and that they can never be forced to gestate an embryo, even if the embryo's fate is especially dire. As Manninen and I will go on to discuss in our joint chapter, the sexual integrity of persons is very significant, much more so than many would have us believe. Indeed, Manninen and I share some deeply rooted convictions about this, and they speak to the gravity of rape and anything on an analogy with it. Nevertheless, I do not hold that requiring that a woman refrain from taking direct action against the child inside her constitutes compelling her to gestate, because the only way she can evacuate the fetus is by exposing it to grave harm through a direct action against it. This does mean that pregnancy is surpassingly unique, and that society must care for pregnant mothers, new mothers, and infants along with the unborn in ways that require more of us.

Nevertheless, the unborn have a place in that last sentence, and an important one, seeing that they are especially vulnerable. Accounts of personhood such as the one Manninen favors tie the acquisition of rights too tightly to phenomenological properties. The troubles with phenomenological properties as bearers of personal identity are, in my view, legion, but among the most problematic is the fact that once phenomenological properties become the bearers of identity, it becomes extremely difficult to explain why people who lack phenomenal experience of harm are genuinely harmed. Of course I hold that such people *are harmed*, but if mental life is the guarantor of identity, how could an event that never made a dent on one's mental life impact one's identity?

Thinkers such as David Boonin have sought refuge in the concept of a dispositional desire, but the concept of a disposition is actually much more at home in the animalist account of personal identity I have discussed. This is because on that account the person is the organism, and the properties that develop or heal as the person develops or heals are possible because of the kind of entity this is, rather than the kind of performances it can put on display. The EMAPI theorist must explain why the resumption of mental life is relevantly different from the initiation of mental life, and this will be difficult. For at any point at which the temporarily comatose patient resumes her mental life, there will be the point days or even moments prior to this when her organism is healing or reinitiating the mental life that was hers. But the only reason we are unsurprised that she *can* resume this mental life is that it is grounded in her organism. Now take the unborn child days or even moments prior to the initiation of her mental life. She has all the capacities so nearly actualizable that her initiation of her mental life is indistinguishable from its resumption had she incurred some kind of minute harm prior to attaining consciousness. Because of this, and because I think the animalist picture remains much more metaphysically parsimonious and plausible than the EMAPI account, I think that the animalist picture gives us the right account of personal identity, and I think that such a picture can, and should, render the verdict that the unborn are persons with the same complement of rights that you and I possess.

Finally, it is worth noting that pro-life thinkers don't always agree about everything. For example, the principle of double effect is widely appealed to in pro-life thinkers, but as to exactly which cases count as legitimate uses of the principle there are often in-house controversies among pro-life thinkers. But this is to be expected when any serious viewpoint is defended by a number of thinkers. Where pro-life thinkers seldom disagree is with regard to cases such as a woman with advanced uterine cancer whose continuance would pose an imminent threat to both her life and the life of the child within her. When this is the case, and all possible measures have been taken to save both mother and child, it is permissible to treat the pathology of the woman even while it is foreknown, but not directly intended, that the child will die as a result of the treatment. Here the goal is to *prevent* the woman's death, since she is the only one who in this case can be saved, not directly to attack the unborn child. So when Manninen brings in the distinction between passive and active euthanasia, I find the point moot, since both are wrong in a patient who can reasonably be saved. Accepting imminent death with serenity can be good, but only when the pathology has advanced to the point where death is genuinely imminent (and cases like these are seldom cases in which the patient is also pregnant).

For most of the readers of this book, western culture has gotten to a point where abortion is regarded as one more elective medical procedure. While for people who identify as pro-life this is distressing, it is also a factor in mitigating the culpability of people who have not yet understood the gravity of abortion. Women who procure abortions can hardly be happy about the choice (though if they misunderstand the gravity of the situation, they may be happy that the choice is available to them). But abortion is the loss of a child. It is a grievous loss, and it can be wished upon no one. Because of this, and because of the mitigating factors that exist in assessing the culpability for women who procure abortions, few pro-life thinkers seriously envisage punishing mothers for abortions. It may be possible to envisage consequences for providers of abortions in a just legal system, but there, too, there are mitigating factors for culpability. One mitigating factor is our current cultural moment. But another mitigating factor is that people have often disagreed about abortion over the course of history and they have done so for reasons that can be articulated and defended. That is, this is one of those issues on which rational people disagree. I hold that the pro-choice position is mistaken about what is morally and legally permissible (in a just society; of course abortion is legally permissible in many places in the raw empirical sense). I believe that the best account of what a person is and the best account of what we owe to one another in a just society entails that the pro-life position is correct. My friend Bertha Alvarez Manninen disagrees with me, and finds the pro-choice position the best one out there on this matter. We nevertheless both trade in the currency of argument and rational discourse and believe that the other is capable of appreciating the other side of the question. This is why we have undertaken to have some civil dialogue on the topic of abortion in this book.

Notes

1 See Book 1, chapter 6 of Aristotle's *Nicomachean Ethics*.
2 Manninen, Chapter 1, p. 22.
3 Manninen, Chapter 1, p. 22.
4 Reader, 2008, "Abortion, Killing, and Maternal Moral Authority," *Hypatia*, 23: 132–149. Reader writes "Mothers take themselves to be responsible for organizing their children's lives until the children take over that function for themselves. This implies that in seeking abortion-as-killing, the mother who cannot go on into the next stage of mothering discharges her maternal responsibility for organizing that whole life by ending it. She does not relinquish responsibility for her fetus's life. Rather, she exercises her maternal moral authority to complete her responsibility early" (143).
5 Manninen, Chapter 1, p. 22.
6 Though the woman's right in this case may be derivative upon the embryo's right to be brought to term (even though the embryo's right to be brought to term does not override the woman's right not to be coerced into gestation).
7 It is worth considering here that this is a different picture of equality than one that, say, Ruth Bader Ginsburg might use when she argues that the abortion right should be grounded in issues that concern, as she quotes a Professor Karst, "women's position in society in relation to men." She further writes "It is not a sufficient answer to charge it all to women's anatomy – a natural, not man-made, phenomenon. Society, not anatomy, 'places a greater stigma on unmarried women who become pregnant than on the men who father their children.' Society expects, but nature does not command, that 'women take the major responsibility … for child care' and that they will stay with their children, bearing nurture and support burdens alone, when fathers deny paternity or otherwise refuse to provide care or financial support for unwanted offspring" (see Ginsburg, 1998, "Some Thoughts on Autonomy and Equality in Relation to *Roe v. Wade*," in *The Abortion Controversy 25 Years After Roe v. Wade: A Reader*, 2nd edition, Louis P. Pojman and Francis J. Beckwith (Belmont: Wadsworth), pp. 105–113 at 110). Some of this is indeed societal (and unjust) rather than anatomical, but I do maintain that, uteruses being what they are, one can't, at least in our current, and foreseeable, state of technology, terminate a pregnancy at most of its stages without doing direct and grave harm to the unborn human person. Society can, and very well should, conceive of some rights in such a way as to compensate for this reality, but it cannot consider the abortion right merely as a "woman's autonomous charge of her full life's course" (110). Rather, I believe that the effort to map a pregnant woman's autonomy onto a man's without remainder, and to characterize a man's autonomy without acknowledgement of his debt to all women is to consider us as human beings to be more atomistic than we actually are.
8 Manninen, Chapter 1, p. 22.
9 See chapter 9 (on the possibility of artificial wombs) of Christopher Kaczor, 2011, *The Ethics of Abortion* (London: Routledge).
10 This may depend on the assumption that we live in a sufficiently large society that would have other ways of ensuring that the child's most basic needs are met.
11 Of course another private vessel would do, but presumably one should deliver the child to such a vessel with reasonable assurance that doing so would keep her out of harm's way.
12 It is also worth noting that this arrangement is not even of the sort where one must give bone marrow or where Henry Fonda must put his hand on your fevered brow to heal you. Although I think some higher level of assistance may be called for in a just society, it is still true that Henry Fonda's refraining is not a direct killing and your tossing the child into the sea is.
13 See United States Office of Population Affairs, 2017, https://www.hhs.gov/opa/about-opa-and-initiatives/embryo-adoption/. Accessed January 11, 2017.
14 See Tadeusz Pacholczyk, 2007, "On the Moral Objectionability of Human Embryo Adoption," in Sarah-Vaughn Brakman and Darlene Fozard Weaver, eds., *The Ethics of Embryo Adoption and the Catholic Tradition* (Dordrecht: Springer), pp. 69–83 at 70.

15 In some pro-life quarters this is not so taken for granted. See, for instance, in addition to Pacholczyk's essay, Mary Geach, 2009, "The Female Act of Allowing an Intromission of Impregnating Kind," in *Human Embryo Adoption: Biotechnology, Marriage, and the Right to Life*, eds. Thomas V. Berg and Edward J. Furton (Philadelphia: The National Catholic Bioethics Center), pp. 251–271 and Helen Watt, 2009, "Becoming Pregnant or Becoming a Mother? Embryo Transfer With or Without a Prior Maternal Relationship," in Berg and Furton, eds., pp. 55–67.
16 Some, such as Pacholczyk, argue that, at the present time, there is no discrete action at all that is good to do about this situation. See Pacholczyk, "On the Moral Objectionability of Human Embryo Adoption," p. 82. Though, it should be noted, there are many pro-life thinkers who argue that embryo adoption is just as commendable as it might seem to many people reading this. In particular, Robert P. George and Christopher Tollefsen's 2011 book *Embryo: A Defense of Human Life*, 2nd edition (Princeton: Witherspoon Institute) takes this tack.
17 See Kaczor, *The Ethics of Abortion*, p. 93.
18 Manninen, Chapter 1, p. 25.
19 See Manninen, 2009, "The Metaphysical Foundations of Reproductive Ethics," *Journal of Applied Philosophy* 26: 190–204 at p. 191.
20 Manninen, "The Metaphysical Foundations of Reproductive Ethics," p. 192.
21 David Boonin discusses an argument he calls the "Kindred Species Argument," for which he is able to find some proponents, but the key to the Kindred Species Argument is the word "kindred," in that the claim is that one should have due solicitude for *one's own* species. While, like Boonin, I'm not sure how much more plausible that argument is, it is relevantly different from an argument that *some* genetic sequence (to which I bear no necessary relation) deserves moral status of its own accord. See Boonin, 2003, *A Defense of Abortion* (Cambridge: Cambridge University Press), pp. 26–27.
22 See chapter 3 of Singer, 1993, *Practical Ethics*, 2nd edition (Cambridge: Cambridge University Press).
23 See George and Tollefsen, *Embryo*, pp. 76–80.
24 Manninen, Chapter 1, p. 31.
25 Manninen, Chapter 1, p. 27.
26 Manninen, Chapter 1, p. 26.
27 See Archard, 2007, "The Wrong of Rape," *The Philosophical Quarterly* 57: 374–393.
28 See Archard, "The Wrong of Rape," p. 378, italics mine.
29 See Archard, "The Wrong of Rape," p. 379.
30 Manninen, Chapter 1, p. 28.
31 Indeed, she writes "Nonsentient beings are not the types of beings to whom we owe moral considerations because nothing at all is important *to them*" (Manninen, Chapter 1, p. 28, italics original).
32 Even if she never becomes aware of it, her sexual integrity has been violated, and I don't think the idea of "things being worse for x" need entail that x is aware of how they are worse for her.
33 Nicola Jane Williams, 2013, in "Possible Persons and the Problem of Prenatal Harm," *Journal of Ethics* 17: 355–385, goes to considerable trouble to explain how, on a psychological account, which seems relevantly similar to Manninen's, we could still talk, in some attenuated way, of fetal harm. With respect, I must admit that the attempt strikes me as a great deal of effort to justify a counterintuitive idea when a simpler account is available. Williams even admits part of this when she notes that "Were we to subscribe to a biological account of personal identity over time the answer to our question would be simple. On such an account it would be the case that foetuses and embryos were already in possession of the feature that grounds claims to both prenatal and personal harms – their organism … On the psychological account however an answer proves a little more elusive" (pp. 363–364).
34 Boonin, *A Defense of Abortion*, pp. 74–75.
35 See Williams, "Possible Persons and the Problem of Prenatal Harm."

36 George and Tollefsen, *Embryo*, p. 79.
37 See Irish Catholic Bishops' Conference, 2012, *Statement by the Standing Committee of the Irish Catholic Bishops' Conference on the equal and inalienable right to life of a mother and her unborn child* at http://www.catholicbishops.ie/2012/11/19/statement-standing-committee-irish-catholic-bishops-conference-equal-inalienable-life-mother-unborn-child/.
38 This is principally, though perhaps not only, because in the case of the salpingectomy, there is only one way to save even one of the parties. Failing that, both are medically likely to die.
39 Procedures that go beyond a salpingectomy to a salpingostomy or the use of methotrexate in the case of ectopic pregnancies are more controversial in some pro-life circles. See, for instance, Marie A. Anderson, et al., 2011, "Ectopic Pregnancy and Catholic Morality," *The National Catholic Bioethics Quarterly* 11: 667–684. The case of the cancerous uterus is generally not controversial. See, for instance, the United States Conference of Catholic Bishops' 2010 statement (*The Distinction Between Direct Abortion and Legitimate Medical Procedures*) after a difficult case in Phoenix, AZ. See: http://www.usccb.org/about/doctrine/publications/upload/direct-abortion-statement2010-06-23.pdf. While the Phoenix case that occasioned the 2010 document remains subject to considerable controversy even within avowedly pro-life camps, the document explicitly mentions the cancerous uterus case as one that is permissible.
40 Manninen, Chapter 1, p. 20.
41 Manninen, Chapter 1, p. 20.
42 Beckwith, 2007, *Defending Life: A Moral and Legal Case Against Abortion Choice* (Cambridge: Cambridge University Press), p. 171.
43 Manninen, Chapter 1, p. 21.
44 See, for instance, Watson, 2015, http://www.bbc.com/news/world-latin-america-32480443.
45 See Pakaluk's 1990 presentation to the Augustine Club of Columbia University, NY, titled "Difficult Questions for Pro-Choice Persons," esp. Question 6 under the heading "Questions for pro-life people, and replies" at https://michaelpakaluk.files.wordpress.com/2012/03/difficult-questions-for-pro-choice-persons.pdf. Robert P. George and Ramesh Pannuru have also argued that we shouldn't punish women for abortions. See George and Pannuru, 2016, "Why We Shouldn't Punish Mothers for Abortion," *National Review*, May 9, at http://www.nationalreview.com/article/435276/abortion-punishment-donald-trump-doctors-mothers-prosecuted.
46 Mackenzie, 1992, "Abortion and Embodiment," *Australasian Journal of Philosophy*, 70: 136–155.
47 This means that I favor Archard's analysis of rape over H.E. Baber's in Baber, 1987, "How Bad is Rape," *Hypatia*, 2: 125–138.
48 The United States Department of Health and Human Services, 2017, takes this line. See https://www.hhs.gov/hipaa/for-professionals/faq/520/does-hipaa-permit-a-health-care-provider-to-disclose-information-if-the-patient-is-a-danger/index.html?language=es.
49 See Francis J. Beckwith, *Defending Life*, p. 162.
50 See George and Pannuru, "Why We Shouldn't Punish Mothers for Abortion."
51 Manninen, Chapter 1, p. 49.
52 See chapter 9 of his *The Ethics of Abortion*.
53 Manninen, Chapter 1, p. 50.
54 See Rachels, 1994, "Active and Passive Euthanasia," in Bonnie Steinbock and Alastair Norcross, eds., *Killing and Letting Die*, second edition (New York: Fordham University Press), pp. 112–119 and Sullivan, 1994, "Active and Passive Euthanasia: An Impertinent Distinction?" in Steinbock and Norcross, *Killing and Letting Die*, pp. 131–138.
55 Philippa Foot, 1994, "The Problem of Abortion and the Doctrine of Double Effect," in Steinbock and Norcross, *Killing and Letting Die*, pp. 266–279 at 270.
56 See, among many possibilities, Patrick McCruden, 2012, "The Moral Object in the 'Phoenix Case': A Defense of Sister McBride's Decision," *Christian Bioethics*, 18: 301–311; Steven J. Jensen, 2014, "Causal Constraints on Intention: A Critique of Tollefsen

on the Phoenix Case," *National Catholic Bioethics Quarterly*, 14: 273–293; and Christopher Tollefsen, 2015, "Double Effect and Two Hard Cases in Medical Ethics," *American Catholic Philosophical Quarterly*, 89: 407–420.
57 Some lay of the land is provided in Anderson, et al., 2011, "Ectopic Pregnancy and Catholic Morality," though it is interesting to note that William E. May is one well-known pro-life thinker who has explicitly changed his mind on the use of methotrexate from at first arguing that its use for ectopic pregnancies was impermissible, and since then, arguing that its use for such purposes is permissible. See May, 2008, *Catholic Bioethics and the Gift of Human Life*, 2nd edition (Huntington: Our Sunday Visitor), pp. 201–202.
58 Manninen, Chapter 1, p. 54.

References

Anderson, Marie A., Fastiggi, Robert, Hargroder, David, et al. 2011. "Ectopic Pregnancy and Catholic Morality." *The National Catholic Bioethics Quarterly*, 11: 667–684.
Archard, David. 2007. "The Wrong of Rape." *The Philosophical Quarterly*, 57: 374–393.
Baber, H.E. 1987. "How Bad is Rape." *Hypatia*, 2: 125–138.
Beckwith, Francis J. 2007. *Defending Life: A Moral and Legal Case Against Abortion Choice*. Cambridge: Cambridge University Press.
Boonin, David. 2003. *A Defense of Abortion*. Cambridge: Cambridge University Press.
Foot, Philippa. 1994. "The Problem of Abortion and the Doctrine of Double Effect." In Steinbock, Bonnie and Norcross, Alastair, eds. *Killing and Letting Die*. 2nd edition. New York: Fordham University, pp. 266–279.
Geach, Mary. 2009. "The Female Act of Allowing an Intromission of Impregnating Kind." In Berg, Thomas V. and Furton, Edward J., eds. *Human Embryo Adoption: Biotechnology, Marriage, and the Right to Life*. Philadelphia: The National Catholic Bioethics Center, pp. 251–271.
George, Robert P. and Pannuru, Ramesh. 2016. "Why We Shouldn't Punish Mothers for Abortion." *National Review*. http://www.nationalreview.com/article/435276/abortion-punishment-donald-trump-doctors-mothers-prosecuted. Accessed September 13, 2017.
George, Robert P. and Tollefsen, Christopher. 2011. *Embryo: A Defense of Human Life*. 2nd edition. Princeton: Witherspoon Institute.
Ginsburg, Ruth Bader. 1998. "Some Thoughts on Autonomy and Equality in Relation to Roe v. Wade." In *The Abortion Controversy 25 Years After Roe v. Wade: A Reader*. 2nd edition. Eds. Louis P. Pojman and Francis J. Beckwith. Belmont: Wadsworth, pp. 105–113.
Irish Catholic Bishops' Conference. 2012. *Statement by the Standing Committee of the Irish Catholic Bishops' Conference on the equal and inalienable right to life of a mother and her unborn child*. http://www.catholicbishops.ie/2012/11/19/statement-standing-committee-irish-catholic-bishops-conference-equal-inalienable-life-mother-unborn-child/. Accessed September 12, 2017.
Jensen, Steven J. 2014. "Causal Constraints on Intention: A Critique of Tollefsen on the Phoenix Case." *National Catholic Bioethics Quarterly*, 14: 273–293.
Kaczor, Christopher. 2011. *The Ethics of Abortion*. London: Routledge.
Mackenzie, Catriona. 1992. "Abortion and Embodiment." *Australasian Journal of Philosophy*, 70. 2: 136–155.
Manninen, Bertha Alvarez. 2009. "The Metaphysical Foundations of Reproductive Ethics." *Journal of Applied Philosophy*, 26: 190–204.
May, William E. 2008. *Catholic Bioethics and the Gift of Human Life*. 2nd edition. Huntington, IN: Our Sunday Visitor.
McCruden, Patrick. 2012. "The Moral Object in the 'Phoenix Case': A Defense of Sister McBride's Decision." *Christian Bioethics*, 18: 301–311.

Pacholczyk, Tadeusz. 2007. "On the Moral Objectionability of Human Embryo Adoption." In Sarah-Vaughn Brakman and Darlene Fozard Weaver, eds., *The Ethics of Embryo Adoption and the Catholic Tradition* (Dordrecht: Springer), pp. 69–83.

Pakaluk, Michael. 1990. "Difficult Questions for Pro-Choice Persons." https://michaelpakaluk.files.wordpress.com/2012/03/difficult-questions-for-pro-choice-persons.pdf. Accessed September 12, 2017.

Rachels, James. 1994. "Active and Passive Euthanasia." In Steinbock, Bonnie and Norcross, Alastair, eds. *Killing and Letting Die*. 2nd edition. New York: Fordham University, pp. 112–119.

Reader, Soran. 2008. "Abortion, Killing, and Maternal Moral Authority." *Hypatia*, 23: 132–149.

Singer, Peter. 1993. *Practical Ethics*. 2nd edition. Cambridge: Cambridge University Press.

Sullivan, Thomas D. 1994. "Active and Passive Euthanasia: An Impertinent Distinction?" In Steinbock, Bonnie and Norcross, Alastair, eds. *Killing and Letting Die*. 2nd edition. New York: Fordham University, pp. 131–138.

Tollefsen, Christopher. 2015. "Double Effect and Two Hard Cases in Medical Ethics." *American Catholic Philosophical Quarterly*, 89: 407–420.

United States Conference of Catholic Bishops. 2010. *The Distinction Between Direct Abortion and Legitimate Medical Procedures*. http://www.usccb.org/about/doctrine/publications/upload/direct-abortion-statement2010-06-23.pdf. Accessed September 13, 2017.

United States Department of Health and Human Services. 2017. "Health Information Privacy." https://www.hhs.gov/hipaa/for-professionals/faq/520/does-hipaa-permit-a-healthcare-provider-to-disclose-information-if-the-patient-is-a-danger/index.html?language=es. Accessed September 13, 2017.

United States Office of Population Affairs. 2017. "Embryo Adoption." https://www.hhs.gov/opa/about-opa/embryo-adoption/index.html. Accessed September 12, 2017.

Watson, Katy. 2015. "The Mothers being criminalized in El Salvador." http://www.bbc.com/news/world-latin-america-32480443. Accessed September 13, 2017.

Watt, Helen. 2009. "Becoming Pregnant or Becoming a Mother? Embryo Transfer With or Without a Prior Maternal Relationship." In Berg, Thomas V. and Furton, Edward J., eds. *Human Embryo Adoption: Biotechnology, Marriage, and the Right to Life*. Philadelphia: The National Catholic Bioethics Center, pp. 55–67.

Williams, Nicola Jane. 2013. "Possible Persons and the Problem of Prenatal Harm." *Journal of Ethics*, 17: 355–385.

5

CONVERGENCES AND DIVERGENCES

Bertha Alvarez Manninen and Jack Mulder, Jr.

The purpose of this book is, largely, two-fold. First, we wanted to present to the reader the respective reasons we are either pro-life (Mulder) or pro-choice (Manninen), and also, we responded to each other's arguments and concerns. In doing so, we hope to have exemplified the principle John Stuart Mill invokes when he writes:

> the only way in which a human being can make some approach to knowing the whole of a subject is by hearing what can be said about it by persons of every variety of opinion, and studying all modes in which it can be looked at by every character of mind. No wise man ever acquired his wisdom in any mode but this; nor is it in the nature of human intellect to become wise in any other manner.[1]

Indeed, we both think that the best way to learn about the strength of your own views and your own convictions is to patiently examine those views from a variety of perspectives, including those with which one disagrees. Mill notes that until we do this, until we submit even our most cherished views to critical scrutiny, "we do not understand the grounds of our opinions."[2]

Moreover, this format is conducive to the second purpose: namely, an illustration of what philosophical and civil dialogue over contentious issues can look like. The purpose of this chapter is to take this latter goal a step further. We are now going to present to the reader something that is rarely seen when it comes to ethical policy debates about abortion: we are actually going to have some of this dialogue in an attempt to find some areas where we, as people of conviction, can find some areas of common ground, even while we differ in other matters. While there will still be areas of disagreements we will discuss, the goal of this chapter is to show our readers not only that we *have* common ground (if that's not surprising enough), but also how we can *build upon* that common ground in an effort to help enact real change in our society concerning abortion.

Both of us have one core issue in common: neither of us *like* abortions, and *both* of us wish that we could construct a society where abortions are far less prevalent. When all philosophical issues are said and done, what could the dialogue look like on other social and policy issues that would allow us a society that is genuinely just? We have decided to focus on three areas where we most think a discussion between pro-choice and pro-life could be fruitful, namely, issues of social and economic justice that often play a role in the reality of abortion, concerns about sexual ethics, and contraception access.

I Issues of social and economic justice

Manninen

Many of my students who identify as "pro-life" will often make exceptions to their anti-abortion stance for cases of rape and incest. Every other abortion is classified as an abortion of "convenience" and is, therefore, deemed selfish and immoral. The term "convenience" in this context is rarely defined, but it is clearly meant as a sweeping negative generalization of why most women procure abortions. But let's take a closer look at those reasons, and then ask what we, as a society, could do to meet the needs of women who choose abortion as a way out of an undesirable state of affairs.

When asked for the reasons why they were seeking abortion, many women, rather than giving a purely "selfish" answer (whatever that term means in this context), gave these reasons instead:

> The reasons patients gave for having an abortion underscored their understanding of the responsibilities of parenthood and family life. The three most common reasons – each cited by three-fourths of patients – were concern for or responsibility to other individuals; the inability to afford a child; and the belief that having a baby would interfere with work, school or the ability to care for dependents. Half said they did not want to be a single parent or were having problems with their husband or partner.[3]

Are such reasons "selfish" or a mere product of convenience? Understanding the plight of single parenthood in the United States, especially single motherhood, renders such concerns perfectly reasonable ones. It is impossible to deny the economic disparities that influence so many women to obtain abortions. In 2014, 49% of women procuring abortions survived on incomes less than the federal poverty level (classified as making less than $11,670 per year for a single adult with no children). 26% have low incomes (100–199% of the federal poverty level). Women who live below the poverty line are about four times as likely to obtain an abortion when compared to women who live 300% above it.[4] Children born to unwed teenage mothers, and the mothers themselves, face a host of difficulties, including an increased risk of failure in school, of poverty, and even of incidences of physical and mental illness.[5]

The United States claims to be a pro-natalist society, but our social policies far from lend themselves to this conclusion. In 1993, President Bill Clinton signed the Family and Medical Leave Act of 1993 into law, which guarantees 12 weeks of *unpaid* maternity leave to new mothers; for women already facing financial difficulties, three months of no income is simply not a realistic possibility. A 2000 FMLA report found that "pay was not just a worry to those on leave but was a barrier to those who needed to take leave. The current survey found that lack of pay was the number one reason workers who needed leave did not take it."[6] Women who decide to have the baby and then have to return back to work immediately to help provide for the child often have to pay for childcare, which can cost several thousands of dollars per year, sometimes as high as $14,000 per year in the most expensive states. For a single parent, this could constitute anywhere between 25% and 53.6% of their annual income.[7]

Single-parent households headed by women often face crippling poverty. A 2015 study illustrated that single mothers were at a far greater risk of living in poverty than single fathers, and that this was exacerbated with every additional child.[8] A 2012 study by David Brady and Rebekah Burroway noted that among affluent democracies, the United States "has the highest rate of poverty among single mothers …"[9] The 2007 Children's Defense Scorecard noted that the 113 members of Congress who have consistently voted against child welfare programs also self-identify as pro-life.[10] Within the past few years, Republicans have often proposed completely defunding Planned Parenthood, despite the fact that one of its primary purposes is to provide reproductive health care and education, and access to contraception, for millions of disadvantaged women. Moreover, Republicans have also advocated withholding all federal funds from the Title X Family Funding programs, whose main role is to provide contraception and reproductive care services specifically to poor women.

Given all this, it is not hard to see why a single woman, unprepared for parenthood, would choose to abort an unplanned pregnancy. Our society is set up in such a way to establish a dire dichotomy for women in this situation: if you aren't already gainfully employed, educated, with a supportive partner, or financially stable, you must choose between either achieving all these things eventually, or becoming a mother. Given this dichotomy, it is unsurprising that, when women are asked why they chose abortion over parenting, their reasons often mainly come down to financial concerns:

> A financial reason (40%) was the most frequently mentioned theme. Six percent of women mentioned this as their only reason for seeking abortion. Most women (38%) cited general financial concerns which included responses such as "financial problems", "don't have the means", "it all boils down to money" and "can't afford to support a child." As one unemployed 42 year old woman

with a monthly household income of a little over $1,000 describes: "[It was] all financial, me not having a job, living off death benefits, dealing with my 14 year old son. I didn't have money to buy a baby spoon."[11]

It seems clear that in many cases the choice to abort is a response to difficult socio-economic circumstances. Therefore, it is likely that we can mitigate the number of abortions by addressing this root cause.

If the eradication of poverty is what would be needed to reduce abortion rates, it seems like the United States would be facing an insurmountable task. Luckily, less radical means can prove effective. It is important to look at countries with low abortion rates, see what they are doing right, and try to emulate those steps here in the United States. If financial concerns are one of the leading reasons women seek abortions, perhaps creating social services and programs that mitigate that need can go even further in reducing abortion rates.

All women, but especially those in financially precarious situations, would benefit from paid maternity leave (indeed, all families would benefit from paid leave for both parents). The United States joins Papua New Guinea, Swaziland, Suriname, Liberia and Lesotho as one of the few countries in the world that do not mandate paid maternity leave. A 2012 study illustrates that paid family leave (which includes parental leave in order to care for a new child) was offered to only 11% of all American workers.[12] In contrast, Canada offers anywhere between 26 and 52 weeks paid maternity leave, while most European nations offer 52 or more weeks of paid parental leave.[13] Government subsidized child care can also go a long way in helping financially strapped families. In California and Washington State, for example, there are programs that help the most disadvantaged pay for childcare. However, the cut-off for eligibility leaves many families struggling; in Washington State, living at 200% above the poverty line, which is still not much, disqualifies a family from subsidies.[14] Most recently, the town of Newburgh Heights in Ohio approved a first-in-the-nation paternal leave program. All city full-time employees are eligible for 6 months of paid leave after the birth or adoption of their new child.

European countries with low abortion rates share some consistent commonalities: not only do they have liberal abortion laws and wide access to contraception and sexual/reproductive education, they have robust social safety programs as well that make the prospect of an unplanned pregnancy, especially amongst young individuals, less daunting and insurmountable. Consider, for example, the Netherlands, which legalized abortion in 1984 but has one of the lowest abortion rates in the world. Contraception is widely available free of charge, but in addition:

> Like most European countries, the Dutch government provides a range of what sociologists call "social" and what reproductive health advocates call "human" rights: the right to housing, healthcare, and a minimum income. Not only do such rights ensure access, if need be, to free contraceptive and abortion services, government supports make coming of age less perilous for both teenagers and parents. This might make the prospect of sex derailing a child's

life less haunting. Ironically, the very lack of such rights and high rates of childhood poverty in the U.S. contributes to high rates of births among teenagers. Without adequate support systems or educational and job opportunities, young people are simply more likely to start parenthood early in life.[15]

Brady and Burroway's 2012 study of 18 affluent democracies illustrated two important pieces of information concerning the financial state of single mothers. First, having a well-educated and employed head of household was a key factor in alleviating poverty:

> Single-mother households with multiple earners, well-educated and older heads of household, and multiple adults are less likely to be poor. Those with no one employed, low-educated and younger heads of household, and multiple children are more likely to be poor.[16]

A second vital factor in alleviating poverty for single mothers is adopting robust social welfare programs:

> Our central conclusion is that generous, comprehensive, and universal welfare states substantially reduce the poverty of single mothers. The welfare state index and universal replacement rate are strongly negatively associated with single-mother poverty. If the United States increased its welfare state index to the cross-national mean or to Sweden's level, the odds of single-mother poverty would decline by a factor of 3.8 or 13.3, respectively. If the United States increased its universal replacement rate to those levels, the odds of single-mother poverty would decline by a factor of 4.5 or 17.9, respectively. As noted earlier, these effect sizes are large in comparison with the individual-level variables. Although policy and demographic debates often focus on altering the behavior or characteristics of single mothers (e.g., encouraging education, employment, having fewer children, and marriage), welfare universalism could be an even more effective anti-poverty strategy.[17]

In other words, when a country guarantees the basic sustenance of its members, the rates of poverty decrease substantially. Alleviating the financial strain on women who are facing the unplanned prospect of parenthood will simultaneously mitigate one of the leading reasons women choose abortion.

Although Brady and Burroway's detailed study provides evidence that welfare states mitigate poverty, especially amongst single mothers, there is not (as of yet) a similar study that shows a direct correlation between welfare states and low abortion rates *per se* (although there is evidence that providing universal healthcare decreases abortion rates[18]). We do, however, have microcosmic evidence from smaller-scale programs that have been implemented in the United States. Pro-life theologian Steve Tracy argues that, while he opposes legal abortion, he fully supports more robust social safety net programs designed to meet the financial, mental, and emotional needs of women facing unplanned pregnancies, and that part of being "pro-life" is to also be "pro-social justice":

> But a proper and robust pro-life posture is that every human being has intrinsic value and possesses innate human rights regardless of age, gender, ethnicity, or social status. This should apply to the born as well as the unborn, citizens and immigrants, rich and poor, pro-life proponents as well as abortion providers and post-abortive women. And we should be particularly careful to protect the human rights of the vulnerable and marginalized.[19]

Tracy argues that society should offer women considering abortion material assistance and social support, in addition to addressing the physical and sexual abuse of women. He writes about a case study that illustrates the practical consequences of putting such services into practice with pregnant teenagers who are contemplating abortions:

> In an article on how to reduce abortions, evangelical ethicist Glen Stassen uses a case study from his former community in Louisville, Kentucky. His wife and one of his parishioners were nurses at Louisville and Jefferson County's Teenage Parents Program (TAPP) for pregnant teenage students. In 1998, the year of this study, the Centers for Disease Control and Prevention reported that in Louisville 75 percent of pregnant teenagers younger than fifteen years old, and 39 percent of teenagers fifteen to nineteen years old, had abortions. In contrast, only 1 percent of the twelve to nineteen year-old girls at TAPP had abortions. Furthermore, these girls had much lower school dropout, drug abuse, and suicide rates than their peers. Almost none of the girls got pregnant again while they were still in school. How did they achieve these stunning results? Stassen explains, "TAPP gave pregnant teenagers a way to continue school while taking care of their babies, and while building an economically viable future. The clear result was that they chose not to have abortions." TAPP provided child care while the girls were in class. The girls each worked one class period each day in the nursery, receiving hands-on expert child care instruction. Social workers provided counseling and helped the girls address individual needs and plan their future. Nurses and doctors provided OB/GYN care and medical counseling. If this case study is any indication, providing material assistance, social support, and addressing abuse are proven ways to dramatically reduce abortions.[20]

From a pro-choice perspective, it is imperative that a woman's reproductive decisions are truly free ones. A woman who is coerced into having an abortion due to financial circumstances, when she otherwise would have chosen to parent the infant, is not free to choose in any meaningful sense of the term – the abortion is not indicative of what she really desires, but rather a response to her fears. Kathy Rudy, a Christian pro-choice feminist, puts it thus:

> I believe that no woman ought to bear a child against her will. I also believe, as a corollary, that no woman ought to be forced into having an abortion (or a sterilization) because she cannot organize enough social and economic resources to have her baby ... Feminists ought to be striving against the things that make childrearing the exclusive burden of women and working toward ways in which raising children receive the support of the wider community ... [similarly] our churches could and should be working to alleviate the injustices that make abortion necessary.[21]

Mulder

Anyone who is familiar with the work of my co-author knows how seamlessly she weaves helpful data and real-life examples into her discussion of the philosophy and ethics of abortion. While I recognize this as a virtue, I am afraid my own deficiencies on this score will likely be thrown into sharp relief in this chapter. Nevertheless, we can both discuss areas where we would like to see improvement, and it is on this topic, the topic of social justice, that Manninen and I have some real commonality. She and I may disagree about abortion itself, but we can agree about a range of evil social conditions that work to increase the incidence of abortion. My own view is that Laurie Shrage is right when she writes that:

> When "pro-life" sentiments are mixed with a libertarian ethic of individual responsibility, the result is a society that imposes only a negative duty not to destroy human lives, while failing to recognize a positive duty to guarantee a minimum standard of living to the resulting parents and children. Such policies acknowledge little social responsibility for families that are vulnerable to poverty and its miserable effects, while adopting policies that result in the creation of greater numbers of vulnerable families.[22]

Since Manninen and I agree that abortion cannot be understood on a societal level as a choice that people make for "selfish" reasons but rather as a choice that is most often made in difficult circumstances, often with a certain very regrettable degree of coercion, we can agree that there is a social mandate for anyone who wishes to call herself "pro-life." What might this social mandate include? The two areas that Manninen addresses most substantially in the above are poverty and family leave (we will discuss contraception a bit more directly in a later section). The United States is clearly in a bad way as it concerns both, and Manninen ably demonstrates it. While I doubt anyone will pretend that transforming the United States, say, into a society with the sort of social safety net Manninen and I would both like to see will be easy, I agree that there should be such a safety net.

While we can agree that poverty plays a deleterious role in the incidence of abortion, race is also a major factor in how life's opportunities are distributed, certainly in the United States.[23] Researchers have found, for instance, that, in the U.S., one of every three African-American children and one of every four Latino children live in poverty, which is twice the rate for white children. Indeed, even after controlling for poverty, education, and unemployment, whites report better overall health than blacks, Latinos, and Asians.[24] I do not know what it is like to be black, Latino, or Asian, but I do know that white people like me have made it extremely difficult, and continue to do so. People who identify as pro-life need to see that the fact that black women are statistically more likely to have an abortion than white women is an indicator precisely of the bad hand that black women have been dealt by structures of systemic racism that continue to impact black and non-white women's (and men's) life chances.[25] To be genuinely pro-life one must educate oneself and others about these structures and find ways to work against them.

This is why it is frustrating to see many who claim to be pro-life agitate and attempt to legislate under the slogan "All Lives Matter." While of course it is true, and no serious party to the issue is denying, *that* all lives matter, the trouble is that such a slogan is co-opting the phrase "Black Lives Matter" in the wake of a rash of deeply disturbing incidents of police homicide with black citizens as the victims. While all of us should grieve these tragedies, all I can say is that in my efforts to listen and learn about how these incidents have impacted black Americans, it has become clear to me that there is a grief and trauma that acutely affects the black community in the wake of these horrific deaths that is far more traumatic and oppressive than the grief that anyone might feel simply for, say, a fellow citizen. Again, I cannot claim to have experienced that particular depth of grief in any kind of direct way. I am, however, a parent of young black, interracially adopted, children and this fact has certainly served as an impetus to me to deepen my own awareness about the reality of anti-black racism.

My concern, therefore, about slogans like "All Lives Matter" is that they do not recognize the grief and trauma that acutely and uniquely affect the black community and so they turn "Black Lives Matter" into a trope that can be exploited for political gains. The move strikes me as akin to finding someone grieving the death of a family member and telling her "yes, isn't it terrible? *Millions* of people die every year!" There are moments when a particular form of injustice, in this case racial injustice, needs to take center stage, and then the only thing that one can do is join in the grief to the extent that it is appropriate, or respectfully remain silent. Abortion is, in my view, a major justice issue, but it has unfortunately become a thorny political issue with well-meaning and intelligent people on each side. It is simply not appropriate to use a setting of grief to manufacture a conversation about another issue, no matter how important it may be.

My point in bringing up race-related issues is simply to say that, just as earlier I argued that abortion is, in my view, a grievous sort of unjust discrimination, pro-lifers need to recognize that turnabout is fair play. If one is to be genuinely pro-life, one must learn to recognize the genus (any unjust discrimination) under which the species (abortion) belongs.[26] White privilege is a reality that many of us who are white have difficulty identifying (and we need to get over that), but, as Naomi Zack has argued, white privilege has its limits in a context where black rights are being grievously violated. She writes "However much it has been a good beginning ... the discourse of white privilege, alone, does not have the gravitas or urgency of either moral principle or social, institutional, and political action. Often (but not always), what is called a 'white privilege' that nonwhites lack, is a *right* that is protected for whites and not for nonwhites."[27]

Zack goes on to explain the vicious cycle that racism creates for racial profiling and ultimately incarceration, as these issues are closely related to recent high-profile homicides.[28] For convenience, I'll simply summarize what I take to be some salient parts of her argument here, in chapter 2 of her earlier cited book:

1. Hateful dispositions toward racial groups are legally unpunishable and historically common.
2. Police officers have these dispositions at roughly the same rate as the rest of the public.
3. Actions that target black people have resulted in the past from this disposition among police, and plausibly still result from it now.
4. Incarceration rates of black people will reflect the fact that they have been targeted for heavy surveillance and unfair treatment.
5. Yet these same incarceration rates fuel continuing perceptions of the criminality of nonwhite racial groups (particularly blacks).
6. Thus, racial profiling will likely continue unchecked unless new measures are taken to curb it.[29]

Zack's argument is not that police officers themselves are each individually to blame for the incidents whose lamentation forms the impetus for her book. Rather, there are structures within the policing system that contribute to the racial problems at work, as well as racist structures in our culture that will infect everything else if not specifically called out and worked against directly. As Zack writes "American police officers and administrators come into the whole crime-race scenario after the race-related facts of incarceration have been established, and their general charge is to act on the basis of those facts."[30]

Moreover, Zack argues, the discretion afforded police officers to neutralize perceived threats to the community (often when the only way to do so is by use of the deadly weapon they're carrying) is broad, and it can belie the fact that the police officer's job is to protect and serve. As an example, a local pastor in my own community, the Rev. Dr. Denise Kingdom-Grier, recently posted on social media that she encountered a police officer who informed her that he was trained to do "one thing," namely, to go home at the end of the night.[31] The trouble is, as she noted, that police officers should be trained in addition to de-escalate situations and to serve even at a significant cost to themselves. Presumably, very many readers of this book can list off individual police officers who have discharged their duties (and done more besides) admirably, as can I. The point, however, is that widespread racism (even operating below one's conscious awareness) combined with a legal system that gives significant leeway to police officers even in situations that are already escalated beyond what they should be is a dangerous cocktail.[32]

Racism is an obvious form of unjust discrimination (or it should be), and we have already had occasion to notice how unjust discrimination works its way into other issues, such as incarceration and, as I have argued, abortion. But that same kind of discrimination has often played a role in incarceration and in the meting out of the death penalty.[33] Despite consistent findings that the death penalty costs more to administer than it costs to apply a sentence of life without parole, states continue to use this method of punishment.[34] There is not space here to argue that the death penalty must be opposed against all comers. I will have to content myself with simply noting that I cannot see my way clear to how an offender absents himself from civil society itself merely by virtue of committing a crime against some set of its members. The vulnerable members of society among us often demand greater solicitude from us.[35] There will always be a brutal, calculating logic that would counsel those in power among us not to care for them. I hold that prisoners and offenders are, perhaps surprisingly to some, among the vulnerable among us. This does not mean that they are the most vulnerable or that they are more vulnerable than their victims. It merely means that they often find their way into crime through poverty-stricken means and that they are often in danger of being ignored by the civil society to which they belong. The suggestion that some of their actions warrant death, and thus the cruel scorn of the community as it sends them that way, strikes me as a failure of the community's responsibility to its members.

I can make sense of the idea that some punishments are more appropriate than others, and that there is some call for punishment for the good of civic order. But we can lose sight of the need for the community to restore its members to healthier and more socially productive lives if we fixate too much on any retributive, rather than rehabilitative, aspects of justice.[36] Recently, I was at a conference on restorative justice organized (remotely) by prisoners who had been positively impacted by a program that gave them a chance to earn a bachelor's degree within the prison walls. The warden of their facility was one of the speakers on one of the panels. Where some other wardens shy away from such a program, this warden could testify to its benefits, both because such programs contribute to the health and wellbeing of the prisoners and because the recidivism rates of those involved drop dramatically, thus costing the state a great deal less in the long run. His words continue to stick with me: "it's the right thing to do, and it's good business."[37]

There are certainly many other ways in which the label "pro-life" should be applied to issues of social concern and of justice. The link I would suggest between them is a concern for the most vulnerable and a repudiation of unjust discrimination, which I see in abortion, racial injustice, and capital punishment, to name just a few. In our day, Pope Francis has repeatedly linked a similar mindset to what he calls the "throwaway culture."[38] Now it is strong language to indict a culture in this way, and I have already said that I do not think it is right to chalk up individual abortions to "selfish" reasons. Nevertheless, to his credit, Pope Francis has argued that, while abortion is problematic on this score, so is our societal failure to "adequately accompany women in very difficult situations, where abortion appears as a quick solution to their profound anguish, especially when the life developing within them is the result of rape or a situation of extreme poverty."[39] Pope Francis himself also links global climate change as a particularly clear example of this "throwaway culture."[40] It should be remembered that it's easy to call these various concerns out in print and much harder consistently to give voice to, and enact, a coherent pro-life viewpoint. Nevertheless, however rare it may be to find someone who embodies each of these "pro-life" concerns, there is, I think, a consistent and coherent worldview on offer for someone who identifies as "pro-life." Manninen and I don't agree about abortion, but we do have significant common ground on a number of social issues that we consider connected to abortion.

II Sexual ethics

Mulder

I teach a course in sexual ethics fairly regularly, and I am very intentional about being even-handed on nearly every major issue we discuss (I'm not even-handed, whatever that would mean, when it comes to issues like sexual violence, of course). In my experience, the students are often less intentional about being even-handed. There are some readings and theses they just don't *want* to entertain. I know something about their aggregate opinions on the issues we discuss because I always give a survey at the beginning of the class. Although I teach at a religiously affiliated institution, my self-selected students do not usually identify with a very conservative set of beliefs about sex, so it isn't that they just can't stomach permissive views of sex. The reality is closer to the contrary.

One of the essays we read, whose argument, I'm sorry to say, is almost never seriously engaged and routinely dismissed without argument, is an article by David Benatar called "Two Views of Sexual Ethics: Promiscuity, Pedophilia, and Rape."[41] Benatar is most commonly associated with the position of anti-natalism, or the view that it is morally wrong to procreate,[42] and he is hardly the archetype of a conservative intellectual. But his position in this piece rings that way to students. This is because Benatar's thesis, while merely a conditional, is, in part, that *if* we take a casual view of sex, according to which "Sexual pleasure … is morally like any other pleasure and may be enjoyed subject only to the usual sorts of moral constraints," *then* it will turn out that we are hard-pressed to explain our opposition to all cases of pedophilia and rape.[43] It will hopefully come as no surprise to the reader that I, along with many others, would opt for the *modus tollens* here to the effect that, *since* pedophilia and rape are clearly wrong, we ought to reject the casual view of sex, but it might be good to explain a bit of Benatar's reasoning here.

The other view of sex (as opposed to the casual view) that Benatar discusses is what he calls "the significance view" which holds that "for sex to be morally acceptable, it must be an expression of (romantic) love. It must, in other words, signify feelings of affection that are commensurate with the intimacy of the sexual activity."[44] While Benatar's point is merely to explain the logical limits of the casual view, he does think that the significance view can explain most of our widely held intuitions about bad sexual activities. For instance, if you think, as advocates of the significance view do, that sex is only permissible in a context in which it communicates deep romantic affection then it will turn out, as it should, that children are not appropriate sexual partners. This is because they are unable to access the deep romantic affections of which sex should be an expression. Thus, pedophiles *objectify* children, treating them as mere means in their wrongheaded pursuit of sexual pleasure because the children are incapable of the mutual intimacy sex should signal. The objector might argue that one could hold a casual view of sex and reject pedophilia because children are incapable of *consent*. But Benatar rightly, in my view, explains that this is not enough.

If there is nothing especially significant about sex, then the child's consent would function in much the same way it would if one were to ask a child if she would like a glass of milk. If the objector rejoins that the child cannot comprehend the health risks associated with sexual activity, then Benatar responds first that not all sex acts carry significant health risks, and second, that parents are generally thought to be able to give proxy consent to activities whose risks children might not fully understand. Benatar further argues that one can only claim that pedophilia induces trauma for the child if one already holds the significance view. The problem is that if the casual view of sex is correct, then psychological trauma is only plausible as a manifestation of taboos that need not be in place. As Benatar writes "At the most, advocates of this view can say that the current psychological harms impose temporary moral constraints on sex with those children who, given their unfortunate puritanical upbringing or circumstances, would experience psychological trauma."[45] The point of *my* bringing up this unpleasant discussion is simply that you get these unpleasant results if you don't realize what I would argue is the true significance of sex.

Similarly, argues Benatar, proponents of the casual view of sex cannot explain why rape is the grievous moral wrong that most of us think it is. It's not really that there are *no* grounds for objecting to rape on the casual view, it's that the grounds that there are will not be sufficient. One could certainly argue that rape is wrong because it involves forcing someone to do something that she does not want to do. The trouble is that saying that fails to account for the special gravity of rape. As Benatar says "The problem, for the defenders of the casual view is, that it need be no more serious an interference than would be forcing someone to eat something for example."[46] Although forcing someone to eat something whose consumption they morally reject (as in the case of an orthodox Jew or Muslim eating pork) could be an analogy, this makes the gravity of rape dependent on the opinions rape victims hold at the time of their rape (since I'm not an orthodox Jew or Muslim, I do not have the same kind of prohibition against eating pork, so forcing me to eat it wouldn't be as serious a wrong). But this seems implausible and fails, again, to understand the grievous moral wrong that rape is.[47]

As we have seen especially in recent years, however, oftentimes the significance of sex and even the gravity of rape can be lost on a culture that treats sex as superficial. As Donna Freitas writes in her research on "hookup culture" among college-aged young adults, "Hookup sex is fast, uncaring, unthinking, and perfunctory. Hookup culture promotes bad sex, boring sex, drunken sex you don't remember, sex you could care less about, sex where desire is absent, sex that you have 'just because everyone else is, too' or that 'just happens.'"[48] This, I think, is relevantly similar to the kind of sex against which Lois Pineau argued there ought to be a legal presumption in regard to the presence or absence of sexual consent.[49] Instead, we have all but *normalized* it. Moreover, as Freitas writes, when alcohol is in the picture, things get even more difficult. She writes,

> When alcohol is the self-medicating medium of choice, the conversation about sexual assault becomes very complicated … Within hookup culture, it is too simplistic to have conversations about date rape and "no means no" since this culture is one that by definition *excludes dating*, almost prohibiting it, while promoting using copious amounts of alcohol. Taken together, it has students not only *not* saying no, but barely saying anything at all, including yes.[50]

All of this is just to say that there are theoretical and practical reasons to worry about the type of sex those of us in contemporary western societies are having and what consequences it might have. In fact, the United States' Centers for Disease Control and Prevention recently completed a report that is worth thinking about in this regard.[51]

The report covered a wide section of United States teens from grades 9–12. One interesting aspect of the report is how teens who have not engaged in any sexual activity (I will use "chaste teens" for brevity) fare. It may be helpful to try to summarize the findings a bit. When it comes to measurably risky behaviors as they concern health in the nationwide findings, chaste teens overwhelmingly score better than their sexually active counterparts.[52] Let me explain. They wear bike helmets and seatbelts more. They ride with intoxicated drivers or themselves drive when drinking alcohol less. They text while driving less. They carry a weapon less. They get in physical fights less. They experience physical dating violence less. They feel sad or hopeless less. They attempt suicide, make suicide plans, and are treated for suicide attempt-related injuries less. They smoke cigarettes or cigars, vape, drink alcohol, binge drink, use marijuana, hallucinogens, cocaine, ecstasy, heroin, methamphetamines, inhalants, and abuse prescriptions less. In regard to dietary behaviors, chaste teens don't necessarily eat fruit or vegetables better than their sexually active counterparts, though the disparities are generally not especially wide. They drink milk a bit more on most measures. They stay away from soda (or pop) better. They drink sports drinks less, but they drink water more. They eat breakfast more regularly. They are physically active in a way that is usually less than but comparable with their heterosexually active peers. Computer usage is a little higher than heterosexually active peers but television watching is lower. Physical education participation and sports participation is a little less than but comparable with heterosexually active peers. Obesity is slightly higher than heterosexually active peers but the numbers on being overweight are lower. Chaste teens score lower for having had asthma, higher for having seen a dentist, and higher for getting eight or more hours of sleep. In general, when it comes to risky or psychologically concerning behaviors, chaste teens are reliably healthier than their sexually active counterparts and their positive habits are generally better than or comparable with their sexually active counterparts.

The report recommends anti-bullying efforts and other measures for the ways it also documents how sexual minorities fare on such measures, and surely any steps taken to eliminate bullying are positive ones. But in terms of strategies that are likely to measurably improve health or limit risky behaviors, is it really that strange to consider strategies for delaying sexual activity? This seems especially relevant since doing so seems logically connected to a healthier assessment of sex as well as empirically correlated in a statistically significant way to a healthier life. Freitas here points out that "The politics around abstinence-only education has turned people off to the possibility that there could be any fruitful, alternative conversation around abstinence aside from the conservative right-wing one … Rather than reclaiming abstinence, or re-envisioning it for more moderate views, we have simply thrown it out altogether."[53] What might it look like if we understood sex as a significant activity that belongs in a mature, committed context commensurate with the intimacy the sexual activity itself signals and instructed young people to reserve it for that context as well?

Doing this, in my view, would also require recognizing that widespread consumption of pornography has further exacerbated our inability to have meaningful sexual relationships.[54] What are some things we know about pornography in this regard? Many, perhaps most, forms of pornography portray women in degrading situations which objectify them and even suggest that they enjoy these situations.[55] A recent study showed that of 304 scenes analyzed in the most popular pornographic films, 88.2% contained physical aggression and 48.7% contained verbal aggression, overwhelmingly targeted at women.[56] Furthermore, pornography's target audience is no secret. Emerging adults are particularly vulnerable to its appeal, and the reason is that their sexual habits and vision are still developing. Also, several peer-reviewed studies suggest that there is a link between pornography, particularly violent pornography (which is common) and sexual assault.[57] Thus, pornography is a "training ground" for "sexual know-how"[58] and the instructions it gives are damaging, both to the ability of its viewers to form meaningful sexual relationships as adults and to their sexual partners, most of whom are women. We also have good reason to believe that pornography is addictive.[59] Moreover, the viewing of pornography among emerging adults is widespread. A recent study found that 87% of young men and 31% of young women reported using pornography.[60] Indeed, some feminist scholars have argued that pornography constitutes the sort of public health crisis that calls for legislative action.[61] While I am sympathetic with that proposal, even if we stop short of legislative action, there is now a great deal of evidence that any culture that blithely accepts pornography is also accepting genuine threats to the health and lives of women, not to mention the potential for healthy intimacy in the future for those who consume it and their partners.

So I think we should promote a vision of sex that does not trivialize it and that does not constantly place it alongside violence against women (as pornography does). Indeed, if possible, there is reason to think that delaying sexual activity for young adults would be a good thing. The obvious next question is "delay it for what?" Here it will be impossible to escape the perception that I am some kind of prude because I do think that it is desirable that young people reserve sexual activity for a committed relationship that they are even ready publicly to own as such without shame or reservation. In short, yes, I do think it is desirable that people delay sexual activity until marriage, but failing that, it would at least be better than the alternative if they could delay it until such time as they can appreciate (more of) the significance of sex.

Here is a reason why I think so. Suppose, as I think plausible, but cannot argue for here, that David Archard's view of the wrong of rape is right, and that non-consensual sexual activity is a grievous wrong because it violates one's deeply held sexual integrity.[62] Archard notes that our deep interest in our sexual integrity is bound up with our being the sexed beings that we inescapably *are*, and rape assaults this, and not just what we *do*. Accordingly, Archard agrees with theorists who claim that rape is "dehumanizing" and, with a bit of license for the metaphysical hyperbole, "soul murder."[63] Now let's dwell on this analysis a bit. Rape, thus construed, is an attempt to violate someone's self, to substitute in her place an object without the dignity she always has, whether this dignity is a matter of concern to her or not. What, then, is consensual intercourse? I submit that it would not be enough to say that consensual sex is neutral with regard to the self about which Archard has argued. Rather, it seems to me that, if we opt for Archard's view, then consensual sex must be the *entrusting* of a person's self to one's sexual partner, not simply because a sexual encounter could turn sour quickly, but because one is choosing a way to manifest one's sexual integrity in choosing a sexual partner, and this is the very interest that rape seemed to threaten.

In consensual sex, one is, in effect, giving a gift of one's sexual integrity to another in a context that can be abused in the blink of an eye. But to whom might one really entrust a value so deeply held? Surely not to someone one has no expectation of seeing again.[64] Indeed, it would be surprising if this gift (on the assumption that its significance is recognized) were given without some temporal promise or understanding attached to it. My own view is that, while we tend to expect that sex is a private act, that act is actually best reserved for a relationship that is characterized by a commitment made in public so that it can be recognized and supported by the community to which the couple belong. Marriage is a solemnizing and a making public of just such a relationship. While there is not space here for me to explain why I think marriage is the best fit for this, I certainly think that it is an option worth exploring, and in any event, long-term committed relationships are likely to be better than short-term casual relationships for reasons I have already discussed. As Caroline J. Simon writes in response to critics of monogamy, "a tenacious trajectory of following through on one's promises is neither arbitrary nor irrational."[65]

The last thing to note here is that this is a book about abortion. While obviously not all sexual activities or relationships are generative, we needn't even discuss the vexed issue of sexual identities and orientations to grant that most sexual relationships have coitus as their culmination and consummation.[66] Insofar as coitus has the potential to be generative, it would certainly help lower abortion rates if coitus took place in relationships in which planned (or welcome) pregnancies were the norm. Needless to say, sexual relationships involving unprepared teens and uncommitted adults have great potential to give rise to unplanned (indeed, unwelcome) pregnancies. So it is hardly irrelevant to consider in what ways our various cultures can foster healthy beliefs and behaviors about sex and its significance. As I've already said, any truly just society needs to be fighting this battle on multiple fronts, so it isn't as if I see an adjustment to our sexual vision as a panacea and, in any event, any progress in adjusting our sexual vision will of course be slow and arduous. But all excellent things are difficult, and a just sexual culture in which fewer unwelcome pregnancies took place would be an excellent thing, both for justice among sexual partners (especially women) and for justice done to the unborn.

Manninen

Many of my more liberal friends are often surprised to hear that I hold rather stereotypically conservative (or, as Mulder put it, "prudish") views about sexuality; I too believe that sexual activity is best confined to committed and loving relationships (whether that be between members of the opposite or the same sex). I am also a big fan of monogamy and sexual exclusivity and faithfulness. There are many reasons why I believe this, some that are probably tied more to personal experiences than philosophical argumentation, but one of the main reasons I hold the views that I do about sexuality also underpins one of the reasons I am pro-choice: our existence as embodied beings makes it so that what happens to our bodies intimately affects what happens to our minds; what happens to our bodies happens to *us*. Embodied experiences, then, are deserving of the utmost care and consideration.

From my perspective, it is precisely because pregnancy involves a significant and intimate experience of enmeshment with another living being (one that can have extreme physical as well as psychological consequences for women) that it is an experience that must be undertaken voluntarily. It is a deep violation of Kant's formula of humanity to disregard a woman's bodily autonomy in this regard, not because you are violating something that *belongs* to her (our bodies are not merely our property), but because you are violating *her*. Violence against the body is violence against the person. And all these same considerations that preclude the ethical permissibility of forced gestation equally preclude the ethical permissibility of forced abortions. Forced abortion is a violent and disturbing instance of bodily intrusion, in addition to involving the killing of a living being that the woman herself likely already regards as her child. This is also one of the many reasons why rape is so ethically abhorrent. In addition to its violent and dehumanizing aspects, it forces a woman into a state of immense bodily intimacy and vulnerability; one that she does not welcome and adamantly rejects.

The upshot of all this is to underscore the vital role our bodies play in our interaction with the world. Because we are embodied beings, all embodied actions affect our psychological states, and vice-versa. Our minds and our bodies exist symbiotically. This helps us understand one important aspect of the sexual experience; as philosopher Sarah Ruddick puts it, sex is an occasion when "we become our bodies; our consciousness becomes bodily experience of bodily activity."[67] Sexual experiences and behavior, therefore, should indeed be subject to ethical discussion and consideration.

While I do not think that this is the time and place for detailed analysis of sexual ethics (as worthy as I think such an endeavor would be), I will add to Mulder's view that there are important reasons to think young adults should probably delay the onset of their sexual experiences. Ethicist Lara Denis, a Kantian scholar, argues ethically good sex should adhere to Kant's formula of humanity; i.e., any instance of sex that treats another person as a mere means, or a mere instrument, to another's sexual pleasure is morally suspect. Despite the prevalent belief that Kant regarded sexual acts as intrinsically immoral, Denis argues that this is not so. Rather, she argues, Kant's concern was finding ways to satisfy our sexual desires ethically: "Our sexual impulse simply presents us with the challenge of finding ways to satisfy it while properly respecting ourselves and others."[68] Thus, a healthy, respectful, and dignified view of sexuality embraces the following virtues:

> A virtuous Kantian agent will be committed to a morality and have the strength to act on that commitment. She will respect herself and others as rational agents. Moreover, she will recognize that how she treats her body reflects whether she values herself as a rational human being. Such an agent will see her body as an extension and a condition of her agency ... Her recognition of her agency's inseparability from her body will shape her decisions about how to use her body, including how to give and receive sexual pleasure with it.[69]

Robert Van Wyk, appealing to Victor Frankl's stages of sexual maturity, offers the following analysis for why teenage sex will often fall short of this Kantian ideal.

> The goal of sexual activity in the first stage is tension reduction. In the second stage sexual activity has an object as well as a goal, namely a partner, but a totally interchangeable partner to be used only as an object. In the third stage the partner is seen as a subject, as a human being, and not merely as an object. In the fourth stage the partner is seen as a unique human being who can be loved in his or her uniqueness. It seems to me that it is impossible, or at least

highly unlikely, for someone at the first or second stage to engage in sexual intercourse without violating Kant's principle.[70]

Furthermore, Van Wyk cites a study that illustrates how many teenagers harbor beliefs about sexuality that clearly violate the ethical demands of respect and dignity.

> One recent study discovered that approximately 70 percent of older teens believed that it was morally permissible to have sexual intercourse with a woman who was too drunk to have much of an idea what she was doing. Another study discovered that 70 percent of high school boys thought there was nothing wrong with a boy lying to a girl and telling her that he was in love with her when he was not, if that would get the girl to have sexual relations with him. So obviously 70 percent of those involved in these surveys were quite willing to disregard Kant's principle of respect.[71]

The popular Netflix series *13 Reasons Why* tells the story of a young high school girl – Hannah Baker – who commits suicide after multiple instances of extreme maltreatment by her high school peers. Several of those instances had to do with violations to her body and sexuality. In a commentary about the show, one of the directors uses rather Kantian language to describe what leads to Hannah's suicidal depression – she was objectified, dehumanized, and treated as a mere instrument to others' sexual desires.

We cannot deny that media presents us with a rather wanton and careless view of sex (in addition to championing images about women's and men's bodies that are ultimately extremely detrimental to young persons' self-esteem). Television shows, music, and films targeted to teens and young adults (e.g., MTV's *Jersey Shore*) bombard them with views of sexuality and sexual intercourse that routinely violate Kantian respect for persons, and treat the experience as a careless game, rather than, as a Ruddick puts it, a bodily extension of our self and our consciousness. Todd Huffman writes that:

> the media have arguably become the leading sex educator in America today. And that's not particularly good news. The sexual content in much of the media today's teens attend to is frequent, glamorized, and consequence free. "Everyone does it" on television and in the movies, or so it seems, yet the need for birth control, the risks of pregnancy or sexually transmitted infections, or the need for responsibility are rarely discussed. Too often children and teens are permitted to view late evening programming these days hypersexualized at times to the degree that many adults feel uncomfortable watching. And too often shows targeting adolescents seem like "Happy Days With Hormones", with sexual intercourse appearing a normative and casual activity even for teens. In these ways the media function as a kind of sexual 'super peer', providing role models of attractive adults and older adolescents engaging in risky

behavior, and putting additional pressure on young people to have sex at a young age."[72]

One study reported that "76% of teenagers indicate that one reason young people have sex is because television shows and movies make it seem normal for teenagers."[73] While television shows are quick to glamorize sex, they less often emphasize any kind of sexual responsibility or sexual morality: "... while more than 50% of shows – and 66% of prime-time shows – contain sexual content, only 9% contain any reference to the possible risks or responsibilities of sexual activity or any reference to contraception, protection, or safer sex."[74]

While I do not think that teaching abstinence with regard to sexual education should be, as Mulder puts it, "thrown out altogether," I also reject the abstinence-only education so many states and socially conservative politician try to enact (though Mulder will discuss his view on contraception below). For example, in 1996 the federal government began the Title V abstinence-only funding program, which devotes millions of dollars in federal funds to schools willing to only teach abstinence in their sex education programs. Interestingly enough, states that endorse abstinence-only education, or no sex education at all, have higher teen pregnancy rates (see, for example, Mississippi and New Mexico) than states that endorse medically accurate and comprehensive sex education, which includes knowledge on the use of contraception, alongside of abstinence (see, for example, New Hampshire and Massachusetts).[75]

As I will argue below, access to contraception and proper contraception education is clearly linked to decreased abortion rates, and I do not think we can have a proper discussion of ethically responsible sex or sex education without the inclusion of contraception (which is used by individuals in committed and loving relationships, as well as by people who are sexually active outside of such relationships). This is perhaps where my idealistic side clashes with my prudential side: I would love to live in a world where no one would engage in any sexual activity that violates the Kantian imperatives of dignity, and that young adults wait until they have found a partner to whom they can, to use Mulder's terminology, fully entrust themselves. But we don't live in that world. And living in our world, practically, means that we have to give young adults the proper tools to engage in sexual activities responsibly. While this should (I think) include instilling in them a view of sexuality that is in line with Kantian ideals of respect for persons, it should also include instructions and education on how to protect themselves from sexually transmitted diseases and, for the purposes of our discussions in this book, curbing the instances of unwanted pregnancies.

I think it is important to always keep in mind that, while many of us engage in recreational, rather than procreative sex, both within the confines of a committed relationship and outside of such relationships, most instances of heterosexual coitus are potentially procreative, even with the proper use of contraception. And there is a certain mystical beauty to this: two persons can come together and engage in an intimate, powerful, uniquely pleasurable embodied and mental act, and from this intimacy create a new being that is simultaneously half of each partner and yet a wholly new individual in its own right. The procreative potential of heterosexual sex is one aspect that can render the experience a wonderful and beautiful one (though procreation is certainly not the only thing, perhaps not even the primary thing, that renders sex significant. Meaningful and virtuous sex can indeed be had without procreative potential or intention – infertile couples, elderly couples, homosexual couples, or just heterosexual couples who have chosen not to procreate can of course engage in sexual experiences that are equally meaningful to potentially procreative heterosexual sex). Keeping that procreative potential in the forefront of one's mind may lead some of us to agree with Mulder's conclusion that we should consider limiting our sexual experiences to those persons with whom we would want to share the responsibility of procreating. Certainly this will not, by itself, eradicate abortions or unwanted pregnancies. Even if I were to choose to only have sex with someone with whom I am willing to procreate does not mean that, in actuality, I want to procreate at the current time, or even ever at all (i.e., I may have chosen to only have sex with my husband, with whom I am willing to parent, but I may not want to parent *right now* or even ever at all, since I may choose to remain child-free). But I do agree that being more particular about our sexual activities may reduce the amount of unplanned or unwanted pregnancies (though, again, there will always be carefully considered and responsible instances of sexual activity that could nevertheless lead to an unplanned pregnancy – contraception can fail for those within committed relationships as well as those who have sex outside of such relationships). At the very least, heterosexual couples should have open, frank, and honest discussions with each other concerning their stance on parenting, contraception, and abortion before engaging in potentially procreative sexual intercourse.

III Contraception

Manninen

As a lead in to discussing the role I think contraception plays for reducing abortion rates, I want to briefly discuss sexual assault, and why the fact that it happens necessitates that abortion remains legal. As long as women are victims of sexual assault, there will be a need for safe abortion access. Despite what some politicians have said, pregnancy as a result of rape is as likely as pregnancy that results from consensual sex. In fact, one study illustrated that "per-incident rape-pregnancy rates exceed per-incident consensual pregnancy rates by a sizable margin"; that is, it may be *more* likely that pregnancy will result from rape than from consensual sex.[76] Several medical reports approximate that, in the United States, the number of pregnancies that result from rape hovers at around 5% amongst cases of one-time sexual intercourse *sans* birth control. That may not sound like a lot, but when broken down into basic numbers, that's thousands of pregnancies per year. For example, in 2012 the Rape, Abuse, Incest, and National Network (RAINN) estimated that about 17,342 pregnancies resulted from sexual assault that year alone.[77] According to the Guttmacher Institute, about 1% of women who procure abortions in the United States do so because they were victims of rape; this still translates to thousands of women who require access to abortion because they were victims of sexual assault.

The decision to keep a child who is the result of sexual assault should lie with the woman alone. However, it is worth considering how difficult life could be for a woman who makes the choice to keep and raise the child. The emotional repercussions can be severe and permanent. Choosing to parent a child who was the product of rape means that one has chosen to permanently identify oneself as a rape victim; "her identity as a mother proceeds directly from her identity as a rape victim. Her child embodies the violence done against her and gives manifest permanence to what she may ache to forget."[78] Some women are indeed able to derive beauty and meaning from their children – one mother writes that having the baby served a therapeutic role in her healing process, though she still worries the extent to which the child will resemble her rapist:

> Now that I have Amula and I have been really successful at being her mom, obviously I know I made the right decision. But at the time, I didn't know that. So it was torture … I had to be a survivor and hit the ground running and take care of this kid … [but] half of her genes are evil … I can do whatever I should as her mom to make her this loving, caring, wonderful person. But in her is the DNA of a person who is really sick, and is that DNA stronger than what I can do?[79]

Other women, however, are never fully able to recover from their trauma, and this manifests itself in the relationship they have with their children. One mother admits to being unable to be as affectionate with her child as she wishes she could be:

> She and I have had conversations about my prickliness, how I pull away. I would never, ever, ever tell her that it has anything to do with her. I always tell her it's because of me, and because my mom pulled away from me. But I don't do it with her brother … Why can't I hug my daughter? I love her, but when she touches me, it feels like hundreds of razor blades scraping across my skin, like I'm going to die.[80]

Another woman notes that "[t]he laughter of my little boy often reminded me of the hideous laughter of this guy as he raped me."[81]

The point here is not to argue that the trauma of being a rape victim, or a child who results from rape, is sufficient to justify abortion – I do not believe that being a product of rape makes one's life intrinsically non-valuable. I agree with pro-life advocates when they say that the child is not to blame for the crimes of his biological father. What I *do* wish to convey is that the decision to parent a child who is the result of rape is a personal, intimate, and deeply affecting one. The only person who can legitimately make that decision is the person who must deal with the repercussions of that decision for the rest of her life, whether that be in favor of aborting or parenting. And whatever decision she makes, either in favor of aborting or parenting, she should live in a society that respects, supports, and nurtures that decision.

Nevertheless, rape and incest are not the leading reasons many women abort, so we must explore what those reasons are and see how addressing them can lead to a reduction in abortion prevalence. We have clear evidence, however, that criminalizing abortions will not contribute to this goal. Multiple studies confirm this. Most recently, a massive 2016 study in the medical journal *The Lancet* illustrates that, while abortion rates are declining in developed countries (which include the United States, Canada, and many European nations), they are not declining, and are slightly increasing, in developing countries (which includes countries in Africa, Asia, and Latin America). Countries with prohibitive abortion laws actually saw a slight *increase* in abortion rates compared with countries where abortions are permitted:

> When countries were grouped according to the grounds under which abortion was legal, we did not find evidence that abortion rates for 2010–14 were associated with the legal status of abortion. The rate was 37 abortions per 1000 women (34–51) where abortion is prohibited altogether or allowed only to save a woman's life, and 34 (29–46) where it is available on request.[82]

Take, for example, these facts about abortion prevalence in different African countries:

> The overall abortion rate in Africa, where the vast majority of abortions are illegal and unsafe, showed no decline between 2003 and 2008, holding at 29 abortions per 1,000 women of child bearing age. The Southern Africa subregion, dominated by South Africa, where abortion was legalized in 1997, has the lowest abortion rate of all African subregions, at 15 per 1,000 women in 2008.[83]

In another example, El Salvador has one of the most restrictive abortion policies in the world: it is prohibited in all circumstances and prison sentences await both the women who procure abortions and those who provide them. Yet according to their Ministry of Health, there were approximately 19,290 clandestine abortions between 2005 and 2008.[84] Prohibiting abortions, by itself, will do little to stop them from happening. But we do have evidence that low-cost or free contraception access, along with accurate sex and reproductive education, contributes to the reduction of abortion rates.

Unsurprisingly, countries with prohibitive abortion laws also have a higher "unmet need for contraception ... and this contributes to the incidence of abortion in countries with restrictive laws."[85] Multiple studies have noted a direct causal connection between the widespread and effective use of contraception and reduced abortion rates. The abovementioned 2016 study published in *The Lancet* concluded that "ensuring access to sexual and reproductive health care could help millions of women avoid unintended pregnancies and ensure access to safe abortion."[86] A 2006 study amongst women undergoing abortions in Scotland concluded that "the challenge for reducing abortion rates lies in improving contraceptive use among the much larger group of women who do not intend to get pregnant but use contraception imperfectly."[87] In a 2012 study, 9,256 adolescents and women, all recruited from two abortion facilities, were given free contraceptive counseling and reversible contraception as part of the Contraception CHOICE Project. As a result:

> We observed a significant reduction in the percentage of abortions that are repeat abortions in the St. Louis region compared to Kansas City and non-metropolitan Missouri (P < 0.001). Abortion rates of the CHOICE cohort were less than half the regional and national rates (P < 0.001). The rate of teenage birth within the CHOICE cohort was 6.3 per 1,000, compared to the U.S. rate of 34.1 per 1,000.[88]

Yet another study found that, between 1988 and 2001, effective contraception use increased by 74% in Russia and, simultaneously, the abortion rate fell by 61%. In the areas of Russia where family planning clinics subsisted (despite a lack of federal funding), abortion rates dropped at a faster rate than in the rest of the country:

> For example, in the region of Dubna, where clinics are still active, the abortion rate is only half of the national average. Vladimir Serov, deputy director of Moscow's Scientific Center for Obstetrics, Gynecology and Perinatology, believes that the government's lack of support for contraceptive services deserves much of the blame for why abortion is still so prevalent in Russia. "Restrictions [on abortion] are useless," asserts Serov. "We need to promote a healthy way of life and family planning."[89]

In America, the importance of providing contraception for the reduction of unplanned pregnancies and abortion rates can be seen in Colorado. According to the Colorado Department of Health and Public Services between 2009 and 2013, the birthrate amongst teenagers fell by 40%, while abortion rates fell by 42%, after the state started providing teenagers and poor women free intrauterine devices.[90] Repeated studies on the relationship between abortion and contraception point to the same conclusion: "The most direct way to reduce abortion rates is to prevent unintended pregnancies by increasing the practice of effective contraception."[91]

It is insufficient to just give out contraception, however – it is important to have accurate information on how to use it effectively, and this is where comprehensive sex and reproductive health education comes into play. A 2008 study from the University of Washington found that teenagers who received such education were approximately 60% less likely to get pregnant, compared to abstinence-only education.[92] A 2011 study noted that the United States "ranks first among developed nations in rates of both teenage pregnancy and sexually transmitted diseases" and that "increasing emphasis on abstinence education is positively correlated with teenage pregnancy and birth rates. This trend remains significant after accounting for socioeconomic status, teen educational attainment, ethnic composition of the teen population, and availability of Medicaid waivers for family planning services in each state."[93] Although the national rate for teen pregnancies has been steadily declining, the states with abstinence-only sex education had higher incidences of teen pregnancy than states with accurate and comprehensive sex education programs. And it isn't just that teens are using contraception effectively – sex education actually aids in delaying the onset of sexual activity in teens.[94] Given the effectiveness of sex education in all these areas, it is disheartening to read the United States' policies on this issue: only 24 states and the District of Colombia require public schools to teach sex education, and only 20 states require that "if provided, sex and/or HIV education must be medically, factually or technically accurate."[95] This means that, in 30 states in the U.S., a public school may teach sex education in a way that is full of lies, scare tactics, or simply faulty medical information.

Mulder

I think it's important to keep in mind something very fundamental about pro-life positions on abortion in this discussion. My own view is that laws against abortion shouldn't be expected or designed to *do* much of anything in regard to stemming the tide of abortions. Abortion is, in my view, a grievous moral and social wrong and it is abhorrent that a state that laid claim to being just would simply hold its tongue about the status of abortion in the hope that doing so would, for whatever culturally limited reasons, scale back the *number* of abortions.[96]

Now I think it's true that accurate sex education is important, and I think it's also right to be concerned that certain taboos have, in some circles, militated against biologically accurate sex education. It's also true, however, that much that presents itself as accurate sex education is pretty permissive about various kinds of sexual and reproductive issues.[97] No doubt one of the goals of the so-called sexual revolution was to liberate people from enforced gender stereotypes and overly rigid roles. This was, and is, an important goal. But between rigid roles for genders and permissive sexual behavior that often treats sex as hookup culture does, it's worth asking how far we have left to go in a pursuit of a just sexual culture. As an example, Freitas writes: "If in the past women have been used as objects for the sexual gratification of men, does this mean that women's triumph lies in the payback of the same? Or do true gains lie somewhere else in the landscape of sexuality and all that surrounds it?"[98] My point is that it's not clear that our current attitudes toward sex have reached an equilibrium that might signify justice rather than simply swinging in the other direction on a pendulum.

At the end of the day, I can't imagine anyone reading this seriously thinks any culture in the world is a fully just and healthy sexual culture.[99] Nor, as my coauthor recognizes, could merely purveying contraceptives on a massive scale be the answer whole and entire. We have a long way to go. To consider how far, just imagine trying to find data on young people who have been taught healthy, non-patriarchal, sexual relationships uninfluenced by pornography and the objectification of women on a massive scale, and who understand their sexuality as a positive good but further as something that is most appropriately mastered in regard to its impulses over time and in a loving, monogamous relationship (the dynamics of which they will have witnessed inside of an intact family)[100] where pleasure plays a role but not the only role. Trying to get at that demographic in contemporary western culture with any precision is likely to devolve into something little more promising than a hunt for the Easter Bunny. When it comes to a just sexual culture, it's just not clear we've tried it.[101] I do think there are things we could do to try a just sexual culture on for size that don't amount to the "scare tactics" Manninen invokes, though I recognize there are excesses in many sex education programs that could lean in that direction.[102]

To begin some more pointed reflections in this final section, I'm going discuss a remark that got (then) Pope Benedict XVI into hot water in 2010. This statement drew the ire of folks primarily on his right. While the Catholic Church's position on contraception (to the effect that artificial contraception should not be used, at least for merely contraceptive purposes)[103] is not taken seriously by many in the academic mainstream,[104] I maintain that it is fitting to take this position up in this dialogue since, while the position is often dismissed, the Catholic tradition does take up the burden of rational argumentation on this point,[105] so it is fitting at least to understand it, or the terms of civil dialogue we have staked out earlier in the book would have been violated. There will, of course, not be space to argue the meaning of this position in detail, but it is worth discussing what dialogue on this point could look like.

Certainly, some methods of pregnancy prevention are more reliable than others, but no method can claim to eliminate the risk of unplanned pregnancy entirely.[106] As the Catholic writer Christopher West has pointed out, there are exactly three things one can do to eliminate the risk of contributing to unplanned pregnancy entirely. One can either (a) abstain from sex (at least, if you are a woman, until you are post-menopause) or remove one's (b) testicles or (c) ovaries.[107] Much of the world assumes that no one will do any of these things, and so looks for the most reliable (if inevitably fallible) ways to diminish the risk of unplanned pregnancy through various contraceptive measures.[108] Pope Benedict was certainly aware of this, but hoped for what he called a greater humanization of sexuality. In 2010, he said:

> Meanwhile, the secular realm itself has developed the so-called ABC Theory: Abstinence-Be Faithful-Condom, where the condom is understood only as a last resort, when the other two points fail to work. This means that the sheer fixation on the condom implies a banalization of sexuality, which, after all, is precisely the dangerous source of the attitude of no longer seeing sexuality as the expression of love … There may be a basis in the case of some individuals, as perhaps when a male prostitute uses a condom, where this can be a first step

in the direction of a moralization, a first assumption of responsibility, on the way toward recovering an awareness that not everything is allowed and that one cannot do whatever one wants.[109]

It is clear in context that the Pope is by no means advocating the use of contraceptives as a "real or moral solution." But many traditional Catholics felt this went too far in that direction.[110] So what might the idea be here?

As we've already mentioned Catholic teaching does not look favorably upon garden-variety usage of contraceptives. To consider this in the light of what I mentioned in my earlier remarks on sexual ethics, if sex is to be an entrusting of oneself to another, it would seem optimal if the trust were complete.[111] That is, it would seem optimal if the gift of the self (through the gift of one's sexual integrity) held nothing back, and resulted in a genuine unity.[112] Because of the view that sex should be a full gift of the self and that contraception cordons off a portion of the self so that it is not given, more recent Catholic thinking on sex has argued that contraception is not so much (or is not only) an "unnatural" act but is more tellingly seen under the species of a duplicitous act, an act that promises a gift of self but does not actually give it.[113]

But what happens when one's actions do not line up with this, what is often felt to be a rather exacting standard? What Pope Benedict mentions here is a situation where a male prostitute decides to use a condom out of a perhaps budding sense of moral responsibility. While this would not, in his view, be an objectively right act, it might show the beginning of a real moral awareness, because it would show a concern for others. That is, when one is already not being abstinent, and when one is already not being faithful to a particular sexual relationship, then it can show genuine, though not yet fully moral concern nevertheless to don a condom with a view to preventing the spread of infection. With perhaps some modifications, this was roughly the strategy taken by the authors and signatories to the 2004 statement by *The Lancet* on common ground in regard to sexual transmission of HIV.[114] While I am not saying that Pope Benedict (or current Pope Francis) himself or Catholics in general could or should agree with every aspect of it, it may be worth consulting this statement for a bit.

What the statement argues is that, first, strategies for combatting sexual transmission of HIV must be sensitive to local and cultural factors and human rights. Moreover, the statement explicitly gives a positive mention of the ABC strategy we discussed earlier. While the statement argues that everyone should have knowledge of these prevention options, "it is not essential that every organization promote all three elements: each can focus on the part(s) they are most comfortable supporting."[115] Next, the statement tailors this approach to different populations. In regard to young people who have not begun to be sexually active, "the first priority should be to encourage abstinence or delay of sexual onset." When young people have already, in effect, made their sexual debut, "returning to abstinence or being mutually faithful with an uninfected partner are the most effective ways of avoiding infection." When talking with sexually active adults, one should promote fidelity to an uninfected partner. When it comes to people at high risk of infection, as with the hypothetical male prostitute Pope Benedict invoked, the statement advocated "correct and consistent condom use, along with approaches, such as avoiding high-risk behaviours or partners." When it is learned that particular young people are already sexually active (and, presumably, have no intention of changing that), "condom use should be supported," according to the statement.[116]

On a person-to-person level one might consider what a conversation might look like between people with competing moral views on this point. In the following imagined conversation, let's assume that A takes something like a traditional Catholic position on sex and contraception and that B is, roughly, the male prostitute we've been discussing. Now imagine that A, following the example of a certain first-century Jew, dines with just such a male prostitute against the gossip and rancor of his peers and develops a friendship with him. Consider this conversation:

A: What do you have planned for this weekend?
B: Nothing you'd want to know about.
A: Have you thought more lately about getting out of that business?
B: Sure, but it's not as simple as just leaving your two weeks' notice. Besides, the money is better than it would be anywhere else I could find work, and I don't believe what you believe about sex.
A: I know, and we've had those conversations. I value our friendship, and I know I can't force your hand. Still, have you at least considered any steps you could take to minimize risks of infection for you and your partners?
B: You mean like using a condom? I've considered it. But wait – I thought you didn't agree with using contraception!
A: I don't, but then I don't agree with extra-marital sex, either, and I can't seem to dissuade you from that. Look, I'll never recommend that you engage in contracepted sex, and I'm certainly not going to start now. But my arguments against extra-marital and even risky sex haven't cut any ice with you to date. It seems I can't get you not to do something I think is morally wrong, but I can at least encourage you to think about your partners as people who are engaging in risky behavior whose risks can be minimized. If you won't turn away from prostitution, it's possible that a condom could be a first step toward minimizing that risk for your partners. Anyway, if you're ever willing to consider leaving this work, I'd like the chance to talk to you, as your friend, about what other options there might be for you.
B: I appreciate you saying that. I'll keep it in mind.

Notice that in this conversation, A's moral standards are not abandoned. Rather, A is merely trying to encourage the moral development of B, whose friend A has become. This, I think, is a version of the strategy of "accompaniment" that Pope Benedict himself invokes and has been taken up, somewhat more controversially in Catholic quarters, by Pope Francis.[117] While these are difficult questions, I maintain that the above conversation is an example of how A, who opposed contraception from a moral point of view, could nevertheless see genuine moral concern at work in its user in a particular case where A's moral convictions are *known but not shared*, and where B is already headed down a bad path whose risks can only be minimized. I doubt this is exactly the "support" of condom usage that the statement from *The Lancet* envisioned, but it is a recognition that non-abortifacient contraceptives could play a role in halting the spread of HIV in particular high-risk scenarios.

But what about contraception and its relevance to abortion? Well, I think there is an analogue here. I do not advocate the outlawing of non-abortifacient contraceptives, and we live in a sufficiently large world where condoms and other contraceptives are no longer especially difficult to find (though this does not guarantee their quality or durability). When adults are already making a decision to engage in sexual activity that is not marked by faithfulness to one partner and that sexual activity has (a) the potential to be generative, and (b) the potential to give rise to a child the partners have no desire to parent, they might consider any potential resulting offspring in much the same way that Pope Benedict suggests the male prostitute might consider his partners he hopes not to infect. Unplanned pregnancies impact the life chances and prospects for happiness of the children born by them, as well as for the women who become pregnant. In saying that, I do not mean to equate belonging, say, to a non-intact family with contracting the HIV virus. But I do want to say that society should want to decrease unplanned pregnancies for the good reasons Manninen and I have already discussed.

This is not a question of advocating contraception. I do not, and would not, advocate or promote engaging in contracepted sex, and only with the qualifications seen above could I agree to its partial role in certain regrettable situations. Indeed, in the conversation above, it is important that B *already knows* A's stance on the morality of contraception. Here one is reminded of then Pope John Paul II's statement that a pro-life politician could support legislation that sought to minimize abortion so long as her opposition to it was clearly understood.[118] So, if one is *already* going to engage in sexual activity that is inadvisable and ultimately (as I think) morally impermissible, it may be a step in one's incomplete moral development to take some steps to reduce the risk of an unplanned pregnancy. That does not mean that the sexual act in question would constitute a morally right action, it merely means that one could do something to mitigate the risks to others affected by this act.[119] Ultimately, though, the far better and more important thing, I believe, would be to encourage a culture in which people engaged in the kind of self-giving sex where pregnancy, when it occurred, was welcomed.

Indeed, just as there are high-risk contexts in which contraceptives can play a role in minimizing infection, there are also contexts in which contraceptives engender a certain risk of their own. Edward C. Green, former director of the AIDS Prevention Research Project at the Harvard Center for Population and Development Studies, has often invoked the danger of "risk compensation" in the sexual transmission of HIV, especially in Africa. In Green's book with Allison

Herling Ruark (then a fellow of the aforementioned center), the two write "Any risk reduction measure has the potential to lead to risk compensation." As an example, Green and Ruark cite the study of Ugandan men who were taught condom use skills and given free condoms over against a control group that only received an informational presentation about AIDS. The men in the first group used more condoms but increased the number of their sexual partners by 31%, whereas the control group decreased the number of their partners.[120] Since condoms have their failure rates, and the reality is that those rates are not insignificant, it is always important to consider the danger of risk compensation, and to consider when behavior changes will be more effective measures for stemming the tide of infection (or unwanted pregnancy).

While there are environments in which contraceptives help to stabilize abortion rates, there are also environments in which increased contraceptive use parallels or travels with increased elective abortion rates. William Newton has argued that, while abortion rates dropped in Russia with the introduction of more widespread usage of contraception, when this happened in Russia, this was an extreme case with very high beginning levels of abortion. In other cases, such as that of Turkey, once contraception and abortion laws were liberalized, rates for both jumped. Once contraceptive use hit a saturation point, abortion levels tapered off, but they never returned to the lower levels at which they began, prior to the abortion and contraception liberalization.[121] Other countries, such as Spain and Ukraine, have a high rate of condom usage but also a high rate of elective abortions.[122] There are some situations in which contraception can serve to diminish abortion rates, but it of course does not, and could not be expected to, *end* abortions. The point here is simply this: in situations that are already morally bad (as in the case of the male prostitute) or extreme (as in the case of Russia), there are roles for contraception to play at a larger societal level, though not every group or person need promote this either directly or in the same way. However, these roles for contraception cannot overshadow the necessary behavioral changes that would need to occur on a societal level if we are to make a dent in the unplanned pregnancies without which we would not be talking quite so much about abortion.

IV Conclusion

In this chapter, we've chosen a set of issues that we see as connected in various ways to abortion. Neither of us are legislators, and even if we were (perish the thought), we have no illusions that legislation is as simple as the two of us talking through our differences and similarities. As the old maxim goes, there are two things no one would want to know the production process for: laws and sausages. Nevertheless, we hope that this chapter allows readers a chance to see where some dialogue is possible between two friends of differing viewpoints, and, perhaps to spur on better discussions about what the next steps could be in what we venture to hope could become a less acrimonious debate. In the brief conclusion that follows, we will offer some assessment of where this discussion has taken us.

Notes

1 John Stuart Mill. 1991. *On Liberty and Other Essays*. New York: Oxford University Press, p. 25.
2 Mill, 1991, p. 42.
3 Guttmacher Institute. 2016. "Induced Abortion in the United States." Available at: https://www.guttmacher.org/fact-sheet/induced-abortion-united-states
4 Guttmacher Institute. 2016. "Abortion Patients More Likely to be Poor in 2014 than 2008." May 10. Available at: https://www.guttmacher.org/news-release/2016/abortion-patients-more-likely-be-poor-2014-2008
5 American Academy of Child and Adolescent Psychiatry. 2004. "When Children Have Children." Available at: http://www.aacap.org/cs/root/facts_for_families/when_children_have_children
6 Department of Labor. 2000. "Balancing the Needs of Families and Employers: Family and Medical Leave Surveys." Available at: https://www.dol.gov/whd/fmla/cover-statement.pdf
7 Child Care Aware of America. 2015. "Parents and the High Cost of Child Care." Available at: http://usa.childcareaware.org/wp-content/uploads/2016/05/Parents-and-the-High-Cost-of-Child-Care-2015-FINAL.pdf
8 Karen Z. Kramer, et al. 2016. "Comparison of Poverty and Income Disparity of Single Mothers and Fathers Across Three Decades: 1990–2010." *Gender Issues*, 33: 22–41.
9 David Brady and Rebekah Burroway. 2012. "Targeting, Universalism, and Single-Mother Poverty: A Multilevel Analysis Across 18 Affluent Democracies." *Demography*, 49.2, p. 719.
10 Steve Tracy. 2010. "Abortion, the Marginalized, and the Vulnerable: A Social Justice Perspective for Reducing Abortion." *Cultural Encounters: A Journal for the Theology of Culture*, 6.2, p. 27.
11 M. Antonia Biggs, et al. 2013. "Understanding Why Women Seek Abortions in the US." *BMC Women's Health*, 13.29, p. 5. Available at: http://www.biomedcentral.com/1472-6874/13/29
12 Robert W. Van Giezen. 2013. "Paid Leave in the Private Industry Over the Past 20 Years." Available at: http://www.bls.gov/opub/btn/volume-2/paid-leave-in-private-industry-over-the-past-20-years.htm
13 World Policy Center. 2016. "Is Paid Leave Available for Mothers of Infants?" Available at: http://worldpolicycenter.org/policies/is-paid-leave-available-for-mothers-of-infants
14 Washington State Department of Social and Health Services. n.d. Available at: https://www.dshs.wa.gov/esa/community-services-offices/child-care-subsidy-program
15 Amy Schalet. 2010. "Sex, Love, and Autonomy in the Teenage Sleepover." *Contexts*, 9.3, p. 20.
16 Brady and Burroway, 2012, p. 738.
17 Brady and Burroway, 2012, p. 738.
18 T.R. Reid. 2010. "Universal Health Care Tends to Cut Abortion Rates." *The Washington Post*. Available at: http://www.washingtonpost.com/wp-dyn/content/article/2010/03/12/AR2010031202287.html
19 Tracy, 2010, p. 28.
20 Tracy, 2010, p. 33.
21 Kathy Rudy. 1996. *Beyond Pro-Life and Pro-Choice: Moral Diversity in the Abortion Debate*. Boston: Beacon Press, pp. 56, 108, and 143.
22 Laurie Shrage. 2003. *Abortion and Social Responsibility: Depolarizing the Debate*. Oxford: Oxford University Press, p. 35.
23 Though I neither mean to nor want to collapse race into, say, class, as I agree that they are different and each significant categories in their own rights.

24 See the National Poverty Center's 2009 policy brief on "The Colors of Poverty" at http://npc.umich.edu/publications/policy_briefs/brief16/.
25 See, for example, Zoe Dutton's 2014 article "Abortion's Racial Gap" in *The Atlantic* at: https://www.theatlantic.com/health/archive/2014/09/abortions-racial-gap/380251/.
26 Though of course there will disputes about what constitutes unjust discrimination.
27 Naomi Zack. 2015. *White Privilege and Black Rights*. Lanham: Rowman and Littlefield, pp. 3–4. Italics in original.
28 Zack dedicates her book to the memory of Oscar Juliuss Grant III, Trayvon Martin, Eric Garner, Michael Brown, and Tamir Rice, among others.
29 This is a summary of some ideas in chapter 2 of Zack's *White Privilege and Black Rights*.
30 Zack, 2015, p. 38.
31 My thanks to the good Reverend Doctor for allowing me to use this example.
32 Here Zack cites the example of Officer Christopher Manney who shot Donte Hamilton (see *White Privilege and Black Rights*, p. 90).
33 A classic study is David C. Baldus, et al., 1990, *Equal Justice and the Death Penalty* (Boston: Northeastern University Press).
34 See Louis J. Palmer. 2008. "Costs of Capital Punishment," in *Encyclopedia of Capital Punishment in the United States* (Jefferson, NC: McFarland, 2nd edition).
35 See, for example, Pope Francis's 2013 apostolic exhortation *Evangelii Gaudium*, 209–216 on the vulnerable, at: http://w2.vatican.va/content/francesco/en/apost_exhortations/documents/papa-francesco_esortazione-ap_20131124_evangelii-gaudium.html.
36 The late U.S. Supreme Court justice Antonin Scalia suggests that "just retribution" is "the principal legitimate purpose" of capital punishment. See Antonin Scalia. 2006. "The Death Penalty is Just," in *The Death Penalty: Opposing Viewpoints*, ed. Dian Andrews Henningfield (Detroit: Greenhaven Press), pp. 16–24 at 23–24.
37 The warden was DeWayne Burton of Richard A. Handlon Correctional Facility as part of the Conference *Hope for Restoration: Radical Hospitality and Prison Reform*; see Saint Benedict Institute, 2017: http://www.saintbenedictinstitute.org/blog/2017/1/27/hope-for-restoration-radical-hospitality-and-prison-reform-upcoming-conference-on-restorative-justice.
38 For a short summary of Pope Francis's concerns about the "throwaway culture," one might consider his January 13 speech of 2014 to diplomats. See Pope Francis, 2014, http://w2.vatican.va/content/francesco/en/speeches/2014/january/documents/papa-francesco_20140113_corpo-diplomatico.html.
39 See *Evangelii Gaudium*, 214.
40 As in Pope Francis's 2015 encyclical *Laudato Si*, at: http://w2.vatican.va/content/francesco/en/encyclicals/documents/papa-francesco_20150524_enciclica-laudato-si.html.
41 David Benatar, 2008, "Two Views of Sexual Ethics," in Alan Soble and Nicholas Power, eds., *The Philosophy of Sex* (Lanham: Rowman and Littlefield), pp. 325–336.
42 See David Benatar. 2006. *Better Never to Have Been: The Harm of Coming Into Existence* (Oxford: Oxford University Press).
43 Benatar, 2008, p. 327.
44 Benatar, 2008, p. 327.
45 Benatar, 2008, p. 329.
46 Benatar, 2008, p. 330.
47 While it would take us too far afield in the context of this chapter to discuss this at length, I think that other related problems plague the accounts other scholars give for what sex itself is. See, for example, Alan Soble, 2008, "Masturbation, Again," in Soble and Nicholas Power, eds., *The Philosophy of Sex*, pp. 75–98 at 94 and Alan Goldman, 2008, "Plain Sex," in Soble and Power, eds, *The Philosophy of Sex*, pp. 55–73 at 57.
48 Donna Freitas. 2013. *The End of Sex: How Hookup Culture is Leaving a Generation Unhappy, Sexually Unfulfilled, and Confused About Intimacy* (New York: Basic Books), p. 2.
49 See Lois Pineau. 1989. "Date Rape," *Law and Philosophy*, 8: 217–243.
50 Donna Freitas, 2013, p. 48.

51 See Center for Disease Control, 2016, "Sexual Identity, Sex of Sexual Contacts, and Health-Related Behaviors Among Students in Grades 9–12 – United States and Selected Sites, 2015," released August 12, 2016. Accessed May 1, 2017 at: https://www.cdc.gov/mmwr/volumes/65/ss/pdfs/ss6509.pdf.
52 It is true that heterosexually active teens score better than homosexually or bisexually active teens nationwide, but commenting on this trend is beyond the scope of my work here.
53 Freitas, 2013, pp. 151–152.
54 Consider Gail Dines's 2016 op-ed, "Is Porn Immoral? That Doesn't Matter: It's a Public Health Crisis," *Washington Post*, April 8, 2016 at: https://www.washingtonpost.com/posteverything/wp/2016/04/08/is-porn-immoral-that-doesnt-matter-its-a-public-health-crisis/?utm_term=.aee631e436f8.
55 See Joan Mason-Grant. 2008. "Pornography as Embodied Practice," in *The Philosophy of Sex*, eds. Alan Soble and Nicholas Power, 5th edition (Lanham: Rowman and Littlefield), pp. 401–418.
56 See Ana J. Bridges, et al. 2010. "Aggression and Sexual Behavior in Best-Selling Pornography Videos: A Content Analysis Update," *Violence Against Women*, 16: 1065–1085.
57 See, for example, Neil M. Malamuth, et al. 2000. "Pornography and Sexual Aggression: Are There Reliable Effects and Can We Understand Them?" *Annual Review of Sex Research*, 11: 26–91.
58 See Mason-Grant, 2008, p. 415.
59 Donald Hilton and Clark Watts. 2011. "Pornography Addiction: A Neuroscience Perspective." *Surgical Neurology International* 2.1: 19.
60 See Jason S. Carroll, et al. 2008. "Generation XXX: Pornography Acceptance and Use Among Emerging Adults," *Journal of Adolescent Research*, 23: 6–30.
61 See, for example, the "Model Antipornography Civil Rights Ordinance" developed in Appendix D in Andrea Dworkin and Catharine A. MacKinnon. 1988. *Pornography and Civil Rights: A New Day for Women's Equality* (Minneapolis, MN: Organizing Against Pornography), pp. 138–142.
62 David Archard. 2007. "The Wrong of Rape." *Philosophical Quarterly*, 57: 374–393.
63 Archard, 2007, p. 393.
64 Unless perhaps the parting is very sad and one partner is off to join a probably deadly war effort.
65 See Caroline Simon. 2012. *Bringing Sex Into Focus: The Quest for Sexual Integrity* (Downers Grove, IL: IVP Academic), p. 52.
66 For a brief but relevant discussion, see, for example, the work of my colleague, prolific psychologist David G. Myers's 2014 essay, "Most Are Straight, Some Are Gay, and Why It Is That Way: The Science of Sexual Orientation." *Modern Believing*, 55: 127–139.
67 Sarah Ruddick. 1975. "Better Sex," in *Analyzing Moral Issues*. Judith Boss (ed.), New York: McGraw Hill, p. 371.
68 Lara Denis. 2007. "Sex and the Virtuous Agent," in *Sex and Ethics: Essays on Sexuality, Virtue, and the Good Life*. Raja Halwani (ed.), New York: Palgrave MacMillan Publishers, p. 47.
69 Denis, 2007, p. 46.
70 Robert Van Wyk. 2011. "The Morality of Teenage Sex and its Implications for Sex Education," in *Sex, Love, and Friendship*. Adrianne Leigh McEvoy (ed.), New York: Rodopi Publishers, p. 45.
71 Van Wyk, 2011, p. 46.
72 Todd Huffman. 2008. "Sexuality in Modern Media: How is it Affecting Our Children", *Eugene Register Guard* (February).
73 Susan Villani. 2001. "Impact of Media on Children and Adolescents: A 10-Year Review of the Research", *Research Update Review*, p. 395.
74 Villani, 2001, p. 395.

75 Kathryn Kost and Stanley Henshaw. 2014. "U.S. Teenage Pregnancies, Births and Abortions, 2010: National and State Trends by Age, Race and Ethnicity." https://www.guttmacher.org/sites/default/files/report_pdf/ustptrends10.pdf
76 Jonathan A. Gottschall and Tiffani A. Gottschall. 2003. "Are per-incident rape-pregnancy rates higher than per-incident consensual pregnancy rates?" *Human Nature*, 14.1: 1–20.
77 Rape, Abuse, and Incest National Network. n.d. "Sexual Assault Victims Statistics." Available at: https://rainn.org/get-information/statistics/sexual-assault-victims
78 Andrew Solomon. 2012. *Far From the Tree: Parents, Children, and the Search for Identity*. New York: Scribner Publishing Company, p. 478.
79 Solomon, 2012, p. 484.
80 Solomon, 2012, p. 511.
81 Solomon, 2012, p. 486.
82 Gilda Sedgh, et al. 2016. "Abortion Incidence between 1990 and 2014: Global, Regional, and Subregional Levels and Trends." *The Lancet*. Available at: http://www.thelancet.com/pdfs/journals/lancet/PIIS0140-6736%2816%2930380-4.pdf. Also see Guttmacher Institute, 2017: https://www.guttmacher.org/fact-sheet/facts-induced-abortion-worldwide
83 Guttmacher Institute. 2012. "Facts on Induced Abortion." Available at: http://www.who.int/reproductivehealth/publications/unsafe_abortion/induced_abortion_2012.pdf
84 Amnesty International. 2014. "Twelve Facts about the abortion ban in El Salvador." Available at: https://www.amnesty.org/en/latest/news/2014/09/twelve-facts-about-abortion-ban-el-salvador/
85 Sedgh et al., 2016.
86 Sedgh et al., 2016.
87 Catherine Schumann and Ann Glasier. 2006. "Measuring Pregnancy Intention and Its Relationship with Contraceptive Use Among Women Undergoing Therapeutic Abortion." *Contraception*, 73.5, p. 520.
88 Jeffrey Peipert, et al. 2012. "Preventing Unintended Pregnancies by Providing No-Cost Contraception." *Obstetrics and Gynecology*, 120.6. Available at: http://www.ncbi.nlm.nih.gov/pmc/articles/PMC4000282/pdf/nihms570177.pdf
89 Amy Deschner and Susan Cohen. 2003. "Contraceptive Use Is Key to Reducing Abortion Worldwide." *The Guttmacher Report on Public Policy*, 6.4. Available at: https://www.guttmacher.org/about/gpr/2003/10/contraceptive-use-key-reducing-abortion-worldwide
90 Sabrina Tavernise. 2015. "Colorado's Effort Against Teenage Pregnancies is a Startling Success." *The New York Times*. Available at: http://www.nytimes.com/2015/07/06/science/colorados-push-against-teenage-pregnancies-is-a-startling-success.html?_r=0
91 John Bongaarts and Charles Westoff. 2000. "The Potential Role of Contraception in Reducing Abortion." *Studies in Family Planning*, 31.2: 193–202, at p. 201.
92 Sexuality Information and Education Council in the United States. 2008. "National Data Shows Comprehensive Sex Education Better at Reducing Teen Pregnancy than Abstinence-Only Programs." Available at: http://www.siecus.org/index.cfm?fuseaction=Feature.showFeature&featureID=1041
93 Kathrin F. Stanger-Hall. 2011. "Abstinence-Only Education and Teen Pregnancy Rates: Why We Need Comprehensive Sex Education in the U.S." *PLoS ONE* 6.10: e24658. Available at: http://journals.plos.org/plosone/article?id=10.1371/journal.pone.0024658
94 Amanda Peterson Beadle. 2012. "Teen Pregnancies Highest in States with Abstinence-Only Policies." Available at: http://thinkprogress.org/health/2012/04/10/461402/teen-pregnancy-sex-education/ Also see: Patten and Livingston, 2016. http://www.pewresearch.org/fact-tank/2016/04/29/why-is-the-teen-birth-rate-falling/
95 National Conference of State Legislatures. 2016. "State Policies on Sex Education in Schools." Available at: http://www.ncsl.org/research/health/state-policies-on-sex-education-in-schools.aspx

96 Mary Anne Warren notes that "the fact that restricting access to abortion has tragic side effects does not, in itself, show that the restrictions are unjustified, since murder is wrong regardless of the consequences of prohibiting it" (see Mary Ann Warren. 1973. "On the Moral and Legal Status of Abortion." *The Monist*, 57: 43–61 at 44). Personally, I would not use the term "murder" here for reasons we've discussed, but it is present in Warren's text.
97 My own view is that, while certainly one can receive various needed health care services at Planned Parenthood, the views it takes of sex are either deftly floating above commitment to any view of sex's significance (in precisely the context in which it would be helpful to reinforce this) or, in some cases, are committed to what I would regard as permissive views on sex. See, for instance, Planned Parenthood's (n.d.) discussion of sex at: https://www.plannedparenthood.org/learn/sex-and-relationships/sex. For instance, we read "Everyone has different sex drives and likes different things when it comes to sex, so don't worry about whether you're 'normal.'" Then Planned Parenthood goes on to list behaviors that are "common" giving every indication that they are quite permissible, including masturbating, oral and anal sex, phone sex, and reading and watching porn.
98 Freitas, 2013, p. 10. The question of whether women accept or are benefited by hookup culture is contested. For a view that neither is the case, see Leah Fessler. 2016. "A lot of women don't enjoy hookup culture – so why do we force ourselves to participate?" in *Quartz*, May 17, 2016 at https://qz.com/685852/hookup-culture/.
99 By "just and healthy sexual culture," I mean, roughly, that practices are encouraged that contribute to clear and explicit consent (particularly relevant to justice) and that sexual practices are encouraged and largely observed that lead to the emotional, physical, and psychological health of their participants (particularly relevant to health). Also, relevant to "culture," I would indicate that if culture were to lend support to this rather than have a hand in the mischief, it would include widespread understanding and rejection of practices that objectify women (and men) and hypersexualize them. Again, I don't expect to be able to call an actual culture "just and healthy" anytime soon.
100 As the study my coauthor cites above notes, one of the strongest predictors of STD diagnosis is a "non-intact family." See Sexuality Information and Education Council in the United States. 2008. "National Data Shows Comprehensive Sex Education Better at Reducing Teen Pregnancy than Abstinence-Only Programs." Available at: http://www.siecus.org/index.cfm?fuseaction=Feature.showFeature&featureID=1041
101 As Elizabeth Anscombe writes, "The trouble with the Christian standard of chastity [though I maintain this needn't be only Christian] is that it isn't and never has been generally lived by; not that it would be profitless if it were. Quite the contrary: it would be colossally productive of earthly happiness" (see "Contraception and Chastity," in Anscombe, 2011, *Faith in a Hard Ground: Essays on Religion, Philosophy and Ethics by G.E.M. Anscombe*, eds. Mary Geach and Luke Gormally (Luton: Andrews UK), pp. 193–214 at 211).
102 Freitas gives some practical tips in the final sections of her book, *The End of Sex*.
103 For a philosophically sophisticated treatment of this theme, see Alexander Pruss. 2000. "Christian Sexual Ethics and Teleological Organicity." *The Thomist*, 64: 71–100. Pruss (2012) has also released a book expanding substantially on his article, namely, *One Body: An Essay in Christian Sexual Ethics* (South Bend: University of Notre Dame Press). On exceptional circumstances, consider the debate in Benedict Guevin and Martin Rhonheimer. 2005. "On the Use of Condoms to Prevent Acquired Immune Deficiency Syndrome." *National Catholic Bioethics Quarterly*, 5: 37–48.
104 Consider, for example, Christopher Hamilton's (2008) essay "Sex" (in Soble and Power, eds, *The Philosophy of Sex*, pp. 99–116 at pp. 100–101), which briskly mentions what it takes, simplistically at best, to be a Catholic view on sex only to rush past it without argument. This is, I'm sorry to say, the norm in mainstream contemporary philosophical discussions of sex.

105 No shortage of Catholic thinkers are willing to argue this point, including Helen Alvaré, Elizabeth Anscombe (until her death), John Finnis, Robert P. George, Christopher Kaczor, Patrick Lee, Alexander Pruss, Christopher Tollefsen, Janet Smith, and many more. The Church claims that its teachings on sexual ethics belong to the domain of the natural order which, according to Church teaching, means that these teachings are capable of being understood and accepted through rational argumentation without benefit of special divine revelation, though it holds that special revelation confirms these teachings (see, for example, Vatican II's *Gaudium et Spes*, 48 at: http://www.vatican.va/archive/hist_councils/ii_vatican_council/documents/vat-ii_cons_19651207_gaudium-et-spes_en.html).

106 Some examples from the United States in regard to contraceptive failure show that, even with perfect usage (consistent and correct as opposed to typical usage) of all contraceptives, a percentage of women experience an unplanned pregnancy within the first year. For example, perfect use of spermicides has an 18% failure rate, perfect use of sponges has a 20% failure rate in parous women and 9% failure rate in nulliparous women, perfect use of a diaphragm has a 6% failure rate, perfect combined use of pill and progestin-only pill has a 0.3% failure rate, as do perfect use of Evra and NuvaRing (Depo-Provera at 0.2%). Interestingly, the Ovulation fertility-based awareness method (based on evaluation of cervical mucus), given perfect usage, has a 3% failure rate and the Symptothermal method (which involves evaluation of cervical mucus and temperature checkpoints) has a perfect usage failure rate of 0.4%. Also interesting is that the failure rate for female sterilization is 0.5%. See James Trussell. 2011. "Contraceptive Failure in the United States." *Contraception*, 83: 397–404.

107 Christopher West. 2004. *Good News about Sex and Marriage: Answers to Your Honest Questions about Catholic Teaching*, revised edition (Cincinnati: Servant Books), p. 120.

108 The claim that periodic abstinence methods are less effective than other models of contraception is often overstated. Here is a characteristic explanation of why that is often the case from Robert T. Kambic, then of the Johns Hopkins School of Hygiene and Public Health: "[Women in a survey] were given 15 choices including the pill, IUD, sterilization and barrier methods. Of interest to us are two choices. Women were asked if they were using 'Rhythm or safe period by calendar,' or if they were using, 'Natural family planning, safe period by temperature or cervical mucus test.' When the results of the survey were tabulated, out of 6,306 women using some form of birth spacing, 221 (3.5%) women said they were using 'rhythm' and 35 (0.6%) were using 'Natural Family Planning.' Fourteen percent (14%) of natural method users were using NFP, and the rest rhythm. These numbers are too small to provide accurate estimates of the numbers of NFP users as opposed to rhythm users, *so NSFG analysts combined the numbers*. This means that they combined the unplanned pregnancies of rhythm and NFP users and calculated that about 20% of women using 'periodic abstinence' became pregnant. The problem is that these results include untrained women, who may or may not have used the method correctly. I conclude that these results are invalid. There is no way that these results can be verified. For prescription method users, one could go to a physician and confirm that the pill was prescribed. For barrier method users, one could ask which pharmacy was visited to purchase the barrier; but for natural method users, a women can say, 'I was using rhythm,' and even her spouse might not be able to confirm it" (see R.T. Kambic. 1999. "The Effectiveness of Natural Family Planning Methods for Birth Spacing: A Comprehensive Review," Hopkins Population Center Papers on Population (October 1999) at: https://jscholarship.library.jhu.edu/bitstream/handle/1774.2/918/WP99-07.htm, italics mine).

109 See Pope Benedict XVI. 2010a. *Light of the World: The Pope, The Church, and the Signs of the Times: A Conversation with Peter Seewald*, trans. Michael J. Miller and Adrian J. Walker (San Francisco: Ignatius Press), pp. 118–119.

110 This prompted a clarification of Pope Benedict's remarks, which I think is quite in accord with the remarks themselves. See Pope Benedict XVI, 2010b: http://www.va

tican.va/roman_curia/congregations/cfaith/documents/rc_con_cfaith_doc_20101221_luce-del-mondo_en.html.
111 The fact that I am talking about "optimal" behavior here does not mean that I hold that morality is merely a matter of approximating an ideal. Even in a theistic context, for instance, St. Thomas Aquinas claims that "we do not offend God except by doing something contrary to our own good." See Aquinas. 1975. *Summa Contra Gentiles*, III.122.2 in *Summa Contra Gentiles: Book Three: Providence Part II*, trans. Vernon J. Bourke (Notre Dame: University of Notre Dame Press), p. 143. Thus, we can understand our good and the good of others as determining those actions that are required, even if what it means for them to be required is that they aim, teleologically, at the right sort of goal.
112 In Pruss's account, the unity is purchased through the coordinated biological activity that aims at reproduction (in coitus) even if, for various health-related reasons, reproduction is not even realistically possible.
113 This is why then Pope John Paul II (1981) referred to this kind of holding back as a "lie" in his apostolic exhortation *Familiaris Consortio*, 11 at: http://w2.vatican.va/content/john-paul-ii/en/apost_exhortations/documents/hf_jp-ii_exh_19811122_familiaris-consortio.html.
114 See Daniel T. Halperin, et al. 2004. "The Time Has Come for Common Ground on Preventing Sexual Transmission of HIV." *The Lancet*, 364: 1913–1915. It is also noteworthy for what follows that Edward C. Green was one of eight people identified as authors of the statement, along with many signatories.
115 Halperin, et al., 2004, p. 1913.
116 Halperin, et al., 2004, p. 1913.
117 See Pope Benedict, 2010a, p. 118 and Pope Francis's 2016 apostolic exhortation *Amoris Laetitia*, esp. chapter 8. See: http://w2.vatican.va/content/francesco/en/apost_exhortations/documents/papa-francesco_esortazione-ap_20160319_amoris-laetitia.html.
118 See the introduction to this book for the passage from the encyclical *Evangelium Vitae* (John Paul II, 1995, 73).
119 Catholic readers might be aided by considering *The Catechism of the Catholic Church*, 1749–1761 and recognizing that this view of contraception would merely diminish the bad circumstances of the act, it would change neither the intention nor the object chosen. It does nothing to make right what is actually wrong. See The *Catechism of the Catholic Church*, n.d., http://www.vatican.va/archive/ENG0015/__P5R.HTM.
120 See Edward Green and Allison Herling Ruark. 2011. *AIDS, Behavior, and Culture: Understanding Evidence-Based Prevention* (Walnut Creek: Left Coast Press), pp. 156–158.
121 William Newton. 2015. "Contraception and Abortion: Fruits of the Same Rotten Tree?" *Linacre Quarterly*, 82: 135–148 at 137–138.
122 See J.L. Dueñas, et al. 2011. "Trends in the Use of Contraceptive Methods and Voluntary Interruption of Pregnancy in the Spanish Population During 1997–2007." *Contraception*, 83: 82–87.

References

American Academy of Child and Adolescent Psychiatry. 2004. "When Children Have Children." Available at: http://www.aacap.org/cs/root/facts_for_families/when_children_have_children

Amnesty International. 2014. "Twelve Facts about the Abortion Ban in El Salvador." Available at: https://www.amnesty.org/en/latest/news/2014/09/twelve-facts-about-abortion-ban-el-salvador/

Anscombe, Elizabeth. 2011. "Contraception and Chastity," in Mary Geach and Luke Gormally (eds), *Faith in a Hard Ground: Essays on Religion, Philosophy and Ethics by G.E.M. Anscombe*. Luton: Andrews UK, pp. 193–214.

Aquinas, St. Thomas. 1975. *Summa Contra Gentiles*, III.122.2 in *Summa Contra Gentiles: Book Three: Providence Part II*. Vernon J. Bourke (trans.) Notre Dame: University of Notre Dame Press.

Archard, David. 2007. "The Wrong of Rape." *Philosophical Quarterly*, 57: 374–393.

Baldus, David C., George Woodworth, and Charles A. Pulaski, Jr. 1990. *Equal Justice and the Death Penalty*. Boston: Northeastern University Press.

Beadle, Amanda Peterson. 2012. "Teen Pregnancies Highest in States with Abstinence-Only Policies." Available at: http://thinkprogress.org/health/2012/04/10/461402/teen-pregnancy-sex-education/

Benatar, David. 2008. "Two Views of Sexual Ethics." In Soble, Alan and Nicholas Power (eds). *The Philosophy of Sex*. Lanham: Rowman and Littlefield, pp. 325–336.

Benatar, David. 2006. *Better Never to Have Been: The Harm of Coming into Existence*. Oxford: Oxford University Press.

Benedict XVI, Pope. 2010a. *Light of the World: The Pope, The Church, and the Signs of the Times: A Conversation with Peter Seewald*, Michael J. Miller and Adrian J. Walker (trans). San Francisco: Ignatius Press.

Benedict XVI, Pope. 2010b. "Note on the Banalization of Sexuality Regarding Certain Interpretations of Light of the World". Available at: http://www.vatican.va/roman_curia/congregations/cfaith/documents/rc_con_cfaith_doc_20101221_luce-del-mondo_en.html

Biggs, M. Antonia, Heather Gould, and Diana Greene Foster. 2013. "Understanding Why Women Seek Abortions in the US." *BMC Women's Health*, 13. 29: 5. Available at: http://www.biomedcentral.com/1472-6874/13/29

Bongaarts, John and Charles Westoff. 2000. "The Potential Role of Contraception in Reducing Abortion." *Studies in Family Planning*, 31. 2: 193–202.

Brady, David and Rebekah Burroway. 2012. "Targeting, Universalism, and Single-Mother Poverty: A Multilevel Analysis Across 18 Affluent Democracies." *Demography*, 49. 2: 719–746.

Bridges, Ana J., Robert Wosnitzer, Erica Scharrer, et al. 2010. "Aggression and Sexual Behavior in Best-Selling Pornography Videos: A Content Analysis Update." *Violence Against Women*, 16: 1065–1085.

Carroll, Jason, Laura M. Padilla-Walker, Larry J. Nelson, et al. 2008. "Generation XXX: Pornography Acceptance and Use Among Emerging Adults." *Journal of Adolescent Research*, 23: 6–30.

Catholic Church. n.d. *Catechism of the Catholic Church*. Available at: http://www.vatican.va/archive/ENG0015/__P5R.HTM

Center for Disease Control. 2016. "Sexual Identity, Sex of Sexual Contacts, and Health-Related Behaviors Among Students in Grades 9–12 – United States and Selected Sites." Available at: https://www.cdc.gov/mmwr/volumes/65/ss/pdfs/ss6509.pdf.

Child Care Aware of America. 2015. "Parents and the High Cost of Child Care." Available at: http://usa.childcareaware.org/wp-content/uploads/2016/05/Parents-and-the-High-Cost-of-Child-Care-2015-FINAL.pdf

Denis, Lara. 2007. "Sex and the Virtuous Agent," in Raja Halwani (ed.), *Sex and Ethics: Essays on Sexuality, Virtue, and the Good Life*. New York: Palgrave MacMillan Publishers, pp. 37–48.

Department of Labor. 2000. "Balancing the Needs of Families and Employers: Family and Medical Leave Surveys." Available at: https://www.dol.gov/whd/fmla/cover-statement.pdf

Deschner, Amy and Susan Cohen. 2003. "Contraceptive Use Is Key to Reducing Abortion Worldwide." *The Guttmacher Report on Public Policy*, 6. 4. Available at: https://www.guttmacher.org/about/gpr/2003/10/contraceptive-use-key-reducing-abortion-worldwide

Dines, Gail. 2016. "Is Porn Immoral? That Doesn't Matter: It's a Public Health Crisis." Available at: https://www.washingtonpost.com/posteverything/wp/2016/04/08/is-porn-immoral-that-doesnt-matter-its-a-public-health-crisis/?utm_term=.aee631e436f8

Dueñas, J.L., Iñaki Lete, Rafael Bermejo, et al. 2011. "Trends in the Use of Contraceptive Methods and Voluntary Interruption of Pregnancy in the Spanish Population during 1997–2007." *Contraception*, 83: 82–87.

Dutton, Zoe. 2014. "Abortion's Racial Gap." *The Atlantic*. Available at: https://www.theatlantic.com/health/archive/2014/09/abortions-racial-gap/380251/.

Dworkin, Andrea and Catharine A. MacKinnon. 1988. *Pornography and Civil Rights: A New Day for Women's Equality*. Minneapolis, MN: Organizing Against Pornography.

Fessler, Leah. 2016. "A Lot of Women Don't Enjoy Hookup Culture – So Why Do We Force Ourselves to Participate?" *Quartz*. Available at: https://qz.com/685852/hookup-culture/.

Francis, Pope. 2016. *Amoris Laetitia*. Available at: http://w2.vatican.va/content/francesco/en/apost_exhortations/documents/papa-francesco_esortazione-ap_20160319_amoris-laetitia.html.

Francis, Pope. 2015. *Laudato Si*. Available at: http://w2.vatican.va/content/francesco/en/encyclicals/documents/papa-francesco_20150524_enciclica-laudato-si.html

Francis, Pope. 2014. "Address of his Holiness Pope Francis to the Members of the Diplomatic Corps Accredited to the Holy See." Available at: http://w2.vatican.va/content/francesco/en/speeches/2014/january/documents/papa-francesco_20140113_corpo-diplomatico.html

Francis, Pope. 2013. *Evangelii Gaudium*. Available at: http://w2.vatican.va/content/francesco/en/apost_exhortations/documents/papa-francesco_esortazione-ap_20131124_evangelii-gaudium.html

Freitas, Donna. 2013. *The End of Sex: How Hookup Culture is Leaving a Generation Unhappy, Sexually Unfulfilled, and Confused About Intimacy*. New York: Basic Books.

Goldman, Alan. 2008. "Plain Sex." In Soble, Alan and Nicholas Power (eds). *The Philosophy of Sex*. Lanham: Rowman and Littlefield, pp. 55–73.

Gottschall, Jonathan and Tiffani A. Gottschall. 2003. "Are Per-incident Rape-pregnancy Rates Higher than Per-incident Consensual Pregnancy Rates?" *Human Nature*, 14. 1: 1–20.

Green, Edward and Allison Herling Ruark. 2011. *AIDS, Behavior, and Culture: Understanding Evidence-Based Prevention*. Walnut Creek: Left Coast Press.

Guevin, Benedict and Martin Rhonheimer. 2005. "On the Use of Condoms to Prevent Acquired Immune Deficiency Syndrome." *National Catholic Bioethics Quarterly*, 5: 37–48.

Guttmacher Institute. 2017. "Induced Abortion Worldwide." https://www.guttmacher.org/fact-sheet/facts-induced-abortion-worldwide

Guttmacher Institute. 2016. "Induced Abortion in the United States." Available at: https://www.guttmacher.org/fact-sheet/induced-abortion-united-states

Guttmacher Institute. 2016. "Abortion Patients More Likely to be Poor in 2014 than 2008." Available at: https://www.guttmacher.org/news-release/2016/abortion-patients-more-likely-be-poor-2014-2008

Guttmacher Institute. 2012. "Facts on Induced Abortion." Available at: http://www.who.int/reproductivehealth/publications/unsafe_abortion/induced_abortion_2012.pdf

Halperin, Daniel T., Markus J. Steiner, Michael M. Cassell, et al. 2004. "The Time Has Come for Common Ground on Preventing Sexual Transmission of HIV." *The Lancet*, 364: 1913–1915.

Hamilton, Christopher. 2008. "Sex." In Soble, Alan and Nicholas Power (eds). *The Philosophy of Sex*. Lanham: Rowman and Littlefield, pp. 99–116.

Hilton, Donald and Clark Watts. 2011. "Pornography Addiction: A Neuroscience Perspective." *Surgical Neurology International* 2. 1: Available at: http://surgicalneurologyint.com/surgicalint-articles/pornography-addiction-a-neuroscience-perspective/

Huffman, Todd. 2008. "Sexuality in Modern Media: How Is It Affecting Our Children?" *Eugene Register Guard*, February.

John Paul II, Pope. 1995. *Evangelium Vitae*. New York, NY: Random House Inc.

John Paul II, Pope. 1981. *Familiaris Consortio*, 11. Available at: http://w2.vatican.va/content/john-paul-ii/en/apost_exhortations/documents/hf_jp-ii_exh_19811122_familiaris-consortio.html

Kambic, R.T. 1999. "The Effectiveness of Natural Family Planning Methods for Birth Spacing: A Comprehensive Review." Hopkins Population Center Papers on Population. Available at: https://jscholarship.library.jhu.edu/bitstream/handle/1774.2/918/WP99-07.htm

Kost, Kathryn and Stanley Henshaw. 2014. "U.S. Teenage Pregnancies, Births and Abortions, 2010: National and State Trends by Age, Race and Ethnicity." https://www.guttmacher.org/sites/default/files/report_pdf/ustptrends10.pdf

Kramer, Karen Z., Laurelle L. Myhra, Virginia S. Zuiker, and Jean W. Bauer. 2016. "Comparison of Poverty and Income Disparity of Single Mothers and Fathers Across Three Decades: 1990–2010." *Gender Issues*, 33: 22–41.

Malamuth, Neil M., Tamara Addison, and Mary Koss. 2000. "Pornography and Sexual Aggression: Are There Reliable Effects and Can We Understand Them?" *Annual Review of Sex Research*, 11: 26–91.

Mason-Grant, Joan. 2008. "Pornography as Embodied Practice," in *The Philosophy of Sex*, ed. Alan Soble and Nicholas Power, 5th edition. Lanham: Rowman and Littlefield, pp. 401–418.

Mill, John Stuart. 1991. *On Liberty and Other Essays*. New York: Oxford University Press.

Myers, David G. 2014. "Most Are Straight, Some Are Gay, and Why It Is That Way: The Science of Sexual Orientation." *Modern Believing*, 55: 127–139.

National Conference of State Legislatures. 2016. "State Policies on Sex Education in Schools." Available at: http://www.ncsl.org/research/health/state-policies-on-sex-education-in-schools.aspx

National Poverty Center. 2009. "The Colors of Poverty: Why Racial and Ethnic Disparities Persist." Available at: http://npc.umich.edu/publications/policy_briefs/brief16/.

Newton, William. 2015. "Contraception and Abortion: Fruits of the same rotten tree?" *Linacre Quarterly*, 82: 135–148.

Palmer, Louis. 2008. "Costs of Capital Punishment," in *Encyclopedia of Capital Punishment in the United States* (2nd ed.). Jefferson, NC: McFarland.

Patten, Eileen and Gretchen Livingston. 2016. "Why is the Teen Birth Rate Falling?" Available at: http://www.pewresearch.org/fact-tank/2016/04/29/why-is-the-teen-birth-rate-falling/

Peipert, Jeffrey, Tessa Madden, Jenifer Allsworth, and Gina Secura. 2012. "Preventing Unintended Pregnancies by Providing No-Cost Contraception." *Obstetrics and Gynecology*, 120. 6. Available at: http://www.ncbi.nlm.nih.gov/pmc/articles/PMC4000282/pdf/nihms570177.pdf

Pineau, Lois. 1989. "Date Rape." *Law and Philosophy*, 8: 217–243.

Planned Parenthood. n.d. "Sex." Available at: https://www.plannedparenthood.org/learn/sex-and-relationships/sex

Pruss, Alexander. 2012. *One Body: An Essay in Christian Sexual Ethics*. South Bend: University of Notre Dame Press.

Pruss, Alexander. 2000. "Christian Sexual Ethics and Teleological Organicity." *The Thomist*, 64: 71–100.

Rape, Abuse, and Incest National Network. n.d. "Sexual Assault Victims Statistics." Available at: https://rainn.org/get-information/statistics/sexual-assault-victims

Reid, T.R. 2010. "Universal Health Care Tends to Cut Abortion Rates." *The Washington Post*. Available at: http://www.washingtonpost.com/wp-dyn/content/article/2010/03/12/AR2010031202287.html

Ruddick, Sarah. 1975. "Better Sex," in Judith Boss (ed.), *Analyzing Moral Issues*. New York: McGraw Hill, pp. 368–377.

Rudy, Kathy. 1996. *Beyond Pro-Life and Pro-Choice: Moral Diversity in the Abortion Debate*. Boston: Beacon Press.

Saint Benedict Institute. 2016. "Hope for Restoration: Radical Hospitality and Prison Reform." http://www.saintbenedictinstitute.org/blog/2017/1/27/hope-for-restoration-radical-hospitality-and-prison-reform-upcoming-conference-on-restorative-justice. Accessed September 13, 2017.

Scalia, Antonin. 2006. "The Death Penalty is Just." In *The Death Penalty: Opposing Viewpoints*. Ed. Dian Andrews Henningfield. Detroit: Greenhaven Press, pp. 16–24.

Schalet, Amy. 2010. "Sex, Love, and Autonomy in the Teenage Sleepover." *Contexts*, 9. 3: 16–21. Available at: http://journals.sagepub.com/doi/pdf/10.1525/ctx.2010.9.3.16

Schuman, Catherine and Ann Glasier. 2006. "Measuring Pregnancy Intention and its Relationship with Contraceptive Use Among Women Undergoing Therapeutic Abortion." *Contraception*, 73. 5: 520–524.

Sedgh, Gilda, Jonathan Bearak, Susheela Singh, et al. 2016. "Abortion Incidence between 1990 and 2014: Global, Regional, and Subregional Levels and Trends." *The Lancet*. Available at: http://www.thelancet.com/pdfs/journals/lancet/PIIS0140-6736%2816%2930380-4.pdf.

Sexuality Information and Education Council in the United States. 2008. "National Data Shows Comprehensive Sex Education Better at Reducing Teen Pregnancy than Abstinence-Only Programs." Available at: http://www.siecus.org/index.cfm?fuseaction=Feature.show Feature&featureID=1041

Shrage, Laurie. 2003. *Abortion and Social Responsibility: Depolarizing the Debate*. Oxford: Oxford University Press.

Simon, Caroline. 2012. *Bringing Sex Into Focus: The Quest for Sexual Integrity*. Downers Grove, IL: IVP Academic.

Soble, Alan. 2008. "Masturbation, Again." In Soble, Alan and Nicholas Power (eds). *The Philosophy of Sex*. Lanham: Rowman and Littlefield, pp. 75–98.

Solomon, Andrew. 2012. *Far from the Tree: Parents, Children, and the Search for Identity*. New York: Scribner Publishing Company.

Stanger-Hall, Kathrin F. 2011. "Abstinence-Only Education and Teen Pregnancy Rates: Why We Need Comprehensive Sex Education in the U.S." *PLoS ONE* 6. 10: e24658. Available at: http://journals.plos.org/plosone/article?id=10.1371/journal.pone.0024658

Tavernise, Sabrina. 2015. "Colorado's Effort Against Teenage Pregnancies is a Startling Success." *The New York Times*. Available at: http://www.nytimes.com/2015/07/06/science/colorados-push-against-teenage-pregnancies-is-a-startling-success.html?_r=0

Tracy, Steve. 2010. "Abortion, the Marginalized, and the Vulnerable: A Social Justice Perspective for Reducing Abortion." *Cultural Encounters: A Journal for the Theology of Culture*, 6. 2: 23–33.

Trussell, James. 2011. "Contraceptive Failure in the United States." *Contraception*, 83: 397–404.

Van Giezen, Robert W. 2013. "Paid Leave in the Private Industry over the Past 20 Years." Available at: http://www.bls.gov/opub/btn/volume-2/paid-leave-in-private-industry-over-the-past-20-years.htm

Van Wyk, Robert. 2011. "The Morality of Teenage Sex and Its Implications for Sex Education," in *Sex, Love, and Friendship*. Adrianne Leigh McEvoy (ed.). New York: Rodopi Publishers, pp. 39–50.

Vatican II. *Gaudium et Spes*, 48. Available at: http://www.vatican.va/archive/hist_councils/ii_vatican_council/documents/vat-ii_cons_19651207_gaudium-et-spes_en.html.

Villani, Susan. 2001. "Impact of Media on Children and Adolescents: A 10-Year Review of the Research." *Journal of the American Academy of Child and Adolescent Psychiatry*, 40. 4: 392–401.

Warren, Mary Anne. 1973. "On the Moral and Legal Status of Abortion." *The Monist*, 57. 1: 43–61.
Washington State Department of Social and Health Services. n.d. Available at: https://www.dshs.wa.gov/esa/community-services-offices/child-care-subsidy-program
West, Christopher. 2004. *Good News about Sex and Marriage: Answers to Your Honest Questions about Catholic Teaching*, revised edition. Cincinnati: Servant Books.
World Policy Center. 2016. "Is Paid Leave Available for Mothers and Infants?" Available at: http://worldpolicycenter.org/policies/is-paid-leave-available-for-mothers-of-infants
Zack, Naomi. 2015. *White Privilege and Black Rights*. Lanham: Rowman and Littlefield.

CONCLUSION

Bertha Alvarez Manninen and Jack Mulder, Jr.

In this book, we have discussed our reasons for being pro-choice and pro-life in regard to the abortion issue. We have also glimpsed some agreement on related issues that, we think, springs from the reasons we take the positions we do. Some recap is probably useful. On a range of issues concerning social justice, we can say we have considerable agreement. We both think that there should be serious societal measures against poverty, for family leave, against racial injustice, for prisoners, against the death penalty, and for our earth and its environment. A "hands-off" approach that seems to characterize some libertarian visions at the level of government strikes both of us as problematic. We also have some common ground on issues of sexual ethics. This is because we both think that delaying sexual activity in young people is an important goal to have, since sex among young people often fails certain basic ethical norms (some as basic as Kantian norms requiring that one's partner be viewed as a full person in her own right). We also agree that popular media has a strongly pedagogical hand in the mischief, as does pornography, and that we cannot reasonably expect healthy sexual behavior from a society whose chief forms of entertainment do not model it.

We have somewhat less agreement when it comes to contraception. We have different viewpoints about the moral status of discrete acts of contraception. Mulder holds that contracepted sex is, ultimately, a kind of duplicity in the very sort of relationship that should signal an unparalleled degree of openness. Manninen sees contraception as simply one way that sexual partners might choose to reduce the potential for infection or unplanned pregnancy. Nevertheless, both of us agree that abstinence should come (at least) highly recommended for young people, although Manninen also believes contraception education should be taught to them right alongside. When people are no longer abstinent, both of us agree that they would do well to be faithful to and monogamous with their sexual partners. When people enter into sexual encounters in which any resulting pregnancy would not be welcome, or when they enter into sexual encounters that simply present greater risk for sexually transmitted infections, Mulder would insist that it behooves them to recognize a couple of things. First, no method of contraception is 100% reliable (and many aren't even very close to that). Contraception does not end unplanned pregnancies and it cannot be expected to do so. Moreover, risk compensation does occur.

Still, when people have already made a decision not to be abstinent and not to be faithful and to engage in sex that puts them or their partners at high risk of infection or of an unplanned (and unwelcome) pregnancy, and they are aware of the risks and concerns, even Mulder can agree that at that point it does little good to rail against contraception. Indeed, when someone is on the point of engaging in risky sexual behavior and will not relent, Mulder would concede that it may show some (perhaps budding) moral awareness to employ some manner of contraception. Mulder insists that this would not entail that the act itself would be morally right, it would merely signal, as (then) Pope Benedict XVI did in 2010, that this may be a way of showing some respect for one's partners and, Mulder suggests, perhaps the situation into which potential offspring might be born.

One would be right to point out that this is hardly a robust agreement between Mulder and Manninen on contraception. Mulder has more nuanced views as to the morality of contraception that Manninen does not share. Yet this discussion may shine a light on some ways to think about contraception in a pluralistic society. As we've discussed before, pro-life and pro-choice people can proceed toward meaningful outcomes in a deliberative democracy even while their horns are locked on certain key issues. If greater emphasis were laid upon abstinence and being faithful to one's sexual partner, and if our culture and forms of entertainment helped us imagine this future better, perhaps there could be more meaningful discussion about what we as a society hope for and worry about when it comes to contraception. It is also worth remembering that, while it is possible for politicians and activists to work toward meaningful outcomes, these are inevitably temporary. Manninen has not come around to Mulder's view and Mulder has not come around to Manninen's view.

Nevertheless, we remain committed to the stance that the long patient path of dialogue is the right one. Without it, we lose respect for one another and can no longer envisage a future worth passing on. In this sense, although we ultimately disagree on the moral and legal status of abortion, we follow John Stuart Mill's suggestion of "giving merited honor to everyone, whatever opinion he may hold, who has calmness to see and honesty to state what his opponents and their opinions really are, exaggerating nothing to their discredit, keeping nothing back which tell … in their favor."[1] We bestow this "honor" not just to each other, but to anyone who is willing to take up any controversial issue with an open mind and with integrity; to really *understand* opposing views charitably, even if they ultimately do not come to accept those views as their own. For us, this book has been a welcome opportunity for old friends to reconnect, work together, and learn from one another, despite the hotly contested nature of the topic. We hope the method of dialogue it employs can inspire more of the same.

Note

1 Mill, 1991, p. 61.

References

Mill, John Stuart. 1991. *On Liberty and Other Essays*. New York: Oxford University Press.

INDEX

ABC Theory of sex 196–197
AIDS/HIV 199–200
Aldana, Carmen 20, 25, 144, 159–160
"All Lives Matter" 179
American College of Obstetricians and Gynecologists 98
animalism 25, 79, 99, 113–120, 122–124, 126, 128, 153, 154, 157, 165
Aquinas, St. Thomas 207n110
Archard, David 155, 169n47
artificial wombs 163, 167n9

Baker, Lynn Rudder 120
Beckwith, Francis: abortion methods 107n110; drunk driving example 40–41; metaphysics 104n16; miscarriages 159; personhood 21, 114, 125; rape or incest pregnancies 130–131
Benatar, David 182–183
Benedict XVI, Pope 196–199, 214
"Black Lives Matter" 179
Boonin, David: desire 105n50, 156, 165; irrelevance of implantation 80; kindred species argument 168n21; personhood 74–76, 114–116, 127; responsibility objection 40–41
Bordo, Susan 38–39
Brady, David and Burroway, Rebecca 174, 176
Burgess, J.A. and Tawia, S.A 31
Burwell v. Hobby Lobby 141–143

Camosy, Charles 4, 6, 102n2
Cannold, Leslie 13, 54
Cantor, Julie D 98
capital punishment 5, 21, 65, 100, 181, 202n35, 213
Carey v. Population Services International 33
casual view of sex 182–183, 189
cognitive account of moral personhood 15–19, 20, 25, 29, 30, 32, 45, 47, 114, 154, 155
conscience rights 12, 97–98
contraception 33, 40, 80–83, 122, 152, 174, 175, 178, 190, 191–200, 213–214; contraceptive failure 206n105; Catholic views of contraception 206n104; types of contraception 142, 206n105, 206n107
Cruzan, Nancy Beth 29–30, 118, 119

Davis v. Davis 22, 150–151
Dawson, Karen 146n11.
Dear, Robert 2
death penalty *see* capital punishment
DeGrazia, David 25, 126–128
Denis, Lara 188
desires: types of desires fetuses may or may not have 16, 75–76, 100, 105n50, 115, 156–158, 165
dialogue 1–5, 7, 8
DiSilvestro, Russell. 114, 116, 145n3, 146n12
double effect 88, 132, 164, 166
Doe v. Doe 48

ectogenesis 134
ectopic pregnancy 37, 66, 77, 83, 87, 158, 163, 164, 169n39, 170n57
Eisenstadt v. Baird 33
embodied mind account of personal identity 25, 29–32, 52, 115, 116, 120, 122, 123, 154–157, 165
embryos: embryogenesis 77–81, 120–122; embryo division/twinning 80, 81, 120; used and unused embryos 22, 150–153
emergency contraception 83, 122, 141, 142
endowment view of personhood 71, 74, 76, 77, 114, 123–125, 154
Ethical and Religious Directives for Catholic Health Care 102n5, 106n77, 107n105
euthanasia 15, 49, 50, 65, 74, 92, 100, 14, 163, 166

family leave 65, 96, 174, 175, 178, 213
Feldman, Susan 46
Feinberg, Joel 26, 155
Flaherty, Judge John P., Jr. 93, 95, 131, 132
Ford, Norman 121
Francis, Pope 4, 181–182, 198
Francke, Linda 13
Freitas, Donna 184, 185, 195, 205n97, 205n101

genetic account of moral personhood 15, 19–25, 32, 47, 153–154
George, Robert P. and Ramesh Pannuru 161, 169n45
George, Robert P. and Tollefsen, Christopher: body–self dualism 79–80; cloning 81; discrimination 75; embryogenesis 78; embryo adoption 168n16; faith-based arguments 69, 104n15; personhood 125, 154, 157
Gillespie, Norman 26
Ginsburg, Ruth Bader 167n7
Giubilini, Alberto 12
Good Samaritan 46, 48, 96, 138
Green, Edward C 207n113
Green, Edward C. and Herling Ruark, Allison 199–200.
Griswold v. Connecticut 33
Gurin, Patricia 2
Guttmacher Institute 58n64, 60n105, 60n106, 146n34, 146n37, 192, 201n3, 201n4, 204n74, 204n81, 204n82, 204n88

Halappanavar, Savita 19, 20, 37, 158
Harris, Lisa 14
"heartbeat legislation". 67–68
Hershenov, David B. and Rose 96–97

Hodgers, Sheila 19–20
hookup culture 184, 195, 205n97
Huffman, Todd 189
Hursthouse, Rosalind 53, 54, 95, 96

implantation 22, 23, 33, 77, 79–81, 83, 120, 134, 141, 142, 143, 151, 153
in vitro fertilization (IVF) 21, 22, 25, 57n38
interest view of moral status 26–32, 52, 115, 156
Irish Catholic Bishops' Conference 158
Irish Protection of Life During Pregnancy Act 19

Jecker, Nancy 44
John Paul II, Pope 7, 9n16, 24, 82, 154, 199, 207n111

Kaczor, Christopher: appearance of embryo 66; artificial wombs 163; capital punishment and euthanasia 108n143; definition of abortion 102n5; endowment vs. performance views 74, 75, 114, 123–125; parenting 34; personhood 71, 78–79; 118–119; rape and incest pregnancies 130; responsibility objection 131; violinist example 95, 135–137
Kant, Immanuel 35–37, 39, 45, 138, 187–190, 214
Kissling, Francis 12

La Fleur, William 9
Little, Margret Olivia 12, 37, 92, 94
LNG EC *see* "morning after pill"
Locke, John 72–74, 78, 79, 83, 99, 104n29, 104n30, 105n35
Lundquist, Caroline 38

Mackenzie, Catriona 51, 89, 90, 96, 129, 145, 160
Marquis, Don 23–25, 57n38, 74, 114, 126, 127
Mathewes-Green, Frederica 96, 107n107
McCloskey, H.J 28
McFall v. Shimp 47–49, 93–94, 131–137, 162
McMahan, Jeff 29, 32, 116, 122
methotrexate 164, 169n39, 170n57
mifepristone 83, 102n5, 141
Mill, John Stuart 7, 172, 214
Minerva, Francesca 12
mizuko kuyo 14
"morning after pill" 83, 122, 141–143
murder: as inappropriate term for abortion 3, 6, 9n12, 20–21, 144, 150, 159, 205n95

218 Index

Nagel, Thomas 27
natural embryo loss 82, 113, 143–145
natural family planning 206n107
neutrality 70, 74
Nobis, Nathan 125

Olson, Eric 25, 118, 120
Ord, Toby 81–82, 143
Overall, Christine 38, 89, 129
ownership 89–90, 128, 151, 160

Pakaluk, Michael 109n141, 160, 161, 169n45
paternalism 99–101
performance view of personhood 71, 74, 75, 83, 114, 116, 127, 154, 157
person essentialism (metaphysical and moral) 113–116, 122–128
personhood amendments 19, 20, 22, 23, 33, 35, 52, 151
Phoenix case 164, 169n39
Picoult, Jodi 44, 161
Pineau, Lois 184
Planned Parenthood 2, 33, 83, 174, 205n96
Planned Parenthood v. Casey 33, 52, 84
pluralism 5, 68–70, 79, 99, 113, 214
Poppema, Suzanne 12
pornography 100, 185–186, 196, 213
post-abortion syndrome 14
poverty 7, 145, 173–178, 179, 181, 182, 214
pregnancy: burdens and complications 20, 34, 37–39, 42, 44, 48; compelled or compulsory 22, 38–39, 41–46, 48, 91–94, 101, 133–138, 151–152, 165; unique state 95–96, 101, 135–136, 138, 151, 159, 187
pro-choice and pro-life: choice of language 5–7
public reason 97, 99, 108n140

R v. Morgentaler 48
Rachels, James 92, 163
racism (or racial justice) 3, 65, 71, 75–76, 122, 125, 136, 178–181
rape *see* sexual assault
Rawls, John 71, 97, 99, 104n17, 108n140
Reader, Soran 1–2, 6, 60n109, 89–91, 109n145, 129, 150, 167n4
Regan, Donald 39, 44, 46, 48
Responsibility Objection 40–43, 59n83, 91, 131
Rickless, Samuel C. 73, 104n30, 105n35

Roe v. Wade 19, 20, 32, 33–35, 49, 70, 84, 103n8, 104n16, 167n7
Ross, Steven 136–137
Ruddick, Sarah 188–189
RU-486 *see* mifepristone

Sagan, Agata, and Singer, Peter 81
salpingectomy 66, 87, 163, 164, 169n38, 169n39
savior siblings 44–45, 161–162
Schiavo, Terri 29, 30, 118
Schwartz, Stephen 43
sentience 16, 17, 23, 26–28, 32, 49, 82, 115, 125, 127, 144, 155–156, 168n31
sex education 189–190, 195
sexual assault 20, 41, 53, 55, 66, 83, 86–87, 89–91, 94, 129–131, 136, 145, 151–152, 155, 160, 169n47, 173, 182, 184, 186, 188, 191–193
sexual ethics 182–191
Shrage, Laurie 178
significance view of sex 182–183
Singer, Peter 11, 16–18, 29, 73, 122, 137, 154
Snyder v. Phelps 52
spontaneous abortion *see* natural embryo loss
Stanford Hospital v. Vega 47
Steinbock, Bonnie 27
Sullivan, Thomas D. 92, 163

Thomson, Judith Jarvis: abortion right does not permit killing 50–52; coat case 86; Henry Fonda case 87; legal implications of Thomson's article 47–52; responsibility objection 40–42, 90; special responsibility objection 42–45; tiny house case 85; violinist example 36–37, 86–87, 94–95, 133, 135–136;
Tiller, George 2, 140
Titanic case 92–93
Tooley, Michael 11, 16, 17, 79, 122
Tracy, Steve 176, 177
Trump, Donald J. 65

Union Pacific Railway Company v. Botsford 47
United States Centers for Disease Control and Prevention 177, 184–185
United States Conference of Catholic Bishops 91, 102n5, 169n39

Van Wyk, Robert 188–189
Vanderford, Marsha 3
Vera Drake 65–66, 67, 98, 101
vulnerability 18, 71, 93, 99–101, 149

Warren, Mary Anne 11, 16, 17, 74, 89, 114, 122, 205n95
West, Christopher 196
West, Robin 44, 49, 90
white privilege 179–180
Wicklund, Susan 8

Williams, Nicola Jane 168n33
Winston v. Lee 47
Wittgenstein, Ludwig 27

Zack, Naomi 103n7, 179–180, 202n27, 202n31

Taylor & Francis eBooks

Helping you to choose the right eBooks for your Library

Add Routledge titles to your library's digital collection today. Taylor and Francis ebooks contains over 50,000 titles in the Humanities, Social Sciences, Behavioural Sciences, Built Environment and Law.

Choose from a range of subject packages or create your own!

Benefits for you
- Free MARC records
- COUNTER-compliant usage statistics
- Flexible purchase and pricing options
- All titles DRM-free.

REQUEST YOUR FREE INSTITUTIONAL TRIAL TODAY

Free Trials Available
We offer free trials to qualifying academic, corporate and government customers.

Benefits for your user
- Off-site, anytime access via Athens or referring URL
- Print or copy pages or chapters
- Full content search
- Bookmark, highlight and annotate text
- Access to thousands of pages of quality research at the click of a button.

eCollections – Choose from over 30 subject eCollections, including:

Archaeology	Language Learning
Architecture	Law
Asian Studies	Literature
Business & Management	Media & Communication
Classical Studies	Middle East Studies
Construction	Music
Creative & Media Arts	Philosophy
Criminology & Criminal Justice	Planning
Economics	Politics
Education	Psychology & Mental Health
Energy	Religion
Engineering	Security
English Language & Linguistics	Social Work
Environment & Sustainability	Sociology
Geography	Sport
Health Studies	Theatre & Performance
History	Tourism, Hospitality & Events

For more information, pricing enquiries or to order a free trial, please contact your local sales team:
www.tandfebooks.com/page/sales

Routledge
Taylor & Francis Group

The home of Routledge books

www.tandfebooks.com